"Important and timely."
James Appathurai, Deputy Assistant Secretary General for Political Affairs and Security Policy, NATO

"This is an utterly fascinating, carefully argued and lucidly drafted analysis of the current global circumstances. Holslag provides a deft, informed and multifaceted argument to explain how the highly optimistic views of the future of world politics failed to materialize after the end of the Cold War."
Sumit Ganguly, Indiana University

"Rich and comprehensive, Jonathan Holslag's book takes readers on a journey of discovery through the major changes in world politics over the past three decades. I will be assigning this book for my undergraduate international relations classes."
Kun-Chin Lin, University of Cambridge

"This wonderfully written book takes the reader on a fascinating journey through the complexity of the last three decades of world politics. Jonathan Holslag connects the dots of a fragmented and scattered global landscape, offering multiple roads to understanding."
Federica Mogherini, Rector of the College of Europe, Former European High Representative for Foreign Affairs

WORLD POLITICS
SINCE 1989

WORLD POLITICS SINCE 1989

Jonathan Holslag

polity

First published in 2021 by Polity Press

Polity Press
65 Bridge Street
Cambridge CB2 1UR, UK

Polity Press
101 Station Landing
Suite 300
Medford, MA 02155, USA

ISBN-13: 978-1-5095-4672-5

A catalogue record for this book is available from the British Library.

Library of Congress Cataloging-in-Publication Data

Names: Holslag, Jonathan, author.
Title: World politics since 1989 / Jonathan Holslag.
Description: Cambridge, UK ; Medford, MA : Polity Press, 2021. | Includes bibliographical references and index. | Summary: "A brilliant account of how the world squandered the opportunities of the post-Cold War era"-- Provided by publisher.
Identifiers: LCCN 2020054809 (print) | LCCN 2020054810 (ebook) | ISBN 9781509546725 (hardback) | ISBN 9781509546749 (epub)
Subjects: LCSH: World politics--20th century. | World politics--21st century.
Classification: LCC D443 .H6435 2021 (print) | LCC D443 (ebook) | DDC 909.83/1--dc23
LC record available at https://lccn.loc.gov/2020054809
LC ebook record available at https://lccn.loc.gov/2020054810

Typeset in 11 on 15 pt Dante by
Servis Filmsetting Ltd, Stockport, Cheshire
Printed and bound in Great Britain by TJ Books Ltd, Padstow, Cornwall

For further information on Polity, visit our website: politybooks.com

CONTENTS

No society is fortunate when its walls are standing while its morals are in ruins.
Scipio

MAPS, FIGURES, AND TABLE

Maps

Figures

Table

THE PENDULUM

WALLPECKERS, THEY WERE CALLED. IN THE WINTER OF 1989, hundreds of wallpeckers or *Mauerspechte* descended on the Berlin Wall. Armed with hammers and chisels, they attacked the imposing barrier of concrete and barbed wire. One year later, the entire Iron Curtain between the Soviet Union and the West came down. It was an electric moment. "A second heart implanted," wrote a student in her diary, "can't breathe any more."[1] From then onwards, the world experienced a period of opening up, of fading political fault lines, diminishing travel restrictions, and lowering barriers against trade. This was the age of globalization, of growing connectivity, commerce, and prosperity, growth that came with the expectation that the remaining vestiges of authoritarianism would make place for freedom.

The high tide of globalization appeared to hold opportunities for all.[2] Emerging powers like South Korea, China, and Vietnam received access to the technology, capital, and consumer markets of rich societies, like the United States, Western Europe, and Japan. Rich citizens benefited from cheap goods, from toys to mobile phones, and specialized into services. Countries in Africa, Latin America, and the Middle East profited from growing raw material exports and investment. Trade propelled specialization between nations and specialization brought more growth to all. It was called a great convergence.[3] There were still threats, to be sure. But these threats were expected to make countries work together. Terrorism, for example, pirates that targeted global shipping, criminals that penetrated digital networks – or pandemics. Experts spoke of security interdependence, of global common goods requiring a common policy.[4] A teenager asked to name the most urgent challenge facing the world would likely mention pollution or climate change.

If there was competition, it would be a peaceful contest for connectivity, conducted by multinationals and start-up companies instead of states and soldiers. Container ships not aircraft carriers shaped the fortune of the major powers. Cheap airlines made city trips affordable. Internet traffic exploded. Global economic production grew. Extreme poverty retreated. Magazines wrote about a renaissance in Africa.[5] "China's arrival has improved Africa's infrastructure and boosted its manufacturing sector," a magazine trumpeted. "Africa's enthusiasm for technology is boosting growth."[6] India with its hundreds of millions of paupers was set to shine. Globalization augured a golden era – or at least an exit from an era of iron.

A missed opportunity

But the pendulum swung back. In 2019, people protested again in the shadow of an imposing wall. It was pulled up along thousands of kilometers of border between the United States and Mexico. It was another milestone in world history, a turning point between a period of opening and a new period of fragmenting. The talk of the day was no longer about globalization but about de-globalization, about sovereignty, and autonomy. The United Kingdom decided to leave the European Union. In the United States, President Donald Trump railed against cosmopolitanism. Despite his turbulent term, two impeachment procedures, his blatant nationalism, his failure to address the devastating corona pandemic, and his rude style, Trump narrowly missed a second term during the elections of 2020. Many Americans continued to support him. The center of the global order, the champion of liberal values, the West itself, was cast adrift. Never had it been so fragmented.

All around, nationalism and authoritarianism were on the offense. In democratic India, Hindu-nationalist politicians exploited resentment against a minority of two hundred million Muslims. In South Africa, the legacy of freedom fighter Nelson Mandela was replaced by nationalism and xenophobia. If competition about territory was sometimes seen as trivial, Iraq invaded Kuwait, India clashed with Pakistan and China over Kashmir, Russia annexed Crimea, a strategically located peninsula in the Black Sea, and China went further and further in trying to control its adjacent seas. Numerous other territorial conflicts remained tense. The world moved from wall to wall.

In 2020, a worldwide outbreak of coronavirus accelerated this evolution. The World Health Organization became a battleground between China and the United States, until Washington ended its membership entirely. Highlighting the nationalist tendency, countries like Germany delayed exports of medical equipment. Instead of joining forces, the major powers unleashed a propaganda war. Exposing their increasing weakness, disaster management in countries like Italy and the United Kingdom turned out to be disastrous. In the United States, militia protested against national government measures to halt the virus. "Tyrants get the rope," protesters yelled outside the capitol building of the State of Michigan. The coronavirus did not cause the decay of political order. It rather took hold of a political body that was in bad shape. Over one hundred armed groups vowed to fight the return of a Democrat to the White House, his alleged attempt to bring in communism, and his attempt to curtail gun ownership. The defeat of President Donald Trump in the elections made Trumpism more defiant.

The return of walls and nationalism cannot be reduced to isolated events, like the presidency of Donald Trump, the departure of the United Kingdom from the European Union, or the corona pandemic. The next chapters will provide evidence of a more fundamental fragmentation. At this point, it suffices to summarize that there was an increase in both economic globalization and democratization in the 1990s. In the following decade, between 2000 and 2009, economic globalization still advanced, but democratization stagnated. Between 2010 and 2020, economic globalization stagnated and democratization receded. At the same time, global military spending surpassed the Cold War record. The number of armed conflicts increased.

So, what happened? How was it lost? How was it lost, the flicker of hope that rude power politics was bound to make place for a benign world order? How could it be that the age of globalization bred so much nationalism?

This question forms the point of departure for this book. The history of the period of globalization, the 30 years roughly between 1989 and 2020, is the story of a lost momentum. For all the growth, it was insufficient to overcome the gravity of power politics and localism.

One of the reasons was that the Western world held immense power, but often lacked wisdom: the wisdom to preserve social cohesion, the wisdom to use the historical wealth to build an attractive economic future, and the wisdom to use power with prudence on the global scene. It was as if those societies, after an arduous upward journey, a journey of toil and sacrifice, came to take their blessings for granted. They no longer had an idea about how to advance either, about what the next stage of development could be. A former South Korean minister once put it to me as follows. "I see the world as a mountain. Countries like mine and China are moving up," he said. "But as we near the top, we see you having a picnic, consuming your wealth, unwilling to move to new heights, and being angry that others now move closer. You yield leadership and blame others for their ambition."[7] The three decades of relative peace in the West were a long-missed opportunity, a crisis of politics, diplomacy, and, in a way, civilization.

As so often in history, it is in a time of prosperity that we find the causes of decay. "They who are in the sinking scale do not easily come off from the habitual prejudices of superior wealth."[8] While the West fell short in preserving and reinventing the historical sources of its wealth, others harbored resentment and used shrewd statecraft to profit from its short-sightedness. What accounted for a lot of the trouble was indeed that the West complacently consumed its prosperity at the pinnacle of world politics, and for a long time ignored the challenges that built up. When it did wake up to the changes, the consequent nationalism made the situation worse. Nationalist remedies were about pretending strength and not about regaining strength. They did not call on citizens to take their responsibility, but put the responsibility on others. Western democracy became an incubator of demagogy.

Harmony contested

There is no single explanation for this upsurge of nationalism and turbulence. It was not just the power shift from the West toward China that caused new uncertainty, nor was it just the failure of capitalism, or the inability to address common challenges, like climate change. Such a one-size-fits-all explanation would make this book perhaps more straightforward, allow it to be summarized in a captivating headline. But would that make us wiser? To understand change in world politics, it is imperative to consider a combination of elements. In fact, one of the things that stand out as a factor contributing to instability, is the failure of politics to deal with complexity, its proclivity for black and white. This book is about connections between different trends. But let us try, at the start, to put up some markers, to identify some themes that recur throughout the chapters.

A first such theme I title "Harmony contested." We need to be cautious describing the period between 1989 and 2020 as a golden age. What looked like a golden age to some remained a challenging time to many others. Developing countries often saw globalization permitting consumers in North America and Europe to benefit from their resources and cheap labor. What the leading powers called just was considered abuse by others; what they considered harmony was a hierarchy. Many countries were dissatisfied, wanted to change that order, to catch up, to grow their own power, and become less dependent on the West. Disgruntlement also struck inside rich countries. After the turn of the century, many citizens in Europe and the United States saw their purchasing power stagnate, while the very rich at the top of their society flourished. In the United States, satisfaction about the state of the country declined. In the West and elsewhere, the frustration about cosmopolitanism had been brewing for years.

What most obviously caused the world to retreat into conflict positions was a profound power shift. This is the second theme. Power is the capacity to make others do what they otherwise would not have done. It is about possessing the economic, political, military, and moral weight to influence behavior. The West became the world's center of power after the collapse of the Soviet Union. For a while, it was able to dictate the rules. Several countries wanted to be part of its orbit of influence, become members of the European Union, join the North Atlantic Treaty Organization (NATO), and participate in the international organizations it dominated. Slowly but surely, this position eroded. Externally, it prompted other powers to contest Western interests, led smaller countries to play the West off against new partners, and in its turn created a defensive backlash in Western capitals. Internally, the loss of power coincided with social distress and the waning of the legitimacy of center politics.

A third theme is the decadence trap. It was the rise of China and the uncertainty it instilled, in a way, that made conflict unavoidable. Still, the focus on China's rise ignores the weakening of the West. Weakness and profligacy are as much the harbingers of friction as growth and ambition. Instead of preserving wealth at home by building more advanced and sustainable industries, large Western markets spent beyond their means on imported raw materials and consumer goods. They piled up debt and made competitors rich. Consumerism and speculation advanced at the expense of civic duty and entrepreneurialism. Fortune turned savage. Wealth was squandered and the free mind subjugated to materialism. The changes in the distribution of hard power followed changes in the soft tissue of morals, enlightenment, dignity, and civilization. Civic engagement, the bedrock of modern state power, crumbled. Communism was an excess of state control. It was supplanted by another excess: reckless consumerism.

A fourth important observation is that the free world made authoritarianism strong. Benefiting the most from Western consumerism was China. Its annual trade surplus with the West grew to hundreds of billions of dollars. Its state capitalist model implied that this trade surplus was used for strategic purposes. The Central Bank hoarded the foreign currency and used it to buy technology, ports, and so forth. China's sterilization policy meant that the West, so to say, had its influence undermined with its own money. Consumerism also came with vast imports of fossil fuel. Europe in particular depended on imports of gas. That bolstered the authoritarianism of Vladimir Putin and his attempt to halt Western influence. Energy imports also helped authoritarian regimes in the Gulf preserve their power and export radical Islamism, despite repeated requests from Washington and European capitals to stop it.

A fifth theme concerns hubris, or excessive self-confidence. Blind faith in military technology led to remote-control interventionism, the assumption that governments could be bombed into obedience, violence be controlled by long-range missile strikes, democracy installed by means of a dysfunctional combination of hard power and humanitarianism. Fortunes were spent on military interventions, in Afghanistan and Iraq. By the time the West came to understand the need for sustained presence and sophisticated engagement, its interest had disappeared altogether. Hubris also marked international cooperation. The West expected other powers to become responsible stakeholders, to subscribe to its rules and to liberalize. But for countries like China, Russia, and Saudi Arabia, cooperation was only a means to serve the end of amassing power. The same was true for political elites in smaller developing countries. For a while, they paid lip service to Western values, yet loathed its double standards and turned their backs as soon as they could.

A sixth current is what I call the school of strife. While the West felt betrayed, others thought that the West had bullied and belittled them long enough. The three decades of relative peace did not usher in a virtuous path along which trade would first demand more political cooperation, then strengthen international organizations, teach citizens that it was more useful to see themselves as part of a world community than to perceive the world narrowly through national interests, and, in the end, change the very genetics of international politics. Countries did indeed find out that it was often easier to grow rich through openness. But at the same time, positive learning was superseded by negative learning. Interventionism taught them that the weak still obey the strong, that economic dependency is selfishly exploited, and that benign intentions can never be taken for granted. What mattered, the weak learned, was sovereignty and power. This school of strife, this negative socialization, left a larger imprint on the outlook of world politics than the school of peace.

A seventh dimension is about the changing nature of power. Not only the distribution of power changed; the nature of power evolved as well. Consider the economy. If economists argued that as long as the cake grew, everybody would benefit, the cake came to look more like a sponge cake. Societies needed much more of it to be saturated. Automation and digitization allowed more to be produced with fewer people. Thus these productivity gains were beneficial. But the benefits went disproportionally to those in possession of capital. Moreover, if the expectation was that productivity allowed citizens to work less, pressure to work harder increased in many countries.[9] Some intellectuals prophesied that technology would help advance humanism, but many humans felt that technology degraded them into robots. The growth–wellbeing gap contributed to social anxiety. While globalization was touted for making products cheaper, the hidden costs of pollution, the devastating consequences of financial speculation, and the social instability caused by exploitation were hardly considered. If liberal thinkers like Adam Smith expected consumers to make rational choices with an eye on their wellbeing, long production chains made such impossible. Globalization became like a smoke screen instead of a facilitator of the enlightened selfishness that Smith and others had in mind. There also existed a widening chasm between the capacity of scientists to find solutions for challenges, like environmental degradation, and the extent to which they were implemented. Hence, for all the technological possibilities, pollution increased, precious resources were exhausted in more precarious environments, and hundreds of millions of citizens still suffered from famine. These were in a way good times, but certainly not the best of times, and for many they were still just bad times.

A last theme is the limit of learning. One of the most interesting observations of the post-Cold War period is that many of the challenges were identified at an early stage, that experts described them in their publications, that governments promised to respond, but that the response was often slow or absent altogether. There was unprecedented information about problems. Yet, action remained underwhelming or mechanical.[10] This had been the case with reports about the erosion of society in the West, the neglect of education, low civic engagement, and destabilizing inequality. It had been the case with studies about the dangers of excessive speculation and the ignoring of investment in key infrastructure. It had been the case also about foreign policy objectives, the fact that the West was making dictators rich only to find them more opposed to Western values. Consider the insight that global warming would cause insecurity and that polluting consumerism was as detrimental to the environment as it was to the strength of Western economies in the long run. There was knowledge, but societies were reluctant to let it shape their decisions. There was light, but societies often seemed to prefer to remain oblivious. So, in the end, there was not much enlightenment.

Is this excessive, to capture eight themes in one book? Some of my reviewers indeed suggested that I narrow the focus. It is a deliberate choice not to do so. Yes, it makes the reading less straightforward. But do the growing polarization in political debates, the difficulty of dealing with complex situations, and the struggle to grasp the causes of our challenges without one-sidely putting the blame on others all show the need for students, opinion leaders, and decision makers to accept that things are not always black and white? The world is an overwhelming place. Nothing is evident. The aim should be to provide clarity without losing sight of complexity.

Gray zone

This book is a history of recent world politics. I wrote it in the first place as a provocation for my students. Such a project always comes with the following question: What might it be important for them to ponder? What is relevant for the diplomats, journalists, entrepreneurs, activists, and politicians of tomorrow to understand about world politics? What is world politics in the first place? Events, some would argue, big, headline-hitting events that shape the outlook of our world, like major wars and large diplomatic conferences. This book certainly pays attention to decisive events, like the fall of the Soviet Union, the terrorist attack against the United States in 2001, and so forth. But at least as important, as was stated before, are incremental changes. Economic change, for instance, which alters the balance of power between countries, changes in consumer choices, which affect the organization of an economy, the productivity of countries, and the allocation of financial wealth. Hence, this work wants to familiarize the reader with the milestones of recent world politics, but also to tell something about the road in between.

A history of world politics cannot be about external politics alone. Some theorists insist on a clear separation between external and internal politics. Kenneth Waltz, an influential thinker about international relations, stated that it is not domestic politics that shapes the behavior of states, but the world system.[11] Whatever the culture, the values, or the constitution of states, he argues, they are forced by the behavior of others to defend their interests. This argument is similar to what I refer to in this book as the school of strife. Russia in the 1990s, for instance, had an interest in replacing the antagonistic policy toward the West with a policy of accommodation and integration. Yet, distrust and a lack of interest on the side of the West, combined with latent nationalism, forced it back to battle modus. The same happened to China. Still, instead of seeing the world as an engine, controlled by mechanical laws, it is indispensable to examine the internal dynamics that help understand why some countries grow their power and why others lose it, what mediates their response to external challenges, in terms of institutions, values, public expectations, and so forth. It adds nuance and clarifies why the seemingly predictable mechanics of certain thinkers does not always work out so predictably.

A study of world politics must give a place to non-state actors: to cities, companies, nongovernmental organizations (NGOs), and opposition movements. States remain immensely powerful actors, but the understanding of their interaction with large companies and international organizations is critical. In the next chapters, for instance, we will discover how Western multinational companies detached from their home market, how they still influenced politicians to adjust their foreign policy regarding international economics, and how this contributed to the altering balance of power between countries. But we also explore how countries like China and Russia clung to state capitalism. They forced large domestic companies to serve the national interest and twisted the arm of Western investors to do the same. Hence, the same large companies that influenced the government in one country were influenced *by* the government in another country.

This instantly explains why experts have remained trapped in an unproductive debate about who influences whom.[12] Influence went in both directions. The one country whose prosperity led it to ignore economic security allowed itself to be influenced by the multinational. The other state whose vulnerability made it put economic security upfront, insisted on preserving influence over the multinational. The same ambivalence applies to international organizations, like the United Nations, the World Trade Organization, and the World Health Organization.[13] While they have some autonomy with regard to states, and states sometimes find multilateral cooperation a relevant way to shore up their legitimacy in the world, these organizations atrophy when powerful states are no longer capable of brokering a mutually beneficial compromise through them. Multilateralism remains power politics by different means.

When Russia gained control over the Crimean Peninsula and staged a proxy war in Eastern Ukraine, newspapers and military staffs suddenly underlined the importance of gray zone conflict or hybrid war.[14] Both concepts imply that states confront each other just below the threshold of a full-blown war. An American general summarized the challenge thus: "We can still win any war, but we have difficulties with anything short of war."[15] In this book, it becomes clear that world politics is always a gray zone. The difference between civilian and military actors is seldom clear. China built merchant ships sturdy enough to carry tanks and used small fishing boats to assert territorial claims. There were many examples of states going guerrilla. Iran supported proxies throughout the region and let them launch missiles against adversaries. Russia paid Afghani fighters to kill American soldiers. China's inducing of foreign companies to give up technological secrets was a very effective way to alter the balance of power and also to make its military stronger. Hybrid and gray are intrinsic to world politics. But, because of technology, the possibilities of information warfare exploded.

Hybrid wars relate to information wars.[16] A clear example of information war concerns the Russian interference with the American elections in 2016. Moscow used social media to spread fake news and to support its favored presidential candidate. But information wars were often more subtle. Authoritarian regimes from the Gulf conducted a permanent campaign against Western societies in order to be seen as trustworthy partners. In international meetings, like the World Economic Forum, they smoothly intermingled with leaders from the West. Through sponsorship of sports clubs, "Emirates" and "Qatar" became brand names. China first pursued a refined public diplomacy to showcase its peaceful intentions and went on to propagate a modern variant of the romantic ideal of the old Silk Road. During the corona pandemic, it tried to profile itself as a savior to other countries.

The battle for hearts and minds can be studied with an eye on the perpetrator, its intentions, and its means. At least as important is to clarify why Western societies were sensitive to misinformation and propaganda. In that regard, the book highlights the importance of the neglect of civic education and fickle patriotism. There was a lot of flag waving in the West, yet few genuine efforts to make citizens understand the risks of authoritarianism, the history of dictatorship, and the sacrifices paid to fight it. Hence, while officers in the armed forces received larger budgets to conduct information war and dedicated government institutions were set up to counter fake news, Western society remained mellow at the core. It was hard to win an information war, when citizens were not dedicated to the truth.

What, then, is the stance of this work toward other allegedly new issues in world politics? Has the age of globalization not genuinely reshaped world politics by making citizens more aware of themes such as the environment, climate change, cyber security, and migration? Thinking about international politics, like thinking in general, is partially contingent. Theory evolves as also the world evolves. Yet, caution is due when it comes to considering themes to be new. The impact of the environment on political stability attracted the attention of kings and thinkers already in ancient times. Cyber security is obviously a new phenomenon. But the struggle for information dominance, whether through messenger networks or the telegraph, has been a perpetual concern. Migration is another issue that has occupied officials and thinkers throughout the centuries, their responses oscillating between openness and disdain for the alleged barbarians. The form changes, but the issues are not entirely new. Environmental change, migration, and technology have shown their capacity to make societies flourish and suffer many times in the past. This is not to downplay their importance, but rather to steer clear of a tendency for exaggeration. There certainly exist perennial forces that shape politics, like the desire of most men and women to settle in a place where it is good to live and to defend that place against outsiders. Some call that the power of proximity, others the pull of provincialism. Only a minority of the world population is cosmopolitan and that makes centrifugal forces powerful.

Readers who expect to find simple critiques will be disappointed. This work identifies flaws of the past generations of political leaders, but also stresses that citizens easily surrendered politics to a class of professional election campaigners. Citizenship hence was reduced to going to vote once every few years and bitterly complaining about their elected politicians in between. Some intellectuals called for participatory democracy, but have citizens truly become ready and willing to participate? This book confirms the crippling gap between poor and rich, the excesses of capitalism, yet also stresses that many who did not belong to the jet set showed the same profit-maximizing behavior at a more modest scale. Lower income groups refused to match their indignation about inequality with action.[17] Instead of supporting the small entrepreneur, they made the giants bigger. Joe six-pack exploited the lack of transparency of globalization, the invisibility of exploitation and abuse, as eagerly as the Wall Street shark. I would bet that if we gave citizens a basic income, as some suggest, they would still spend it on the same multinationals, watch the same billionaire soccer players. If one only applies ethics on the income side and not on the expenditure side, can we expect the economy to become better? Or take the criticism about China. The reader will discover the cunning statecraft of China. Instead of blaming China for the economic problems in the developed world, however, this book explains how Beijing essentially aligned its own policy that focused on industrialization with Western governments that were primarily concerned about consumption.

Nor should this work be expected to be prophetic. It emphasizes a lost momentum for the Western world, its weakening, but does not predict its collapse. Yes, democracy is in bad shape. In fact, there has been an endless stream of warnings. In 1974, the German Chancellor Willy Brandt famously remarked: "Western Europe has only twenty or thirty more years of democracy left in it; after that it will slide, engineless and rudderless, under the surrounding sea of dictatorship."[18] One cannot deny the feeling that Western politics is on a slippery slope, that the *rota fortunae* now inevitably shrieks toward distress and uncertainty. One cannot disagree with the assessment that dignity retreats from the assemblies, that big business is tremendously influential, and that policy is frequently about sterile economics instead of the deeper chords of identity and pride that form a nation.[19] Yet, in many countries democracy remained resilient and all around the world activists shed their blood for political liberty. For all the dynamism, authoritarian states also remain fragile and often lack the freedom that is so crucial for innovation.[20] I can thus not conclude at this stage whether Western liberalism will die, whether the Western world will be eclipsed by the authoritarian countries, as Brandt suggested. Thirty years is a wavelet in history, a few books in a long line of library shelves. I do not even think our times were so exceptional; they were different. All I can conclude is that the West has lost a golden opportunity to grow stronger, that it has saddled the next generations with formidable challenges, that the world became more divided, and that other powers can take advantage of it.

So, the reader should not expect this book to be a long opinion article with a single idea and everything organized accordingly. It consists of different themes that are studied throughout the chapters, themes that are inseparable. It is mostly chronological. The chronological approach sometimes leads to repetition. The reader will, for example, discover that the incapacity of the West to deal with the growing instability of the South comes back in different periods. They will also find that while some warnings were already audible in the late 1980s – about the impact of social inequality on the resilience of Western society, for instance, or the consequences of underinvestment for economic power – politicians were still seen to be incapable of addressing these issues in the 1990s and the subsequent two decades.

This repetition, the recurrence of a problem and statements of concern, helps the reader understand themes like the limits of learning or the decadence trap. Oftentimes, we did have the scientific reports about the challenges and we even had clues about solutions, yet were too slow to react. We knew that consumerism and the sorry state of citizenship were rendering Western society vulnerable in a competitive world. Books were written about the matter and important leaders signaled their worry, decade after decade. Yet, to make a rich society change track, so it would appear, is like trying to change the course of a mammoth tanker whose rudder is broken. If there is repetition in this book, let it be an affirmation of inertia.

The account takes the reader back and forth between different viewpoints. The book approaches world politics from the viewpoint of the West, roughly defined as North America and Europe, but also looks at the West from the perspective of other parts of the world. This is required to understand how tensions built up, how common challenges, like financial instability, were approached with different interests in mind. The book takes an interest in the internal causes of the difficulties of the West, but also in its foreign policy, the way Western experts evaluated its effectiveness, and the way non-Western voices commented on it. The reader will be introduced to Western assessments of world security, but also to Russian, Chinese, Indian, and various African interpretations. Hence, this project draws from multiple sources. It builds on various previous studies, but also reviews policy documents, integrates insights from personal conversations, and includes figures from multiple databases. The merit of the book lies thus not so much in sensational revelations, but in bringing information from many sources together, combining viewpoints, and connecting aspects of world politics that are often treated separately: connecting the dots.

The result is a broad canvas of events and personalities, connected through different themes. This approach is somewhat at loggerheads with today's more common approach of looking at history through the lens of small events or personalities. In those cases, one can look at history as through a drop of water: through something very tiny, one obtains an all-around panorama. This is indeed a very enchanting way of writing, allowing readers to identify themselves with personalities or to be offered salient anecdotes, to smell and feel history. Yet, sometimes, it is also important to look at the world as it is: a murky and vast complex of intrigues, partnerships, and conflicts.

This book will therefore be less an elegant miniature and more a panorama that invites the reader on certain occasions to study facets in detail and then again to take a few steps back to see the bigger picture, to gaze through one perspective and then to take another viewpoint. It is a more demanding approach, less straightforward perhaps, but an approach that encourages the reader to master the complexity that is inherent to world politics. It will not be easy to read this work leisurely. Pages are rather packed with information and sometimes one will have to turn back to keep seeing the plot. While this book certainly has flaws, it needs to be read with this purpose in mind.

Outline

The book consists of 12 chapters. A very short first chapter documents the move of the pendulum with data. It became fashionable for optimistic intellectuals to display charts that had only one destination: up. Optimism is a moral duty, it was said. There was indeed reason to be optimistic. The chapter shows growth in production and trade, a decrease also of extreme poverty. Yet, it recommends prudence and seeing these positive trends next to more worrying developments.

How was the transition from the Cold War to a new age perceived? What was the mood in the world at this dramatic moment of change around 1990? These are the central questions in chapters 2 and 3. The second chapter explains that the fall of the Soviet Union was not a victory of the West. Yes, the West became uncontested in terms of power. And, yes, one famous essay proclaimed the end of history. Yet, that same essay also warned that the end of history would be an unhappy time and make many in the West long for identity. The end of the Cold War triggered a moment of introspection.

The third chapter takes an alternative viewpoint. It looks at the world from the perspective of other societies. Russia, for instance, was still tottering between the old certainty of Soviet nationalism and the new uncertainty of democracy. In China, reformism was balanced by a commitment to fight Westernization, to keep control over the economy, and to contest American dominance. In the Middle East, the main experiment of democracy, Turkey, struggled, while the authoritarian countries showed no interest in liberalization. In the Global South, prominent thinkers were critical of Western liberalism. Hence, the turning point around 1990 was a defeat of Soviet communism, but certainly not yet a victory of Western liberalism. Chapters 2 and 3 form the overture and set the scene.

The next three chapters survey world politics between the end of the Cold War and the turn of the century. This is, so to say, the first act. Chapter 4 explains how the liberalism advocated by the West became a façade. It became a façade because the pledges of Western leaders to strike a balance between openness and protection, the Third Way, as it was called, were not matched by their deeds. In the United States, President Bill Clinton promised to create a more humane economy, but inequality exploded. While American society became more dependent on imported goods, distributed by megamalls like Walmart, the government started to sell massive amounts of debt overseas. In the European Union, integration advanced, but citizens were hesitant. While rightist nationalism was quarantined, the gains of the open market were not clear to all citizens. Similar contradictions, chapter 5 explains, were visible in security policy. While the West pretended to stand for the promotion of democracy, it opted for remote-control bombings with limited ambition to help create the conditions for lasting democracy on the ground.

If the West expected its partners to adjust to Western values, China made it clear that the West had better mind its own business. Beijing played Western companies against one another. The American president stated that he hated his China policy, yet insisted that his country had to continue to try to "improve" China. At the same time, Western investors turned their back on India. Russia emerged from the 1990s disillusioned. Less than a decade after the fall of the Soviet Union, longing for strong central power returned and the fight against NATO rekindled. In the Middle East, a dramatic intervention was launched against Iraq. Afterwards, the West found itself actively protecting authoritarian regimes. Hence, chapter 6 concludes, the West failed to lead and started making its rivals rich. The 1990s were a period of fast growth and confidence, epitomized by television series like *Friends* and *Sex and the City*, but the pillars of that prosperity were starting to corrode.

The following three chapters discuss the period between the bursting of the Dotcom bubble around the year 2000 and the terrorist attacks around the turn of the century and the height of a new financial crisis in 2009. This forms the second act. Chapter 7 concentrates on the ongoing failure to strengthen Western society from inside. Economically, the West literally moved from one crisis to another without learning its lesson. It was awash with capital, but hardly used it to invest in the vital tissue of its society. It created new bubbles that caused the so-called subprime crisis in the United States and the Eurozone crisis. In the wake of the dramatic terrorist attacks in 2001, American patriotism was promoted, but it became flimsy. Companies claimed to be more ethical, yet sourced more and more from countries with lax environmental and social standards.

Chapter 8 takes stock of Western foreign policy. American foreign policy became a combination of a dysfunctional crusade against terrorism and an ineffective campaign to advance globalization. The global war on terror, with interventions in Afghanistan and Iraq, was badly planned, came at a staggering financial cost, and destroyed what was left of international legitimacy. While soldiers were being killed on the frontline, governments kept befriending the very states that sponsored radical Islam. Europe tried to profile itself more as a soft power, but also undermined its principles with an opportunistic stance toward various authoritarian regimes. The West failed to reform international economic governance, so that competitors like China asserted themselves as alternative partners. The leadership of the West was challenged primarily by its own inconsistent policies.

The next chapter clarifies how this high age of globalization coincided with a growing contestation of Western influence. China and the Gulf States banked on Western consumerism; other developing countries banked on Chinese growth. China emerged as Asia's most powerful country. India and Japan were left behind; other Asian countries were pitted against one another. Russia, too, aimed at a sphere of influence. Countries in the Middle East consolidated autocracy and armed themselves to the teeth. In the Global South, a large part of the revenues from the commodity boom disappeared. Extreme poverty, slums, and precarious employment remained widespread. The situation proved an incubator of war, terrorism, and new great power rivalry.

The final act, also consisting of three chapters, examines the period between 2010 and 2019. This period gave the Western world more relief. Politicians could pride themselves that the financial crisis had not turned into an economic Armageddon and that there was recovery. Still, large parts of society remained unconvinced. The social fabric of the United States and Europe continued to corrode. In Europe, the common currency was saved, but citizens remained skeptical and entrepreneurs reluctant to invest. The response to migration also undermined the credibility of pragmatic politicians. The mood of confidence of the 1990s gave way to uncertainty. As rightist demagogues were on the march, pragmatic politicians were seen mourning the death of the ideals they themselves had buried. But now, at least, they could blame nationalists for that malfeasance.

Chapter 11 shows that the West could still not rebalance its ties with China, despite more assertive nationalism and the corona pandemic revealing the downside of long supply chains. It also betrayed the call for democracy of the Arab Spring and fell back into its habit of sponsoring dictators as a quick fix for instability. The rise of the Islamic State led to an inconsistent military response that mainly repressed insecurity in the Middle East. Military strains were visible in regard to Russia and China. Both countries deployed missiles and other systems to deny access to their neighborhoods. The West completely destroyed what was left of its prominent role in international global governance. This was a period of international abdication.

The world order that came forth was fragmented and turbulent. As a result of the rise of China, the old geopolitical dilemma of the main maritime power, the United States, facing a new continental power, China, returned. Xi Jinping destroyed the last hope that trade would make his country democratic. Many Asian countries saw no option but to accept China as an inevitable partner. South Asia remained a waiting room of globalization, overshadowed by China. Africa became once again an arena of great power rivalry. Three important forces came to shape world politics: the relative decline of the West, a demographic explosion in a context of poverty in the South, and the rise of China. Amidst all this, regional powers, from Russia, through Turkey, to Saudi Arabia, hedged their bets. They reduced Western influence so as to protect their national interests more assertively. The new order was immensely fragile. There was strife between states and strife inside states. Thirty years after the world pulled down the Berlin Wall, new walls and fissures emerged everywhere.

OVERTURE

CHAPTER 1

PROGRESS

AFTER HAVING READ THROUGH THE INTRODUCTION, SOME READERS might have grown impatient. Why should we question the progress made during the decades that followed the end of the Cold War? In terms of trade, growth, and prosperity, this was a golden age! Indeed, it was so. Just consider figure 1.1. Between 1990 and 2019, world trade increased almost sixfold. Gross production grew fourfold. The number of people living in extreme poverty, below US$1.9 per day, decreased by 70 percent. In absolute terms, the number of very poor people decreased from about 1.9 billion people in 1990 to around 600 million in 2019. One can clearly recognize a few economic dips in the chart; in 2001, for example, in 2009, and in 2015. Yet, each time, the global economy recovered. For all the doomsday preaching, there was no global depression. Despite the dips, recent history remained an upward curve.

Readers might recall the arguments of optimistic thinkers. Steven Pinker described globalization as a cosmic force, born out of the age of enlightenment.[1] With some dramatic charts, he argued that globalization improved health, prosperity, security, and wellbeing. This is also the argument that the late Swedish scientist Hans Rosling made in *Factfulness*.[2] His data about receding conflict and advancing wellbeing pop up in numerous presentations of other opinion makers, politicians, and business leaders. Yuval Noah Harari is another acclaimed writer who made the argument that the world has still become a better and more peaceful place.[3] This is the moment for

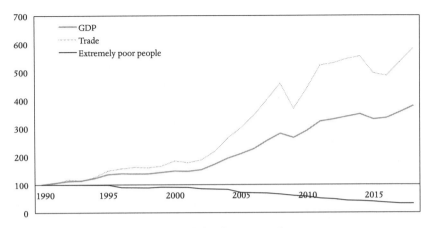

Figure 1.1   World development indicators (%)

Note: Trade concerns world exports of goods and services, extremely poor people concerns
the estimated number of people living below the US$1.9 PPP per day threshold.
Source: World Development Indicators (WDI).

humans, he wrote, to move beyond materialistic needs, to use technology to develop their talents, and to emerge like a godlike creature. These
optimists are particularly compelling because they advance their case in a
seemingly rational and scientific way, supported by loads of data.

The aim of this chapter is not to disregard progress. The aim is to put
optimistic observations into perspective. We cannot relativize everything.
Even if the poverty rate were to be reduced, still hundreds of millions of
people would live in destitution. This is a humanitarian tragedy and a security challenge. It suffices, that out of the poor masses a tiny fraction grows
angry or opportunistic enough to pick up a weapon, for an entire region to
sink into anarchy. Nothing is more devastating to stability than the combination of masses of poor and a few greedy warlords. The data in this chapter
call for nuance. Believers in progress should not just look back to see how
mankind advanced, but take into consideration the flaws and the errors.
The chapter is also a scene setter. It introduces important trends before
they are explained in detail in the following chapters. These include the
weakening of the West, the limits of globalization, the divergence between
China and the rest of the developing world, enduring insecurity, and environmental distress.

Table 1.1. Basic indicators of Western power (%)

	1990s	2000s	2010s
Global population	13	12	11
Gross domestic product	61	54	48
Manufacturing	53	47	34
Satisfaction about the state of the country	40	38	26
Export destination	35	33	26
Foreign lending	61	82	39
Foreign direct investment	73	71	51
Military spending	68	65	50

Sources: WDI, IMF, SIPRI, UNCTAD.
Note: The West is defined as the United States and Western Europe. "Satisfaction about the state of the country" relates to the US only.

The weakening of the West

In the 1990s, the West represented 60 percent of the world's economic production and 50 percent of its manufacturing, with around 13 percent of the world's population (see table 1.1). In the subsequent decades, that dominance diminished. It coincided with a decrease of public satisfaction with the state of the country (US only) and of trust in politics.

Economic weakening has important external consequences. The smaller a country's share in the world economy, the more difficult it becomes to wield influence, because partner countries find alternative customers for their exports, alternative lenders, and alternative investors. In the last decade, table 1.1 shows, an average country still had around 26 percent of exports bound for the West, 39 percent of its loans coming from the West, and 51 percent of its foreign investment. The West remained a crucial economic partner. But its position was clearly eroded. This was also true for its military power. The global preponderance enjoyed in the years after the Cold War drew to an end and this relative weakening inevitably empowered other countries as security actors.

Despite economic decline, Western economies were resilient. Trade grew and so did domestic production. But it is clear that economic growth between 2010 and 2019 remained slower than in the previous 20 years (figure 1.2). The resilience of trade, an important element of globalization, did

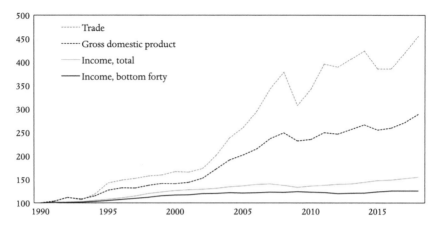

Figure 1.2   Selected growth indicators for the West (%)

Note: Figures for EU28 and US. All income figures are inflation-adjusted. The income
figures for the bottom 40 concern the unweighted average of real disposable incomes for
the US, the UK, France, and Germany.

Sources: WDI, BEA, SOEP, INSEE.

not always coincide with strong production growth. Western countries
participated intensively in globalization, but their economies started to
grow more slowly. There was also a large gap between globalization and
production on the one hand, and the real disposable income of households on the other. The real disposable income is what households can
spend, corrected for inflation. If incomes increase, but products and rent
become more expensive, the *real* disposable income increases much more
slowly or might even decrease. Particularly the poorest 40 percent suffered. Their real disposable income has had virtually no growth since
2000. Over the 30 years, their real disposable income growth was just
25 percent.

Western countries experienced a decline of their power and a growing
gap between economic growth and purchasing power. The full impact of
this weakening was mitigated by growing external debt. The majority of
Western countries imported more than they exported. Later, we will discover that these imports primarily concern fuels from Russia and the Gulf
States, consumer goods from China, and cars alongside other machines
from Germany. If we accumulate the current account deficit throughout
the three decades, it amounts to US$14 trillion, five times the size of the

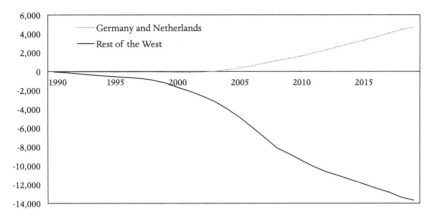

Figure 1.3   The evolution of the net international investment position
(US$ bn)
Note: US and EU countries. Germany and the Netherlands are set apart given their
exceptionally large surplus.
Source: WDI.

economy of the United Kingdom (figure 1.3). The current account includes trade and investment incomes. Germany and the Netherlands were key exceptions with large surpluses. Large, structural deficits can spark painful adjustment crises in the long run. Think of the tale by Jean de La Fontaine, about the ant and the grasshopper. When the cold winter kicks in and the industrious ant is not willing to help, the vulnerability of the grasshopper becomes visible.

The limits of globalization

The erosion of economic power notwithstanding, the West remained an important consumer market. In the 1990s, a core foreign policy theme was conditional engagement: access to the Western market in exchange for accepting Western rules and values, including free trade, democracy, and the rule of law. Striking, however, was that the countries profiting the most from the age of globalization and the openness of the West were not the democratic countries.

Authoritarian countries, especially China, rapidly expanded their share in Western imports from 15 percent in 1990 to 34 percent in

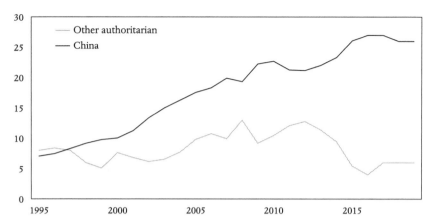

Figure 1.4 Share of authoritarian countries in total imports of EU and US (%, EU is extra-EU)

Note: Coding for authoritarianism based on World Governance Indicators (accountability and rule of law).
Sources: WGI and UNCTAD.

2012 (figure 1.4). The countries growing their export revenues from the West the most were thus not necessarily free, democratic countries, but often authoritarian countries. Conditional engagement was self-deception.

Figure 1.5 shows that economic openness advanced between 1990 and 2010. Afterwards, its advance slowed significantly and even tapered off. More remarkable is the fact that political openness hardly increased during these 30 years. Of all the countries in the world, at most 46 percent could be defined as free. Of all the people in the world, at most 40 percent lived in a liberal democracy. The peak of democratization was around 2008. Afterwards, not only did economic globalization stagnate, but democracy receded slowly as well. There is thus not much evidence that globalization promoted democracy in the world. Economic openness, if it ever truly existed, did not lead to political openness. Still, this tune was repeated by Western politicians again and again.

While the world was celebrating the high age of globalization, even physical walls returned. Altogether, over 13,000 kilometers of walls and border fences were built between 1990 and 2019 (figure 1.6). By comparison, the Berlin Wall was just 155 kilometers long; the whole Iron Curtain,

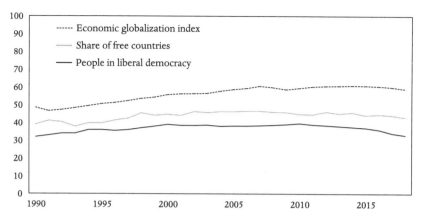

Figure 1.5 Economic and political globalization: economic globalization index, share of free countries, and share of world population living in liberal democracies (%)

Sources: KOF, Freedom House, Anna Lührmann, Sandra Grahn, Richard Morgan, Shreeya Pillai, and Staffan I. Lindberg, 2019. State of the world 2018: Democracy facing global challenges. *Democratization*, 26(6), 895–915.

the fault line between the Soviet Union and the West, was about 6,800 kilometers. Walls have emerged in every region: Europe, Asia, Africa, and the Americas. The idea that commerce would level out borders and barriers has thus not materialized. Nationalism never entirely vanished. Memories of previous wars and territorial disputes continued to hang as a dark shadow over trading states like China, South Korea, and Japan. In Europe, despite decades of integration, center politicians continued to struggle with nationalist parties and the vast majority of citizens still identified themselves more as national citizens than as European ones.

China vs Global South

During the early post-Cold War period, there was enthusiasm about the rise of the Global South, about Africa, South Asia, and Latin America. But this area was eclipsed by China. China's growth was the fruit of the hard work of hundreds of millions of citizens and a government that did a better job in attracting the foreign investment that came with technology and experience. This had important consequences.

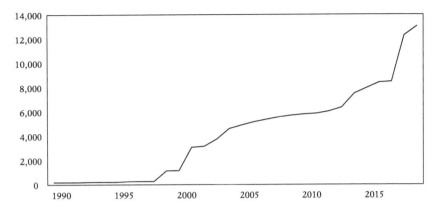

Figure 1.6   Accumulated length of border fences and walls (km)

Source: Verified news sources. For instance: India building new "steel fence" along Pakistan, Bangla borders. *Economic Times,* January 10, 2020; Tom Head, 2020. SA's new R37m border fence with Zimbabwe badly damaged. *The South Africa,* April 13, 2020; Ilan Greenberg, 2006. Kazakhstan: Fence for part of Uzbek border. *The New York Times,* October 20, 2006.

The Global South remained beset by poverty. The World Bank stressed that the $1.90 poverty threshold is too low to measure economic distress and proposed higher thresholds. Figure 1.7 shows the number of people below the threshold of US\$5.2 per day. US\$5.2 per day barely covers food purchases and basic needs. It is not extreme poverty, but it remains poverty. The number of people in the Global South, Africa, Latin America, and South Asia living below this threshold grew by about 500 million.

A critical problem for the Global South concerned the limited availability of jobs. Once more, the difference from China was striking. Between 1990 and 2019, China's population between 15 and 64 years of age increased by 245 million. At the same time, it created 207 million additional jobs. Between 1990 and 2019, the combined population between 15 and 64 years of age in Africa and South Asia increased by 870 million. But the total number of jobs only increased by 170 million. In 2019, 16 percent of the South Asian population between 15 and 64 years was employed, 15 percent in Africa. Many thus remained dependent on self-employment in agriculture or informal employment in cities (figure 1.8). Yet, subsistence

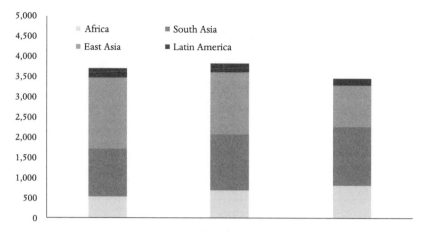

Figure 1.7   People living below US$5.2 PPP per day (million)
Source: WDI.

farming in the agricultural sector was threatened by climate change, water shortage, and cheap products exported by the West, and the informal sector in the cities by inflation, crime, and cheaper goods dumped from China.

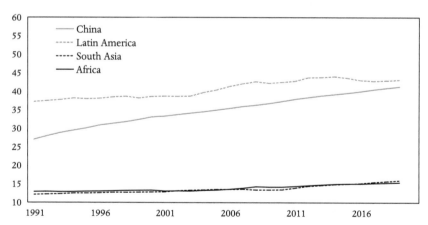

Figure 1.8   People employed as share of people between 15 and 64 years old (%)
Source: WDI.

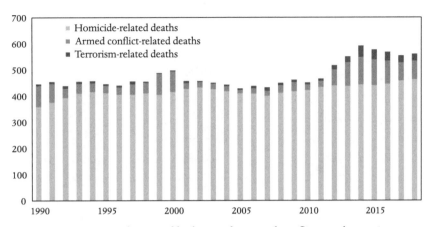

Figure 1.9   Deaths caused by homicide, armed conflicts, and terrorism
(thousands)
Note: All data are approximate.
Sources: UCPD, WDI, GTD.

Security

Economic uncertainty is an incubator of insecurity. It is often argued that
the world has never been safer than during the high age of globalization.
This is correct. In many countries, the homicide rate, which is the number
of murders compared to the total population, decreased. Compared to
the brutally violent first half of the twentieth century, fewer people were
killed in wars. In absolute terms, however, the number of people killed by
violence slightly increased, particularly between 2010 and 2019 (figure 1.9).
Organized crime, rebellion, and terrorism infested large parts of the world.
There can be discussion about the degree to which, for instance, murders
and terrorist incidents are now more frequently reported. The fact remains
that over half a million people were killed by violence each year. In relation
to the population, the death rate dropped. Yet still, many people lived in the
dark shadow of endemic violence.

Figure 1.10 shows that globalization has not advanced security throughout the world. Between 1990 and 2004, the number of armed conflicts
decreased, but rebounded in the following 15 years. The number of wars
remained small. The most lethal wars were those in the Democratic
Republic of Congo, Rwanda, Syria, Sudan, Afghanistan, and Iraq. Many of

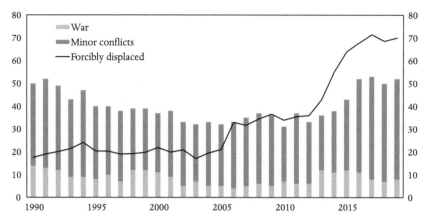

Figure 1.10   Number of armed conflicts (left axis) and forcibly displaced people
(million, right axis)

Note: Major wars have at least 1,000 battle-related deaths.
Source: UCPD.

these conflicts were protracted and lasted many years, so that international
attention diminished. Highlighting the increase in conflict is the number of
forcibly displaced people. These include refugees and people who are forced
to leave their home but remain inside the country. Between 2004 and 2017,
the number of forcibly displaced people more than doubled. The majority
were located in Africa and the Middle East.

Global military spending, calculated in constant American dollars, also
bounced back to Cold War levels (figure 1.11). Most countries reduced the
number of soldiers, but spent much more on modern weapons systems.
The United States intervened in Afghanistan and Iraq. The Western global
war on terror became one of the most expensive military campaigns in
recent history. Russia used military force to repel the West from what
was left of the Soviet sphere of influence. China embarked on a massive military build-up to drive the United States out of its adjacent seas.
Thousands of ballistic missiles were deployed as a cheap deterrent against
US naval prowess. Major geopolitical tensions resurfaced between close
trading partners, like China and the United States, and Russia and Western
Europe.

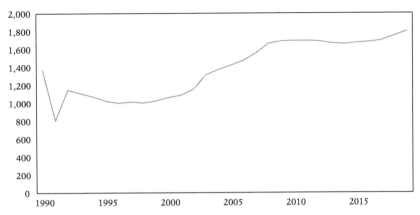

Figure 1.11   Global military spending (constant US$ bn)
Source: SIPRI.

Environment

Citizens were consistently concerned about pollution. In 1990, long before Greta Thunberg started the school strike against climate change, hundreds of thousands of protesters gathered on the Mall in Washington, DC to celebrate Earth Day. Movie star Tom Cruise addressed them: "We see many walls come tumbling down this year. With the walls down, we can all see what we have in common: our planet."[4]

That same year, a Swiss physicist proposed to mitigate global warming by putting a mirror in space to deflect the sun's heat. "How to solve the CO2 problem without tears," scientists challenged themselves.[5] In 1993, Bill Clinton was one of the first presidential candidates in the United States to embrace climate change and the environment as key themes in his campaign. But the CO_2 problem was not solved. Since 1990, CO_2 emissions grew by about 70 percent and the CO_2 efficiency of the world economy hardly increased (figure 1.12).

Or consider transportation. Globalization was often said to be a more efficient way of production. But one factor that was seldom considered in measuring its success concerned transportation. Transportation is a key emitter of polluting gases, but it also causes traffic jams and requires a lot of space for roads, warehouses, and so forth.

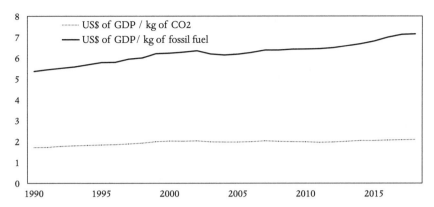

Figure 1.12 Fueling economic growth: Global US$ of GDP per kg of CO$_2$ emitted and kg of fossil fuel consumed (kg/constant 2010 US$)
Source: WDI.

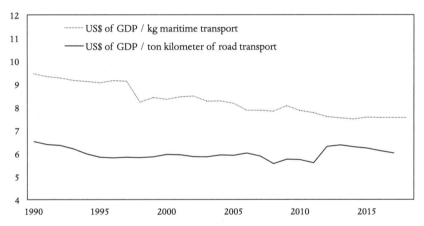

Figure 1.13 Global US$ of GDP per kg of transport (kg/constant 2010 US$)
Source: WDI.

Between 1990 and 2019, figure 1.13 shows, the global economy became significantly less efficient in terms of transportation. There were thus more ships, container stacks, trucks, vans, and warehouses for smaller gains in production.

A final indicator that hints at the limited impact of innovation and technology is the disposal of waste. We do not have consistent data for the total global waste pile. We do know that the disposed waste in European countries decreased, that it remained stable in the United

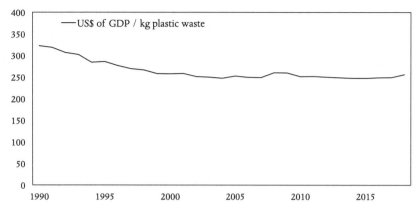

Figure 1.14   GDP per kg plastic waste (kg/constant 2010 US$)
Source: WDI and UN Baseline Report on Plastic Waste.

States, and that it increased spectacularly in many developing countries. We do have data, however, for global plastic waste, summarized in figure 1.14. While recycling of plastic waste was almost negligible in the early 1990s, the global share of reused plastic waste climbed to slightly below a quarter in 2020. Yet, the total disposed plastic waste, burned or put into landfill, almost trebled. Overall, the world economy became less, not more, economical in using plastics. The global production per kilogram of plastic waste decreased in the 1990s and remained flat in the following two decades.

Perspective

In sum, the question is not so much whether there has been progress in the post-Cold War period. The question is rather how we evaluate the degree of progress in spreading democracy, social dignity, security, and sustainable production in comparison to the spectacular high tide of economic globalization, the opportunity to exchange technology and ideas, and so forth. Progress optimists often magnify the positive trend by comparing everything with the growing world population. Compared with the growing world population, fewer people get killed. Compared with the growing world population, one can mitigate many trends. But if we really care about progress, it is fairer to ask whether we advanced enough in comparison with to the economic opportunities that were present than to ask whether we advanced in comparison with the number of people that live on the planet. From that perspective, many curves remained remarkably flat.

CHAPTER 2

A DOUBTFUL VICTORY

"IT IS IN OUR HANDS TO LEAVE THESE DARK MACHINES BEHIND, IN THE dark ages where they belong and to press forward to cap a historic movement toward a long era of peace."[1] This was how American President George H. W. Bush described the end of the Cold War. Technology was overwhelming tyranny, he reasoned, so that the age of information would be an age of liberation. British Prime Minister Margaret Thatcher echoed his optimism: "Our policies have brought unparalleled prosperity."[2] As McDonald's opened its first franchise in Russia, Hollywood movies were tolerated by the theocracy in Tehran, and crowds kept descending on the Berlin Wall to hack pieces of concrete as a souvenir, liberalism appeared to become an irresistible guide to world politics.

This chapter captures the mood in the West at this decisive moment in the late 1980s and early 1990s. It measures its advantages, but also traces back worries, about the neglect of infrastructure, the decadence trap, with wealth decoupling from virtue, economic growth predating on the environment, the prospect of decline if the West did not respond to the ambitions of new competitors. The victory of the West, we will discover, was perceived as a doubtful victory. Some of these challenges, indeed, were present at an earlier stage. The 1970s formed a watershed between the 30 years of growth after World War II and a subsequent period of decay. Yet, still, it was at the end of the Cold War that the West had its hands free to address those challenges.

The Cold War

But what was the Cold War in the first place? In the early 1980s, a soldier in a bunker near Moscow was alerted to an incoming American missile. The alert came at a sensitive time. For months, the United States had been testing the resolve of the Soviet Union by deploying nuclear-capable bombers and submarines close to its borders. A Korean passenger plane, mistakenly identified as an American military aircraft, had just been shot down. Now, this soldier in his bunker saw an intercontinental ballistic missile heading toward his country. That was at least what satellites and computers made of it. The incoming missile was in reality nothing more than the sun reflected by clouds. Luckily, the duty officer also assumed it was a false alarm. This was the Cold War: the permanent threat of mass destruction by tens of thousands of nuclear weapons.

Close calls like this were common. They showed that if the war between the two superpowers ever became hot, the whole world would burn in a nuclear apocalypse. This threat hung over the world like a permanent storm cloud. In its shadow, the global order remained a patchwork of regional battlegrounds, like Southeast Asia, the Middle East, and Africa, and a few havens of relative peace. It was a breath-taking joust between the United States and the Soviet Union, a clash of titans over geopolitical interests, with the Soviets seeking to expand their influence across Eurasia, and Washington seeking to stop it – a conflict over ideology, technological leadership, economic dominance, and military supremacy. It was a period of physical walls, barriers that halted both people and trade, and mental walls, separating ideas. The Cold War lasted over 40 years.

Rather suddenly, the skies cleared. In 1985, the Secretary General of the Communist Party, Mikhail Gorbachev, and American President Ronald Reagan had made overtures and met for the first time in Geneva. That year also, Mikhail Gorbachev avowed that the rigid Soviet system needed openness and reform. Glasnost and perestroika became the keywords in Russian policy reform. In 1987, he allowed private ownership, followed by the relaxing of control over smaller Soviet republics in 1988, and first attempts toward democratization in 1989. That year, Soviet troops withdrew after a decade of deployment in Afghanistan. The dismantling of a bastion of authoritarianism had started.

Dictatorship was also defied in other parts of the world. In 1987, direct elections had peacefully ended a decade of military rule in South Korea. The same year, Taiwan, which already had moved toward economic openness, lifted martial law. In Singapore, strongman Lee Kuan Yew partially democratized the city state and prepared to step down. In 1989, tens of thousands of students assembled in Beijing to call for democracy. Despite brutal suppression, these Tiananmen protests made it appear that economic growth would make democratization irresistible. Also in 1989, elections ended military rule in Turkey. In Iran, Akbar Rafsanjani was elected president with an agenda of opening up, also toward the West.

Opportunity to lead

1989 and 1990 were years of excitement, of electricity in the living rooms of hundreds of millions of households when the images of the collapsing Soviet Empire reached them. The West entered a moment without peer rivals, a unipolar moment. With 6 percent of the world population, the countries around the Atlantic Basin controlled over 60 percent of the world's economic production and trade. An average citizen here was twice as rich as a person in Russia, ten times richer than a Chinese, and 14 times wealthier than someone living in Africa or South Asia. Over 50 percent of manufacturing was located in the West. Western countries hosted all top universities and owned 60 percent of the world's patents.[3] Whether one lived in Boston, New York, London, Amsterdam, or Paris, one could see the emergence of a global elite that understood the same language, watched the same movies, and used the same brands. Its networking power, the capability of weaving large markets, was unequaled. It represented around 40 percent of the world's shipping fleet, half of the largest multinationals, 70 percent of all large aircraft, and 90 percent of the internet traffic. At the center of this web of commerce and information sat the United States, the universal spider.

With the Soviets on the ropes, the United States was freed from its most important geopolitical concern: the menace of a Eurasian Leviathan. This geopolitical fixation had its roots far back in history, more precisely in the resistance to Great Britain as its imperial overlord. The American

Declaration of Independence in 1776 was only the beginning of that struggle. In 1814, British troops burned the White House. It was this event, alongside a persistent European presence in the western hemisphere, that led to the Monroe Doctrine, prescribing the United States to keep rivals at a distance. Since then, Washington has kept a wary eye on the appearance of any Eurasian rival capable of projecting power into the Atlantic and Pacific Ocean, and, hence, of menacing the American continent. This had been the case first with Great Britain in the nineteenth century, then with Germany and Japan in the early twentieth century, and subsequently with the Soviet Union during the Cold War. Each time, these actors had first sprung up as Eurasian powers, forged onwards into the oceans, and extended their power to the shores of the American continent.

Hence, the United States pursued absolute security on the American continent, predominance in its flanking oceans, as well as the preservation of a first line of defense against Eurasian powers in Western Europe and East Asia (map 2.1). After the collapse of the Soviet Union, this strategy was almost fulfilled. America's neighborhood was secure. If in the north, Canada figured as a loyal seafood supplier, Mexico in the south could be considered its low-income seafood processor. Both countries had around 80 percent of their exports bound for the United States. The North American Free Trade Agreement, NAFTA, signed in 1988, institutionalized these commercial relations. The United States preserved a mutual defense pact with most of the Latin American countries, the Rio Treaty, and had a controlling stake in the Inter-American Development Bank, the IDB. The adjoining two oceans were patrolled by the world's largest navy and American companies controlled many of the undersea cables and satellites that provided connectivity with Europe and East Asia.

In Western Europe, American security interests were guarded by the North Atlantic Treaty Organization (NATO). The alliance was founded in 1949 to defend the liberal world, America's European sphere of influence, against communism. "Determined to safeguard the freedom, common heritage and civilisation of their peoples, founded on the principles of democracy, individual liberty and the rule of law," its preamble said.[4] Article five provided for mutual assistance if one of the members ever came under attack. Washington traditionally provided most of the alliance's budget. It

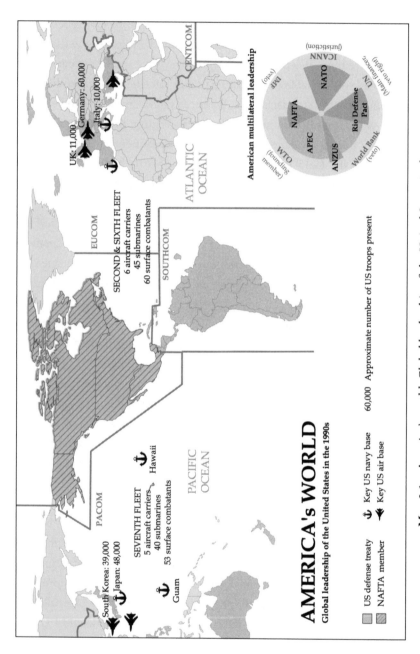

AMERICA's WORLD
Global leadership of the United States in the 1990s

South Korea: 39,000
Japan: 48,000

SEVENTH FLEET
5 aircraft carriers
40 submarines
53 surface combatants

Guam

Hawaii

PACOM

PACIFIC
OCEAN

SECOND & SIXTH FLEET
6 aircraft carriers
45 submarines
60 surface combatants

EUCOM

SOUTHCOM

ATLANTIC
OCEAN

CENTCOM

UK: 11,000
Germany: 60,000
Italy: 10,000

☐ US defense treaty

▨ NAFTA member

⚓ Key US navy base

♆ Key US air base

60,000 Approximate number of US troops present

American multilateral leadership

ICANN
(jurisdiction)

NATO

UN
(veto right)

Rio Defense
Pact

ANZUS

World Bank
(veto)

APEC

WTO
(founding
member)

NAFTA

IMF
(veto)

Map 2.1   America's world: Global leadership of the United States in the 1990s

delivered the Supreme Allied Commander Europe, or SACEUR, a four-star general for whom most European four-stars would jump up if he entered a meeting room. Some considered the SACEUR the American equivalent of the proconsuls dispatched by ancient Rome to its provinces. The United States maintained large numbers of troops in Europe and was indispensable for vital systems like satellite communication, missile defense, and transport aircraft.

There were certainly tensions between Washington and Western Europe. The United States believed that European countries did not spend enough on the alliance and came to see Europe as an economic competitor. The European Economic Community (EEC) steadily expanded. In 1987, the European Single Act gave more responsibilities to its common institutions and aimed to create an open internal market. Yet, the United States itself was a co-founder of the European project, considering it key to checking the Soviets after World War II.[5] More recently, European enlargement proved useful to prevent weak countries, like Greece, from drifting toward Moscow, and to give others, like Turkey, the prospect of stronger ties with the West. If Washington lamented that Europe did not spend enough on the military alliance, Europe became important as the main external buyer of American government debt. There were rows between the two sides of the Atlantic, but these remained family rows.

The situation was similar in East Asia. Here, Washington's first line of defense consisted of Japan, South Korea, Taiwan, the Philippines, Australia, New Zealand, Singapore, and Thailand. They curbed the Eurasian communist powers like a line of maritime strongholds. In 1989, these Asian partners represented three quarters of the region's economic output. The United States had over 100,000 troops in the area. It possessed military facilities in South Korea, Japan, and the Philippines. From there, its warships and aircraft patrolled the area. Relations with these countries could be tense. Trade frictions with Japan were recurrent and the Japanese abhorred American military presence. Like with Europe, Washington found that Tokyo could do more to bolster the security partnership. Japan, too, compensated American security commitments by buying American government bonds. The Plaza Accord of 1985 stipulated that Japan would not let its currency depreciate in a way that hurt American exports. Japan was helpful in providing support to other American partners, like Pakistan, or countries that could otherwise drift into the orbit of Beijing and Moscow, like Cambodia and Vietnam. Japan and the United States were the main contributors to the Asian Development Bank (ADB). In 1989, the web of partnerships was strengthened by the establishment of APEC, the forum for Asia Pacific Economic Cooperation.

Beyond these two bulwarks in Europe and East Asia, Washington radiated its influence through international organizations. It had a veto right in the world's two most important financial institutions: the World Bank Group and the International Monetary Fund. These Bretton Woods institutions were founded in 1944 with the aim of stabilizing financial markets and preventing economic nationalism. The World Bank Group included important specialized affiliates, like a tribunal for international investment disputes and an investment guarantee agency. They all had their headquarters in Washington, DC. A third pillar in the Bretton Woods was foreseen, but did not materialize: the International Trade Organization. It was replaced in 1947 by the General Agreement on Tariffs and Trade, GATT. During the Cold War, the three served as a counterweight to economic initiatives of the Soviets and to advance the Washington Consensus. Coined in 1989, the Washington Consensus concerned the idea, creed almost, that growth required deregulation, low trade barriers, freely floating national currencies, commodity prices set by the international market, dismantlement of state-owned enterprises, and even the privatization of public services altogether.

Openness was the key to growth. Such structural adjustment toward openness became a condition for developing countries to receive aid. The Bretton Woods institutions proposed structural adjustment programs. Washington, together with Europe and Japan, also shaped the agenda of a raft of technical bodies that set global standards for digital communication, aerospace, and pharmaceutical products. If the Cold War still provided an alternative to the West, reality was now summarized as TINA: There is no alternative. This was, in fact, a triple TINA. There was no alternative for the West as a partner, no alternative for the West as an investor, and no alternative to neoliberal policy prescriptions of the West.

In the final years of the Cold War, Western economic influence spread without impediment and so did its military power. Western power projection capacity was unmatched. The Soviets too had long-range strike capacity, but this functioned more as a nuclear deterrence. Out of the world's 25 aircraft carriers, 20 were owned by Western countries, 15 by the United States. The United States operated many more very large transport aircraft and had started building a formidable new fleet of destroyers and cruisers that plied the world's oceans. In 1989, NATO defense spending surpassed that of all other countries in the world, the crumbling Soviet Union and China included. Operation Desert Storm, the rain of cruise missiles unleashed in Iraq in 1991, the strikes by stealth bombers, and the speed with which the whole expedition was executed, had just shown how obliterating Western hard power could be. This was a high-tech blitzkrieg.

So, with the Soviet Union in trouble, the whole world appeared to have become the periphery of the West. The center of the emerging new world order would be the United States. It accounted for one third of the global economy and was bordered by two countries that could not threaten it. The Atlantic and Pacific Oceans functioned like a moat around this fortress, guarded by aircraft carrier battle groups. On the other sides of the oceans lay a second line of defense, a line of allied countries that depended on American security and were also tied to the United States by means of commerce, capital, and culture. With Desert Storm, the United States and its partners demonstrated that they could strike overwhelmingly in even the remotest corner of the world. The predominance of organizations like the World Bank and multinationals as providers of capital to almost any country beyond the ring of allies in the Atlantic and the Pacific showed that there was no longer a genuine alternative to the West as an economic partner. Even if officials downplayed the term zealously, the United States arose as a global hegemon.

Economic fragility

The scene seemed set for a long age of Western dominance and the spreading of liberalism. For years, Soviet citizens were literally risking their lives to escape to the West. Its leaders in Moscow recognized failure. The ending of the Cold War kept the United States as the sole protagonist in the spotlight. But the protagonist was bedazzled. It was not even sure of its script.

The situation was one of ambivalence: of unabashed strength on the one hand and, on the other hand, doubt that it would last. Rather than being celebrative, there was an odd feeling of gloom. Especially in the United Kingdom and the United States, the shortcomings of a decade of neoliberal reforms by the governments of Margaret Thatcher (1979–90) and Ronald Reagan (1981–9), marked by privatization and liberalization, had become undeniable. This neoliberalism was a reaction against high unemployment and high inflation in the 1970s. In the United States, only half of the population was satisfied with the state of the nation and confidence in democracy slowly retreated.[6]

The West struggled. It struggled with turbulence outside and disorientation inside. While Thatcher proclaimed the glory of global Britain, hundreds of thousands of citizens demonstrated in London against economic uncertainty and privatization. Confirming the dismal state of the economy, the pound nosedived. Far-right parties gained ground on the European continent. The United States experienced a mini stock market crash in 1989, encountered a bigger one in the autumn of 1990, and subsequently went into recession. Saddening stories appeared about poverty in cities like Detroit. "Most of the neighborhoods appear to be the victims of bombardment – houses burned and vacant, buildings crumbling, whole city blocks overrun with weeds and the carcasses of discarded automobiles," a reporter put it. "Shopping streets are depressing avenues – banks converted into fundamentalist churches, party stores with bars and boards on their windows and, here and there, a barbecue joint or saloon."[7]

Not only in Detroit was the infrastructure dilapidated. In New York, the iconic Williamsburg Bridge between Manhattan and Brooklyn was closed because of neglect. America's cities looked old and fragile due to a decade of accumulated neglect. In the 1980s, a lot of infrastructure in the United States and the United Kingdom had been privatized. While previous generations sacrificed labor and capital to expand public infrastructure, built bridges, schools, and hospitals, Western countries started to shift spending from investment to consumption. Labor shifted from construction and manufacturing to banks, shops, and other services. The share of investment in America's GDP had dropped from 25 percent in 1980 to 19 percent in 1990. The situation was similar in the United Kingdom. "Historians will come to doubt our national sanity," a British politician alerted.[8] The situation was a little better on the European continent, with France investing in high-speed trains, the Netherlands spending on flood defenses, and new ports and airports being opened throughout the region.[9] Experts worried about a tendency to harvest the benefits from investments made by previous generations without making sufficient new investments to secure prosperity for the next generations.

Besides underinvestment in public infrastructure, economists questioned whether there was sufficient investment in manufacturing. Since the late 1980s, manufacturing growth in the United Kingdom and the United States had stalled. Growth of investment in factories had dropped significantly compared to earlier decades. This all happened at a moment when the consumption of manufactured goods increased. Strong national currencies benefited consumers of goods, because they made imports cheaper, but came as a challenge to local producers of goods. Optimist economists stated that the shift toward services made the economy competitive and that growth of information technology kept the West ahead of its rivals. They also stated that the reduction of manufacturing in places like Detroit need not be a problem, as long as new jobs were created in services elsewhere. Growth would continue, but in different sectors and in different regions.

Critics, however, suggested that an economy could not survive on services alone: "A service economy is a balanced one where all sectors – agricultural, manufacturing and services – are viable even though the great majority of people may work in one area."[10] Another concern was the abandoning of so-called basic industries, like steel and assembling. Instead of making factories more efficient and environmentally sustainable, the production of such goods was outsourced to countries with laxer social and environmental standards.[11] It was an immense contradiction that the same economists who declared their faith in a free market that propelled efficiency gains accepted that rich governments forced polluting companies to close and that poor governments encouraged polluting companies to invest. It was a contradiction also that those who repeated their trust in progress found it normal that even in the twentieth century poor countries needed to pass through a stage of economic and environmental exploitation first. New services, like real estate and finance, were embraced with the same ease in the West as so-called sunset industries were demoted, disregarding the fact that Western citizens could still not imagine a life without basic goods like cotton, polymers, or aluminum.

A critical part of Western society that also suffered from low investment was education. In the 1980s, President Ronald Reagan had wanted to abolish the federal education department altogether, leaving schools to be managed by local governments and dependent on private financing. Neoliberal puritans posited that free education would be better. From a more opportunistic viewpoint, privatization and decentralization were meant to reduce costs. In the United States and the United Kingdom, privatization added to polarization. While schools had once been considered a social blender, they now contributed to segregation.[12] With good education reserved for a small group of rich students, experts warned of a tide of mediocrity. Civic education, crucial for democracies to show that they were truly superior to communist societies, had fallen into disarray.[13] Robust civics instruction, usually organized into three mandatory high-school courses, had been left to atrophy. Large groups of children were left behind, children getting second-rate education in third-rate schools.[14] Child labor returned to parts of the United States.[15] Ten subway stops from the lavish apartments around Central Park, New York, poor school pupils were seen doing worse than their parents: "Bleeding gums, impacted teeth, and rotting teeth are routine matters for the children in the South Bronx. Children get used to feeling constant pain. They go to sleep with it."[16]

For many Western countries, the 1980s were a period of decreasing investment, dwindling saving rates, and increasing household consumption. One of the comments of liberal economists about the Soviet planned economy was that it misallocated capital to sectors that did not make the country more productive. Now it could be questioned whether capitalism was not leading to the misallocation of capital in the West. How could it be that giant shopping malls were erected, yet there was no money to build schools and maintain bridges? How could it be that the rich were spending lavishly on yachts and penthouses, yet millions of poor children were ignored, hardly received quality education, and, hence, would not in any way help the economy to grow stronger? A berth for a yacht in New York could cost as much as US$2 million a year, enough to pay for about

500 children at elementary school. When asked about his single apartment worth US$12 million in downtown Manhattan, the property owner, a future American president, said: "While I cannot honestly say I need an 80-foot-long living room, I do get a kick out of having one."[17] How could it be that privatization in the 1980s had made the average American or British citizen spend more on healthcare and other public services, yet with their quality being in decline? Should it really be taken for granted that capitalism was superior?

The growing consumption in several Western countries coincided with growing external debt. As they imported more than they exported, some of the imports had to be pre-financed. But President Ronald Reagan had explained this as a sign of strength. After all, he argued, it implied that countries like the United States were creditworthy enough for foreigners to advance money.[18] You can only borrow large quantities of money if you are strong. Many economists agreed, but suggested some conditions.[19] America and other deficit countries could use the foreign money and cheap imported consumer goods as an opportunity to invest in innovative industries, education, and infrastructure. If not, some experts warned, growing debt combined with a weakened economy would mean repayment problems in the future. Even the position of the United States as the leading economy and the American dollar as the leading currency could be at risk.[20] Why, after all, would one accept American dollars to build financial reserves if the American economy was set to weaken in the long run? One economist referred to the dilemma as the morning-after problem.[21]

A first source of uncertainty about the ability of the West to preserve its power and its position at the center of world politics concerned, thus, the downside of neoliberalism. The retreat of the state, advocated by politicians like Ronald Reagan and Margaret Thatcher, had affected the vital tissue of American and British society. The shopping malls erected against the backdrop of decaying public infrastructure, manufacturing, and schools also exemplified how much this neoliberalism strayed from the Enlightenment beliefs that lay at the origins of liberal thought. Whereas the original liberal thinkers emphasized the need for the emancipation of the mind and civilization, this neoliberalism was about the creation and satisfaction of new material needs. Statesmen in the past stressed the importance of active citizenship and of education. "Patriotism, virtue and wisdom," one reads in the Federalist Papers.[22] Neoliberalism reduced citizens to consumers. It did not set them free, nor empower them, as some neoliberal intellectuals maintained. Instead, it left them to the influence of corporate Leviathans, their advertisements, their role models, and the banality of their media channels.

Previous generations of leaders called for frugality. But now, families and nations spent beyond their means. In previous times, also, leaders warned against the sort of capitalism that bred large inequality and ignored the objective of a strong society. "It is a bad thing for a nation to admire the false standard of success and there can be no falser standard than that set by the deification of material wealth," President Theodore Roosevelt had warned.[23] Was Western society even that free? Soviet citizens lived in a dictatorship that denied them fundamental freedoms, including the freedom to choose how to live their lives. While these freedoms were guaranteed in the West, Westerners had come to face some serious challenges concerning their own lives, in particular the moral dimension of their lives. On the one hand, they ended up living in a system that educated them less about morals and citizenship, yet, on the other hand, heavily influenced by commercial publicity, powerful retail chains, and mass media with their own ideas of what lifestyle ought to be. There were, of course, differences inside the West, but in the core of the Western world – the United States and the United Kingdom – neoliberalism had made the spirit of the Founding Fathers and the liberal ideal of emancipation fall on many citizens like a worn-out cloak. It surely was not always better in the past, but many wondered whether the abandoning of the ideals would help build a better future.

Decadence

Wealth without virtue breads decadence. Decadence in its turn is the precursor of decline. Historians who had studied the rise and fall of great powers saw resemblances between the internal weakening of the late Roman Empire and the West. They were also familiar with the words of the Roman historian Sallust and theologian Saint Augustine that the abolition of external adversaries and the removal of the necessity to be alert was followed by disasters arising from prosperity, greed, and inequality.[24] So, if the collapse of the Soviet Union already presented an opportunity, it would at best be a pause in which to remedy these internal economic problems.[25]

Even such pause was considered by some to be more a curse than a blessing. The problem of a breathing space, contended the historian Paul Kennedy, is that one feels less pressured to tackle challenges.[26] He made a comparison with the late-Victorian age, during and after which Britain constantly staggered from one crisis to the next. Decline is not necessarily a collapse. Decline can also be slow, with moments of recovery that allow politicians to dismiss the warnings of critics. Decline can be subtle, encouraging leaders to go on with laissez-faire policies, and citizens to enjoy their prosperity without worrying about the erosion of their productivity and wealth. The harsh confrontation with reality is thereby postponed for another generation or so. Kennedy, who in earlier years investigated the phenomenon of imperial overstretch, the fact that global interests were growing too much in comparison to the means to secure them, now highlighted the moral dimension. Like many historians who wrote about the fate of great powers, he saw decadence as the main threat, describing his country drifting lazily downstream, putting out the boathook to avoid an occasional collision.

Moral decay was also what the influential economist John Kenneth Galbraith saw around him. He had previously outlined how a small part of private America had become outrageously rich, while the public sector remained outrageously poor. The problem, he saw, was economics. But the cause was the dissipating of virtue and ethics, the erosion of the values that America's Founding Fathers embodied. Materialism among youngsters was on the rise, as figure 2.1 shows. Other virtues, like the pursuit of a meaningful philosophy in life, retreated. "Whether the problem be that of a burgeoning population and of space in which to live with peace and grace, or whether it be the depletion of the materials which nature has stocked in the earth's crust and which have been drawn upon more heavily in this century than in all previous time together, or whether it be that of occupying minds no longer committed to the stockpiling of consumer goods,"

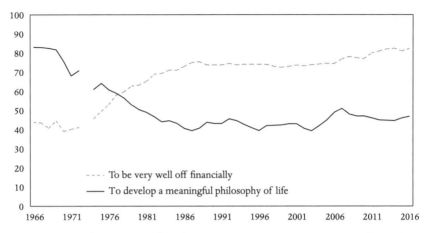

Figure 2.1   The purpose of studying among American university students (%)
Source: UCLA Freshmen Survey.

he advocated, "the basic demand on America will be on its resources of intelligence, and education."[27] Hence, without educational renaissance, without moral renaissance, and without morals and virtue, no power can go on to lead.

Whole generations had learned to hate communism, yet not to understand democracy. In 1990, only about 6 percent of American high school students had a proper understanding of their country's institutions. The majority did not know that Congress made laws, or what checks and balances were about.[28] The philosopher Alan Bloom found a dismal lack of critical thought. He called it the closing of the American mind.[29] American students might not have faced the propaganda and the censorship, but they were not sufficiently equipped to treat information critically either. Hence, they could be more inclined to advance understanding through basic instincts than through logic and critical thinking. Absent the clear rival of the Cold War, citizens were left with abstract ideas of good and evil, and a poor understanding of the common good.

There was more. Francis Fukuyama, a professor who had famously declared the victory of liberalism, cautioned that the victory of liberalism could be devastating. Instead of being triumphalist, his essay "The End of History" predicted that this moment would presage a somber time. The more liberalism and postmodernism advanced, he asserted, the more they would elicit nostalgia for the time when history existed, the time that called for daring, courage, imagination, and idealism.[30] Human beings, he tried to say, expected more of life than just economic calculation, the solving of technical problems, and the satisfaction of consumer demands. This harkened back to the thinking of the European existentialists in between the two world wars. They saw in the progress of materialism a risk of both radicalism and decline, of a society of primitive socialized men without identity, sometimes leisurely consuming, at other times feverishly searching for an affirmation of one's corner.[31] Thus he wrote:

> The end of history will be a very sad time. The struggle for recognition, the willingness to risk one's life for a purely abstract goal, the worldwide ideological struggle that called forth daring, courage, imagination, and idealism, will be replaced by economic calculation, the endless solving of technical problems, environmental concerns, and the satisfaction of sophisticated consumer demands. In the post-historical period, there will be neither art nor philosophy, just the perpetual caretaking of the museum of human history. I can feel in myself, and see in others around me, a powerful nostalgia for the time when history existed.[32]

Western liberalism became materialism. Progress was measured by the degree not to which the world advanced human dignity, but to which it encouraged people to consume. Pope John Paul II stated that if Marxist materialism had failed to succeed, liberal capitalism was bound to fail to meet the profound aspirations of humanity. "Some have seen the fall of Communism in Eastern Europe as a victory of liberal capitalism and now see the latter as the only road, forgetting the very limited contribution it makes to a full human life, let alone the devastating consequences it has for the third world."[33] French President François Mitterrand put it thus: "It would be disastrous to assist one cultural model to become universal. Will we allow that the law of money, the forces of technology, will succeed in what totalitarian regimes failed to do?"[34]

Even die-hard proponents of capitalism stated that the advance of Western economic and political values would not succeed without a deeper moral and cultural code. "It needs the energies of the creative imagination as expressed in religion and the arts," Irving Kristol stated. "It is crucial to the lives of all our citizens, as of all human beings at all times, that they encounter a world that possesses a transcendent meaning, in which the human experience makes sense."[35] Sociologist Seymour Martin Lipset posited that spreading democracy could provoke a backlash. Promoting economic liberalism is important, he stated, but not enough. Democracy requires inclusive prosperity, meritocracy, culture, civic education, moderation, and emancipated citizens. He warned: "Do not count on all the world's democracies lasting."[36]

Others took as evidence of the moral crisis the growing inequality, particularly in the United States and the United Kingdom. A leading economist calculated that the richest 1 percent had amassed 70 percent of the rise in family income in the 1980s. Wallace Peterson found the real income of a worker in 1990 to be 20 percent lower than in 1973.[37] *Newsweek* ran an article that scathingly confronted America with its poverty. "Nineteen nations have better infant mortality rates than the United States. The infant death rate in Japan is less than half the American rate," it summarized. "The infant death rate in the nation's capital, and in Detroit and Baltimore, is humiliatingly close to a Third World rate. Nothing that happens in Bangladesh should be as interesting to Americans as the fact that a boy born in Harlem today has a lower life expectancy than a boy born in Bangladesh."[38] Rich coastal Democrat America sometimes replaced the backward communists with narrow-minded rural deplorables. Rich and Republican America often replaced the backward communists as their principal enemies with backward poor.[39]

Many of these backward communities consisted of immigrants. Hence, doubts grew about the image of Western society as a multicultural melting pot. The idea of such cultural blending originated from the time of Henry Ford. During an opening ceremony of a school for migrant workers in 1917, Ford let foreigners in native dress descend into a large black vessel named "The American melting pot." That was a little more than 70 years earlier, when the United States felt confident and strong. By the 1980s, the melting pot was no longer melting.[40] This was also the case in Europe. Throughout the West, immigrants lagged behind in terms of education and prosperity. The frustration about the failing integration of immigrants was enforced by a growing fear of Islam. "The Muslims are Coming!" a magazine ran as a cover story.[41] Next to the title, whose initial version was titled "Out Go the Commies, In Come the Muslims," was a picture of a dozen Arabs riding camels in a desert. As the far right gained ground, center politicians panicked. The French presidential candidate Jacques Chirac claimed to understand the feelings of workers who were tired of the smell and noise of immigrants.[42] After the clash with communism, the Western world was brewing its own internal clash of civilizations.[43]

It was also feared that unrestrained capitalism would be catastrophic for the environment. Economists lamented the fact that prices of products in supermarkets did not include external costs.[44] While companies tried to compete by pricing products as cheaply as possible, they transferred the cost of pollution to tax payers. Private investors took the profits of capitalism; society was expected to pay for its problems. Such a distorted market, the criticism went, discouraged producers from innovating, from implementing more sustainable technologies, and from reducing the waste of precious resources. Raw materialism, it was called. This concern was not new. The Club of Rome, a group of political and corporate influencers, had concluded that there were limits to growth. It derided the mismanagement of the world economy, including the diffusion of toxic substances, the acidification of lakes, the cutting of forests, and global warming.[45] At the Rio Summit in 1992, its secretary-general said: "One part of the world cannot live in an orgy of unrestrained consumption where the rest destroys its environment just to survive. No one is immune from the effects of the other." A real free market would redress these market failures. This concern occupied the public at large. In different surveys, the environment was identified as a priority.[46]

The end of the Cold War was not a victorious period. There were concerns about the state of Western society, its economy, and its democracy. The West was seen as being on a slippery slope, a slippery slope down. A first critique that resonated through the Western world at the beginning of the 1990s was that the capitalist system had flaws. Inequality could become as problematic a misallocation of production factors as the forced misallocation that brought communism to a collapse. The consequent question that many asked was whether the West still had the moral leadership to solve that problem or whether it had already grown too complacent. Either way, it could not afford paralysis. The Soviet Union might have disappeared; the unipolar moment of almost uncontested power could be very brief in a world where new competitors continuously tried to improve their position. Barely had the cheers about the collapse of the Soviet Union subsided, or opinion makers predicted that Western power was set to decline, than preponderance would soon make way for a new stage of competition. Complacency, consumerism, and persistent provincialism would make matters worse.

Challenges on the horizon?

Concerns about the internal problems thus led to concerns about the position of the West in the world. The United States had the power resources to lead. Trade and investment made countries more dependent on one another. But interdependence required Americans to have an open attitude toward the world, to invest in international institutions.[47] It was questioned whether the United States was able to act like a leader, not so much because of its natural penchant for isolationism, but because internal uncertainty aggravated a tendency to introversion.[48] Books whose covers promised American leadership carried sobering analyses inside, monodies about America's economic fragility and how it all crippled its capability to compete with new economic challengers.[49]

The Organization for Economic Cooperation and Development, OECD, echoed this concern. "It is alarming," it remarked, "at least for anyone living in Western Europe or North America, in that the focus of world economic power will shift inexorably . . . towards the Far East."[50] It was no moment for self-satisfaction when Western households were falling for Asian ingenuity: Nintendo's Gameboy, Sony's Walkman, and Toyota SUVs. In spite of Japan having entered a decade of slow growth, manufacturers remained strong. On the one hand, it sourced from cheap countries like China. On the other hand, Japan demonstrated that, confronted with competition and a mature home market, rich countries could upgrade instead of relocating, by investing in technology, quality, and automation.[51] Instead of running trade deficits, Japan preserved modest surpluses. And in Japan's wake followed other markets: South Korea, Taiwan – and China.

The fall of the Iron Curtain reinforced the idea that communication would bring commerce and cooperation. Soft power, or the ability of a state to attract, would grow more important. Virtual power, the ability to innovate, to establish strong brands, and to profit from the resources and cheap labor elsewhere was presented as an efficient way for the West to continue to lead. Confidence was drawn also from European integration. A dozen countries kept going further in economic integration. They were ready to pass sovereignty on matters like customs to supranational institutions.[52] Some saw the European experience leading to a deeper transformation, a transformation of the mind. Instead of being fixated with sovereignty, citizens came to see themselves as Europeans. Identities changed and so did the very nature of power politics. The predators, who bloodily fought each other for centuries, had become herbivores. Anarchy is what states make of it.[53] If Europe could do it, why could the rest of the world not follow?

This optimistic notion, however, was criticized. Had the Europeans truly become herbivores? Member states retained sovereignty on matters like security and foreign policy. And while they had become more civilized toward one another, they were still seen as predators elsewhere. In the United States, diplomats cautioned that in spite of the swollen language about values, its moral credibility was limited. While the world looked benign through the lens of economic liberalism and the constructivist idea of world citizenship, the existing order also meant inferiority and exploitation to others. Hence, friction would be inevitable. "The West should not expect the world to become a more peace loving or free place," wrote an academic. "The future does not promise to be more tranquil. . . . The day of the dictator is not over and many nations are ruled by repressive governments. . . . We still live in an anarchic international order."[54] While the Central Intelligence Agency was criticized for having failed to predict the fall of the Soviet Union, it did provide intelligence assessments about the risk of instability in the Middle East and Africa, and uncertainty about China and Russia's future.[55] The Department of Defense drafted an internal vision document that stated the need for "convincing potential competitors that they need not aspire to a greater role or pursue a more aggressive posture to protect their legitimate interests."[56]

Western societies were aware that the unipolar moment was shaky. But was the West ready to act upon it? The most skeptical assessment was that the Western world was set to follow the fate of declining empires in the past. Had the United States not arrived at the point where Venice was around 1500, Holland around 1660, and Britain around 1873? The watershed between rise and fall. Declinists referred to the Soviets challenging American technological leadership with the launch of the Sputnik in 1957, the oil crisis of 1973, President Ronald Reagan's unwillingness to address fiscal and trade deficits when they were still small in the 1980s.[57] The productivity edge relative to that of rival states had begun to fritter away but the costs of preserving global influence did not diminish.[58] "Today America is where Britain was around the turn of the century," one renowned economist asserted. "Rome lasted a thousand years, the British Empire about 200; why are we slipping after about 50 years?"[59]

Future

The end of the Cold War did not lead to the expectation that the history of war, dictatorship, and exploitation had reached its end. Neither was everyone convinced that the West would lead. Its weaknesses were numerous. Neoliberalism, in theory, held that citizens were encouraged by competition to give society their best. In practice, policies of neoliberalism had coincided with growing external debt, the decay of infrastructure, and diminishing interest in manufacturing. While it surely pressured people to work harder, it was less evident whether it empowered them as citizens. Other competitors loomed on the horizon. Not only pundits vented their concern. Opinion polls showed that only half of Americans were satisfied with the state of the nation. In 1989 and 1990, only about 40 percent of Americans expected the future to become better while 25 percent believed it would be worse. The Soviet Union might have been defeated, but it did not feel like a victory of the West: neither to the public, nor to many of its opinion leaders. It presented an opportunity, as the West had unequaled power. But would it be able to use it in a way that would restore confidence? Would it use its power advantage to redress some of the internal challenges? Would it be able to use its power to try to shape a world that was more hospitable to its ideals?

CHAPTER 3

THE NEW ORDER
SEEN FROM ELSEWHERE

THE DOWNFALL OF THE SOVIET UNION DEPRIVED RUSSIA OF ITS imperial crust. Alongside 14 other Soviet states, it was required to completely reorient its domestic and foreign policy. This was also true for other protagonists. India, for instance, had been closer to the Soviet Union, because of American support for its rival, Pakistan. For China, the Soviet Union had long loomed as a rival on the northern and western border. Smaller countries too needed to respond to the situation. The Soviets had been an important donor of aid, especially to countries like Cuba and Vietnam.[1] They were the world's largest arms supplier.[2] The Council for Mutual Economic Assistance, COMECON, included several developing countries, like Ethiopia, Mozambique, Laos, and Nicaragua. COMECON held the capitalist West responsible for the poverty in the South and championed a new international order. That promise was now gone. The Iranian religious leader wrote a letter to Moscow, proposing that only Islam could rescue his decaying empire. "It is clear to everybody," he observed, "that from now on communism will only be found in the museums of world political history."[3]

The ending of the Cold War period, we have seen, was a moment of introspection in the West, introspection about some internal problems, about the resilience of democracy, and about its position in the world. If there was already so much uncertainty in the West about the future and about some of the liberal values that its leaders underlined in their discourses, what, then, to expect of the rest of the world? As Western citizens were already critical of the state of the free market and democracy at home, what were the views of other states, such as Russia whose leaders were promising to replace communist dictatorship by some sort of democracy? And what to expect of China, a country that counted 1.1 billion people and whose leaders had just been confronted with massive uprisings. Of India, a country of 900 million citizens, the biggest existing, yet also one of the poorest, democracies in the world? This chapter starts by surveying three important regional powers: Russia, China, and India. It then focuses on four regions: Middle East, Latin America, Africa, and Southeast Asia. How did countries perceive Western power, the Washington Consensus? What did the world order surrounding the West look like? What were the aspirations, the weaknesses, and the strengths?

The new Mongols

A diary of a collaborator of Gorbachev gives a glimpse of how the downfall of the Soviet Union was experienced at the center of power. His entry of September 11, 1989: "If we create stability, it will be the end of perestroika. Stability is stagnation. A revolution must have instability."[4] On October 23, 1989, he wrote: "The Party is no longer recognized as a governing body. The Soviets continue to be helpless."[5] "The Berlin Wall has fallen," he jotted on November 10, 1989. "An entire era in the history of the 'socialist system' has come to an end," he continues. "This is no longer a matter of socialism, but of a change in the world balance of powers, the end of Yalta, the end of Stalin's legacy."[6]

Just after the fall, General Secretary Mikhail Gorbachev (1985–91) gave an address in Paris. "We are leaving behind a totalitarian regime, the most powerful totalitarian regime in the world, which had relied not only on political tools, exploiting the monopoly position of one party, but also on totalitarian domination of state property," he proclaimed. "You realize what a monster it was!"[7] Gorbachev envisioned the Soviet Union to be part of what he referred to as the European house. The best guarantee for security, he thought, was no longer an empire, as the Soviet Union was before, but integration into the West. Gorbachev practiced what he preached. He started major reforms – glasnost and perestroika. In 1989, the first parliamentary elections were held, followed by regional elections, and presidential elections. In December 1991, the red flag with the golden hammer and the sickle disappeared from the rooftop of the Grand Kremlin Palace in Moscow.

As hopeful as Gorbachev sounded, Russian citizens grappled with the unfolding cataclysm. The first declaration of independence in Estonia in 1988, the first major protests in Poland in 1989, followed by more unrest in Hungary, East Germany, Bulgaria, Czechoslovakia, and Romania, the start of the fall of the Berlin Wall in November 1989, the law of April 1990 that allowed republics to secede, the dramatic coup attempt by Russian nationalists in the summer of 1990, all these events unfolding in a persistent political turmoil. In a few years, the number of citizens over which Moscow ruled halved from 290 million to 150 million.

Not all Russians were convinced that the Soviet Union had been the dreadful monster Gorbachev talked about. Surveys showed that even if there was a small liberal-minded segment of the population, there was still a sizable conservative and nationalist fraction. The majority of the Russian population was caught hesitantly in the middle, with a penchant, however, for strong leadership.[8] While democracy was established institutionally, the Russians still had to be convinced of its merits. Having lived under authoritarian rule for decades, the influence of communism on every aspect of their lives was a heavy legacy. In the first presidential ballot, held in 1991, Boris Yeltsin, the champion of democracy, won with only 59 percent of the votes.

Nationalists and conservatives fiercely attacked the pro-Western promises of Yeltsin. Was Russia going to be allowed into the European house? How earnest was the West in its hope to see Russia emerge as a stable state? Absent guarantees, nationalists assumed, Russia would soon again discover the core geopolitical rationale for building an empire, as it was once summarized by Tsarina Catherine the Great. The best way to secure borders, she claimed, was to expand them. How was Moscow going to secure the millions of Russians that now lived in newly established republics? Even the most outspoken critic of the Soviet regime, the novelist Aleksandr Solzhenitsyn, proposed that the borders of the new Russian Federation be adjusted southward to include compatriots that lived in Central Asia

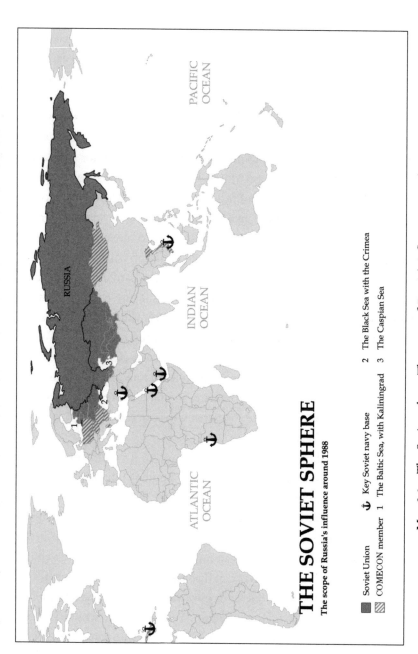

THE SOVIET SPHERE

The scope of Russia's influence around 1988

■ Soviet Union   ⚓ Key Soviet navy base   2   The Black Sea with the Crimea
▨ COMECON member   1   The Baltic Sea, with Kaliningrad   3   The Caspian Sea

Map 3.1   The Soviet sphere: The scope of Russia's influence around 1988

and that the Slav republics of Ukraine and Belarus remained in union with their Russian brethren. Solzhenitsyn had survived the Soviet Gulags, the forced labor camps in Siberia, but distrusted the West. President Yeltsin too warned that Russia would reserve to itself the right to adjust borders with breakaway republics. "Russia will not agree to give away these territories just like that."[9]

From the days of Tsar Peter the Great, Russia had fought for these lands as gateways to the seas. Control over the Baltic and the Black Sea would deny hostile powers the ability to use them as a staging point for aggression. With the fall of the Soviet Union, Russia had lost its dominance over these gateways. The consequent geopolitical fixation became the opposite of the geopolitical aspirations of the United States. The United States sought to lock up continental Eurasian powers like Russia into the inner seas; Russia itself strived to use the inner seas as a staging point to contest its maritime rivals. This sensitivity became visible in 1991, when hardliners singlehandedly tried to regain control over the Baltic States. More complex was the situation in the Black Sea. Sebastopol, on the Crimean Peninsula, was an important navy port. In 1992, a Russian-backed group orchestrated a referendum to split Crimea from Ukraine. "Are you for an independent Republic of Crimea in union with other states?" the referendum asked. It failed. But a few weeks later the Russian parliament annulled an agreement of 1954 that yielded Crimea to Ukraine. Moscow's mayor stated that Ukrainian independence was illegal altogether.

Russia made it abundantly clear from the outset: it would never permit Ukraine to distance itself too far. A country of 52 million inhabitants, Ukraine was strategically important for the Black Sea fleet, but also as an industrial hub, and as the cradle of the Russian Orthodox Church. Moscow had made Ukraine feel its dependence on Russian energy and supported strikes in the eastern region, Donbass. The Russian minorities there were aggrieved not only at the devastating economic crisis that raged in the country, but also at the increasingly nationalistic line of its government. Even Washington had warned Kiev against suicidal nationalism. What position would Ukraine obtain in between the West and Russia? The issue was particularly pertinent, because the West did not have the slightest idea how it could help stabilize the country. The government in Kiev was not only nationalistic, it was also notoriously corrupt, racist, and had a tendency to silence opponents. It wanted a large army of half a million soldiers, but mishandled the economy. "It has done nothing except pay lip service to reforms," a World Bank official reported.[10]

During the first years, the nationalist call for the restoration of a Russian sphere of influence and resistance against the West was spearheaded by Vladimir Zhirinovsky. He gained a minority of the votes during the first presidential election. Zhirinovsky dreamed openly of bringing Russia to the shores of the Indian Ocean and the Mediterranean, to make it dominate the Arctic. Zhirinovsky was an eccentric figure. But in his shadow, there were numerous officials and military officers who also felt uncomfortable with what to them seemed to be a one-sided overture. "I had nothing but regret for the loss of the Soviet Union's position in Europe, although intellectually I understood that a position based on walls and water barriers cannot exist forever," a young KGB officer registered. "But I wanted something different to rise in its place and nothing different was proposed. That is what hurt. All we did was toss everything away and leave."[11] Russia was in limbo. A reform-minded president had promised a better future facing West. But in other parts of society, a new chapter in Russia's century-old story of insecurity and humiliation had opened. After the Mongols, the British Empire, the German Empire, the American Empire, Russians saw the beginning of a new struggle against foreign rivals.

Elsewhere in Eastern Europe, the disappearance of the oppressor caused doubt. Yes, the East Germans shot off fireworks and partied on Berlin's Alexanderplatz the night before the reunification with the West. In the Czech Republic, the first free elections had a turnout of 96 percent. "Back to Europe!" election posters exclaimed. Yet, the trailblazers of reform were skeptical of the West. Václav Havel, the opposition leader in former Czechoslovakia, railed at Western consumerism, the fact that unabated commercial advertisement could be as imposing as propaganda, and that Western capitalism lacked a human touch.[12] He and Lech Wałęsa, who led a peaceful resistance movement against the Soviet leaders from the Polish port city of Gdansk, also predicted that the road of reform would be arduous: "We are coming in as heroes, but in the end, when they realised what a mess we are in and how little we can do about it, they will railroad us, tarred and feathered, out of town."[13] Progress, they repeated, would depend not just on freedom, but on the capacity to bend freedom into human emancipation.[14] An East German writer insisted that Western capitalism would bring both freedom and fear. "The countless embraces at the wall were fired by alcohol, and ended that way, in headache," he stated. "Ever since then, the man from the West has appeared as the force behind rising rents, eviction orders, as an arrogant know-it-all, as a babbling salesman."[15]

This philosophical chasm aside, the newly independent countries faced many other obstacles on the road to reform: the lack of a true opposition, economic stress, the Soviet legacy of civil distrust, and poor work ethics. The attempt to build market-based and democratic states in Eastern Europe was compared to trying to recuperate different ingredients from a Soviet goulash. Others pointed at the huge tension between the democratic activism of a small elite on the one hand, and civic passiveness as well as conservatism on the other.[16] Like in Russia, an intelligentsia had claimed liberty. The majority of the people still wondered what liberty would bring, not so much what they themselves could do with it. Freedom, seen as the unknown, frightened citizens throughout the decaying Soviet Union. For now, a progressive elite seized momentum, but powerful forces, wanting to hold on to power and to the past, did not subside.

China's Goddess of Democracy

In Asia, social transformation was compared to a flock of flying geese. Every time a new country took the lead in economic reform, this new leader drew the whole region further ahead. This had started with the industrialization of Japan, was followed by the four Asian Tigers – South Korea, Taiwan, Hong Kong, and Singapore – and then by the largest of all: China. On the one hand, this pattern entailed a transfer of investment from rich Asian countries to poorer ones, investment that required countries to open their economies. On the other hand, the flying geese pattern stimulated the betterment of governance and, albeit more slowly, political openness. By the early 1990s, some East Asian countries had embraced democracy. Asia would always remain Asia. Western liberalism would always be interpreted

through the lens of Asian values. But there was at least enough convergence, in terms of economic interests and norms, to allow competition to
remain peaceful and pragmatic. The main question now was whether this
would also apply to China.

China's outlook in the early 1990s was still more that of a farm than
that of a factory. Three quarters of its population lived in the countryside. Pudong, which would harbor Shanghai's first high-rise offices, was
a mosquito-infested wetland. Chinese domestic production remained ten
times smaller than Japan's. While its industry grew by 10 percent annually
and over ten million citizens moved to cities each year, China remained a
fragile nation. The United States, for example, could deploy its navy ships
all the way up to the coast without the Chinese armed forces being able to
detect them. The West could send arms to Taiwan ignoring the insistence
of Beijing that the island remained part of the Chinese motherland. The
fragility also became clear during the student uprising of 1989. Millions of
students called for democracy, freedom, and accountability. At Tiananmen
Square in Beijing, protesters had erected a Goddess of Democracy, ten
meters tall, made of paper and cardboard.

The Tiananmen Square protests were a make-or-break moment for the
Communist Party of China. A brief debate took place over whether to give
in to the students or to clamp down. In the end, the Party leadership decided
that enough was enough. Martial law was declared. On June 3, 1989, the
crackdown commenced. "The army is ordered to spare none," a British
diplomat reported from Beijing. "Four wounded girl students begged for
their lives but were bayoneted."[17] The Party's traditional line was that nothing mattered more than stability. Despite diplomats cabling the bloodshed
in detail, Western governments showed empathy to the argument that
stability had to come first and that only the Party could guarantee it. The
American government dispatched the national security advisor to explain
that sanctions would be imposed but that they were for domestic consumption. "President Bush," an internal Pentagon document explained,
"has a deep personal desire to see the friendship between the Chinese and
American people maintained and strengthened."[18]

Friendship was not mutual. The Chinese leadership considered the
United States a rival. It thought democracy, as imposed by America, was

incompatible with the determination to preserve the monopoly of the Communist Party. The leadership perceived the very existence of Western democracy as a challenge to its legitimacy. The narrative of interdependence and cooperation allowed the West to weaken China by supporting dissidents and minorities.[19]

This threat perception did not disappear with the arrival of a new generation of leaders. Between 1949 and 1976, Mao Zedong led China. He was succeeded by Deng Xiaoping (1978–89), praised, still today, for the opening up of China to foreign investors. Now, a third generation of leaders, led by Jiang Zemin (1989–2002), came to the forefront. Deng reminded him that the goal remained to achieve superiority over capitalism, not to succumb to it. If Western imperialists, Deng found, expected this next generation to yield to a slow and peaceful evolution toward democracy, the Party would make sure that those next generations would be properly disciplined. Regime survival was key.

Hence, the new leadership stuck to authoritarianism. It spoke of Western bourgeois liberalism as a recipe for cultural nihilism.[20] Jiang Zemin considered Western society decadent. If it infected China, it would never grow strong. "Many people who do not understand history often believe that they can enjoy the life of developed capitalist countries as soon as the capitalist system has been adopted and the parliamentary democracy of the West has been fully copied," he explained. "These people do not understand how much toil and sweat of the laboring people was exploited during the period when primitive accumulation of capital was made." [21] Jiang proclaimed that the West plotted regime change and confused people's minds.[22] So rather than exposing Chinese citizens to the capitalist West, the task was patriotic education – and to keep dissidents under the thumb. A new state security law was introduced. It gave police forces broader powers to arrest critics. There would be no Chinese Gorbachev.

In the minds of Chinese leaders, the struggle that Mao Zedong had launched against the hegemony of the West continued. It had to be won by changing the balance of power. On the one hand, power meant growth and prosperity to keep the nation satisfied. On the other hand, it entailed the conversion of a part of that wealth to wield influence and develop military prowess to keep rivals at a distance. Like Russian strategists prescribed that the control of inner seas was vital for the security of the state, Chinese strategists proposed that they needed their own sphere of influence.

China, too, had its geopolitical trauma of being bullied via the sea. Its Century of Humiliation started in the nineteenth century, when the last imperial dynasty succumbed to the maritime power of Britain during the Opium Wars. The reference to a painful past was cemented into the heart of official discourse. While the leadership stated that China would not seek hegemony, it was made clear that the pushback of American and Japanese military power was decisive to keep China secure and to reclaim control over so-called lost territory: Hong Kong, Taiwan, the South China Sea, the East China Sea, and so forth.

China wanted a new great wall to stop rivals: this time at sea. Already in the 1980s, the influential general Liu Huaqing had drawn a map that gave an impression of how this Chinese sphere of influence ought to look. By 2010, the Chinese military had to be dominant as far as a first island chain that included Taiwan and the Japanese archipelago. By 2020, it needed to steam up to the second island chain, including the American stronghold, Guam. By 2040, it had to alter the balance of power in the entire Western Pacific. It was nothing less than a Chinese version of the Monroe Doctrine and a sustained attempt to break the influence of adversaries in its backyard. Just like the American Monroe Doctrine was rooted in the recollection of aggression by British troops that culminated in the burning of the White House in 1814, Chinese history books explained that the imperialists were able to torch the Summer Palace in 1860 because the Qing Empire was too weak to keep their gunboats at bay.

Even if President Bush quickly tried to rebuild relations after the Tiananmen Square protests, Beijing was not at all convinced by his proposal of building a new, cooperative world order. That order, the reasoning was, meant nothing more than new world domination, a Pax Americana.[23] Openness and interdependence were in the interest of the strong, a thin guise for the continuation of the exploitation of the weak.[24] The harmony that President Bush talked about was a hierarchy that needed to be upended.[25] The objective was to make the country strong. As Jiang Zemin put it: "The lofty mission of defending the country's territorial sovereignty over the land and in the air, as well as its rights and interests on the sea;

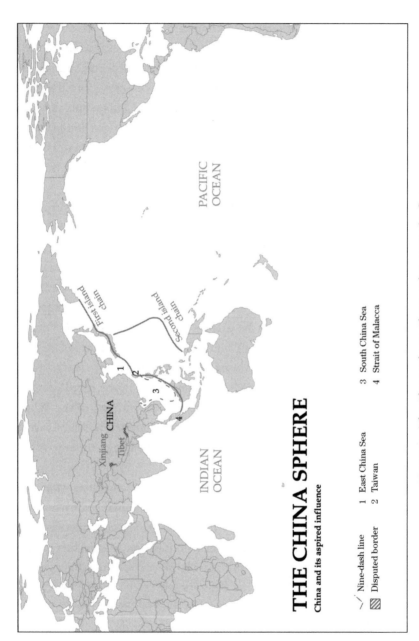

THE CHINA SPHERE

China and its aspired influence

⟋ Nine-dash line   1 East China Sea   3 South China Sea

▨ Disputed border   2 Taiwan   4 Strait of Malacca

Map 3.2 The China sphere: China and its aspired influence

should safeguard the unification and security of the motherland."[26] Still, Beijing decided to accept Western proposals for cooperation. Cooperation and dialogue gave China the necessary breathing space to grow its power. It had also learned from the Soviet collapse that confrontation and arms races could lead to exhaustion, especially in a poor country like China.

The plan was to let the West engage China, but certainly not to adjust in accordance with Western demands; to integrate into the world economy, but not to lose sight of core national interests. This meant Beijing's readiness to embrace those aspects of the engagement that it perceived as serving the country's development. But it also meant rejecting those elements the government considered interfered with or even hampered its development. In a nutshell, open up to economic engagement, but remain closed to political cooperation along with human rights, democracy, and the rule of law. China wanted to have it both ways: the pursuit of trade and the preservation of dictatorship. And it could have it both ways. Foreign investors restlessly searched for new opportunities and cheap labor.

Foreign investors could set up shop, yet always with an eye on China's independent growth and national industries. State-owned enterprises did not have to be discarded; they needed to be reformed, be made more competitive. From the early 1990s, the Party started to focus on so-called pillar industries, key companies that would slowly rival foreign multinationals. Wu Bangguo spoke of a national team. "International economic confrontations show that if a country has several large companies or groups it will be assured of maintaining a certain market share and a position in the international economic order," he said. "In the next century our nation's position in the international economic order will be to a large extent determined by the position of our nation's large enterprises and groups."[27] Foreign companies would be welcomed on the condition that they formed joint ventures that allowed China to retain control, to take hold of their technology, and to oblige them to reinvest their profits into China. Cooperation was a means, not an end.

Lotus in a mud pond

Russia felt a geopolitical necessity to preserve its influence beyond its new borders; China to project power in the adjacent seas. India sensed that it was ordained to become the most powerful nation in the Indian Ocean. A giant southward protuberance of the Eurasian landmass, India is a natural bulwark along the maritime lifelines between Eastern Asia, Africa, and Europe. But like the other major powers, it had a history of humiliation that made India fixated with projecting influence beyond its borders and particularly into the contiguous seas. Whichever power controls the Indian Ocean, it was held, has India's seaborne trade at its mercy and so its independence. Delhi already had built itself a track record of interventions in that neighborhood, in Sri Lanka, for instance, and in the Maldives. It was in this quest for regional dominance that the United States loomed as a troublemaker rather than an ally. The United States had long supported India's neighbor and main rival, Pakistan, and also preserved several military strongholds in the Indian Ocean.[28] Exhibiting this tension, Delhi defied Washington in the run-up to the invasion of Iraq and praised Saddam Hussein.

India was frequently considered an evident counterweight against China. It was large and had a history of border conflicts with its northern neighbor. Still, the Indian elite had a penchant for suspicion of the West. For decades, it had held on to the doctrine of non-alignment or abstaining from alliances with the major powers of the Cold War. This was maintained after the collapse of the Soviet Union. Strategically, India wanted to emerge as a power in its own right, not to be a deputy. Ideologically, India clung to the tradition of swadeshi, or self-sustainment, economic nationalism, and resistance to Western capitalism. Swadeshi was a brainchild of Mahatma Gandhi. Gandhi, the leader of the Indian independence movement against British colonial rule in the first half of the century, still inspired many, like farmers, who had started a satyagraha, a non-violent action against the seed products of Western multinationals, or students who took aim at American food chains. Getting a Pizza Hut next to the Kremlin was easier than setting up a Pizza Hut next to an Indian marketplace. Indian corporate bosses even became allies of Marxist parties as they were the best guarantee against global competition. So, despite a shared legacy of democracy, a big rift loomed between India and the West.

The gulf was set to become wider. While the Chinese economy raced ahead and exports boomed, India struggled with a large trade deficit and government debt. There were promising industries in information technology, but they remained like the buds of lotus flowers in a mud pond. While the West showed itself lenient toward the Chinese Communist Party's crackdown on the Tiananmen Square protests, it took the Indian government head-on as the latter grappled with a severe economic crisis. In 1989, American aid was suspended. In 1990, a senior US official called Indian economic policy flawed. The International Monetary Fund was reluctant to throw a financial lifeline. In the summer of 1991, the Indian Central Bank had to airlift 47 tons of gold into the vaults of the Bank of England as collateral for a foreign loan. A deadlock followed. The more the West wanted to see genuine liberalization, the more Indians disparaged it as new imperialism and the return to the time of the East India Company. The commerce minister told parliament that he insisted on economic independence; his predecessor inveighed against the arrogance of the West. And so, the country of almost 900 million people exited the Cold War period in a state of economic disarray.

This economic deadlock and the ensuing crisis were the nail in the coffin of the Indian Congress Party. Once led by Mahatma Gandhi, the Congress Party long held the promise of a secular union, transcending the division between the Hindu majority, Muslims, and other minorities, and overcoming the differences between castes. It might have failed to liberalize economically, been protectionist and nationalist, but at least its nationalism was somewhat inclusive toward different religious groups. At least, also, it remained democratic, unlike the dominance of the military in Pakistan and the one-party regime in China. Since Indian independence, Congress had been the largest party. Now, India fragmented. Between 1989 and 1991, it had four different governments. Local parties gained ground in elections and so did Hindu parties. Hindu parties promised some economic reform, but the price paid was religious polarization, the establishment, as some judged, of the tyranny of the Hindu majority.[29]

Between the biggest democracy of the world and the biggest dictatorship

in the world, the West chose the latter. This was a choice of conveni-
ence. Beijing had a clear political vision; Delhi was marred by instability. In
China, the Party forced people to adjust, to relocate, to change jobs; in the
absence of a clear perspective on jobs created by foreign companies, Indian
democratic parties could do none of that. While India opted for overt protectionism, China cleverly pursued economic nationalism under the guise
of reform. And while Indian leaders felt pressured to be openly critical of
liberalization, the Chinese propagated capitalism in the short term just as
they quietly contemplated the victory of socialist dictatorship in the long
run. If India antagonized, China charmed.

A vicious circle followed. The more India slid into chaos, the less foreign
investors were inclined to contribute to its growth. And chaos there was.
Religious strife spread like wildfire. A thousand mutinies, as the writer
V. S. Naipaul put it. Hundreds of citizens were killed in violence between
Hindus and Muslims. Mobs attacked trains, set houses ablaze, and besieged
underequipped soldiers with knives and clubs. Politicians of the leading
Hindu party, the BJP, called for a rejuvenation of Hindu culture and the
demolition of an important mosque in Ajodhya. More extreme movements
and parties openly flirted with the work of the Guru M. S. Golwalkar, who
considered Adolf Hitler's racial purification an example. If that were not
enough, parts of the country were scourged by leftist rebels, the so-called
Naxalites, and secessionists all around the country. India was a struggling
democracy.

Russia, China, and India: the three main non-Western powers struggled,
each in their own way. China held the best cards. Despite the Tiananmen
Square protests, its Communist Party remained in control and had turned
the country into a magnet for foreign investors. Russia was licking its
wounds and India grappled with economic and political turmoil. While the
three powers conducted their own struggle, they all distrusted the West.
Economic independence, preserving a sphere of influence, and diplomatic
autonomy were important to them. The new world order did not mean a
world run on Western values, a belief Moscow, Beijing and Delhi shared.
It would be a multipolar order where sovereignty and diversity in values
were respected. In the case of China, any hope of political liberalization
had been eradicated. While both Deng and Jiang were praised as reform-

ers, their number one concern remained the defense of the monopoly of the Communist Party. In Russia, President Yeltsin faced widespread public skepticism about democracy as well as a conservative elite that considered some of his reforms as the selling out of the country to the West. This was also true in India. Even if criticism in this country was not so much directed against democracy, some believed that democracy had to be dominated by the Hindu majority. Many found that democracy did not have to mean the embrace of the free market, and most Indians thought that the United States had to be kept at a distance.

The journey of the Middle East

Russia and India were not the only struggling democracies. Turkey was another example of a large, fragile democracy. "Is the Turkish rose still capable of blooming?" the director of the Turkish-American business chamber asked.[30] On the one hand, Turkey was a poster child of liberal reform. In 1989, a newly elected civilian president ended almost a decade of military rule. Turgut Özal, a former World Bank official, privatized state-owned companies, liberalized capital flows, championed membership of the European Union, stressed the importance of Turkey's membership of NATO, and supported the American intervention in neighboring Iraq.

And yet, these steps toward opening up did not lead Turkey to bloom. Foreign investors stayed away because they had alternative low-income opportunities inside the European Community. Lacking the development of a competitive industry, Turkey ran a large trade deficit with Western countries, on top of a deficit that was a result of growing energy imports. All this led to volatility, with speculative capital flowing in, the currency moving up and down, inflation, and high unemployment. As public resistance to economic liberalization grew, President Özal increasingly tended to sidestep parliament and bolster his position through privileged ties with large corporate conglomerates.[31] The risks had long been clear. "If the economy fails to prosper," the CIA warned, "Ozal's government will come under pressure from the military and the public and could fall."[32]

Turkey was the only large country in the Middle East that held promise for democracy and the free market. But many asked whether that was really what the West was looking for in the region. For more than a decade, the United States had maintained close relations with the authoritarian leader of Iraq, Saddam Hussein (1979–2003), in spite of his use of chemical weapons against the Kurdish minority. It was only when President Hussein invaded the neighboring country Kuwait, and hence could come to control a very large part of the region's oil, that the West stopped him. Operation Desert Storm called a halt to the ambitions of President Hussein abroad, not to his brutal rule at home.

Meanwhile, the United States had established very close economic, military, and political ties with the authoritarian leaders of Saudi Arabia. President Bush was spotted watching baseball with the Egyptian strongman Hosni Mubarak and met with Syrian dictator Hafez Assad. The main objective, whether it concerned operation Desert Storm in Iraq or the development of political relations with other countries, was not the advancing of the rule of law, as the American president claimed. It was rather the preservation of a balance of power between the region's protagonists. America wanted to preserve its role as arbiter of the balance of power, part of a broader strategy to preserve world leadership.[33] This entailed preventing any single power from becoming dominant, guaranteeing access to the region's oil, which were about one quarter of America's total imports, controlling some of the maritime chokepoints, as well as punishing anyone who challenged the status quo and American leadership. This also implied repelling Saddam Hussein's expansionism, while keeping a check on its main adversary: Iran.

For Iran, the West had become a threat since it supported a coup against popular Prime Minister Mohammad Mosaddegh in 1953 and replaced him with a puppet. From then onwards, anti-Western resentment simmered and culminated in the Iranian Revolution of 1979. Supreme religious leader Grand Ayatollah Ruhollah Khomeini made anti-Americanism the hallmark of his reign. After his death in 1989, successor Ali Hosseini Khamenei left some space for reform. The new Grand Ayatollah's strategy for the survival of the religious regime consisted of several elements. These included balancing moderate reformers against conservatives, avoiding collision with the United States, yet still turning public attention toward useful adversaries like Israel, and continuing to fight against geopolitical isolation by supporting Hezbollah in Lebanon, the Assad regime in Syria, Shia minorities in Pakistan and Saudi Arabia, Shia and Kurdish opponents of Saddam Hussein in Iraq, and projecting its influence in the Persian Gulf. Like so many Persian empires in the past, Iran's geopolitical aspiration was to create a sphere of influence from the Mediterranean to the mountain passes that give way to Southern and Eastern Asia, and from the Caucasus to the Indian Ocean.

The Middle East was a conglomerate of mostly authoritarian states. It was the result of 80 years of struggle to handle the power vacuum that the dismantling of the Ottoman Empire left in 1919. The authoritarian sultans that once wielded control from Tunis to Baghdad and from the Black Sea to the Gulf of Aden were replaced by authoritarian leaders that ruled as Western proxies over small parts of that previous empire, first for Britain, and then for the United States. Some of them had tried to replace the United States with the Soviet Union during the Cold War, but now the United States became the only possible overlord. The region's leaders were expected to help preserve American power; Washington instead took their oil and delivered weapons, which seemed like a mutually beneficial arrangement, at least as far as the leadership on both ends was concerned.

Underneath this realpolitik, however, a current of disillusionment gathered strength. The situation in the Middle East was brilliantly described in a novel by Naguib Mahfouz. In *Journey*, the main character becomes disenchanted with the poverty and ignorance in his country. He first journeys to the land of sunrise, where he finds the old tribal structures to be morally superior to his homeland, yet economically backward. Then he travels to a land of authoritarian bewilderment, a land of wealth and liberty, akin to Europe, which he leaves because of its lack of values.[34] Millions of citizens in the Middle East wandered. Like Mahfouz, many were unconvinced by the West as the promised land. Unlike Mahfouz, many returned to Islam. Radical Islam became like a liberation movement against alleged exploitation with the fiat of Western capitalists and against the perceived humiliation of Muslims by the America-backed state of Israel. Whether it concerned Shia Iran, the Sunnite Muslim Brothers in Egypt, or the nascent movement of Al-Qaeda, the rallying cry was similar: it was time for the so-called Western infidels and their proxies to pack their bags. In 1988, Osama bin Laden left nothing to the imagination in the following fatwa:

> The Arabian Peninsula has never, since God made it flat, created its desert, and encircled it with seas, been stormed by any forces like the crusader armies. They spread like locusts, eating its riches and wiping out its plantations . . . We, with God's help, call on every Muslim who believes in God and wishes to be rewarded to comply with God's order to kill the Americans and plunder their money wherever and whenever they find it.[35]

The plagues of Africa

The Cold War left a painful legacy on the African continent. Proxy wars were conducted between the Western and Soviet camps. Compared to the Middle East, Africa remained marginal in the new world order. There were no nuclear weapons, no key allies like Israel that could be threatened, no crucial maritime lifelines that needed to be protected. Seas and desert insulated it from the West. "With the end of the Cold War, Africa has lost whatever political luster it may have once had," an African political scientist wrote.[36] As Soviet aid vanished, regimes on the continent got into trouble, one after the other. European-ruled African territories had freed themselves, but were left with dysfunctional governments. On top of that, a global glut in the supply of commodities like coffee and cocoa caused prices to drop dramatically in the late 1980s. The region slid into recession. Poverty and famine were on the rise. Demonstrating the gloom, the French newspaper *Le Monde* ran a series of reports titled the "Plagues of Africa."

The West hardly felt a necessity to engage with it. Investment remained stagnant and so did development aid. With the removal of Soviet influence, however, it could lecture African countries on democracy and liberalization like never before. During a summit meeting with African heads of state, French President François Mitterrand, said to be dreaming of democracy in Africa, posited that "France will link its entire contribution effort to efforts made to move in the direction of greater freedom. "Aid will be more lukewarm toward regimes which conduct themselves in an authoritarian manner without accepting evolution toward democracy; it will be enthusiastic for those which take the step with courage."[37] The World Bank and the International Monetary Fund kept pressuring countries toward structural adjustment: opening up in exchange for loans. It often led economic circumstances to evolve from bad to worse. In Rwanda, for example, the government used Western loans to boost military spending, while it simultaneously reduced support for poor coffee farmers. In Ivory Coast, foreign loans enabled the president to build a cathedral in his birth town, yet at the same time he phased out support for cocoa farmers and sold state assets to French companies. Nigeria also liberalized, the main victors being its corrupt military elite and foreign oil companies. One Nigerian dissident summarized it:

> Politics is seen as a way of gaining access to fantastic wealth, and this government has carried it to an extreme. Nigeria has many fine lawyers, but the judiciary is tainted by trials settled with bribes. It has fine academics, but universities are tarnished by the trade in diplomas. It has respected chiefs, but the nobility has been mocked by the sale of chieftaincy titles. In many ways, the institution that has suffered the most under this military government is the military itself. Military men are not soldiers anymore.[38]

A silent compact seemed to be in the making. On the one side, Western financers paid lip service to liberal reform. On the other side, African elites used these reforms in a way that prolonged self-enrichment. It led to a peculiar situation. African politicians legitimately criticized the devastating consequences of exposing weak economies to wildly fluctuating global commodity prices. The president of Ivory Coast, for instance, incessantly condemned international speculators. Yet, this criticism was also a form of demagoguery to distract attention from their own corruption. In other cases, criticism of structural adjustment served more as a defense against international criticism of socialist economic policy. The Tanzanian President Julius Nyerere, whom one could hardly accuse of corruption, put it thus: "We are not earning any more foreign exchange with the World Bank and the International Monetary Fund running the economy." He continued: "In my day, inflation was 28–30 percent a year. Now it is 22 percent. I do not see much success."[39] Nyerere's statement summarized the continent's situation well: it was stuck between socialism, neoliberalism, and corruption.

"Morality matters and right ultimately is profitable," orated South African Archbishop Desmond Tutu.[40] Yet, few knew how to act upon it. The early 1990s did see new democratic movements and attempts toward ending strife. Peace talks and political transition started in Botswana, Mozambique, Ethiopia, and several other countries. But how would democratization be supported by economic development? Political reform first was the assumption in the West. Preserving power democratically was not evident with economies dependent on the capricious market prices of commodities like coffee and cocoa, with farmers facing a torrent of agricultural goods that the West had in excess, and with few investors interested in setting up factories. One intellectual warned of farcical democracies.[41] The South African leader, Nelson Mandela, released in 1990 after having spent 27 years in prison for his fight against Apartheid, urged caution against the instability that fast liberalization could cause. While the West, the World Bank and the International Monetary Fund demanded that countries dismantle state intervention in exchange for support, Mandela proposed the nationalization of mines, banks, and industries, and showed himself very critical of America's role in the world.

Thinkers tried to take the debate about Africa's position in the global order beyond economics and politics. There would be no African rebirth if the continent did not rediscover its roots. The Cameroonian writer Axelle Kabou urged that the continent had to stop importing Western notions of state and development.[42] In his novel *Things Fall Apart*, the Nigerian writer Chinua Achebe cautioned against materialism and the anonymity of Western society. "It seemed as if the very soul of the tribe wept for a great evil that was coming," he wrote, "its own death."[43] One of the most powerful criticisms of Westernization came from the first African recipient of the Nobel Prize for Literature, Wole Soyinka. In a speech during a conference sponsored by the World Bank, he argued that African capitals risked becoming impoverished imitations of New York or Chicago. Echoing Francis Fukuyama's warnings for the West, Soyinka observed that the average African was becoming an unhappy materialist. He compared him to a foreigner standing for the first time in front of a Western shop window:

> He has never seen such consumer items in his entire existence. Indeed, the totality of such items that she has encountered in a lifetime does not match what she is now staring at in a single shop window, and the street is of course taken up with unlimited replications of such luxury. The visitor scratches herself to ensure that she has not died, then woken up in paradise. The society into which this alien has stepped is, however, not merely at home with such goodies; every individual in that society now considers their acquisition the primary goal of existence . . . That culture, in order to guarantee productivity at home, is vigorously exported.
>
> Entire generations of a totally different culture, and usually of less affluent societies, are inducted into this unequal exchange. Being usually the scions of privileged families, they gravitate into positions of influence on national economic policies and executive positions. Soon, the self-respecting youth dare not be seen without a Walkman. The hybrid shuts out the world and enters another world, so wrapped up in that world that he sometimes steps into the gutter or fails to hear the warning sounds of a speeding vehicle and crosses the road at a fatal instant. . . . Feeding the foreign consumerist machine becomes a way of life."[44]

As these debates unfolded, a new generation of warlords saw that the combination of cheap Soviet weapons, access to precious commodities, like diamonds, and the manipulating of the destitute young men would be more solid pillars of power than democracy, trade liberalism, or culture. Their gangs cultivated a Kalashnikov lifestyle. Radical Islam took root here too. In the North of Nigeria, poor farmers changed their name to Saddam and brandished posters of the Iraqi dictator, whom they considered a hero. The authoritarian leadership of Sudan imposed Islamic law, the Sharia, on non-Muslims. Radical Islamic movements commenced to operate in the Horn of Africa.

Maquilas

In Latin America, the United States had long prevented democracy from taking root. Elections were acceptable, as long as they empowered politicians that respected the interests of the United States. This was particularly so in Central America. In 1984, presidential elections in Nicaragua, proclaimed fair by international observers, were won by a leftist leader. President Ronald Reagan called it a Soviet scam, imposed a trade embargo, and supported far-right opponents. America also interfered in Guatemala, Panama, Grenada, and Honduras, supporting strongmen to suppress ideas harming American interests. Still, democracy advanced. Brazil and Argentina were no longer ruled by military leaders. Dictator Augusto Pinochet had left the scene in Chile. Finally, some Central American countries, like El Salvador and Nicaragua, appeared to be on the road to democracy. In Latin America as well, the question remained how democracy would thrive in a context of agony.

By 1990, the population of Latin America was nearly 450 million people, the majority living in poverty. Throughout the previous ten years, production per capita in the region had slightly decreased. It was a lost decade. Agriculture was in crisis. Much more than in Africa, agriculture was dominated by megafarms that produced bananas, pineapples, soy and other cash crops for export. There was less precarious subsistence farming, but more precarious seasonal labor. The remaining smallholders had to compete against large volumes of imported wheat and food products from the United States.

Cocaine and other drugs became tempting alternatives. Organized crime grew and homicide rates soared in the 1980s. Millions of people left the countryside to live in megacities. Slums were growing incredibly fast. Most governments were so indebted that a significant share of their tax incomes was used to pay foreign lenders. They were pushed to open their markets. For some, like Chile, this liberalization brought growth. For others, like Mexico and Bolivia, the results were disappointing. Mexico had millions of citizens toiling in so-called maquilas, sweatshops for export, yet still incurred large trade deficits.[45]

It dawned in Washington that the situation was perilous. As one expert remarked: "The democratic trend, while broad, is very fragile, vulnerable to economic collapse, social strain and political extremism."[46] *The New York Times* put it thus: "In country after country, falling living standards are breeding a hopelessness that is beginning to translate into ominous political decay."[47] The Peruvian economist Hernando de Soto warned that countries were not turning to the liberal policy prescriptions of the World Bank and the International Monetary Fund because they worked, but because they did not have any other option, and that populist policies would soon return.[48] "We do not know how to reconcile the markets with policies that will ameliorate poverty, misery and injustice," wrote sociologist-politician Fernando Cardoso.[49]

Many others from the Latin American intelligentsia urged that capitalism be made more social. The author Mario Vargas Llosa argued that social corrections had to give capitalism the human face it needs to promote social change and preserve legitimacy.[50] The rector of the University of Central America, Father Ignacio Ellacuria, insisted again and again that no democracy would thrive if the norms the West considered universal did not help advance human dignity. "As a mechanism the market is efficient, but like all mechanisms it lacks both conscience and compassion," stated the writer Octavio Paz in his Nobel lecture. "We must find a way of integrating it into society so that it expresses the social contract and becomes an instrument of justice and fairness. . . . A society possessed by the frantic need to produce more in order to consume more tends to reduce ideas, feelings, art, love, friendship and people themselves to consumer products. Everything becomes a thing to be bought, used and then thrown in the rubbish dump."[51]

The region's largest states were engulfed in violence. In Mexico, President Carlos Salinas had privatized companies and trimmed trade tariffs, but only half of his labor force had formal work. Each year, around half a million Mexicans migrated to the United States. Homicide rates remained high. Several prominent members of opposition parties were killed. In Colombia, homicide rates and the number of mass killings peaked. In 1990, students called for a referendum to end the violence between the government, crime syndicates, and paramilitary groups like the Revolutionary Armed Forces of Colombia (FARC). Yet, a low turnout hinted at popular skepticism toward the prospect of peace. In Argentina, President Carlos Menem prioritized close relations with the United States. His economic liberalization efforts came at the expense of political liberty. Menem sidestepped the parliament, clipped the wings of the judicial branch, monopolized mass media, and let his police forces commit arbitrary arrests and killings almost with impunity.

In Peru, President Alberto Fujimori executed the liberalization prescribed by the International Monetary Fund, a policy called the Fujishock, yet showed disdain for parliament. He would ultimately dissolve it a move scarcely criticized by the United States. In Brazil, a country of 150 million, homicide rates also increased. A liberal government had slashed import restrictions, but inflation and unemployment soon again fed popular disillusionment. One of the politicians promising to restore order was Jair Bolsonaro, who openly mulled over the return of military rule. "We will never resolve serious national problems with this irresponsible democracy," he said. "Real democracy is food on the table, the ability to plan your life, the ability to walk on the street without getting mugged."[52]

Subic Bay

Democracy was not particularly highly rated in Southeast Asia either. Lee Kuan Yew, the mastermind who turned Singapore from an impoverished backwater into a first world city state, wasted no opportunity to caution other countries that, while Western capitalism might present opportunities, its obsession with individualism had to be shunned and the state had to remain firmly in control. Southeast Asia on the threshold of the 1990s included ten countries with a population of over 400 million people. It formed the gateway between the Pacific and the Indian Ocean. That presented trade opportunities, but also the interest of great powers.

Like Western Europe, Southeast Asia formed a small tailpiece of the Eurasian landmass. But it lacked prosperity and regional cooperation. Attempts were made. From 1967, the Philippines, Indonesia, Thailand, Singapore, and Malaysia were part of the Association of Southeast Asian Nations, ASEAN. It was formed mainly as a balance against communism in the Cold War, the Soviets, China, and Vietnam. Now, it was also bent on advancing regional economic cooperation, and overtures were made to Vietnam to join. The Vietnamese themselves, traditional recipient of aid from Moscow, quickly seized the opportunity. Following the demise of its sponsor, it ended a war with neighboring Cambodia and started mending ties with Beijing, Washington, and other countries. In 1990, foreign investors were welcomed. "After the Cold War, we can't rely on anyone and must be friends with everyone."[53]

The region remained unstable, having to cope with the legacy of the Cold War divisions. There were border disputes both in the South China Sea and on the continent. Authoritarianism was the most common form of government. In Vietnam, a communist party ruled. Cambodia proclaimed itself a one-party free trade state. Thailand was ruled by a general. He was replaced in a coup by yet another general, who welcomed Western money but not democracy. In the Philippines, a democratically elected president highlighted human rights, but during her term, the United States was forced to close its navy base in Subic Bay. In Indonesia, a country of 180 million people, Suharto had ruled for three decades. He preserved security ties with the United States, but clung to economic nationalism, cultivated his credentials as a Muslim, and did not refrain from using chemical weapons to stamp out secessionism, as in Timor and Aceh.[54] Malaysia had a democracy, but its prime minister showed himself skeptical of political liberalism and followed the Singaporean example of state capitalism. Myanmar was led by a military junta, lyrically called the State Peace and Development Council. For the West, the foremost concern had long been to contain communism, not to promote openness. Now, the region lost its strategic relevance so that Japan became the region's main partner and China recognized as the potential leader for the future.

Structural violence

The disappearance of the world order led to disorientation. The merits of Western leadership, democracy, and economic liberalism as the viable way forward were looked at with skepticism. Russian distrust of the West remained, but the new government's assumption was that if you cannot beat the enemy, you join him. In China, the idea was rather: join the enemy to beat him. It considered economic cooperation necessary to amass power to be able to compete in the long run. Smaller countries also tried to find ways to selectively benefit from the West without fully embracing its values and interests. Many countries were forced to embrace Western leadership in the short run, yet determined to resist it in the long run. Skepticism was also audible elsewhere.

International governmental organizations warned that deregulation could expedite social distress.[55] A war of words erupted between World Bank economists. UNICEF, the United Nations' Children's Fund, had concluded that children and poor households were often fiercely hit by deregulation, as food prices became more capricious, for instance, or social protection disappeared. Adjustment, it proposed, had to show compassion.[56] Thinkers proposed that Western or American hegemony was unjust and destabilizing. Johan Galtung argued that even if the traditional control of land became less important, the world would be marred by structural violence: economic exploitation, discrimination, and exclusion. Immanuel Wallerstein followed that line of thought but asserted that the imperial center, the West, would soon see capitalism hit its economic, environmental, and social limits. Samir Amin proposed that poor countries free themselves of their dependency and delink from unfair globalization.

In 1990, the West gazed with uncertainty towards the changing world and the changing world gazed back at it with even deeper uncertainty. The clear division of the Cold War was about to disappear. What emerged instead was an international outlook characterized by a single superpower, supported by a Pacific and Atlantic ring of partners, and a large number of regional and lesser powers seeking to come to grips with the crisis of the Soviet Union. Even as the only possible major economic partner, the West was distrusted. The persistent nationalism and geopolitical tensions around the globe made it unlikely that the end of the Cold War would usher in a period of cooperation, reconciliation, and, ultimately, prosperity, where individuals and communities could lead meaningful, sustainable lives. Economic difficulties and the fragility of political institutions also made it doubtful that democracy would affirm itself easily.

It had taken Western countries centuries to democratize, a process that coincided with industrialization, which in its turn supported rich cities and sound state structures. Both conditions remained absent in large parts of the world. In a global context burdened by the legacy of the Cold War, it became clear that liberalism, capitalism, and free trade in the way the West had been promoting them as the new irresistible guidance for world politics, faced skepticism. This was the case inside the West and beyond. Capitalism was widely disparaged as the viable solution for a new post-Cold War world, given its emphasis on markets and material pursuit, perceived to be serving interests at the expense of moral values. Claims that capitalism lacked compassion were often justified. Introspection was therefore indispensable to help find ways to preserve the legitimacy of a Western-led global system. But that did not happen. In the next chapters, we will discover how the many concerns at the outset of the post-Cold War period were ignored and how the West undermined its own position at the center of the global order.

ACT 1 (1989–2000)

CHAPTER 4

MISSED OPPORTUNITIES

T HE ROMAN HISTORIAN LIVY WROTE THAT IT IS IN TIMES OF PROS-
PERITY and growth that societies ignore the shaky fundaments
on which their prosperity rests. The 1990s were such a time. The West,
notwithstanding its preponderance, faced internal and external challenges. While decision makers acknowledged them, their introspection
was shallow. Vigor to change course was limited. Between 1990 and 2000,
many problems grew larger. In the core of the Western world, formed
by the United States and the European Union, the social and economic
situation became more unbalanced. Growth, this chapter shows, made
adjustment less urgent. There were countries with a more sustainable
and balanced economic model, in Northwestern Europe, in countries like
the Netherlands, Denmark, and Sweden. Europe continued to integrate,
prepared for enlargement, and introduced its own currency. Yet, each
step of integration required governments to go to their hesitant elec-
torates and public support did not keep pace with the political push for
cooperation.

The detaching of America Inc.

Citizens in the West experienced the 1990s as a golden age. After a slow
start, economic growth kicked in. The news that mesmerized people was
not about crises but about scandals, like popstar Michael Jackson's alleged

molestation of young boys, the murder trial of football player O. J. Simpson, and President Bill Clinton's affair with one of his interns. Big problems looked remote. Households, including the poor, saw their income increase. Consumption goods, like textiles, food, and fuel became more affordable, so that money could be spent on gadgets, a somewhat bigger car, and middle-class brands.

This was the time of the first personal computers, the Gameboy, the Walkman, and the first affordable mobile phones, of aerodynamically designed family cars, like the Ford Focus, and fashion brands like Tommy Hilfiger. Television series like *Friends* and *Sex and the City* idealized adult life as a carefree continuation of the teenage years: Livin' la vida loca! Despite the criticism by intellectuals, the belief in the economic superiority of the West was firmly established in government circles. While Microsoft and Apple had grown into large multinationals, a new generation of giants was already in the making in American garages and campus dorms: Amazon, Google, and Facebook.

Still, it is in the pleasant and comfortable 1990s that we find causes of weakening, particularly in the United States. Bill Clinton (1993–2001) arrived in the White House with the promise to put a human face to the economy. One of his first proposals was to tax the rich a little more and yet also limit welfare benefits at the same time. The Clinton administration could ride an economic high tide that had started just before its inauguration in 1993. During the remainder of the 1990s, the American economy grew impressively. Unemployment fell and the administration could pride itself on lowering the public budget deficit. Yet, while the government budget deficit decreased, the whole nation consumed beyond its means. Not only credit card spending surged.[1] America also saw its external debt expand. As it imported more than it exported, it meant that other countries pre-financed American consumption.

Growing consumption often causes prices to go up. This is the law of supply and demand. It was not the case, though, in the United States, because products could be imported cheaply. World energy production was outstripping demand. Supermarkets tapped into products from low-wage countries like China and Mexico. At the same time, interest rates were kept high, so that foreign capital flowed in and helped spark a boom in the

American stock market. That in turn benefited American shareholders and thus encouraged consumption further. The trade deficit and external debt grew steadily. Yet, the treasury secretary stated that critics of the deficit did not know what they were talking about. It was the size of the American market that attracted capital and made developing countries desperate to export to it. So, the whole trade deficit, he continued, was a meaningless concept. Foreign credit was a good thing.

Still, there was an undeniable downside. Borrowing from international markets indeed did not need to be a problem if more was invested in industries that make the economy more productive, so that the debt could be repaid in the long run. That did not happen. Private investment growth in manufacturing slowed and was overtaken by investment in retail, banking, and real estate. This situation also accounts for the very slow spreading of productivity gains in the information technology sector to the rest of the economy: the so-called IT productivity paradox. Why should American companies invest in more efficient factories at home when goods could be cheaply imported? While American research centers realized scientific breakthroughs in information technology, the country imported far more IT goods and services than it exported.[2] Moreover, private and public investment in research and development, as a share of its total domestic production, dropped in the first half of the 1990s. There was a second negative effect: the overheating of the stock market. While investment in manufacturing or in public infrastructure was modest, the value of IT champions on the stock market grew almost threefold between 1995 and 1999. It formed a bubble that had to burst and the inflow of foreign capital made it even larger.

It coincided with a third phenomenon: the slow detachment of American companies from their home market. While the American government annually sold US$60 billion of bonds to foreign creditors and high interest rates attracted billions more to the American capital market, American companies themselves relocated more of their capital abroad (figure 4.1): a diversification of investment risk, it was explained. In reality, many investors went offshore. By 1999, 27 percent of all direct investment overseas was in holdings; 16 percent was in holdings in tax havens, like Switzerland, the Netherlands, Luxembourg, and the Bermuda Islands. If 60 percent

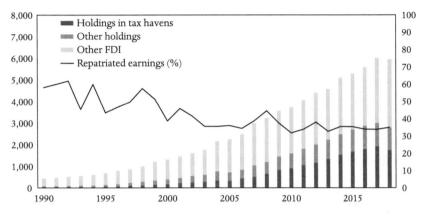

Figure 4.1 The detaching of America Inc.: American foreign direct investment (US$ bn, left axis) and the share of foreign direct investment earnings repatriated (%, right axis)

Source: BEA.

of overseas profit on investment was still being repatriated in 1990, this declined to 50 percent in 1999. American investors restlessly searched for higher returns. Investment funds scavenged the world for profit. Interest rates in the United States were around 5 percent. Profits on debt products could still be higher in weak countries. Information technology allowed a faster response to changes in the value of currencies, commodity prices, and so forth. They called on the American government for diplomatic backing and to bail them out at times of crisis. This search for foreign markets, we will discover, shaped American foreign policy.

American hollow

In 1990, 23 percent of American citizens were satisfied with the state of the economy; in 1999 this was 71 percent. Growth in the 1990s appeared to be a tide that lifted all boats. Poverty dropped, th e number of citizens depending on welfare decreased. Crime rates went down. But not all boats were lifted equally. Inequality increased. While the richest 1 percent claimed 10 percent of the national income in 1990, this increased to 20 percent in 1999. The rich benefited disproportionally from the stock market's growth and the large bonuses in the IT sector, while the middle class saw much less benefit from the IT boom.

While dedicated programs had led to a decrease in the poverty among African-Americans, close to three million white American families, primarily in isolated rural areas, lived in poverty by the end of the decade.[3] The documentary *American Hollow* brought the gripping story of one of these families. It lived a hidden existence in the Appalachians and saw no opportunity to break the spiral of poverty. "You cannot go to places without money, so another great day in shithole." It was in the rural hinterland also that the number of working poor continued to increase and that citizens felt left behind by coastal cities like New York and San Francisco.[4] Despite economic growth and despite high consumer confidence, Americans were less happy at the end of the decade than at the beginning. There was more loneliness, more pressure at work, and longer commuting times. While the economy grew, the social fabric frayed. Interestingly, American citizens put forward morals, the decline of family cohesion, and education as their most important concerns.[5]

The 1990s were a missed opportunity in another way. While citizens again and again expressed their desire for more time with their loved ones, for a sustainable economy, and care for those who need it, the government made no effort to better explain how citizens could help make these ideas happen.[6] Despite the intuitive longing for a humane society, they were not told how to build it. They were left adrift in a society where the main influencers tried to sell *things* and materialism continued to advance. As parents worked longer days, schools became bigger, more anonymous, and yet burdened with more responsibilities. "I believe that somehow every student in every college of the United States," a prominent historian wrote, "ought to be taught fundamental lessons that say democracy is precious, democracy is perishable, democracy requires active attention and that democracy requires hard work."[7]

The opposite happened. Pedagogues saw an overall decline in the quality of civic and history education.[8] Industrial education, it was called.[9] The retreat of broad knowledge of ethics, history, literature, arts, and science, a leading pedagogue concluded, would undermine a democracy that depended on the judgments of the masses.[10] It also abraded important attitudes, like honesty, responsibility, curiosity, industry, kindness, empathy, and courage. Youngsters were pushed deeper into an abyss of nihilism. And, indeed, civic engagement did decline. It was as if the United States ignored the many experts that had highlighted the premonition of the Founding Fathers that no democracy survives without civic duty.[11] Youngsters participated less in school debates or student elections, refrained from voluntary work, took less interest in politics, and spent more time alone than with friends and family.[12]

The 1990s bred a generation without public passion, a generation for whom conscious ignorance had become a way of life. It bred an elite that pursued wealth but had limited civic duty, and, if it could, did not keep its wealth inside the country but took it to a tax haven. The corporate elite consisted also less and less of industrialists, stakeholders of the real economy. In the 1990s, its place was taken more and more by stock market brokers, financial directors, and celebrities. It was not an elite that led by example, aspiring to economic growth to strengthen the nation, but, as President Theodore Roosevelt had warned, an elite recklessly deifying material wealth.

The spirit, tragic almost, was magisterially captured in one of the protagonists in Jonathan Franzen's *The Corrections*: Gary. "Gary wanted to enjoy being a man of wealth and leisure, but the country was making it none too easy," he put it. "All around him, millions of newly minted American millionaires were engaged in the identical pursuit of feeling extraordinary – of buying the perfect Victorian, of skiing the virgin slope, of knowing the chef personally, of locating the beach that had no footprints. There were further tens of millions of young Americans who didn't have money but were nonetheless chasing the Perfect Cool."[13]

Eurostar

The European Union presented itself as a humane alternative. As an international actor, it aspired to become a civilian power that replaced the threat of force with multilateral cooperation. As a society, it prided itself on being a civilized power, dedicated to social justice, and in that way superior to naked capitalism. Some considered this to be part of a lasting effort to escape from Europe's war trap. German Chancellor Helmut Kohl (1982–98), whose brother was killed in World War II, and French President François

Mitterrand (1981–95), who had been a prisoner of war himself, both propounded repeatedly that peace must not be taken for granted. "The policy of European integration is a question of war and peace."[14] The president of the European Commission put it even more firmly: "If we do not succeed with political union, the historical decline of Europe which began with the First World War will resume."[15]

With the passing of that political generation, new leaders shifted the emphasis to Europe as the vanguard of the third way. The best way to preserve stability, they claimed, was to strike a balance between entrepreneurship and social corrections. European integration advanced. The Maastricht Treaty gave more responsibility to the European institutions. The Schengen Agreement opened borders and most of the member states accepted the euro as a common currency. New member states joined. Yet, European citizens were still unconvinced. Fewer than half of them supported European membership or found that their country had benefited from the Union. In the years before its introduction of the euro, for instance, just half of the citizens supported the common currency.

The most important challenge for Europe in the 1990s concerned the unification of Germany. Germany had to overcome an immense gap between the rich West and the poor East. The operation each year demanded over US$100 billion of support for the impoverished citizens that had lived on the eastern side of the Iron Curtain. The impact on regional income disparity, however, was modest. The implications of German reunification went beyond the country's borders. While reunification meant addressing the weakness of the East, the rest of Europe feared the return of German strength.

A second concern related to the euro. After reunification, Germany became the largest economy. Hence, it had to be enmeshed even more strongly into the common market and one of the traditional symbols of German power, the strong Deutsche Mark, had to be replaced by the common currency. The euro was introduced in 1999. Economists warned that if the euro limited destabilizing competitive devaluations between countries, it could cause new instability if it was not soon completed by fiscal integration, a common government budget, and, in the end, a political union. A common currency introduced in a large market that showed important disparities and without proper rebalancing mechanisms, whether that be smooth labor movement from poor to rich places or capital movement from rich to poor places, was bound for trouble.

And the regional disparities did remain large, which brings us to a third important challenge. As with the rift between the American hinterland and the thriving areas on the coast, Europe also had difficulties in addressing regional differences, in spite of dedicated cohesion funds.[16] The northwest, with countries like the Netherlands, Denmark, Sweden, and Finland, became Europe's San Francisco Bay. These places were high on happiness and wellbeing. Companies like Nokia and Philips were technology leaders. German regions like Bavaria and North Rhine-Westphalia benefited from the European export market to grow car- and machine-building industries. London consolidated its position as a leading financial hub. Regional economic differences have always existed. But for a political project founded on the ideal of cohesion and with the ambition to have its own monetary union, it did not bode well. For now, most of the consequences were political. Some regions, like the north and south of France, showed their anger by voting for the far right. Sometimes, rich regions made it clear that there had been enough patience with the poor. This was the case with populist political parties like Lega Nord in Italy and Vlaams Blok in Belgium.

A fourth challenge that started to become visible was the political expression of a significant undercurrent of Euroscepticism. Citizens experienced the introduction of the euro and the ending of border controls. Few related these changes to the quest for lasting peace or human dignity. Whereas European integration, its giant market, its unprecedented openness, its common standards, and its common currency was appealing to those mobile and strong, it caused mixed feelings and even opposition among those who longed for security and fellowship. The prospect of future enlargement toward the east and accepting more poorer countries led to an outcry of protectionism. A new group of intellectuals echoed these feelings. It took aim at the elite in Brussels or their national elites who allegedly set aside native culture for multiculturalism, the working man for big business. In France, Gaullist politicians called for a return to a Europe of strong states. In Italy, Forza Italia and the Lega Nord were keen on European funding and even supported enlargement, but also opposed more power for the European institutions. The Eurosceptics mixed anger with nostalgia, nationalism with opportunism.

It is in this context also that a fifth problem kept imposing itself: the persistent doubt about European integration in the United Kingdom. In the United Kingdom, 18 years of Conservative rule had coincided with a slump in manufacturing, low productivity, sinking education standards, an increase in crime rates, and decline in many regions outside London.[17] When a new social-democrat prime minister, Tony Blair (1997–2007), promised to follow the third way and that everyone could be a winner, conservatives highlighted the dreadful state of the country, the surveys that showed that only a minority of students still paid attention to British heroes like Churchill, the advance of McDonald's at the expense of the authentic pub, and behold, the alleged threat of the European Union to traditional fox hunting.[18] They called it a disgrace when the Royal Yacht, towed away by a German tugboat for decommissioning, caused the Queen to shed a tear.[19] "This great country was tricked, conned, and cheated into joining a Union, which has been disastrous for her economy, her world standing, her true interests and her God-given independence."[20] To halt decline, they vented, Britain had to have its borders back and get out of the European Union. Sovereignty sharing, at the core of the European project, lost its appeal; it was time to reflect on taking sovereignty back.

By the late 1990s, over three quarters of European citizens found that politics had become too complicated, that the integration of immigrants had failed, and that center parties that still dominated European politics could not be trusted.[21] But whether it concerned the far right, the Eurosceptics, or leftist protesters, the response of the political center was not to try to get to grips with the causes of their concerns. Their response was to cordon them off. The far right was put into quarantine, critics of the European Union disparaged as ignorant protectionists. As economic growth accelerated in the second half of the 1990s and consumer confidence was restored, the impetus to resolve some of the downsides of European integration diminished. The center parties even raised the stakes. While only a minority of the population supported eastward enlargement, toward former communist countries including the three Baltic States, the Czech Republic, Slovakia, Poland, and Hungary, the process was continued nevertheless. Politicians reasoned that access to Europe was the only way for the former Soviet countries to become stable and that this was in the interest of all. Citizens doubted. Many saw enlargement as a group of poor countries endangering their established way of life, requiring massive investments, and making the Union too large to govern. Integration looked like a Eurostar high-speed train rushing by in the distance.

Carry on

There are enduring themes in political history. The gap between political promise and reality, for example, the tensions between those flourishing and those being left behind. What made the 1990s particular in terms of Western politics was the growing gap between consumer confidence and political distrust. While citizens happily spent, they seemed to sense that something was amiss. A second particularity was that seldom before in recent history had there been such a gap between the pretense of politicians to be compassionate, their appeal to the moral high ground of peace and harmony, and the reluctance to act upon it. A third observation was the wide gap between politicians' support for economic globalization and the reluctance of citizens. Finally, there were new symptoms of weakening. If the neoliberal policies of the 1980s were criticized, third way politics coincided with growing external debt. Yet, for now, there was enough growth and enough confidence for the center politician to carry on. Foreign policy, as we will see, was a continuation of it.

rationale for European integration. The European Union also had to have a common external policy. The Maastricht Treaty established foreign and security policy as a key pillar. In the Maastricht Treaty, signed in 1992, the 12 member states of the European Union also sketched out the normative guidelines of a common foreign policy. It codified common values like democracy, the rule of law, and human rights as priorities for the development of the Union's foreign relations.[2] Previously the heads of government had called the promotion of human rights and free trade relations "essential" elements in their foreign policy.[3] Only an open world, the assumption was, would advance security.

On the other side of the Atlantic, the American National Security Strategy of 1990 claimed to be a vision shaped by the Magna Carta and the Universal Declaration of Human Rights. Security advisors in the White House spoke of a blue area of market democracy that had to be enlarged. Policy would be about principle more than power. This line was set out under President George H. W. Bush and preserved under President Clinton in his first National Security Strategy of 1994. Power was almost taken for granted. The United States, this document proposed, still had a vital interest in preventing any hostile power from dominating the Eurasian land mass.[4] The United States also had to continue to be able to fight two major wars simultaneously.[5] But for now, no peer rival loomed on the horizon.

The main security threats were the proliferation of nuclear weapons to rogue and unstable states. Even if certain powers were to rise, like China or an invigorated European Union, the assumption was that their intentions could be made less hostile by coaxing them into democracy, free trade, and human rights. If Western principles could spread, shifts in the balance of power had to cause less concern. The promotion of democracy was central.[6] "Our national security strategy is based on enlarging the community of market democracies," the 1994 National Security Strategy stated. "The more that democracy and political and economic liberalization take hold in the world, particularly in countries of geostrategic importance to us, the safer our nation is likely to be and the more our people are likely to prosper."[7]

But how was this to be reconciled with economic interests? "Economy at the heart of foreign policy," as it was summarized. American foreign economic policy in the 1990s started as a promise to make globalization more humane for the poor, yet ended up rescuing large investors for whom globalization had become an opportunity to speculate on a worldwide scale. As a presidential candidate, Bill Clinton had called for the improvement of labor rights in Mexico. He proposed an American industrial policy to bring manufacturing back. One of his first initiatives was indeed to propose an agreement on labor cooperation. The president also favored a social clause in new global trade rules, wished the world economy to become more environment-friendly, and to bring human rights into the debate. "We must ensure that economic policies provide protection for the environment and promote the well-being of workers," he said. This echoed the concerns of American public opinion. A majority favored tying human rights to trade and paying more attention to labor rights.[8] The American public also consistently favored tariffs to protect local jobs.[9] The popular view of the European Union was as a group of spoiled societies dependent on American protection, of Japan as an unfair trading partner, and of the free trade schemes with Mexico as a sell-out of jobs.[10] This was in contrast with the policy elite that saw Japan and Europe as crucial allies.

There were different opportunities to strike a balance between free trade and adjustments, but they were missed. Before the North American Free Trade Agreement (NAFTA), with Mexico and Canada entered into force in 1994, the parties adopted an agreement on labor cooperation, but it did not set any minimum standards and its petition procedure had no impact. During the Uruguay Round, the negotiations that had to transform the Global Agreement on Tariffs and Trade, GATT, into a more capable World Trade Organization, almost all ambitions to include social and environmental rules were ditched. Despite interest also from European countries, large transnational companies, together with the governments of developing countries, lobbied against it. They argued that poor societies would not be able to catch up if they were denied more lax social and environmental standards. Critics cautioned that this could allow authoritarian countries to ignore labor rights and unleash a race to the bottom by the West.[11] When the World Trade Organization, or WTO, was founded, in 1995, it did leave members the possibility to implement social and environmental rules, yet sought to prevent them from impeding trade.[12] In its negotiations with China, the world's largest authoritarian economy, the Clinton administration dropped the principle that trade would be linked to human rights. Conditionality disappeared.

There were several explanations for this turn. Clinton had tried to win votes with a promise for a humane economy. As a governor, however, he had previously shown himself lax on social and environmental standards. Besides this personal ambivalence, multinational companies had set their eyes on overseas markets and had much more lobbying power than the many small producers that struggled to survive at home. The retail sector particularly sought to source cheap products from Asia and Mexico. President Clinton's spouse Hillary had been on the board of Walmart, the largest retailer, which had built itself a reputation for suppressing labor unions, and owned a significant number of Walmart shares. During his first presidential campaign, Clinton accepted funding from various companies that pressured for relaxing conditions on trade with China.[13] Top positions in his team were taken by free-traders.[14]

The Clinton administration now wanted a voluntarist trade policy. "To turn mutual assured destruction into mutual assured prosperity," it was explained.[15] Along the way, the human dimension moved entirely to the background. Only trade remained. This could be seen as a continuation of the neoliberal trade policy of previous administrations, the fact that a large number of the policy makers had been influenced by the Chicago School, the belief that there was no alternative to open markets, and that American interests were best served by unrestrained economic openness, disregarding unfair competition. To sustain the consumption boom, America needed cheap goods from China and oil from the Gulf States – whether the regimes were authoritarian or not.

The new IT companies also required a global market. They needed low-wage countries to assemble computers and mobile phones. They set their eyes on other societies to export to. "We have passed the point where we can sustain prosperity on sales just within the United States," the Secretary of State said.[16] In this regard, Washington was particularly keen on the protection of patents and other intellectual property. It was the main sponsor of TRIPS, a worldwide treaty on trade-related intellectual property rights. TRIPS implied that signatories would protect each other's patents. It also pushed hard for the General Agreement on Trade in Services, GATS. Services, like banks, insurance, and telecom providers, were increasingly important in American exports. Washington successfully resisted calls to have the United Nations oversee the internet, which could restrain companies like Google and Yahoo, and made an American organization, called ICANN, responsible for the allocation of domain names.[17] ICANN, the Internet Corporation for Assigned Names and Numbers, was a non-profit organization bound to American law. "We have to be at the center of every vital global network," said the president.[18] This all made it clear that, contrary to the social and environmental standards, Washington could get its own way – if it wished to.

The influence of American transnational companies on trade policy and the limitations of ethical concerns also became manifest during the Banana War that started in 1998. The European Union offered to several poor Caribbean countries the opportunity to export bananas on favorable terms, but the banana multinational Chiquita prodded the American government to consider this discrimination and to slap taxes on French cheese, Scottish cashmere, and telecommunication producers. So, the main goal of American trade in the 1990s seemed to be to guarantee the import of cheap consumer goods, as well as to increase access for American tech champions and allow them to dominate the digital sphere.

The digital revolution also transformed capitalism. It made the transfers faster and more globalized. It also detached the investment managers even further from the real economy. "You're looking at electronic screens. When I watch my children playing Nintendo or Sega or Pokemon or whatever the current game is, it's analogous," a fund manager explained. "There's an electronic screen. . . . [Y]ou're playing with this game with your imagination. In essence, you're not out in the field experiencing the changes in employment and agricultural harvests or things like that, you're looking at a distillation of all the indicators about that process over an electronic screen."[19]

Moral hazard

Hence, another objective concerned access for American capital. Policy makers were initially cautious about the possible speculation that financial liberalism might lead to. They explored the possibility of a multilateral framework to limit tax evasion. "It is vital that we put an end to international tax practices that encourage tax evasion and distort capital flows."[20] Yet, pressure from Wall Street was immense. Investment funds, like Goldman Sachs and Blackstone Group, were the largest sponsors of Bill Clinton's presidential campaign. Linkages between such funds and the influential Treasury were so close that experts spoke of a Wall Street Treasury complex.

Along the way, the government backtracked and laid out that it was not in the interest of the United States to stifle tax competition. Overall, it wanted "full market access" to banks, brokers, and funds.[21] In the International Monetary Fund, where Washington had the majority of the votes, it proposed to make financial support to developing countries conditional on the liberalization of capital markets.[22] This was despite the fact that the founders of the IMF had warned that the flow of capital must not be allowed to become an independent and possibly disruptive force.[23] The American public too loathed this flight to fiscal havens and financial speculation.

One of the first destinations of speculative capital was Mexico. The Mexican government issued billions of bonds and, despite the economy being in deep trouble, large investment funds continued to pour in as they could earn interest of 15 percent and more, until the bubble burst in 1995. The American government demanded that the IMF lead a bailout of over US$50 billion, which had to allow Mexico to repay predominantly American lenders. Many economists warned of the moral hazard: if speculators were rescued by the government they would just go on. It was like socialism for the rich. But the Treasury stated that Mexico was unique and that American stability was at risk.

The next target became Russia, another struggling economy with government bonds with high interest rates. "Russia was the ultimate moral hazard," said an official of one of the biggest investment funds. "The general view was that it was too big or too nuclear to fail, that the West would put money in as far as the eye can see. It gave foreign investors a feeling of complacency."[24] After this bubble burst too, the IMF weighed in. Speculators moved on, to Asia, where they invested over US$150 billion. "Why should we care? We are protected," a banker uttered.[25] The problem with Asian countries was often that, prodded by the West, investment was left in and taken out freely, but the banking sector and financial policy were fragile. But weakness, for speculators, means high profits from high interest rates, at least until the bubble bursts, or, even more cynically, an opportunity to speculate on the burst.

The Asian financial crisis of 1997 and 1998 was devastating. It dealt a blow to the credibility of the United States. In the negotiations about a bailout with South Korea, private American funds had a seat at the table, alongside the IMF. The Korean government was forced to sell companies at fire-sale prices. In Indonesia, the government had to abandon support for the domestic car and aircraft industries. Remarks of the American trade representative left nothing to the imagination. He called the crisis a golden opportunity for the West to use the IMF as a "battering ram" to gain advantage.[26] It also undermined trust in capitalism and Western policy prescriptions, especially because countries that had liberalized financial markets were wrecked by the crisis, while China, which still had a regulated capital market, was much less affected by the financial crises. Still, the IMF asserted that financial openness was worth the risk.[27] The United States also continued to press the Fund to require members to stick to financial liberalization. It is better, a Treasury official maintained, that money tries to get into a country than that no money tries to move in.[28]

American foreign economic policy was a combination of Walmart, Microsoft, and Goldman Sachs. It celebrated globalization and paid less attention to its downside. Concerns about social justice, the fate of smaller producers that tried to make a living inside the United States, and financial stability moved to the background. Criticism of this approach grew, also in the West. When the trade ministers of the WTO met in Seattle in 1999, tens of thousands of protesters came out against naked capitalism and globalization. Polls showed that a vast majority of Americans feared that globalization would lead to job losses and favored barriers to prevent the import of cheap goods from affecting the labor market.[29] A majority also favored corrections to reduce the gap between rich and poor at home.[30] Similar sentiments were expressed in Western Europe. So, despite a decade of high growth in the United States, concerns about the impact of trade remained widespread and a minority of about 30 percent even opposed free trade altogether.

Cruise missiles

During the Cold War, the West stated the importance of promoting democracy and liberty. It sensed that it was easier said than done, yet could explain that the Soviets were pushing back on it and that pragmatism was due. After the Cold War, it still stated the importance of promoting democracy, but this time there was no rival to blame for setbacks. The administration of George H. W. Bush concluded that the advancing of democracy in Eastern Europe was partly due to its sustained overseas military presence. He vowed to adopt a forward-leaning defense policy and to respond more assertively to threats to Western values.[31] The Clinton administration continued this policy. It put emphasis on the importance of a global presence to respond to humanitarian challenges. This was the apogee of liberal and humanitarian interventionism.

There was, however, an immense gap between ideals and reality. The West enjoyed an unprecedented military advantage. Absent a peer rival, some openly questioned whether the United States still had to be capable of fighting two major wars simultaneously.[32] One military commander stated that he was running out of demons to fight.[33] NATO countries represented half of the world's defense spending. The United States alone kept hundreds of thousands of troops overseas. Its defense budget remained three times larger than that of China and Russia combined. It led the so-called revolution in military affairs, the pursuit of dominance on the global battlefield by means of networking, precision, range, speed, and stealth. Nothing represented this more than the F-117, the black bomber that was almost invisible to radar, the Tomahawk cruise missile that could strike targets as far as 1,500 kilometers away, and the aircraft carrier battle groups.

America's military force was overwhelming. But threats, like unstable states, civil wars, and terrorism required a measured and sustained effort, rather than overwhelming force. A civil war could upend a state in a few days. But to rebuild one, let alone a democratic one, proved immensely difficult. The question was also how much sacrifice Western citizens were ready to make. Many of the so-called teacup wars in the 1990s took place in countries that they were hardly familiar with.[34] For the military, the diplomatic service, and the political leadership, it was not evident how to come to grips with this new situation. Over 20 drafts were needed before the first national security strategy of the Clinton administration was released. The main question was how much risk the West was willing to take to slowly adjust reality to its ideals of liberty and democracy.

During the Gulf War of 1990, it would have taken American tanks less than about a day to roll from the battlefields in the south onwards to the palaces of the dictator Saddam Hussein in Baghdad. But despite President Bush's call for a new era of freedom in the Middle East, the dictator was allowed to stay. In the years that followed, American military presence in the region was not meant to promote democracy, but to protect autocrats. In 1998, when the West grew concerned about Saddam Hussein's weapons of mass destruction, Western countries launched a pinprick attack, with missiles and aircraft, yet still with no clear design for how to deal with the strongman in the long run.

In 1991, a military coup was staged in Haiti, a small Central American island state, about one thousand kilometers off the coast of Florida. The Bush administration denounced it, but refused to intervene. As the military rule caused an exodus of refugees and provided a sanctuary to drug traffickers, the Clinton administration launched Operation Restore Democracy. Close to 20,000 troops were deployed in 1994. They were deployed to topple the junta, but without a strategy to restore democracy. As soon as the American troops decamped in 1996, it again became manifest how feeble state structures were. A deadlock between the president and the parliament developed, crime once more engulfed the slums of the capital Port-au-Prince, and the people became bitter and disillusioned.

In 1990, a civil war in Somalia escalated. The stream of horror stories, as well as the fear of contagion to other countries, prompted the Bush administration to send in 25,000 troops to restore order as part of a UN mission. But the rebels were defiant and struck back. In 1993, President Clinton approved an elite force operation to take out the rebel leaders. But the underestimation of civilian resistance, the unpreparedness for urban warfare in the urban maze of Mogadishu, and the lack of protection against rocket-propelled grenades caused the operation to fail and Washington to pull out. At almost exactly the same moment, genocide started in Rwanda. Over 15,000 civilians were massacred each week. Western intelligence services knew that a genocide was in the making, but if troops were deployed to the Central African country, they were sent to evacuate Western citizens and to protect embassies, not so much to protect local people. The State Department initially prohibited calling the tragedy a genocide.

The most dramatic example was the Yugoslav Wars: the conflict between Serbia and other countries of the former Federal Republic of Yugoslavia, like Croatia and Bosnia. "We don't have a dog in this fight," said the American Secretary of State.[35] Estimations showed that at least 100,000 soldiers would be needed to stabilize the Balkans. Besides, the Serbs were not threatening vital interests. The initial American approach was to call for unity. Yet, intelligence reports warned that there was a growing risk of war. European countries were divided. The French proposed economic incentives to avoid conflict. Britain and Greece were reluctant to criticize Belgrade. Peace conferences were convened and a first unarmed European monitoring mission deployed. But violence increased. By the autumn of 1991 thousands of people had been killed in Serbian attacks against Croatia. By now, the idea of unity had been ditched and replaced by plans to form new states along ethnic lines: Serbia, Croatia, and Slovenia. These ethnic lines were very complex: What would happen to Bosnia, whose demographic map of Serbs and Bosnians was said to resemble a Jackson Pollock painting? In 1992, the UN deployed a first monitoring mission, including many British troops.

In the spring of 1992, thousands of civilians were killed in the siege of the Bosnian capital Sarajevo. Sanctions were imposed on Serbia. They made no impression. A flight interdiction was imposed. It was violated. A UN peacekeeping mission was deployed. It was powerless. Serbia defied the superpower. The death toll climbed. Washington proposed air strikes and arming Serbia's rivals. European countries, having peacekeepers on the ground, refused. In 1995, Serbia readied for a decisive push for victory. It took UN peacekeepers hostage and allowed 8,000 Bosnians to be massacred right under the nose of UN troops near the city of Srebrenica. In a video-taped conversation with the Bosnian-Serbian warlord, the UN commander humiliatingly pleaded for Serbian assistance because his troops had run out of fuel and provision: "I would like to thank the Serbian authorities for the good treatment."[36]

This was a turning point. Washington now took the lead, its credibility at stake. Bosnia was a cancer eating away at American credibility.[37] London and Paris were still reluctant, but consented to a NATO air campaign against Serbia and to replace the toothless UN mission with a NATO force. The war now drew to an end in Bosnia, Croatia, and Slovenia, but the settlement left the status of the Serbian Province of Kosovo unresolved. In 1998, the Kosovo Liberation Army started attacking Serbian troops, which led to harsh retaliations by Serbia. NATO decided to act, despite opposition from Russia and China. It launched a new bombing campaign. But after two months of bombing, Serbia continued its offensive, hoping for Russian support. Only when it became clear that Russia would not come to the rescue did Belgrade accept a peace agreement and NATO peacekeepers were deployed.

Several factors conditioned Western interventions. Politicians needed quick results. They were programmed by elections to look only a few years ahead in their own country, and could not be expected to look far ahead in distant countries. The absence of direct security threats and real-time reporting made their societies risk-averse and impatient to see results. Fast fighting became the military equivalent of fast food. The debacles of the early 1990s led the West to be more afraid of entanglement in overseas operations. The killing of American soldiers in Somalia, the execution of Belgian paratroopers in Rwanda, left a deep scar. "This was the lowest point of my presidency," President Clinton would reveal. "It was a goddamned nightmare. I felt personally responsible for that kid's body being dragged through the streets."[38]

Washington's priority, and also of many European countries, became to avoid putting boots on the ground. President George H. W. Bush had warned his successor of the consequences of such restraint: "Our leadership around the world is eroded by a stop-and-start policy of hesitancy."[39] But in Congress, it was the Republican Party of Bush that campaigned for restraint, especially toward interventions in civil wars, and even more so toward the participation in UN peacekeeping missions. "There is an extraordinary contradiction between enlarging democracy and defending human rights around the world, and what is actually being done," an expert concluded. "It is a minimalist policy with maximalist, very lofty language."[40]

More than ever, America resorted to remote-control engagement, a policy that turned to long-range attacks, more to show that it could strike back than with the resolve to address the causes of the security threat. In 1995, Washington ordered a massive bombing campaign against the Serbian government. As long as it assumed that no ground troops would follow, Belgrade remained as defiant as the warlords in Somalia a few years earlier. In 1996, the response against Saddam Hussein's atrocious campaign against the Kurds was again one of missiles. Against the Al-Qaeda bombings of embassies in East Africa in 1998: more missiles. Against Saddam Hussein's chemical weapons program: missiles. And against the Serbian attacks in Kosovo, the year after: missiles and bombing. During the campaign above Kosovo, a new weapon was deployed. The B-2 was the most expensive bomber ever built and executed its strikes directly from air force bases on the American continent. During the Yugoslav Wars, the American military also started developing the first plans to deploy unmanned aerial vehicles with missiles. "Distant maneuver" became the priority in the Pentagon's vision for the future battlefield: more precise warfighting with better integrated weapons from a greater distance.[41]

Sanctions were the economic equivalent of cruise missiles. In the best case, they were part of an earnest strategy to change the course of action of the targeted country. Most of the time, they reflected the refusal to engage comprehensively. By the late 1990s, over half of the world population in a total of 75 countries was subject to unilateral coercive economic measures.[42] The vast majority of those sanctions were imposed by the United States. Their main function was to signal anger at an acceptable cost. Reviews of unilateral economic sanctions showed their limitations. An American government report concluded that sanctions only had a chance of success if they were supported by many other countries, if they were endorsed by international organizations, if they were part of a comprehensive political strategy for the target country, if the population was spared, and if the position of the targeted government was undermined.[43] Nevertheless, sanctions continued to be imposed without these conditions being fulfilled. As a result, they added to the humanitarian crisis in Haiti and weakened the Bosnian resistance movements in the Yugoslav Wars. Rather than causing North Korea, Iran, or Pakistan to drop their nuclear ambitions, they confirmed the image of the United States as an adversary and the conviction that weapons of mass destruction were needed to stop it. Moreover, the sanctions, and their extraterritorial effect on non-American companies, caused widespread frustration among allies.

Contradictions

Western foreign policy was a large contradiction. It was a contradiction between the declared goal of democracy promotion and, as the crisis in Haiti and many African countries showed, the unwillingness to provide the sustained and comprehensive support to give democracy a chance. Spending on development cooperation, for example, decreased in the 1990s. There was a contradiction between the promise of Western governments to make global markets more humane and the fact that their fight for social and environmental standards was much less energetic than their fight for binding rules for the liberalization of trade and capital markets. There was a contradiction also between the claim of global leadership and the growing penchant for remote-control engagement, the kind of engagement that relies more on long-range missiles and sanctions than on true dedication and sacrifices on the ground, the engagement that views the world more through the lenses of satellites and spy planes than through sophisticated understanding of the complexity of history, social organization, and economic realities on the ground.

Another paradox existed between the apparent internationalism of the Clinton administration and its unwillingness to abandon unilateralism. The European Union had incorporated multilateralism into its political genetics. That was not the case with the United States. Despite its call for free trade, the United States never relinquished the right to impose unilateral trade measures. The main instrument in this regard was the infamous section 301 of a trade act from the 1970s. It gave the president the right to retaliate against any trade-damaging trade restriction. At the very moment that the World Trade Organization was established, a 301 procedure was launched against Japanese car makers and Chinese toy producers. While President George H. W. Bush opposed using the instrument, it was embraced by the Clinton administration.

If the Republicans were somewhat more inclined toward free trade multilateralism than the Democrats, it was the opposite in other matters. In 1994, President Clinton declared his support for the continuation of the Anti-Ballistic Missile Treaty, which limits the defensive systems against ballistic missiles, but the Senate, which was dominated by the Republicans, urged to end it. In 1996, President Clinton signed the Comprehensive Test-Ban Treaty, the CTBT, which prohibited nuclear experimental explosions, but the Senate refused to ratify it. In 1997, the President accepted the Kyoto Protocol to mitigate climate change, but the Senate balked. In 1998, the White House was positive about a convention banning discrimination against women, but could not get it endorsed. The Senate also remained critical of the United Nations. If the majority of American citizens were favorable toward the United Nations, it was harshly criticized for its poor record by Republicans.[44]

Tensions also grew inside NATO. NATO was an unequal alliance. The United States controlled its command structure and the Europeans depended entirely on American support. This had become painfully visible in the wars in Bosnia and Kosovo. Without American assistance, there would have been no intervention. As the ending of the Cold War encouraged the Europeans to lower their defense spending, this imbalance became still more pronounced. In Washington, it caused politicians to complain louder and louder that Europe was freeriding on America's military preponderance, yet challenged it economically with its growing internal market.

In Europe, it led to the critique that the alliance had become a subcontractor of Washington, a guise for American unilateralism. The French and Germans questioned whether NATO could operate without authorization of the United Nations, whereas the Americans insisted that no such approval was needed if the security of one of the allies was threatened. In discussions about a new strategic concept, the United States also wanted the organization to play a more global role, beyond Europe. But many European countries resisted that too. It was questioned publicly whether the alliance would even survive, given those tensions and the fact that the main emerging powers were all located in East Asia.

In 1998, the American Secretary of State Madeleine Albright made a strong statement: "If we have to use force, it is because we are America," she said. "We are the indispensable nation. We stand tall and we see further than other countries into the future."[45] The assertion was typical of the internationalist style of the Clinton administration, a continuation almost of the ideal of America as a chosen nation but now with a global responsibility to stamp out dictatorship and protectionism. But whether it concerned trade, security, or international governance, cleavages were visible, within the Western world, between America and its liberal allies, and even more so between the proclaimed principles and what happened in reality.

CHAPTER 6

MAKING RIVALS RICH

THE 1990S WERE A STRATEGIC PAUSE FOR THE WEST. ABSENT MAJOR challengers, it could repair some of its internal weaknesses and assist countries whenever they embraced liberal values. It could both bolster its power and advance its principles. Yet, as we observed, the opposite happened. The previous chapter clarified that the West did not show leadership abroad convincingly. The foreign policy discourse was interventionist and moralizing. Desert Storm in Iraq was explained as an effort to halt barbaric dictatorship.[1] But most subsequent military interventions revealed the limited capabilities of Europe and the preference of the United States for remote-control engagement. While Western-led organizations like the IMF were established to preserve monetary stability, the reckless push for financial liberalization undermined the legitimacy of the United States as a financial power. Trade policy was half-hearted and triggered growing criticism.

The West hardly profited from its pause. Moreover, while the Cold War was all about containing adversaries, this chapter elucidates that Western preponderance made it reckless toward countries that were still weak but had the potential to become regional powers. In the 1990s, the West started making authoritarian states strong. Instead of globalization being the precursor of democracy, it empowered dictatorships. Instead of upgrading its own industries, the West allowed the technology and knowhow to empower state capitalist countries like China. Instead of strengthening its position by reducing dependence on imports of raw materials, it kept flooding authoritarian countries with oil money. Multinational companies continued to go offshore, corroborating what the French Emperor Napoleon Bonaparte once stated: money knows no fatherland. As governments declared that capitalism had to be made more responsible, capitalism most of all wanted to escape.

"I hate our China policy!"

In the 1990s, China was led by President Jiang Zemin (1989–2002). He was considered a liberal, as he insisted on economic opening up and had a more extrovert lifestyle than his predecessor, Deng Xiaoping. Jiang listened to Elvis Presley, watched Hollywood movies, and danced with the French First Lady during a state visit. He courted the West to increase trust, to foster cooperation, and to steer clear of confrontation. During the 1990s, the Chinese economy grew around 10 percent annually. Its construction boom, with flagship projects like the Three Gorges Dam and the skyscrapers of Shanghai, required more steel and concrete than all other Asian countries together.

China's economic appeal made many Western governments turn a blind eye to the carnage of the Tiananmen crisis of 1989. An official expressed it thus: "China has enormous potential as a market for American goods and services."[2] President George H. W. Bush trusted to his diary: "I am sending signals to China that we want the relationship to stay intact."[3] The capitals reasoned that it was not in their interest to see China retreat or destabilize. After all, it had nuclear weapons and was a permanent member of the Security Council.[4] There was also a genuine belief that China could be changed.

Engagement: that would be the preferred approach, both for Europe and the United States, under both President Bush and President Clinton. Trade, investment, and access to Western markets would pave the way for gradual liberalization. "No nation," so it went, "has yet discovered a way to import the world's goods and services while stopping foreign ideas at the border."[5] Through engagement, the explanation was, China could slowly transform into an open society like Taiwan and Hong Kong.[6] The tail would wag the dog. The vast middle class now forming in China, predicted a politician,

almost assured the triumph of democracy. At the same time, Western lead-
ers would raise human rights with China. The religious leader of the restless
Chinese region Tibet, the Dalai Lama, was received in the White House.
Congress and the European Parliament could go on to criticize Beijing. The
American Navy would show its flag to contest China's claim on the adjacent
seas.

The Chinese leaders, we discovered in previous chapters, had made it
crystal-clear that they wanted to counter this. The Party wished to retain its
monopoly on power. Propaganda remained in place. Economic opening up
would be allowed only to the degree that it contributed to a strong national
industry. China built special investment zones not to yield the domestic
market to foreigners, but to make foreigners transfer technology to domestic companies. Selective openness in the short term was but a means in the
pursuit of power and independence in the long run. China pushed back on
human rights. Western human rights envoys were mocked as gentlemen
making a living out of lecturing and meddling in others' internal affairs.[7] In
1993, Chinese officials told the United States to mind its own problems with
black minorities. A year later, they demanded Washington withdraw its
support for a resolution in the United Nations that criticized China's track
record on political reforms, and arrested dissidents the evening before the
Secretary of State arrived in Beijing.

Even if its economy remained small, fragile, and dependent on foreign
knowhow, China tested the resolve and unity of the Western world. After
France signed a deal with Taiwan to supply fighter jets, China retaliated
against French companies. Meanwhile, it concluded billions of deals with
Germany, which, after Chinese pressure, canceled a delivery of warships
to Taiwan. German Chancellor Helmut Kohl explained: "It is left to every
country to make its own decision."[8] In 1996, France, close to signing a
contract for the export of passenger planes to China, backtracked from supporting a critical resolution in the UN Human Rights Commission, while
China severed trade relations with sponsors of the resolution like Denmark
and the Netherlands.[9] "When President Jacques Chirac arrives in Beijing in a
few weeks, I am sure that he will be rewarded for that stance," commented
an executive.[10] That year, Chinese citizens, close to the government, sponsored the Democratic Party in the American presidential elections. China

played on the divisions, sought weak spots, and drove a wedge between the United States and Europe.[11]

Instead of allowing the West to keep a check on China, China searched for ways to check Western influence. Inside the inner crowd of the Communist Party, the leadership was firm: "In press and publicity work we must adhere to the principle of upholding the Party spirit, we should tighten control over the press and publishing," Jiang Zemin said. "We should do away with all factors destabilizing stability, oppose bourgeois liberalization, and guard against infiltration, subversion, and separatist activities carried out by international and domestic hostile forces."[12] Toward external audiences, however, the message was more direct. Consider this excerpt from a speech by Jiang given in New York:

> We believe that without democracy there can be no modernization. We will ensure that our people hold democratic elections, make policy decisions democratically, carry out democratic management and supervision and enjoy extensive rights and freedoms under the law while giving greater play to their creativity and their sense of being the masters of state affairs. We will continue to safeguard the dignity of the constitution and other laws, further improve the legal system, strengthen supervision on government organs and leading officials at all levels to ensure that all work of the country is carried out according to law. The goal of our political restructuring is to build socialist democracy with Chinese characteristics.[13]

Not everyone in the West was blind to the risk. In 1992, the American Department of Commerce reported that China had stopped living up to its promise to lift import barriers. "Should China ever flower as a market worth pursuing," a corporate leader wrote, "the Chinese will simply grab it for themselves."[14] By 1994, the American Secretary of State judged that the West was making Beijing one of the most difficult leading actors on the world stage. President Clinton was even more blunt. "I hate our China policy!" he was reported as saying, "I wish I was running against our China policy. I mean . . . we change our commercial policy and what has it changed?"[15] There were incessant reports about human rights issues, like the destruction of mosques in Xinjiang and forced abortions among ethnic minority groups. Intelligence services warned that Western technology was being used to bolster Chinese military capabilities and that it was building up its presence on disputed islands in the South China Sea.[16] Intelligence services warned – literally – that the "betrayal" of constructive engagement, the decoupling thus of trade and political reform, could lead to more intransigence, nationalism, and assertiveness.[17]

What emerged was a situation in which the Chinese party remained dedicated to defending its principles of social dictatorship but the West relinquished its own principles of liberalization. Already by 1991, the economic sanctions that followed the Tiananmen protests had been relaxed. China was accorded most-favored nation status in trade, which meant that Washington had to treat it like any other trade partner. Presidents Bush and Clinton abandoned the idea of tying Chinese access to the American market to human rights. The limitations on sharing militarily sensitive technology, another repercussion of the Tiananmen uprising, were relaxed. In the 1996 elections, Clinton championed a tough China policy. Yet, one of the first decisions of his second term was to permit the People's Republic to buy supercomputers and, despite the misgivings of the State Department, to cooperate in satellite technology. The same was the case in Europe. The European Union initiated a human rights dialogue with China. But when Beijing suspended it the following year, Europe let it happen. The European institutions were left dealing with the thorny issue of human rights while the member states prioritized business.

Worse was yet to come. In 1996, Beijing punished Taiwan for reaching out to the United States by lobbing missiles into the Taiwan Strait. This was the so-called Taiwan missile crisis. A senior Chinese military officer warned Washington to stay out. In the 1950s, he said, you three times threatened nuclear strikes on China. "You could do that because we could not hit back. Now we can. In the end, you care a lot more about Los Angeles than Taipei."[18] Intelligence services found that China had increased its military presence in the South China Sea. It helped countries like Pakistan and Iran develop nuclear weapons. Beijing also remained outspoken about America's alleged pursuit of hegemony. A Chinese defense minister stated: "Hostile international forces have never abandoned their strategic plot to westernize and split China."[19]

Throughout the 1990s, China reduced the number of troops, but did so with the aim of making its armed forces more capable, investing in technology, and repelling adversaries by means of asymmetric deterrence, including hundreds of missiles and electronic warfare.[20] America's high-tech warfare in the Balkans and in Iraq encouraged Beijing in this pursuit. If American missiles could penetrate Serbian or Iraqi defenses, so could they evade Chinese defenses. In 1999, an American plane mistakenly dropped a bomb on the Chinese Embassy in Belgrade, killing three citizens. It was clear that China looked at the West as a strategic adversary, despite the fact that the United States and the European Union referred to China as a strategic economic partner.

Even the economic partnership was lukewarm. Trade officials criticized China's unwillingness to open key sectors to foreign companies and the forced technology transfers. When China showed its interest in joining the World Trade Organization, officials and experts warned of larger trade deficits. One Congressman spoke of delusion and appeasement. China, he thought, was an expansionist power, openly hostile to the ideals of human dignity and freedom. The European Parliament, too, was critical. It called for military transparency, fair treatment of ethnic minorities, and the cessation of support for the military junta in Myanmar.[21] The European Economic and Social Committee demanded respect for civil society organizations, labor movements, and human rights.[22]

But companies were too keen. Boeing, Airbus, Volkswagen, General Motors: they all had set up shop. China's interest in joining the World Trade Organization was seen by Western governments as an important opportunity to impel it toward openness and to empower reformists. "This agreement gains us better access to China's market in every sector from agriculture to telecommunications to automobiles," it was explained. "There is simply no better way right now to encourage China to choose deeper economic reform and respect for the rule of law."[23] Notwithstanding China building its Digital Great Firewall, a system of online censorship, the supposed benefits of digital trade were highlighted. "More people interacting through companies, through e-mail, through the 4 million Chinese that by the year 2000 will be on the Internet."[24]

"The question is not simply whether we approve or disapprove of

China's practices," said President Clinton. "The question is what can we do to improve them?"[25] His Secretary of State saw it slightly differently and highlighted the aversion of the corporate world to the human rights agenda. During a visit to Beijing, he confided to his diary: "After consuming their sweet rolls, representatives of American companies took the floor and blasted me for pressing the Chinese on human rights."[26] In 1999, after months of furious lobbying by large companies and despite fierce resistance of labor unions, Washington agreed on permanent normal trade relations with China and started negotiations to allow China to join the World Trade Organization.

In China's shadow

In the contest between Chinese authoritarianism and Indian democracy, the latter stood no chance. The reform-minded Prime Minister Narasimha Rao, who was able to govern the full five years between 1991 and 1995, failed to convince investors that India was an alternative to China. During his term, India attracted only one tenth of the investments that flowed into China. Rao did try to follow the prescriptions of the IMF to end a financial crisis and to kick-start industrialization. He devalued the rupee, reduced tariffs, and opened up to foreign investment. But he had to tread carefully. If state industries and subsidies for farmers were dismantled before alternative jobs were created in modern manufacturing or services firms, social unrest would increase and drive poor Indians deeper into the arms of Hindu radicals and local parties. Reform had, Rao put it, to be carried out by stealth. At the end of his term, Rao satisfied neither foreign investors nor his citizens. Motorola, which planned a big investment, decided to go to China. At the same time, the fallout of the financial crisis and subsequent austerity measures had mostly affected the poor.

It was no surprise, then, that the 1996 elections led the main Hindu party, BJP, to once more accuse the Rao government of sacrificing the people's interests to foreigners. It protested fiercely against the decision to award an energy project to an American company and forced Kentucky Fried Chicken to close after two flies were discovered in the kitchen of one of its franchises. Hindu radicals protested against Western decadence and consumerism. The

BJP jumped on an alleged miracle of a statue of the god Ganesha drinking milk. In reality it was an effect of capillary action. Nevertheless, the party claimed that it was a prophecy that India should become a pure Hindu nation. "Saffronization," it was called. BJP-related movements staged a crusade against Muslims and Christians. "India is a country of Hindus," a leaflet said. "Our religion of Rama and Krishna is pious. To convert or leave it is a sin." Another piece of propaganda put it thus: "Caution Hindus! Beware of inhuman deeds of Muslims. Muslims are destroying Hindu community by demolishing houses, slaughtering cows and making Hindu girls elope. Crime, drugs, terrorism are Muslim's empire."[27]

The BJP won the 1996 elections with a call for Hindutva, but failed to form a coalition. Three years of political turbulence followed, during which India irked the West with the testing of a nuclear weapon and a brief war fought with Pakistan. During this Kargil crisis, in the summer of 1999, tens of thousands of Indian and Pakistani soldiers were sent to the contested region of Kashmir. Showing India's weakness, its military ran out of ammunition in three weeks.[28] New elections that year allowed the BJP to form a more solid government. Its promise was an India shining.

The United States had long favored Pakistan as a partner. During the Cold War, it supplied the country's military regime with weapons and nuclear technology. From 1988, Pakistan was led by civilian governments. The military retained its dominance through the control of a large part of the economy and pursued its own foreign policy. It made itself indispensable by stoking up rivalry with India and controlling the mountainous border area with Afghanistan. It was this role as gatekeeper to Afghanistan, the soft underbelly of the Soviet Union, that had made it a partner for the United States in the past. But if supporting the mujahedin, the Islamic fighters, in Afghanistan had proved useful during the Cold War, it subsequently had become a source of discontent. In the 1990s, the American government pushed the Pakistani civilian governments to end support for the Taliban, but the military kept supporting it. The Taliban conquered the capital Kabul in 1996. "Pakistan has not been responsive to our requests that it use its full influence on the Taliban to surrender Bin Laden," a diplomatic cable suggested, and accused Pakistan of training terrorists to fight India in Kashmir.[29] It was the military that pushed for the development of nuclear weapons, for which China now provided most of the knowhow. It was the military also that, behind the back of the civilian government, orchestrated a showdown with India over Kashmir during the Kargil crisis.[30] It was the military, led by General Pervez Musharraf, that once more toppled a civilian leader when he became too critical. Pakistan entered the first decade following the Cold War as a country that was at least superficially run by civilians; it exited the decade again as a military regime. It was an army with a state.

The outlook in South Asia was dire. With a population that grew by 20 million annually, it could not be ignored. Yet, if it was the intention of the West to stop nuclear proliferation, there were now two new nuclear powers. Instead of flourishing democracies, Pakistan returned to military rule and India was run by Hindu nationalists. Under President Clinton, a section for South Asian affairs was established in the State Department. But beyond the failed attempt to halt nuclear proliferation, South Asia was not a priority. Although the Indian Ocean became increasingly important for shipping between East Asia and Europe, the countries on its coasts remained marginalized in international trade networks and ignored by investors. In Sri Lanka, a devastating civil war raged between the Tamil Tigers and the Sinhalese majority. In Nepal, the oppressive monarchy came under attack from marginalized populaces in the south and Maoist rebels. In Bangladesh, the three main parties used gangs and the regular military to retain power. In Afghanistan, the Taliban brutally imposed Islamic sharia law and provided sanctuary to Osama bin Laden, already one of the most wanted terrorists. Countries from the Gulf financed the Pakistani military and the Pakistani military financed Islamic madrassa schools throughout the region. The more the region was overlooked in the new globalization and the deeper it sank into poverty, the more it became prone to nationalism, religious radicalism, and strife. For now, it was an economic backwater, but it would soon impose itself as a major source of global insecurity.

Southeast Asia appeared to be better placed to benefit from globalization. Geographically, the region formed an extension of the long East Asian beltway of industrial growth that stretched from South Korea to Hong Kong. Transformed into a first world trading state, Singapore had already established itself as a beacon of prosperity. By the early 1990s, Southeast

Asian countries were settling their Cold War disputes. Vietnam had pulled its troops out of neighboring Cambodia. Many border disputes were solved or brought for settlement to the International Court of Justice. ASEAN, the Association of Southeast Asian Nations, was joined by Vietnam, Laos, Myanmar, and Cambodia. ASEAN did not yet have the ambition to become as densely integrated as the European Union. With more informal political contacts and by putting economic cooperation upfront, it first of all sought to continue to build confidence and to compete as a bloc with China.[31] Most of the countries also wanted autonomy from the United States. Only a market of scale with the diminution of internal trade tariffs would allow countries to steadily enhance "the quality of the life of its people and human development."[32]

Interpretations of human development varied though. In most states, it meant development under authoritarian rule. Myanmar was governed by a junta, the State Law and Order Restoration Council, that rejected the 1990 election results and repressed dissidents. Laos, Cambodia, and Brunei were ruled by authoritarian regimes. In Vietnam, the Communist Party held sway. In Indonesia, Suharto ruled with a heavy hand. He was criticized for corruption and abandoning cautious reform for the protection of favored corporate groups. The Singaporean leader Lee Kwan Yew stated that the success of Singapore was only possible because his government had preserved order. In Thailand, the 1990s started with two years of military repression. Even after a popular, democratic leader was elected in 1992, a military constitution remained in place. The Philippines was about the only country that could be considered democratic. And even there, the public demanded a more robust response to proliferating crime and rebellions in Mindanao. If ASEAN entertained hopes of regional integration, it was primarily with an eye to preserving regime stability, not to spreading democracy.

But like Southern Asia, the ten were unable to withstand China's growing might. Throughout the 1990s, China attracted about twice as much foreign investment as the ASEAN bloc. Most countries held on to backward industries. The few countries that already had some manufacturing, like Malaysia and the Philippines, two processing hubs for electronic goods, lost their position to China's coastal provinces. Except Singapore, they all ran growing trade deficits. Large foreign funds started to speculate on currency fluctuations. During the financial crisis of 1997 and 1998, which struck in Thailand, Indonesia, the Philippines, and Malaysia, over US$100 billion of speculative investment was pulled out of the region.[33] Recession followed. The consequent fall of Suharto in Indonesia offered some hope that the financial crisis might be a moment of democratization.[34] Others assumed that it showed the need for more regional cooperation.[35] But this all remained doubtful.

Less doubtful was the shattering impact of the financial crisis on the legitimacy of the West. The Thai prime minister stated that the World Bank and the International Monetary Fund had become unreliable.[36] His Malaysian counterpart chided the West for reckless capitalism. Singapore, traditionally close to the US, did not spare its criticism: "The IMF was seen by some as a tool of the US to achieve the latter's political objectives," said the prime minister. "Some Asian countries, for example, blame the Asian financial crisis on western pressures to uncritically and prematurely open up their economies and adopt American economic and political models and mores."[37]

China emerged from the crisis as a victor, particularly because the other regional leader, Japan, seemed unable to live up to its role as traditional partner. "Japan needs to worry about its own self-interest," its prime minister stated. "We are certainly not arrogant enough to think that we can take the role of locomotive for Asia."[38] China's controls on foreign investment had prevented speculation. It also did not let its own currency depreciate. We are a safe island for stability, President Jiang Zemin declared. It provided loans to Thailand, floated the idea of a free trade area, and cultivated the expectation that it would provide the investment that Japan and the West had failed to deliver. "ASEAN will be a priority market for China's investment," it was explained, "especially if a closer economic relationship between the two sides could be established."[39]

It formed a perfect storm. In the previous years, China had irked the Philippines with the construction of facilities on the disputed Paracel Islands, and Vietnam by starting to drill for oil in contested waters. Now, it presented itself as an economic partner. If China initially remained reluctant to engage in regional formats, it now tried to shape regional forums to the benefit of its national interests.[40] It became clear also that this would be the end of the hope that ASEAN would be a counterweight. This was a turning point. As trade grew much faster with China, the crisis aggravated internal instability. Radical Islamists struck in the south of Thailand, in Indonesia, and in the Philippines. Jemaah Islamiyah, a Southeast Asian militant extremist Islamist rebel group, vowed to establish an Islamic realm of Southeast Asia.

Boris and George

The situation in China, Asia's emerging leading power, was not at all inconvenient to the West. While it paid lip service to democratic ideals, companies could pursue commercial opportunities, and the Communist Party kept the country stable. The situation in Russia was different. Here, the challenge was not to promote liberal values, but to demonstrate to 150 million Russian citizens that liberalism would be better than communism. The Russians remained divided. In 1990, they voted as many democratic reformers as conservatives into parliament. In the countryside and in small towns, the majority continued to favor communism above democracy and the free market.[41] A hard core of communists and nationalists resolved on fighting Russia's alleged sell-out to the West. Democracy and the free market had to be built in a context of chaos and disorientation.

The clock was ticking. A coup attempt of conservative hardliners just before the presidential elections in 1991 showed how precarious the situation was. At the same time, Russia quickly ran out of money to pay its debt, for its imports, and its millions of public servants. How could Russia be helped? Contacts between the White House and the Kremlin were strong. "We call each other on the telephone," Yeltsin explained. "We say Boris and George."[42] But Republicans in Washington urged their government not to give a blank check. The European states were preoccupied with the unification of Germany and quarreled about how close the partnership with Russia should be. While Moscow pushed for a tight partnership, fears emerged that even a weak Russia could upset the European project and the balance of power if it became too closely involved. In the wake of the coup of 1991, the G7 countries, a forum of the largest economies, agreed on a large aid package, yet details about how large exactly it would be and what it entailed remained unclear. The stakes were clear. "If this democratic revolution is defeated," the American president stated, "it could plunge us into a world more dangerous in some respects than the dark years of the Cold War."[43] Still, it was left to technocrats of the IMF to make it work. Those technocrats convinced Boris Yeltsin that it was time for another shock: the shock of economic liberalization.

There was no precedent for the transition from so large a command economy to a market economy. Price controls were abolished and the state sector dismantled. The results were indeed shocking. In January 1992 alone, consumer prices grew fivefold. During the Soviet times, money was unimportant. Now, it was everything. Russian conservatives started to push back. Yeltsin, however, demanded special authorities. A political crisis emerged between him and his opponents. In the summer of 1993, Yeltsin dissolved parliament. Parliament in turn deposed the president. Hard-line conservatives occupied the parliament building and the equally obstinate president went all the way to exhaust his executive power. The showdown reached its climax with the army ordered to attack the parliament building, the closure of dissident newspapers, the abolition of several other organizations, and several decrees that strengthened Yeltsin's power. "Russia needs order," Yeltsin decided. Russian democratization hence started with a purge. Recognizing that the shock therapy of the IMF had caused a backlash and seeing the beginning of a potential slide back into authoritarianism, the West panicked. During the American elections, Bill Clinton accused the Bush administration of siding with stability over democratic change.

But what was to be done next? Yeltsin had bolstered his presidential powers, but ultranationalists had won the parliamentary ballot in the winter of 1993. In Washington, now president Bill Clinton judged that it was time for less shock and more therapy. He granted over US$1 billion in aid – to help Russia sell state-owned industries, to buy American grain, and to repair pipelines. To most Russians, however, the shock had become permanent, while the therapy was commonly explained as an attempt by the West to help itself and advance its economic interests. As many as 90 percent of Russians now lived in poverty and incomes continued to shrink almost 10 percent annually. Life became a void and nothing showed this better than a new extreme wave in Russian art: Moscow Actionism. The artist Alexander

Brener, wearing only boxing gloves and shorts on an icy winter day, challenged Boris Yeltsin to come out to fight him. In a gallery, a life-size cream cake of Lenin's corpse was offered to guests. Moscow Actionism was all about blasphemy, nudism, and self-mutilation, the smashing of icons and the questioning of everything that looked certain.

Yeltsin expressed his skepticism. "Boris in Russian means fighting and struggling without result," he avowed.[44] Russia slithered further into economic trouble. Oligarchs bought lucrative parts of dismantled state enterprises for almost nothing. Crime took control of the streets. Yet, in conversations with Yeltsin, the American government put most of the attention on security: the risk of Russian nuclear assets falling into the hands of criminals, Russia's relations with Iran, and the dismantling of Russian strategic weapons. The European Union mostly focused its dialogues and aid on privatization, energy cooperation, and the safety of Russian nuclear installations. Support for poverty relief, governance, and democratic transition remained minimal.[45] European countries were reluctant to accept Russia as a member of GATT or to consider Moscow's proposal for a common trade zone.

Russian citizens grew disillusioned with the transition of their country and the role of the West. While Russian oligarchs flaunted their wealth, Western investment funds and oil companies were seen as vultures circling around a corpse. Hence, nationalists continued to lambast Yeltsin for having fallen prostrate to Western imperialists. In the American Congress, at the same time, Clinton was pilloried for being soft on Russia. Republicans pushed for the enlargement of NATO and missile defense systems in Europe. Slowly, the strategic distrust that had characterized the Cold War came back, but now with the frontline 700 kilometers eastward, right on Russia's doorstep. The growing distrust was articulated firmly in an internal document drafted by the ministry of defense:

> Western misdeeds include: attempting to force inappropriate reform medicine down Russia's throat while failing to give real help to the ailing economy, stealing Russia's markets, including blocking the sale of arms and nuclear technology, endeavouring to turn Russia into an economic colony, a provider of cheap raw materials and a market for dumping, inciting Ukraine

and other states against Russia; trying to limit Russian influence in the Transcaucasus and Central Asia with a view to controlling energy sources and transit routes; encouraging Balts and others to repress Russian minorities; establishing military and political hegemony through the expansion of NATO and the crushing of such Russian friends as Iraq and Serbia; perhaps even encouraging the disintegration of the Russian state.[46]

The West did accept the inclusion of Russia into the G7, which became the G8, and GATT. Still, it dawned on the Russians that they would never be part of a European house. If Russia had put its hope on the OSCE, the Organization for Security and Co-operation in Europe, becoming the main forum for security affairs, it was clear that the West clung to NATO and that Russia would at best become a partner. While Russia could only take notice of how it was sidelined in the recent crises in the Middle East and the Balkans, fringe countries like Poland and the Baltic States became increasingly alarmed over the resilience of Russian nationalists, persistent references to Crimea, Russia's military intervention in the Caucasian state Chechnya, and a new Military Doctrine that affirmed a determination to keep troops in the near abroad. Russia had tried to strengthen the CST, a Collective Security Treaty signed in 1992, partially in response to NATO, and created a union with Belarus.

While Clinton insisted on Russian strategic disarmament and nuclear safety, President Yeltsin begged at least to postpone NATO enlargement and offered security guarantees to every country that wanted to join the alliance. "I see nothing but humiliation if you proceed," he said. "How do you think it looks to us if one block continues to exist while the Warsaw Pact has been abolished? It is a new form of encirclement."[47] Clinton explained that he would do nothing to accelerate enlargement but could not stop it either. The Republicans made it an issue. The people of Central Europe were desperate to join the alliance and feared the return of hardliners in Moscow. "They are not sure what is going to happen in Russia if you're not around."[48] Thanks to the quasi-monopolization of Russian media, Yeltsin narrowly won the presidential elections of 1996.

In the following years, he and Clinton tried to reduce tensions by temporizing NATO enlargement, instituting a NATO–Russia Council, and confidence building in the Black and Baltic Seas. When Russia was wracked by a new financial crisis in 1998, Clinton urged the IMF to show flexibility to avoid adding fuel to the fire of Russian nationalists. Still, by then, disillusionment in Russia had become complete. With household incomes halved and the country in disarray, Russians saw with anger how the West launched another attack on Iraq, despite its objection in the UN Security Council, and how Poland, Hungary, and the Czech Republic joined NATO in 1999 and how the alliance launched an attack against one of Russia's main allies in the Balkans. For now, liberalization was considered in Russia as a pathway toward chaos.

Bling bling conservatism

Politics in the Middle East was anarchy in the shadow of American dominance. The regional powers continuously balanced against one another, but the United States became the ultimate balance holder. This was famously summarized by former US Secretary of State Henry Kissinger, who had commented on the strife between Iran and Iraq as follows: "It's a pity they can't both lose."[49] The outcome of any regional conflict depended on America lobbing its weight onto one of the scales. There were two certainties: the alliance with Israel and the distrust toward Iran. Otherwise, Washington was ambivalent: "We have no opinion on the Arab-Arab conflicts."[50]

Why, then, did the West respond so forcefully against Iraq in 1990? The Iraq War mobilized close to 1.5 million soldiers. It was a dramatic showdown. CNN brought live footing of burning oil wells, bursts of air defense batteries above Baghdad, and endless lines of blackened carcasses of military vehicles along the highway to Basra – the Highway of Death. The West first of all fought the war because it could afford it. There was no longer a Soviet Union capable of throwing its weight behind Iraq. It also intervened because Iraq threatened to control the oil reserves of Kuwait, because that would upset the regional balance of power, and because the regime had gone too far in its provocations. The Iraq War did not presage the end of regional disorder, but its continuation, with the difference that the United States more firmly asserted itself. After the Iraq War, it homeported warships in Bahrain, and proposed to station tanks in Kuwait, Qatar, and the

United Arab Emirates. Over 35,000 American troops remained in the region. Disorder was a guarantee for Western influence. The strategy seemed to be to keep countries exhausting each other, yet not to let the struggle cause war or regime collapse.

The protagonists in this arena were Saudi Arabia, Iran, Iraq, Egypt, Israel, and Turkey. The playgrounds were the Levant, the Persian Gulf, and the Islamic communities worldwide. Each pretender had its own advantages and weaknesses. Saudi Arabia had a small population. Yet, thanks to its oil exports, it had the largest economy and the largest military budget. Home to the holy cities of Mecca and Medina, the country considered itself the leader of the Sunnite Islamic community. By comparison, Iran's population was three times as large, but its economy was weaker and its defense spending throughout the 1990s half that of Saudi Arabia. Iran, however, prided itself on its ancient Persian roots and its leadership of the Shia Islamic community. Israel was a demographic dwarf yet an economic and technological powerhouse and a military leviathan. In terms of population, economic prowess, and military spending, Turkey was most comparable to Iran, but it had a completely different diplomatic, religious, and political orientation – and no oil. Out of these, Egypt was the weakest. It had the largest population marred in poverty and became increasingly susceptible to external influence. Iraq, still under the rule of Saddam Hussein, remained a power to be reckoned with. In between there were small, yet often very ambitious, countries, like Oman, Qatar, the United Arab Emirates, Bahrain, Kuwait, Jordan, Syria, and Lebanon.

With Saddam Hussein temporarily reined in as the region's troublemaker, attention shifted back to Iran, a sworn rival of the United States, a major threat to Israel, and the main challenger to the regional leadership of Saudi Arabia. Iran itself, however, had changed, at least to some extent. It had remained neutral during the Gulf War. Its new president, Akbar Rafsanjani (1989–97), preached moderation and reform. Yet, at the same time, there was still the conservative religious regime. There was evidence also that those conservatives pursued nuclear weapons, working with China and Russia to set up nuclear facilities, and obtaining missile technology from North Korea. It bought submarines from Russia, patrol boats from China, and anti-ship missiles that could close the Strait of Hormuz off to oil tankers.

While the Iranian side was ambivalent, the Western response was too. Washington, retaliating against Tehran's nuclear ambitions and a terrorist attack by an Iranian proxy, made American oil companies leave, but their stakes were bought by European competitors. In 1997, Iran elected an even more reformist president, Mohammad Khatami (1997–2005). In an unprecedented overture, he gave an interview to CNN, quoting Alexis de Tocqueville, praising the American Declaration of Independence, and expressing his regret for having hurt American feelings. He vowed to cease support for certain Islamic terrorist groups. Yet, the perception of the United States, Israel, and Saudi Arabia was that Khatami's words did not matter. "He was sincere, but he had no influence."[51] More significant to them was the desire of the conservatives and the Revolutionary Guard to preserve their position and to acquire nuclear weapons. But by showing skepticism to Khatami, Washington and its allies made it impossible for the Iranian president to bolster his position regarding conservative hardliners.

Israel felt it was the main target of Iran's nuclear program and feared that nuclear missiles would be ready by 2000. Until then, Iran had waged a guerrilla war against Israel, sponsoring Hezbollah in Lebanon and the Palestinian Hamas. The more these proxies threatened Israel, the more Israel reinforced its capabilities to strike back. By the early 1990s, it had around 100 nuclear warheads as a strategic deterrent. Its conventional military was the region's most capable. Its jets flew above Lebanon with impunity. Its intelligence service, Mossad, hunted down state enemies throughout the world. The main approach to dealing with threats, however, was to take land: the Golan Heights as a defense against Hezbollah, and a whole range of settlements, roads, and corridors to project power into the two Palestinian areas: Gaza and the West Bank. Only bulldozers will draw borders, it was said. Some hardliners called it a policy of strangulation.[52]

The Palestinian question remained another important bone of contention in the region. The more Palestinian houses were bulldozed and the more Israeli settlements were built, the more Israel tried to close off the Palestinian areas, the bigger the economic suffering, and the more numerous the personal tragedies, the more radical the Palestinians became. This was what made peace impossible. From the moment that Israel and the Palestine Liberation Organization (PLO) had signed the Oslo I Accord in

1993, the latter lost its influence to the much more radical Hamas. "How did these Palestinian negotiators accept such a grotesque distortion of the reality?" its leader asked. Oslo was like a kiss of death to Palestinian moderates. Hamas' devastating suicide bombings in turn gave the pretext to Tel Aviv to continue to deploy bulldozers and soldiers. The harsher the Israeli policy, the more it allowed radical preachers to decry alleged Western imperialism and violent Zionism.

Saudi Arabia bolstered its position as another powerhouse. After the threat of Iraq, it was the growing alarm at Iran's nuclear ambitions that permitted Saudi Arabia to become an indispensable partner to the West, despite being probably more conservative culturally and less open politically. In 1992, reformists called on the Saudi king to address corruption and the wasteful spending of the hundreds of princes of the dynasty. Instead of their demands being considered, they were being imprisoned. Religious minorities, like Christians and Shia, were persecuted, and a new law on government continued to curtail freedom of speech and assembly.

The Saudi ambassador in Washington, at the same time, went hunting with President Bush and even tutored his son. During the American presidential elections, Bush was accused of coddling dictators, but Bill Clinton himself also had pursued a Saudi donation for a university in his home state. His new administration went all out to make American firms win contracts for jets, military equipment, and telecom systems. So did European competitors. Clinton even gave in to Saudi pressure to withdraw the nomination of an ambassador who had been critical of the monarchy. The commerce secretary rebuked critics of trade with Riyadh as unsophisticated people causing unnecessary alarm. But when Washington asked for support for negotiations with Palestine, to shoulder more of the financial burden for the deployment of American troops in the Persian Gulf, and to curb the proliferation of nuclear weapons, to limit support for radical Islam, and to investigate a terrorist attack in 1997, the king balked. During one visit in 1995, the Secretary of State was left waiting for six hours. Meanwhile, Western intelligence services reported persistently close ties between Riyadh and terrorist groups.[53]

The downsides of the Western policy in the Middle East became increasingly clear, also in Egypt. In Egypt, the United States supported the government of Hosni Mubarak (1981–2011) in spite of rigged elections and laws that restrained independent media and organizations. Mubarak did not tolerate democratization. He claimed to give priority to stability. But stability was undermined because repression and poverty drove millions of Egyptians into the arms of the Muslim Brotherhood and violent Islamist groups that were sponsored by the very states that America protected in the Gulf. Egyptian terrorists masterminded two bomb attacks on the American embassies in Kenya and Tanzania in 1998.

While the West had tens of thousands of soldiers deployed, kept a warry eye on Iran and Iraq, and imported each year over US$20 billion of oil from the region, the Gulf States had unleashed a stealth campaign against the West. They sought to counter Western values through the financing of conservative Islam. Internally, there was no tendency whatsoever toward political reform. Saudi Arabia was a case in point, but the smaller states also clung to authoritarianism. Oman was an absolute monarchy, the United Arab Emirates was governed by a council of sheikhs, and Qatar by an emir. Often the leadership tried to have it both ways. They showed that they could rapidly modernize the economy, get all the trappings of consumerism, and keep an autocracy at the same time.

It was bling bling conservatism. On the one hand, they wanted to be part of the West, by spending lavishly in Paris and London, on yachts with blonde Scandinavian girls as crew, and on Italian luxury cars. On the other hand, they sought prestige in the Islamic world. They needed to address the criticism that they had tainted the Islamic community by accepting American troops. Qatar Charity had become one of Osama bin Laden's sponsors, and financed terrorists in Sudan, Chechnya, Libya, Lebanon, Palestine, Mali, and Europe.[54] The country became notorious for its ambivalent policy of hosting different peace conferences and sponsoring violent Jihad.[55] In 1996, Qatar founded Al Jazeera to fight the dominance of Western television channels. Saudi Arabia stripped Osama bin Laden of his citizenship but still spent billions each year on Islamic schools, constructing mosques, and sending radical preachers as far as Senegal and the Philippines. Petro-Islam, some called it: the strategy of using oil dollars earned from the West to combat the very values of the West. In 1999, the Saudi crown prince released two extremist scholars, one of whom was the popular Safar al-Hawali. Hawali had to promise to no longer criticize the Saudi monarchy, but he could go on to lash out at the West, which he did, continuing to refer to the West as infidels and aggressors, yet also mocking the state of its society:

> In America there is a totally mad fundamentalist current that seeks to hasten the second-coming of Christ, and who are prepared to do the stupidest thing in the world in order to achieve it. . . . What more proof do we need when we have seen them commit mass suicide, and bomb federal installations, as well as forming militias? . . . They follow no system of logic or reason . . . [and] exercise a remarkable influence on society [through] media . . . and . . . government [representatives]. Secular thinkers in America know that it is nearly impossible to change the backwards beliefs of these people, since their intellectual foundation has been totally destroyed.[56]

This undercurrent of conservatism, its influence on politics, and the reluctance of the political leadership to curb it did not go unnoticed by Western diplomats and intelligence services.[57] The response, however, was muted, certainly compared to the tough answer to Iran and Iraq.

Kalashnikov lifestyle

The end of the Cold War had left a power vacuum on the African continent. It was filled with anarchy. In the 1990s, conflicts in Africa cost at least five million lives. There were more elections, to be sure, but half of them were unfair.[58] There were about five attempted coups each year and four state failures.[59] The World Bank and the International Monetary Fund congratulated themselves for the many adjustment programs that they carried out. Still, the lack of interest from foreign investors and the collapse of commodity prices meant that few of the reforms helped contribute to growth. State spending was reduced, but there came no alternative from the private sector.

In fact, throughout the decade, African economic production per capita decreased by 13 percent. Some of the governments held on to former colonial overlords, like the dictators Omar Bongo in Gabon and Paul Biya in Cameroon. Many more governments collapsed and had dictatorship replaced by warlords. In Congo, the regime of Mobutu Sese Seko was top-pled by Laurent Kabila, a warlord. All one needs to start a rebellion, Kabila explained, is a mobile phone and US$10,000 in cash. Kalashnikov machine guns from former Soviet countries were almost free. That allowed warlords like Kabila to gain control over parts of the economy, like diamond mines, areas where gold and other precious metals were found, or just the local farmers that could be exploited.

Africa's civil wars were orgies of violence. In Rwanda, the Hutu major-ity killed at least half a million Tutsis in 1994 alone. In neighboring Congo, war took the lives of more than two million people in 1998 and 1999. Once one rebel leader was forced to a peace agreement, a handful of lieutenants resumed the fighting. War was profitable. This way, one of the main rebel groups in the civil war in Congo atomized into at least a dozen factions. Rebel groups operated across the border. In the mid-1990s, Central Africa, the Horn, and the coast of the Gulf of Guinea had become porous battle-fields. Regional powers also interfered. The Congolese rebellion of 1996 was supported by Uganda, Rwanda, and Burundi, whereas the Kabila govern-ment had the backing of Angola, Chad, Sudan, and Zimbabwe. South Africa meddled in the internal affairs of Mozambique and Namibia. Nigeria saw itself as the sheriff of West Africa.

It was one thing to advise states on how to liberalize their economy, it was another to rebuild states. There were few jobs to offer to demobilized soldiers or alternatives to the billions earned from looting by their leaders. Meanwhile, the African population grew by about twenty million per year. The sheer magnitude of the challenge led to Africa fatigue. Western public opinion had completely turned against intervention after Belgian soldiers were massacred in Rwanda and American soldiers in Somalia. In addition, the economic and strategic relevance of Africa was limited. In 1995, the American government bluntly stated that it had "very little traditional stra-tegic interest in Africa."[60] As a result, Western countries provided only 3 percent of the personnel to UN peacekeeping missions. The idea became to help the Africans help themselves. Capacity building and ownership: these were the main policies. Hence, hundreds of millions were put at the disposal of regional African organizations, like the African Union and the Economic Community of West African States (ECOWAS). By the end of the 1990s, many civil wars still raged on. From the persistent power vacuum emerged two new realities: the spreading of radical Islam and the growing presence of China.

"West Africa is becoming the symbol of worldwide demographic, environmental, and societal stress, in which criminal anarchy emerges as the real strategic danger," the American journalist Robert D. Kaplan wrote. "Disease, overpopulation, unprovoked crime, scarcity of resources, refugee migrations, the increasing erosion of nation-states and international borders, and the empowerment of private armies, security firms, and international drug cartels are now most tellingly demonstrated through a West African prism."[61] He forgot radical Islam. Radical Islam, propagated by the Gulf States, allowed a continuation of warlord economics with the blessing of God, to build on the anti-Western resentment, and to take revenge on decades of discrimination by elites that favored Christians and secularists. In West Africa, this clash oftentimes coincided with the divide between predominantly Islamic pastoralists in the north and farmers in the south.

Besides radical Islam, the strategic vacuum allowed China to slowly tap into Africa as a source of minerals and an export market. In 1996, President Jiang Zemin visited six African countries and promised an Africa-first policy, with more investment and aid. The first Chinese adventure seekers arrived, setting up shops and starting small mines. In their wake, gigantic state-owned enterprises prepared to make inroads that would profoundly change the situation and create hopes of an African renaissance of some sort, and "Made in China."

Failing to lead

China's search for trade opportunities amidst the backdrop of war and poverty in Africa brings together two of the most important storylines of the 1990s: the success of China and the struggle of the Global South. The rise of China followed the typical pattern that rising trading powers had followed in the past. A strong government, in this case the Communist Party, controlled the market, pursued an ambitious industrial policy, protected infant industries, and tried to learn from the stronger ones and to open foreign markets, like in Southeast Asia, as its factories grew larger. State capitalism was not new, but it was implemented on an unprecedented scale by a Communist Party that did not want to end up like the Soviet Union.

India and many others in the Global South tried to follow that example, striking a balance between openness and protection, but were not successful. The international power vacuum left by the Soviet Union led to a difficult transition in the South. Former client states needed to realign their policies and the urgency for the West to spend on its own clients dissipated somewhat. Many strongmen came into difficulties so that in their case a domestic power vacuum emerged, which was frequently filled by warlordism. One cannot preserve stability, let alone build a democracy in a context of destitution, and the consequent spiral in which poverty breeds strife and strife more poverty is very difficult to stop. West and Central Africa became deadly battlegrounds. It is likely that over five million Africans died in conflicts between 1990 and 1999. By comparison, about 120,000 people were killed in the Yugoslav Wars, less than 100,000 during the Gulf War. The most important conflicts were thus not always the ones the international community paid most attention to.

The most intriguing feature of the 1990s was that the West was seen wasting the opportunity to lead, to preserve the power to work toward its values, to strengthen democracy, and to lift its marketplace to new heights, more sustainable and more humane. The warnings against complacency were audible from the dawning of the unipolar moment. But the opposite happened. Consumerism trumped civic duty. Factories were often relocated instead of being replaced by better alternatives. Politicians like Bill Clinton were popular and presented themselves as civilized, and were considered defenders of the free world.

Their policies, however, only did a little to link social and environmental values to trade, to curb excessive speculation, the flowing of capital to tax havens, and to stop the consumerism that in the long run could predate on the nation's wealth and make adversaries stronger. They were voluntarist in their style; opportunist in their political practice. As a result, more and more capital started flowing to countries that openly defied the West, its power and its values. And Western leaders knew it, wrote it in their diaries, confided it to advisors. This policy fed misgivings and contempt, contempt about double standards, the inability to help maintain financial stability,

ACT 2 (2000–2010)

CHAPTER 7

DISREGARD AND DECADENCE

T HE 1990S WERE A MISSED OPPORTUNITY FOR THE WEST TO CONSOLI-
DATE its position in the world, to reinforce its internal cohesion,
and to preserve its power. The defeat of communism, steady growth, and
robust consumer confidence had made it less urgent to act. This changed.
By the turn of the century, one incident after another exposed defects in
Western internal and external economic policy. Financial crises in Mexico,
Russia, and Asia had delegitimized Western economic leadership. They
had also showed that a large part of investment capital had gone rogue. In
2001, a new financial crisis broke loose, this time in the West. Hundreds of
billions of dollars were lost on the stock markets. After several such economic setbacks, one would expect governments, companies, and citizens to
change track. The opposite happened. Between 2000 and 2009, this chapter
explains, imbalances were allowed to grow larger.

Disregard and decadence struck. A first imbalance existed between the
availability of capital and the extent to which it was spent to make societies stronger, like on schools, public infrastructure, and so forth. A second
imbalance was visible between the eagerness to consume and the readiness
to pay for it. In countries like the United States, the United Kingdom, Italy,
Portugal, and Greece, the share of household consumption in the total
economy surpassed 60 percent. The West, in a way, specialized in consumption. The external deficit of both the United States and the European
Union grew. A third disparity existed between morals and materialism.

While citizens pretended to be more patriotic, their consumer behavior weakened the country. Companies claimed to be more environmentally friendly and ethical, yet sourced more and more from countries with lax environmental and social standards. A fourth imbalance concerned the growing gap between winners and losers, rich and poor, wealthy and stagnant regions. These economic divisions in turn added to political divisions – between states and inside their borders. The pillars of Western power fissured further.

What emerged as a result of this latter divide was a battle between those who favored openness and those who promised protection, protection against migration, against different cultures, and so forth. But it was a fake battle. The pragmatic politician who stressed the need for openness and to defend the moral high ground of democracy, free trade, and tolerance, the mainstream politician who could still ignore the extreme parties as a marginal affair; that politician was often a polite coward. He merely acted against the forces that undermined the market, like financial speculation, the consumerism that put quantity before quality, and the multinationals that sourced from state capitalist countries like China while evading taxes at home. He did not act either against the decline of civic engagement and the persistent neglect of civic education. At the same time, his rival, the self-proclaimed patriotic politician, refused to confront his followers with the inconvenient fact that identity and prosperity were undermined by their own behavior. Rightist politicians vowed to defend Western civilization against new barbarians, yet their rude style was sometimes no less barbaric. Center politics and nationalists engaged in shadowboxing: a waste of energy.

Disneyland

For the United States, the new decade started with two important events. In 2000, the stock market crashed. For over five years, a speculation bulge had built up in the shares of information technology companies. At some point, it was possible for start-ups to raise millions without even having a product, let alone a profit. In 1999, the stock of Qualcomm, a producer of computer chips, became 20 times more expensive. "Such is the exuberance on Wall

Street," it was observed, "that only a brave man insists that the American stock market is overdue for a crash."[1] At the origins of the exuberance was an irrational interest in information technology. It sufficed to have .COM in the name of a company for it to be hyped. This was stoked up by new digital news channels that reported each and every second about investment moves of large funds.

Money flooded the market and interest rates were low. Companies more frequently paid their workers in shares. The economic boom also made workers less loyal. Many even quit their jobs altogether to become full-time stock market traders.[2] There was a growing reverence for wealthy business people. Investment bankers became protagonists in movies like *American Psycho* and *Boiler Room*: "Nobody wants to work for it anymore. There's no honor in taking the after-school job. Honor is in the dollar, kid. So, I went the white boy way of slinging crack rock. I became a stock-broker."[3]

The government did not try to stop it. On the contrary, officials glorified the success of technology companies. So, the market crashed. Shares of internet companies lost US$1.8 trillion of their value. One would expect the crash to be a reminder that while the country had grown immensely rich, it used that wealth recklessly. Yet, with the same ease that investors, magazines helped cause the hype, they relativized the significance of the crash: "It is a cleansing process," explained an investor. "To have some branches grow and bear fruit, you have to trim others."[4]

There was a second dramatic moment. On September 11, 2001, terrorists struck at the heart of American power. The terrorist organization Al-Qaeda smashed two passenger planes into the symbol of capitalism, the Twin Towers in New York, and a third plane into the Pentagon, the center of military power. A fourth plane, on its way to hit Capitol Hill, was taken down by a passenger revolt against the terrorist hijackers. Almost 3,000 people died in the attacks. After the attacks, President George W. Bush (2001–9) called on Americans to retake their normal lives and to go on consuming. "Get down to Disney World," he said. "Take your families and enjoy life."[5] He repeated that message throughout his presidency. "I encourage you all to go shopping more."[6] Consumerism became a synonym for patriotism. Consuming the Americans did: Household consumption became yet more important in the American economy. Consumption was made easier. The credit card had already made it easier to shop. The combination of the credit card and online stores made it irresistible. It was not necessity that propelled buying, but impulse.[7] Americans spent on smarter electronic gadgets, on bigger SUVs, and on larger houses. Bigger houses required still more gadgets.[8] In 2005, an American comedian painted the following picture of his society:

These people, these people are efficient, professional, compulsive consumers. It's their civic duty. Consumption. It's the new national pastime. Fuck baseball. It's consumption. The only true lasting American value that's left. Buying things. People spending money they don't have on things they don't need. So, they can max out their credit cards and spend the rest of their lives paying 18 percent interest on something that cost $12.50. And they didn't like it when they got it home anyway!

But if you talk to one of them about this, if you isolate one of them, you sit them down rationally, and you talk to them about the low IQ's and the dumb behavior and the bad decisions. Right away they start talking about education. Education. They say: We need more money for education. We need more books. More teachers. More classrooms. More schools. We need more testing for the kids. You say to them: Well, you know, we've tried all of that and the kids still can't pass the tests. They say: Don't you worry about that. We're going to lower the passing grades.[9]

While consumption could have been a hedge to support new and sustainable industries at home, American consumers continued to import fossil fuels and low-cost goods. American petroleum imports increased from US$90 billion in 2000 to US$210 billion in 2009. The deficit in trade in consumer goods climbed to US$650 billion. Many of these imported goods were not made to last. During the decade, the volume of textile and electronics thrown away by Americans doubled.[10] It was made to break. The same happened with residential housing. Americans borrowed more for their houses, but many were plywood palazzos, made at best to just outlive their owners.[11] After junk food, America spearheaded junk consumer goods, and now also specialized in junk houses: the McMansion.

Large retail chains, like Walmart and Tesco, used their power as door-keepers to consumers to force manufacturers to produce cheaper.[12] One of the examples was the iconic American jeans brand Levi's. In 2003, Levi's closed its last factory in the United States. It had already been pressured by Walmart to start a cheaper brand; now the brand relocated its entire pro-duction to low-wage countries. Levi's started employing cheaper workers, using cheaper cotton fiber, and saved on rivets and stitching. The quality of a pair of Levi's pants decreased, but not their price. What happened was that in the price structure, there was a shift from paying American workers to branding and publicity.[13]

This degrading of quality was bad for manufacturing in the United States, but it was also bad for consumers. If cheap pants were thought to benefit poor consumers, their low quality meant that consumers just needed to buy more pants with a shorter life. The jobs in large chains like Walmart were of poor quality too and paid less than the previous jobs in Levi's factories. More junk products and more junk jobs: that was the Walmart effect. In 2004, Walmart received the Corporate Patriotism Award. A senior economic advisor in the White House said in justification: "Outsourcing is just a new way of doing international trade. More things are tradable than were tradable in the past and that's a good thing."[14]

Subprime (also known as "not good")

Instead of making the country strong, as one could expect patriots to do, this stage of American consumerism made the country weaker. Growth was about size and quantity, less about quality. Compared to other indus-trialized countries, the United States became a laggard in setting efficiency and quality standards, for cars, for instance, but also for electronics. The American government vowed to harness technology to make manufactur-ing more sustainable. But instead of going green, so to say, it was going to China.

America prided itself on information technology companies, like Microsoft and Google, on its lead in software development. But it still merely used these innovations to increase the productivity of its economy, so that the IT productivity paradox continued to be present. During the decade, American factories did not increase their investment in software, whereas it grew in countries like Japan and Germany.[15] Europe and Japan also invested more in automation and robotization. American companies invested almost as much in factories abroad as in the modernization of factories at home.[16] Investment flowed to other sectors, like real estate and retail sectors. Investment in stores grew twice as fast as investment in factories.

The more households consumed, the more investment fell, and not only in the manufacturing sector. During the 1990s, the neglect of public infrastructure had already become manifest. That neglect continued and public investment decreased further. Experts warned that the shortfall had become a security concern. Infrastructure could break down and not be able to withstand natural disasters. "For the safety and security of our families, we can no longer afford to ignore the congested roads, aging dams, broken water mains, and deficient bridges we face every day."[17] They were proven right. In 2005, a hurricane struck the City of New Orleans and killed many citizens. It was found that many of the pump houses, barriers, and water mains were too old or badly built. Still, after Hurricane Katrina, public investment in infrastructure continued to fall. There were not only security consequences. Underinvestment also put a brake on innovation and entrepreneurship. America's competitors rapidly modernized their infrastructure. Broadband penetration in East Asian countries, for instance, surpassed America's.

The stock market crash of 2000 could have been a warning to divert capital and technology into more durable industries – and to improve the quality of what families spent most of their money on. The response was different. Corporate America turned to services, cheap workers overseas, and tax havens. A trailblazer of this strategy was General Electric. Initially, the company was a producer of household electronics. From the late 1990s, it shifted to high-end products, like hospital scanners and wind power turbines. Half of that was produced in the United States. Over 40 percent of its revenues came from services. The majority of these services revenues were generated from banking and real estate activities. In 2009, General Electric possessed close to US$560 billion in financial assets, about a fourth of it parked in tax havens. On its profits, well in excess of US$10 billion per year, the company paid no taxes. On the contrary, it claimed tax benefits. The company hired a dream team of government insiders, from the Treasury, the federal fiscal service, and committees responsible for taxation in Congress. The leadership explained that it was not swindling the state, but only applied the rules, and needed to optimize its taxation in order to stay competitive. Wealth would otherwise go to non-American competitors.

Like with Bush's comments about consumption, unpatriotic policy was presented as an act of patriotism. Optimists maintained that companies like General Electric showed that American economic power had gone virtual. Instead of producing goods, they claimed, the American economy would now grow rich by selling high-tech, services, and royalties, such as brands and knowhow. Compared to the small returns on some hundreds of thousands of workers, argued *The Economist*, you get huge returns on the ideas produced by Apple in California. "People like Bill Gates and Steve Jobs have all the upsides of Carnegie and Ford without the downsides."[18]

The data revealed a different reality. During the decade, the United States incurred an annual trade deficit, not a surplus, in high-tech products of around US$60 billion. The selling of intellectual property earned the country an annual surplus of US$50 billion. It also earned around US$130 billion annually from investment abroad and from exporting services. But even those royalties, services, and investment incomes combined were not sufficient to pay for the growing imports of energy and consumer goods. Consequently, the overall deficit kept climbing and America's external debt grew by US$545 billion per year, thus much more than in the 1990s. American economic power did not so much go virtual; it slowly evaporated.

As a result, the United States was being hollowed out financially. This trend was already visible in the 1990s. Now, it accelerated. Between 2000 and 2009, the government sold around US$5 trillion in bonds to other countries. The most important buyer was China. At the same time that the Chinese government lent money to the American government, private American investors transferred US$1.5 trillion to overseas bank accounts, US$3.5 trillion to overseas stock markets, and US$2 trillion to other countries in the form of foreign direct investment. A large amount of this foreign direct investment was in holdings in fiscal havens. Less than half of the incomes on these foreign investments was repatriated (see again figure 4.1 on page 94).

By 2009, close to US$1 trillion of American capital was parked in tax havens, causing a loss of around US$50 billion in tax revenue. Hearings in Congress were organized, statements of indignation relayed to the millions of families that did pay taxes. Yet, the government refused to deal with the matter. The external debt, it stated, was the consequence of a "global savings glut" and why should these savings not benefit the American economy? The detachment of companies was justified as an effort to remain competitive, the exodus of capital as a necessity to diversify risk.

The external debt created an aberrant idea of wealth. The selling of government bonds allowed the government to pay contractors and civil servants, who in turn could go on to spend on consumer goods, services, and real estate. This debt trap became more vicious because the external commitment to lend allowed the United States to keep interest rates low. That made it easier to borrow for houses. As borrowing was made easier, housing prices increased, and grew the appetite for even larger loans. Between 2000 and 2009, housing prices increased by 50 percent. Many families borrowed more than they could afford or than their houses were worth. In this regard, too, the government allowed housing debt to increase, mortgages to be turned into opaque financial debt derivatives that promised significant returns to investors.

Capital was again sloshed into a bubble, a double bubble: one of exuberantly high housing prices and one of artificially high returns on junk mortgages. The latter were euphemistically called "subprime." So, while the exodus of private capital on the one hand was a clear no-confidence vote, the real estate surge kept home owners, fund managers, and speculators optimistic for the eight years in between the Dotcom bubble burst and the bankruptcy of banks that had invested deeply into the junk mortgages, like Lehman Brothers. The bankruptcy of Lehman Brothers in 2008 sparked the so-called Great Recession. It would take the economy five years to recover from the crash.[19]

The audacity of hope

The 1990s were a missed opportunity to reform the economy at a time of growth. The decade that followed, with its two major crises, the Dotcom crisis of 2000 and the Great Recession that started in 2008, was a period of slowdown. Despite the capital glut, investment in important infrastructure and manufacturing increased more slowly than before. Productivity growth tapered off. Still, it did not prompt serious rebalancing, away from external debt, overconsumption, and speculation, toward investments that would help uphold competitiveness in the long run: infrastructure, education, and productive industries.

There were new entrepreneurs who skyrocketed into the stratosphere of billionaires because they led innovation. But the contribution of many others was less clear. Americans were paying more to medical specialists, without medical services getting better, more to insurance companies without them providing more security, more on bonuses without banks becoming better run, more to real estate brokers without property becoming more durable.[20] A dog walker in Manhattan could earn US$230 a day, a personal trainer US$300 per hour, a hairdresser US$800 per cut.[21] Meanwhile, teachers struggled and saw their incomes stagnate. Money trickled down. But it was a perverse trickledown.

President George W. Bush championed compassionate conservatism, combining personal duty with care for the weakest. This led him to introduce a bill that provided more assistance for needy children, the "No Child Left Behind Act." Still, income inequality continued to grow, yet slower than in the 1990s. The problem was rather that the real disposable income of the poorest decreased (figure 7.1).[22] It dropped by 10 percent between 2000 and 2009. If in the 1990s American industries were still growing more jobs inside the country than abroad, this was now reversed. More workers were hired in American factories abroad. Unemployment peaked. By the end of the decade, one fifth of Americans lived in poverty.[23] The share of working poor in the labor force increased from just over 4 percent in 2000 to 7 percent in 2009. "I've never lived around poor people and I don't know what they think," President Bush himself avowed. "I really don't know what they think. I'm a white Republican guy who doesn't get it."[24]

The collapse of economic confidence was dramatic. In 2000, 70 percent of Americans were satisfied about the state of the country; this was below 10 percent in 2009. The dean of the Harvard Business School warned that the corporate elite had slid into an unprecedented legitimacy crisis.

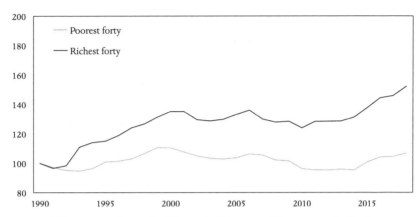

Figure 7.1   Growth of household income (%, constant dollars)
Source: US Census.

"To regain society's trust," he wrote, "business leaders must embrace a way of looking at their role that goes beyond their responsibility to the shareholder to include a civic and personal commitment to their duty as institutional custodians."[25]

Political confidence diminished too. As steadily as political trust grew in the late 1990s, figure 7.2 shows it declined in the decade that followed. By 2009, only about one fifth of Americans said they trusted government. Political anger was especially high in the African-American community, more than a quarter of whom lived in poverty, among the impoverished Hispanics in the South, and the poor non-Hispanic whites in the Midwest. While the majority of citizens were still said to be politically moderate, there were two important ideological shifts. The divide between the Democratic coastal states and the Republican states in the hinterland sharpened. This Republican hinterland also vented its anger much more audibly. "A spectre is haunting the liberal elites of New York and Washington," wrote a conservative commentator, "the spectre of a young, attractive, unapologetic conservatism, rising out of the American countryside."[26]

Conservative movements like Alt Right and the Tea Party started luring large crowds. Rightist talk radio stations attracted millions of listeners and conservative television hosts gained popularity by lambasting immigration and blaming Washington for everything from taxes

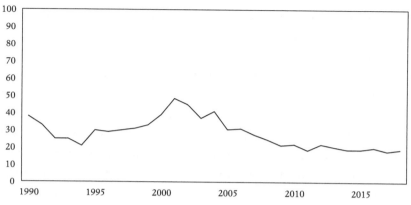

Figure 7.2   Trust in government (%)
Source: Gallup.

to gay marriage. They abhorred the compassionate conservatism of President Bush. To look after oneself, to keep government at bay, and to own a gun were aspirations that connected the rich Texas ranch owner and the destitute white shack dweller. Bush did not confront these hard conservatives, he danced around them, claiming to oppose same-sex marriage, yet tolerating states that approved it; resisting stem-cell research and again leaving the door open for states to finance it. He said he would sign but not push gun restrictions and bent to pressure from the gun owners to allow assault weapons to be offered to civilians. The hard conservatives were a minority, but they were gaining hold of the Republican Party.

After the terrorist attacks of 2001, American flags appeared everywhere: on roofs, as bumper stickers, and on letter boxes. The more flags were flown, the fewer Americans knew what the flag stood for. President George W. Bush liked to refer to the wisdom of the Founding Fathers, and had promised to spend more on education and civic engagement. Yet public spending on education hardly grew.[27] Colleges are cheating their students, a conservative columnist put it: "In 1777, John Adams wrote to his son about the importance of education. He said it was necessary to teach the next generation about America's founding principles in order to preserve the freedom and independence so many of his fellow countrymen sacrificed to achieve."[28] By ignoring the importance of values such as virtue, civic participation and social justice, the foundation of democracy was becoming shaky.[29]

Against that backdrop, the Americans chose a new president: Barack Obama, the first African-American president. He campaigned with a message of hope. "The road ahead will be long," he spoke. "Our climb will be steep. We may not get there in one year or even in one term. But, America, I have never been more hopeful than I am tonight that we will get there."[30] When the president-elect was inaugurated, over one million citizens watched the ceremony on the National Mall. Obama spoke to the nation with rare eloquence and majesty, soothing almost, like a preacher. Would he also be able to repair his wounded country? His election confirmed the division in the country. Never was the presidential approval rate across the fault line between Democrats and Republicans so polarized.[31] Never also had there been such a large difference in the enthusiasm for the president between poor African-Americans and white rich conservatives.

Europe's elastic run

Bicycle lanes, wind farms, and the welfare state: these were the symbols of Europe as a humane alternative to American capitalism. With the creation of a common market, the largest in the world, the introduction of a common currency, a common space program, and steps toward a common foreign policy, Europe appeared to mature into a world power in its own right and, why not, capable of defying the United States in the long run. The United States of Europe. The reality, however, remained complex. Citizens, figure 7.3 shows, were still tepid about the European project. The more elites pushed for openness, the more nationalists pushed back, stirring resentment against technocratic cosmopolitanism, migration, and Islam.

Large political projects always grapple with estrangement between decision makers and the people. But the problem in Europe was made worse, because its decision making was largely anonymous. With rare exceptions, European institutions had no charismatic political leaders. Brussels looked like *Das Schloss* of Franz Kafka: imposing, intrusive, yet

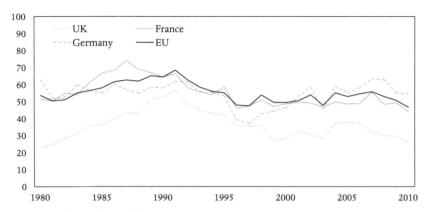

Figure 7.3 "EU membership is a good thing for my country"
(% of respondents agreeing)
Source: Eurobarometer. Dataset discontinued in 2011.

completely separated from the villagers. Trust was dealt a blow when it became clear that a European Commissioner had appointed her dentist as a paid advisor. Stories came out about the luxurious offices of Members of the European Parliament, their private limo service, their high salaries, other generous allowances – and even a cut-price monthly ration of a drug to enhance potency. To many citizens, it was like a UFO had landed in Brussels, with officials speaking an incomprehensible language and a headquarters that, indeed, looked like a UFO. When the European Commission reopened its expensive headquarters, journalists joked that the blinds on the inside were there for officials to shut themselves off from the real world outside. It made Brussels a perfect target for new nationalists. An important ingredient in their identity politics was to set the common people, the villagers in Kafka's book, against the technocrats of the castle.

During elections, the pro-European center parties yielded ground to Eurosceptic parties. While still small, these parties were vocal and pressured the center, in much the same way as the Tea Party did in the United States. A referendum in Ireland decided against more power for European institutions. In another referendum, the Danes voted against introducing the common currency, the euro. These were important signals, but muddling through appeared the only way forward. Proponents of the European project recognized the danger. "There is a widespread sense of unease about Europe, about loss of national identity, and about an EU that increasingly intrudes into their everyday lives," a Dutch foreign minister cautioned.[32] A progressive German politician complained that Europe was becoming "stranger and more incomprehensible."[33]

But an incomprehensible compromise was considered preferable to a return to fragmentation. Better a fog of words than, to paraphrase the Prussian strategist Karl von Clausewitz, the fog of war. Still, the fog of words made citizens lose track. In 2001, the heads of state agreed on a highly complicated voting system for the European Council, but added a declaration to the treaty that it was imperative to improve transparency, to better reflect public opinion, and to engage in a debate with citizens. The enlargement of Europe, however, caused it to be even more incomprehensible. The bargaining between 15 and later 27 countries led to deals that were verbose and vague. The harder the center politicians pressed for new treaties, the harder a new generation of skeptics pushed back. Nationalists mixed the anger at bureaucratic despotism with frustration about cosmopolitan arrogance. One of them was the Dutch politician Pim Fortuyn. He promised to give his country back to his citizens and fiercely criticized the cosmopolitanism of the mainstream politicians:

> The Prime Minister of the UK, Tony Blair, whirls around the world like an American Secretary of State. He meddles with everything. He is the self-proclaimed, uncontrolled minister of a fictitious world government. In every region, Blair pretends to know best and lectures on human rights. Those who stand in his way are bombed. He is a dangerous man. The world is full of anger. This demands pragmatism, restraint, and the respect for sovereignty, not the current naivety and arrogance.[34]

Nationalists could exploit a second factor: the fear that European enlargement would damage national prosperity. In 2004, it was agreed to enlarge the group of 15 countries to 25, and in 2007 to 27. Their accession was necessary, so it was thought, because they would otherwise fall into instability. Political leaders also explained the economic stakes. The European market would expand from 380 million consumers to almost 500 million. In the United Kingdom, the prime minister reasoned that growth would be lower without migration and enlargement. The same in Germany, where the chancellor claimed that German companies depended on enlargement and needed access to new markets.

Enlargement caused tensions in both the old and new member states. Western European citizens were not convinced by the reasons given by politicians to justify enlargement. Only a quarter were strongly in favor of enlargement; the rest did not have a particular opinion.[35] Citizens appreciated the importance of enlargement for preserving peace and security in Europe yet feared that it would come at a high price, complicate decision making, further increase the gap between citizens and institutions, and require large sums of financial aid. About 10 percent were willing to accept many immigrants from poorer member states, 40 percent some, and close to 50 percent few or none.[36] A few years after the new member states joined, the population in several countries, like Austria, France, Finland, and the United Kingdom found that enlargement had had a negative impact.[37] In the East, Havel and Wałęsa had warned of a difficult process. A sizable minority in the new member states were against accession. Questions of identity emerged, whereby the newcomers found it difficult to identify with the European dimension. Rather than a political project, Europe was also frequently seen in the East as a cash cow. Officials took note of the skepticism, but insisted that enlargement was inevitable and that more had to be done to convince people of it.[38]

A third factor concerned mobility and migration more broadly. The European population remained much less mobile than, for example, the population of the United States. The migration flows from Eastern Europe were small compared to American internal migration. So, while goods traveled easily across borders, this was less the case with people. Throughout the decade still only one third of European citizens traveled abroad and only about 1 percent of the student population spent time in a school in a different member state. Only 15 percent had relatives living in another country. The benefits of the open market that companies saw were less clear to the majority of citizens. Most Europeans thought that migration would be bad for employment.[39] The benefits of openness that the mobile elite enjoyed were much more modest in other segments of the society, parts of the society that were more exposed to the downside of openness, like the influx of cheap migrant workers. While European cosmopolitanism advanced, more and more citizens started to fall for nationalism. "The gates are flooded and anybody can have access to England and join in," declared the popular singer Morrissey. "The higher the influx into England the more the British identity disappears. Travel to England and you have no idea where you are."[40]

The debate about migration became inextricable from the debate about Islam. Even mainstream thinkers predicted that the failure of multiculturalism, the growing segregation between natives and immigrants would cause trouble.[41] In many countries, the integration of previous waves of immigrants, predominantly from North Africa and Turkey, was only a partial success. That was revealed by, among other things, disappointing results in schools and in the labor market. Hence, the perception grew that immigrants benefited from the European welfare state, but did not contribute to it.

Worse still, stories came out about violent gangs and parts of cities that had become no-go zones for the police. The other side of that narrative was that minority groups felt discriminated against and targeted by the police. Children playing football were allegedly forced to undergo arbitrary controls. Law enforcers were unable to differentiate between a hard core of criminals and others. America had its black ghettos, Europe its North-African ghettos. Anger festered. In 2005, the outskirts of Paris burned. Thousands of cars were destroyed. In 2006, riots broke out in migrant communities around Brussels.

The Islamic community also became particularly visible. If its mosques and dress had already revealed its growth, terrorist attacks put it in the spotlight: the killing of a Dutch filmmaker, train bombings in Madrid, bombings in London, and an attack against soldiers in Milan. It led to a double sense of insecurity. On the one hand, Islam became inextricably linked with terrorism. On the other hand, it confronted Europe with its own lack of identity. While Islamic communities were closely knit, most of the rest of European society had turned its back on its churches and frayed as a result of individualism and materialism.

The materialism was pleasant and distressing at the same time. Europe became a vast wide openness, a borderless marketplace, a lowland of utilitarianism without clear symbols of pride. Islam was the perfect excuse for native European citizens to disregard that they themselves had launched the most devastating attack against what was left of their local culture, identity, and diversity by replacing it with a monotone landscape of global brands, lifestyles, food, and so forth. This contradiction, this flimsy patriotism as we saw it in the United States, was not new. Yet, like on the other side of the Atlantic, it became more pressing.

"We were aware of the doubt," explained a former head of government, "but we believed that progress in itself would allow us to continue to make progress."[42] Whether it concerned the discussion about bureaucratic despotism, enlargement, migration, or multiculturalism, European politics became an elastic run. The more center politicians forged ahead, the harder the pullback. Those fond of integration could celebrate that the 1999 Amsterdam Treaty turned more competences over to the European institutions, that the euro started to circulate in 2002, that ten more countries joined in 2004, that two more became members in 2007, and that the European Union consequently became the largest market. The nationalists could point at the threat of openness and the loss of control. What followed was another unproductive dispute in which the so-called moderates failed to see that their project had indeed become a sterile, commerce-driven, culturally empty land and the nationalists refused to see that their incessant blaming of others took away from those who deplored the loss of identity the responsibility to reinvent it.

Eurozone

The main test from the viewpoint of the center parties was to demonstrate that economic openness was a good thing and that the introduction of the euro made citizens better off. Slightly more than half of the citizens in countries that had adopted the euro thought it a good thing. The European market did deliver more prosperity. Between 2003 and 2008, household income increased, even in the poorer countries. The value of the euro climbed steadily against the dollar. Still, economists continued to point the finger at the fragility of the whole economic construction.

When it came to innovation, Europe became a champion of noble intentions. In 2000, the member states pledged to spend 3 percent of GDP on research and development. It was still below 2 percent by 2009. "A failure," admitted the Swedish Prime Minister. Europe vowed to strengthen its manufacturing, but investment in this strategic sector grew by less than half the rate of the 1990s. The members pledged to become leaders in clean energy and sustainable development. They did reach their renewable energy targets. They also did become leaders in sustainable technologies. Still, the production of these technologies expanded faster in East Asia. Europe sponsored the innovation and the installation of renewable energy systems, but failed to retain leadership in their production.

That was not the only disappointment. Like the United States, Europe chose to outsource polluting industries to developing countries instead of growing a more sustainable industry at home. China became an important supplier. By 2009, Europe had a US$150 billion trade deficit with China. While the outsourcing of industrial production helped reduce the consumption of fossil fuels, this mitigation was almost entirely offset by the growing number of cars on the road. Between 2000 and 2009, petroleum imports trebled.[43] This caused the European Union to run an overall trade deficit with the rest of the world. Many member states incurred growing external debt while their internal productivity disappointed.

The most important source of concern, however, was the common currency, the euro.[44] Greece joined the currency zone with fraudulent statistics. With the help of foreign investors, it turned a part of its debt into murky derivatives, the same way American banks turned subprime mortgages into derivative financial products. The large government deficits of France and Germany, despite violating the European budget rules, remained unpunished.[45] After the introduction of the euro, the gap between deficit and surplus countries grew further. Germany, Austria, and the Netherlands ran big trade surpluses. If they had still had their national currencies, such export advantage would be partially leveled off, as the inflow of money from trade would push up the value of the national currency and make exports expensive. The monetary union suppressed that correction. Italy,

Spain, Greece, Portugal, and Ireland ran growing deficits. In their case, the euro prevented a devaluation that would have made imports more expensive and exports competitive.

The imperfect monetary union that economists had warned of in the 1990s became a reality. A lot of money flowed from the surplus countries to the deficit countries. This is typical for a monetary union.[46] But like in the United States, this external capital rarely made the weak economies more productive. Why, for instance, would one build factories in Greece, if the country could perfectly be serviced from Germany? Why invest in modern farming in Italy, if vast volumes of tomatoes were grown in gas-heated greenhouses in the Netherlands? So, instead, Dutch and German investors bought government bonds, which allowed the Greek and Italian government to pay their employees, and those employees to continue to spend on German imports.

Given the fact that Greece was a member of the Eurozone, and thus backed by the European Central Bank, the interest rates on these government bonds remained low and no longer reflected the inherent weakness of the Greek economy: high consumption with low investment in productivity. Athens continued to produce fake accounts to cover up the dismal state of its economy. A lot of money from the north also flowed to speculation in the real estate sector, in apartment blocks on the Spanish coast, for example. These examples simplify the situation, but make clear the main flaw of the Eurozone: the investment from the north was not used to boost productivity in the south.

In 2009, the bubble burst. The consequent European debt crisis revealed the weakness of the deficit countries, but also exposed the fragility of the main surplus state: Germany. Germany had transformed from an economic laggard into an export powerhouse and started to generate large trade surpluses. In 2008, its trade surplus was US$270 billion. Part of that surplus was the result of austerity in public spending and the labor market, a subsequent dip in imports, and more competitive exports. That advantage was thus further increased by the effect of the euro, but also by the entering of the new member states. In the years following their accession, German exports to the Baltic and Central European countries doubled. Germany emerged as the main beneficiary of European integration.

Amidst this export boom, Germany missed an important opportunity to consolidate its position. While German companies and banks were hoarding trillions of euros, there was no vision for how to invest them in a way that would allow Germany to retain its leadership, let alone for how it could sustain its main export markets: the weaker European economies. German politicians certainly were right to criticize the fraught economic governance of countries like Greece, but they did not offer an alternative either. Meanwhile, German investors continued to inflate the bubble. While the German industrial companies disdained the poorer European countries, they started to revel in the idea of becoming a global economic power. In Munich, the airport doubled its capacity with a new terminal. In Frankfurt, a new runway was built. Volkswagen vowed to become the world's largest car maker, Siemens the largest machine builder.[47]

That success story was to be written mostly outside Europe. Volkswagen saw the Chinese market as the arena where Toyota had to be surpassed. Siemens wanted to tap into the endless pool of Chinese engineers. "Six Chinese engineers cost as much as one German engineer and they work 2,600 hours per year," its president explained.[48] The new German industrial miracle to some extent was built in cities like Munich, but even more so in cities like Shanghai. During the decade, net investments in factories in Germany increased by about US$8 billion. Investment in factories abroad expanded by US$40 billion.[49] A lot of the income from these investments abroad was also reinvested abroad. Compared to its massive exports, Germany also did not spend a lot on research and development, certainly not compared to other European countries like Finland, Sweden and Denmark, or on its public infrastructure. It was also still a question whether Germany really had become a global champion, or whether it had just benefited disproportionately from the European market. Sixty percent of its export and investment revenues still came from European countries. Either way, while German multinationals tried to go global, local challenges remained. The wealth gap between the West and the former Soviet East hardly shrank during the decade.[50] Poverty increased.

The rest of Europe saw Germany re-emerge as the most powerful country and some of its businessmen flaunted their power. Many Germans did not feel powerful at all. There was confidence in the corporate headquarters around Munich, skepticism still in most of the rest of the country. Already before the eruption of the crisis in 2009, it contributed to tensions with other member states. After criticism of his economic policy, the Italian Prime Minister Silvio Berlusconi called a German politician a Nazi camp guard. "There is a man producing a film on Nazi concentration camps," he said. "I shall put you forward for the role of Capo."[51] Behind closed doors, French officials criticized Germany for dumping its products and abusing the common currency. They argued that Germany had incurred budget deficits for a long time, that it did not need to lecture, and that the European Central Bank had to devalue the euro. Paris was under growing public pressure. Consumer confidence in France had dropped steadily from the peak in the late 1990s and far-right nationalists remained vocal. Berlin struck back. Officials insisted that fiscal guidelines needed to be respected and that France was protectionist. It also reached out to the United Kingdom, hoping to find in London an ally to protect European free trade against alleged French chauvinism.

Prosperity had become the most important argument for center politicians to make the case for Europe. For several years, the euro and the deepening market appeared to deliver just that. There were flaws in the whole economic construction. They were known but not resolved. Imbalances between deficit and surplus countries grew bigger. Yet, the biggest surplus country did not really use the windfall in exports to make its economy stronger in the long run. Like in the United States, capital flows also nourished bubbles in real estate and the financial sector.

The more unbalanced the market became, the larger also the political tensions. Even if they detested the nationalists on the right, many center politicians turned out to have comparably strong protectionist tendencies when economic interests were at stake. In the end, the predicted crisis erupted. In the summer of 2009, lenders turned against Greece. Now it was not just banks that risked bankruptcy, but a sovereign state. It would take countries almost eight years to recover from the Eurozone crisis. Optimists maintained that the EU's very survival demonstrated its resilience; skeptics argued that this was merely a cadaveric spasm.

I am Jesus

European center politicians took an immense gamble of going against the concerns of their constituencies about the impact of enlargement and by introducing a currency that was not supported by sufficiently strong instruments to organize the financial markets. They made another gamble: to promise a third way, between naked capitalism and socialism. Citizens would be encouraged by the market to work. The government would provide in the form of social services. In the more liberal countries, it entailed a social safety net. In welfare states this also included healthcare, pensions, and education. In many countries, though, this formula flopped.

From an economic viewpoint, the full or partial privatization of services, like healthcare insurances and public transportation, seldom led to efficiency gains. Like in the United States, it made such services more expensive without quality improvement. From a social viewpoint, the third way was not very successful either. Economic growth did not lead to a significant decrease in unemployment. Augmenting housing prices, energy costs, and spending on insurance caused the real disposable income to grow three times more slowly than in the 1990s. In many countries, poverty spread.

An important test case of the third way was the United Kingdom. While not a part of the Eurozone, it too slipped into an economic crisis. The population came to feel that the gleeful promise of Prime Minister Tony Blair (1997–2007) to chart a third way between capitalism and socialism was not kept. During the decade, the British economy did grow steadily. Still, poverty levels, which declined during the 1990s, remained steady at around 20 percent.[52] The poor were disillusioned and spoke of betrayal. Even the elite had to acknowledge that the third road appeared to be a dead end. *The Economist* reported on the shocking living conditions of the underclass. "The wind whips along unending concrete walls that are uniformly grey and permanently damp," it wrote. "The stairwells reek of urine and cheap disinfectant and the smell of decaying rubbish wafts from the disposal chutes."[53]

Government debt increased, but the quality of public education, public transportation, and security decreased.[54] In 2004, the British education minister touted that children during the Blair years were the best-educated generation in the nation's history, but international tests showed that pupils' skills deteriorated and that education inequality did not diminish.[55] External debt surged rapidly, but investment in manufacturing remained stagnant. If anything grew, it was the financial services and real estate sector in the City of London.

In many countries, social insecurity increased, despite modest economic growth and despite promises of politicians to preserve it. Moreover, the growth of public debt in the second half of the decade also made it uncertain whether this commitment could be sustained in the long run. There was another important downside of the third way and the welfare state. The countries with the most generous welfare systems, the role models of trust and solidarity, showed themselves less solidary toward the outside. In elections in the Netherlands and Denmark, two poster children of tolerance and solidarity, the far right gained about 10 percent of the votes. In Sweden, too, a rightist party was established. There were several explanations. The wealth and welfare systems of these countries attracted large numbers of migrants and refugees that were accused of abusing solidarity. The welfare system could also not prevent that, around rich cities like Amsterdam, Copenhagen, and Stockholm, the poor white population lived in areas where the majority of immigrants settled. The presence of a generous welfare state, a society with strong social cohesion, thus also came with the desire to defend it.

The protectionist reflex was thus visible in rich and poor countries; countries high on social cohesion and low on social cohesion. Like in the United States, though, the call to defend the country's wealth, its social model, and its identity, went without self-reflection and a new generation of rightist populists also skillfully put the blame on others: immigrants and the European institutions. Hence, in Europe too, it happened that while a growing number of citizens called to defend the nation's wealth and identity, they helped undermine it, by spending on multinational brands, like the furniture retailer Ikea and the fashion chain Zara, brands that sourced almost all their goods from low-wage countries like China and Bangladesh. They spent vastly on companies that hardly paid taxes and stretched labor rules to the limits. Ryanair, for example, carried only five million passengers in 2000 but almost 70 million in 2009. It was the Walmart of flying. It was consumer behavior that undermined the welfare state.

Ikea registered spectacular growth figures. Its vast blue and yellow stores mushroomed. They were often surrounded by a sea of tarmac, so that visitors could drive the maximum of goods back home. Many of its products were sourced from poor countries, like Bangladesh, China, and Vietnam, but marketed with a Scandinavian knack for design and sustainability. Cheap became chic. Cities called it an honor to host an Ikea store. Like with Walmart, the consumers were so captivated by the low prices that they did not consider the high indirect costs of Ikea's business model. Each Ikea shop that opened had negative effects on shops selling similar products and created almost no opportunities for local manufacturers.[56] China is Ikea's biggest purchasing country.[57] The annual number of containers shipped for Ikea from Asia to Europe may have been between 300,000 and 400,000.[58] That equated to 40 very large container ships fully loaded. This intercontinental shipping alone emitted around 700,000 tons of carbon dioxide. Ikea tried to brand itself as an ethical company. Its bookkeeping was of a different nature. Most Ikea stores were indirectly owned by a Dutch tax-non-profit-making legal entity dedicated to "innovation in the field of architectural and interior design."[59] The foundation paid no taxes. Through Ikea, European consumers contributed to the exodus of smaller shops from city centers, the decay of industrial production, the replacement of diverse craftsmanship by a monoculture of products like Ivar and Billy, and the financial sorrows of their government. Ikea was perhaps just one example, but it was a big example.

Europeans felt that their society was threatened from the outside, but a more important threat came from inside. Despite calls for civic renewal, civic engagement continued to recede, the turnout of youngsters in elections to drop, and the time spent with families and friends to shrink. Across Europe, civic engagement was still limited to three hours a week.[60] About one third of 14-year-old students were found to be unable to interpret a simple election leaflet, close to half of these students incapable of distinguishing a democracy from another system.[61] In Britain, young citizens seemed to be carried away as much by voting for Big Brother, a popular television program, as they were ready to vote during the elections.[62] Despite posh elite schools and universities, Britain's teenagers turned out to be among the most badly behaved in Europe. In 2009, the BBC broadcast a documentary titled "The Death of Respect." A prominent theologian and politician put it thus: "Concepts like duty, obligation, responsibility and honour have come to seem antiquated . . . Conscience has been outsourced, delegated away."[63]

Between 2000 and 2009, center parties held on to their power. Nationalist parties advanced in Austria, Belgium, Denmark, Finland, Hungary, and the Netherlands, but usually did not represent more than 15 percent of the voters. The new rightist populists were boisterous, but not big. In Flanders, the far-right party distributed pork sausages before a school with many Muslim children. In the Netherlands, the leader of the far right referred to politicians as "Crazy Ella" and called the Muslim veil a "head mop." A rightist British politician referred to key European officials as "pygmies" and a "damp rag." In Italy, Prime Minister Berlusconi called himself the Jesus Christ of politics and glorified the superiority of European civilization, but his television channels were almost unmatched in the absence of culture, not to mention the disdain shown to women who were portrayed as objects that could be bought almost. The self-proclaimed defenders of European civilization turned discourtesy into their trademark. Some center politicians responded in kind. A Belgian liberal referred to the far right as dung beetles; the Dutch Prime Minister called them tasteless. Rightist politicians tried to win voters with disrespect and contempt, but center politicians themselves lost their citizens with pale technocratic promises that were not fulfilled and by chiding citizens who voted for populists instead of handling their concerns.

Legitimacy

Between 2000 and 2009, from crisis to crisis, the Western world lost more of its power. Its wealth was increasingly consumed instead of being used to improve its social and economic resilience. Its share in global economic production decreased from 57 percent in 2000 to 52 percent in 2009. Both the United States and the European Union incurred growing deficits on the current account. While still small compared to their overall economies, these deficits mirrored the imbalances between consumption and the readiness to invest, between wealth and the wisdom to spend it with an eye on the future, between the pretense of building green and local industries,

CHAPTER 8

A FOREIGN POLICY OF
RECKLESSNESS

I N THE 1990S, IT WAS DIFFICULT TO IDENTIFY THE MOST PRESSING SECURITY threat. With the end of the Cold War, direct security threats to the West had vanished. In 2001, the American Secretary of State proclaimed that it was hard to avoid a permanent state of optimism and glee when surveying the state of the world. One month after his assertion, on September 11, terrorists struck New York and Washington. In the following years, Western foreign policy, in particular in the United States, became a peculiar combination of a dysfunctional crusade against terrorism and an ineffective campaign to advance globalization.

Globalization held that political borders became less relevant. Globalization, at least from the viewpoint of Western capitals, also implied that values of openness, free trade, and democracy would spread further. The difference between Europe and the United States was not about *whether* values had to be promoted but about *how* that had to be done. The administration of George W. Bush resorted to hard military power and unilateralism. In contrast, Europe preached soft, normative power. "When people are looking for new ways to ensure their well-being, peace, prosperity," the president of the European Commission stated, "the European experience has a great deal to offer the world."[1]

In the high age of globalization, the West further undercut its position. The combination of a new clear threat, unchecked military power, and an almost messianic world view in Washington meant that the small remote-control interventions of the 1990s were replaced by two massive yet reckless ground campaigns that overstretched the military capabilities of the United States and its allies. In many parts of the world, not least in the Middle East, the United States, not the terrorists, were perceived as rogue. The Western world also fissured internally.

On top of the internal social and economic problems came growing tensions between Europe and the United States. The two, for instance, bickered over the importance of international organizations. Inside these institutions, Western leadership retreated further, in the financial institutions, and in the forums on trade. Trade policy was so heedless that it left the way open for key competitors, like China, to step in. Western capitals once again pondered measures to prevent authoritarian countries from turning low social and environmental standards into a competitive advantage, but desisted from implementing them. As a result, globalization helped make authoritarian countries rich. Western policy was about growing its consumerism to the limits, and the authoritarian countries ruthlessly seized it as an opportunity to grow their power.

Hubris

Western foreign policy in the 1990s was characterized by remote-control interventionism. It remained interventionist in the following decade. What became different, however, was that the capitals now stressed the fight against evil instead of the fight for justice. Interventionism also became more assertive. Officials spoke of the need for regime change and preventive war, or the capability to counter threats before they became imminent. The most important difference concerned the magnitude of the interventions. Consider the last years of the Clinton administration. In 2000, around 80,000 American soldiers were involved in operations in 12 countries. In the following years, the number of soldiers deployed in overseas operations was about 200,000.[2] The cost of these missions inevitably increased. Not least the human cost. During the 1990s, 208 American soldiers died in combat. Given the focus on missile and air strikes, there were fewer boots on the ground and hence fewer casualties. In the following decade, between 2000 and 2009, the missiles still flew, but the deployment of large numbers of ground troops cost the lives of 4,632 soldiers.[3] About US\$110 billion was spent on foreign operations, US\$110 billion each year.[4] As a share of the American economy, military expenditure grew from 4 to 6 percent. The theaters of these operations were the areas the most remote from the American continent: the Middle East and Central Asia. American troops could not be farther from home.

"Write this down," President George W. Bush said. "Afghanistan and Iraq will lead that part of the world to democracy."[5] The new stage of robust interventionism was not the result of a new grand vision. It was the result of political miscalculation, mission creep, and hubris. After the terrorist attacks, the Pentagon first proposed to launch distant strikes, followed by small teams of special forces that would hunt down the terrorists, and finally to deploy an international stabilization force. In any case, the military did not want to become drawn into the kind of exhausting ground war that had exhausted the Soviet Union in the 1980s.

When the military operation in Afghanistan started, in October 2001, four aircraft carriers, hundreds of advanced aircraft, and about 10,000 ground troops engaged about 50,000 Afghani fighters that were mostly equipped with horses, Kalashnikovs, and rocket-propelled grenades. But it was not clear what victory would mean. Was it about killing the terrorist leaders? Defeating Al-Qaeda, the Taliban? Restoring order in the country? Western forces attacked stronghold after stronghold. Some of their adversaries retreated across the porous border with Pakistan; others blended back into the villages as civilians. They changed their black turbans for white ones, biding their time to strike back. By December 2001, the American defense minister imagined the war to be over and asked for advice on how to preserve presence afterwards.[6]

While some American elite troops were withdrawn, the mission in Afghanistan widened. An international conference in Bonn stated the objective of rebuilding the state. If Washington reiterated that it did not want to engage in a grinding stabilization mission, more and more of its troops were used to support the feeble government that was installed in the capital Kabul. More and more American troops were also assigned to the International Security Assistance Force, ISAF, and this stabilization mission ventured further and further from Kabul.[7]

Unsettled by the first campaigns, the Taliban commenced a counter-offensive using improvised explosives, quick raids, and attacks under the cover of night. In 2003, violence started to spread throughout the country.[8] Northern warlords, who were supposed to fight on the side of the coalition, attacked each other. The mayhem made it easier for the Taliban to find more new recruits than ever before. The United States also deployed in Pakistan, but was unable to gain the full cooperation of the Pakistani military and to oversee the mountainous frontier province.

Before the United States went to war in Afghanistan, the entourage of George W. Bush had set its sights on another country: Iraq. Senior officials found that President Clinton had been too soft on the Iraqi leader Saddam Hussein and not exhausted the mandate given by the Iraq Liberation Act of 1998 to topple the strongman. A first motivation of the Bush team was political: to show that the new president had more courage. It reflected the agenda of a group of neoconservative thinkers that made it to the inner core of the Bush administration and despised faint-hearted humanitarianism. Their main concern: reassert American preponderance.[9] "We are an empire now, and when we act, we create our own reality," a Bush aide was reported bragging. "And while you are studying that reality, judiciously, as you will, we will act again, creating other new realities, which you can study too, and that's how things will sort out. We are history's actors and you, all of you, will be left to just study what we do."[10]

President Bush himself was said to be more ideological than his predecessor, quicker to anger, and less given to shades of gray.[11] So, more black versus white. Like President Ronald Reagan in the 1980s, Bush and his collaborators divided the world into good and evil.[12] This political calculus was supported by strategic arguments. Saddam Hussein, they thought, might pass weapons of mass destruction to terrorists. He might develop nuclear weapons which would make it harder to confront him at a later stage.[13] The elimination of the Iraqi threat could also permit the United States to lower its costly military presence in the region.[14] There was a very strong ideological, political, and strategic push for war and regime change. By the summer of 2001, President Bush agreed that Iraq had to be liberated. The only opponent inside the government was the Secretary of State. The terrorist attacks strengthened the hawks in their conviction that Saddam had to go. The initial success in pushing back the Taliban also strengthened it in the conviction that a shock and awe intervention would make the war in Iraq short and effective.

It was the political elite that wished to go into Iraq, not the military. Pentagon reports stated that a war against Saddam Hussein could be won, but that his army should not be underestimated, and that the stabilization efforts would be immense. The military said that the vision of the politicians required half a million of troops and long-lasting presence for stabilization. The defense minister demanded this be reduced. So, the initial deployment would number around 180,000 troops. "Do not attack Saddam," a former senior official wrote. "There would be an explosion of outrage against us, . . . the results could well destabilize Arab regimes . . . and could even swell the ranks of the terrorists."[15]

As the generals were commanded to make ready their plans, the civilians in the administration tried to convince the international community of the threat of weapons of mass destruction. "We don't want the smoking gun to be a mushroom cloud," said the national security advisor.[16] "Simply stated, there is no doubt that Saddam Hussein now has weapons of mass destruction," stated the vice-president.[17] Most countries were unconvinced. European allies refused to join. Major powers like China, India, and Russia opposed it. In early 2003, the sole senior official that was skeptical of the war plans, Secretary of State Colin Powell, was sent to the UN Security Council with false intelligence about biological and chemical weapons. Even without the backing of the United Nations, Washington resolved on going to war. In March 2003, it began. Baghdad fell in less than three weeks. "Mission accomplished," the president proclaimed on board an aircraft carrier.[18]

The fight in Iraq and Afghanistan only hardened. At the moment that the Taliban launched a counteroffensive in Afghanistan, a bout of violence erupted in Iraq: an endless sequence of suicide bombings and reprisals. Thousands of soldiers from Saddam Hussein's army, predominantly Sunnis, were sacked by the allied forces. Aggrieved and impoverished, they used their weapons to survive and resist. Many joined terrorist movements, like Al-Qaeda. In both countries, insurgents mutilated and massacred civilians that refused to cooperate. They attacked Red Cross hospitals. Several foreign prisoners of war were tortured to death.

This could still be explained as a campaign of intimidation to expel a superior foreign invader. More difficult to explain for the Western countries that promised justice and liberation were the photographs that emanated from Guantanamo Bay: lines of suspected terrorists, blindfolded and kneeling in orange jumpsuits. Or the pictures from the Abu Ghraib Prison with American soldiers posing thumbs up next to a killed captive, a pyramid of naked Iraqis, and a naked inmate on a leash. These images destroyed whatever was left of the promise to bring justice. The more Iraqis and Afghani turned against the West, the more the coalition made use of drones, private security companies, aggressive nightly searches, and intimidating fortresses on wheels, like the Cougar, an infantry vehicle weighing 14 tons. If the idea was to win the hearts and minds, instead it harvested fear and aversion.

In both Iraq and Afghanistan citizens wanted the foreigners out. Fundamentalism and terrorism became a way to resist Western oppressors and at the same time a guise to make money in a warzone. Throughout the Middle East and the Islamic world, perceptions of the West became very negative. Al-Qaeda and the Taliban recruited record numbers and inspired radicals across the globe.[19] New attacks, like in Madrid in 2004, in London in 2005, and in Mumbai in 2008, confirmed that the war against terrorism was not won. Countries that had supported the United States faced a popular backlash. The Pakistani military came to see Washington as arrogant, interested only in saving its face in Afghanistan. Turkey saw a surge of popular anti-Americanism and its politicians loathed Washington's lack of understanding of its fear of a Greater Kurdistan. Saudi Arabia, which had opposed the invasion of Iraq from the beginning, complained that America allowed the Shias in Iraq to be used as proxies by its rival, Iran. The fallout of the two failing interventions came on top of the existing frustration at American support for Israel and its new hard-line Prime Minister, Benjamin Netanyahu. America was losing its wars, it was losing money, and it was losing the Middle East.

The interventions did not bring democracy either. In 2004, the first presidential elections were held in Afghanistan. The Western-backed candidate won with slightly more than half of the votes and almost no backing from Uzbek and Tajik minorities. The next presidential ballot in 2009 showed that public support had further dissipated. Parliament became just a new battleground for the habitual warlords. In Iraq, parliamentary elections were held in 2005.[20] They also displayed the internal tensions that Saddam Hussein had suppressed, divisions between the Shia majority and the Sunnis, the tension between the central government and the secessionist aspirations of the Kurds in the north, and the centrifugal forces of a society that was still dominated by clans and tribes.

The generals in Washington realized that they were more hated than Saddam Hussein or the Taliban. The Pentagon tried to correct this.[21] General David Petraeus ordered his troops to put the local population first, to get out of their fortresses, and to patrol on foot. "Living among the people is essential to securing them and defeating the insurgents."[22] Anthropologists were hired to help the soldiers understand culture and customs. This counterinsurgency required more troops. But the damage was done and the military was already overstretched. In 2006 alone, the two wars cost US$120 billion. Ships, aircraft, and other vehicles had to be diverted from the Asia-Pacific, where China became more assertive. Almost all combat units were deployed.[23] Half of the American soldiers rated their morale as low and complained about exceedingly long tours. Recruitment standards were lowered to keep the units filled.

The majority of Americans thought the Iraq War to be a mistake. The new stage of interventionism was also entirely at loggerheads with the main concern of the neoconservatives: to maximize American power. In such logic, one would expect wars to pay for themselves, the resources of these countries to be claimed. But whereas Washington spent billions on the war, much of the Iraqi oil and the Afghani minerals were taken by competitors. China came to control most of the biggest oilfields in Iraq and the largest copper mine in Afghanistan. The neoconservatives, in a way, had enough arrogance to start a war, not to profit from it. In 2009, while the government was reaching out to China, Iran, and Russia, the Iraqi parliament voted in law that instructed the coalition to leave within two years. Most disturbing of all, the mastermind of the terrorist attacks, Osama Bin Laden, was still not caught. The invasion of Afghanistan became the biggest, the most expensive, and the most disappointing manhunt in history.

Chocolate makers

Two unsuccessful wars damaged the image and position of the West in the world. The growing rift between the two sides of the Atlantic about how to handle world affairs and the fraying of multilateralism came on top of that. The United States and European powers diverged on whether or not to intervene in Iraq, as well as on the role of international organizations in addressing global challenges. Often, it looked like a clash between Mars and Venus, between unilateralism and multilateralism.[24] Despite its criticism of American unilateralism and frustration about America assertively throwing its military might around, Europe failed to become a strong international actor in its own right. The intention to become less dependent on America's military power did not materialize. The aspiration to become a normative power was equally defied.

In 2001, when the United States started its retaliation against Al-Qaeda in Afghanistan, it received sympathy and support. Russia, for instance, opened its airspace to American military aircraft. China promised to cooperate. The coalition in Afghanistan mustered troop contributions from 60 nations. Two years later, Washington had squandered all that credit. When it invaded Iraq, only three countries joined: the United Kingdom, Poland, and, reluctantly, Australia. America became a lone superpower. The transatlantic partnership was dealt a serious blow too. Whatever European capital President George W. Bush visited, he encountered protests. France and Germany led the European resistance against American unilateralism. Besides the partnership with the United States, Europe built alternative strategic partnerships with China, Russia, Japan, and other regional powers. Paris and Berlin openly advocated a multipolar world, hence ending the role of America as the sole superpower. Europe emphasized the importance of international rules, multilateralism, and respect for common values. If the world had become a global village, its two most notable inhabitants were caught fighting in plain sight.

The European Union repeatedly stressed the importance of international organizations. In contrast, the neoconservatives in Washington deliberately sought to upend them. Why would a superpower let itself be tied like a Gulliver to rules and institutions? To the Clinton administration, international organizations were useful, because they helped radiate influence, bolster American legitimacy as the policeman of the world, and make the world more predictable. Less so thus in the case of the Bush administration, which found that other countries benefited disproportionately and limited America's freedom of action. Consider the Kyoto Protocol, signed in 1997 to curb the emission of greenhouse gases. The American Senate never ratified it and the Bush Presidency abandoned it altogether. "A treaty that does not include China and exempts developing countries from tough standards while penalizing American industry cannot possibly be in America's national interest."[25] In 2001, it departed from the Anti-Ballistic Missile Treaty. "It hinders our government's ability to develop ways to protect our people from future terrorist or rogue state missile attacks."[26] In 2002, it refused to join the International Criminal Court, because it feared prosecution of American soldiers abroad. The same year, it withdrew support for the United Nations Population Fund because of its position on abortion. In 2004, Washington assigned a new ambassador to the United Nations who had attacked its very relevance. "There is no such thing as the United Nations," he had written. "There is an international community that occasionally can be led by the only real power left in the world and that is the United States."[27] America attacked its position at the center of global governance.

As a result of the friction, several European countries wanted to rebalance the transatlantic partnership. France, Germany, and some smaller member states proposed that the European Union should establish a more ambitious defense policy. In 2002, Europe threw its weight behind discussions about the responsibility to protect, R2P, a concept that was to empower the United Nations in peacemaking and replace the unilateralist right to intervene. In 2003, the European Union issued its first common security strategy, titled "A Secure Europe in a Better World."[28] Its aim was to offer an alternative to America's fixation with hard military power and unilateralism. It read:

> Our security and prosperity increasingly depend on an effective multilateral system. The Union aims to develop a stronger international society, well-functioning international institutions . . . and a rule-based international order. The best protection for our security is a world of well-governed democratic States.

"Chocolate makers," the Americans chided at the Europeans, skeptical that the ambitions on paper would materialize. They were right. Europe established joint battle groups, but they were never deployed. It vowed to set up an independent military command, but it never became operational. It also promised to reduce its reliance on the United States, but European defense spending dropped. There were some joint projects to develop defense systems, but member states continued to defend their own defense industries. Most of all, there was no common vision about security interests, threats, priorities, and approaches, so that many European countries continued to follow the lead of the United States, deeper into the quagmire of Afghanistan, and, after a while, also into the quicksand of Iraq. Europe remained a military midget.

Also as a civilian power, Europe staggered. The idea at the core of its common foreign policy was to promote peace and prosperity through Europeanization, the creation of a sphere of values. This had happened primarily through enlargement. Candidate members, as we have seen, had to subscribe to numerous rules. Accession negotiations were opened with Turkey and Macedonia; Serbia, Montenegro, and Albania were ready to follow. The sphere of Europeanization that followed consisted of looser association agreements in which trade with the European market came with clauses on human rights and democracy.[29] By 2009, Europe had signed 12 such agreements. Trade advanced, political values less so. There were successes. Morocco, instigated by Europe, modernized its prisons. Tiny Moldova signed up to an action plan on human rights.

But political conditions were hardly enforced. Egyptian strongman Hosni Mubarak was one of the main recipients of aid. His neighbor, Muammar Gaddafi, flanked by female bodyguards, was welcomed to pitch his Bedouin tent in Brussels and Rome. Member states prioritized exports to their weaker neighbors, refused to coordinate at European level on matters like investment and development aid. Common European foreign policy was common in name only. At critical moments, it was still the United States that stepped into the limelight. During Georgia's Rose Revolution in 2003, American flags were flying over the masses of protesters. The same was true during the Ukrainian Orange Revolution of 2004. While America was seen as the liberator, Germany was showing sympathy for Moscow's line that the West had to stay out. In the escalating tensions between Israel and Palestine, Europe had no weight to throw onto the scales.

Antagonized by American arrogance, Europe pretended to put itself on a moral high ground, but its foreign policy remained opportunistic. It included human rights clauses in cooperation agreements, but seldom acted upon them. What was more: it actively reached out to human rights abusers to invest. London became a magnet for authoritarian countries. Governments were aware of it, tolerated it, and even encouraged it. British Prime Minister Tony Blair cut capital gains taxes to attract foreign capital. "The new world rewards those who are open to it," he claimed. "Foreign investment improves our economy."[30] The mayor of London wheedled money out of the Gulf States to build a new airport on platforms in the Thames Estuary, and Chinese investors were invited to discover London as their gateway to Europe. Russian oligarchs were among the first to discover London as a safe haven and spent on expensive real estate. British football became a playground for sponsors from authoritarian countries. A Russian oligarch bought Chelsea, a Thai billionaire close to the King bought Leicester, and a prince from the Emirates acquired Manchester City. The United Arab Emirates became a financer of the London School of Economics and a member of Saudi Arabia's ruling family financed an Islamic studies center at Cambridge. British auction houses sold European antique treasures to wealthy billionaires from Asia by the container load. "Thank you for reminding me about Christie's," the Emir of Qatar reportedly said to the British Queen during a state visit. One Qatari sheikh spent one billion dollars in a single year.[31] Business first, Prime Minister Blair thought, when he broke the law by abandoning an investigation into a large business fraud with Saudi Arabia.[32]

London built itself the reputation of an economic brothel, not only for oligarchs and princes, but also for shadowy firms for whom the lax solvency laws were an opportunity to borrow large sums and then to declare bankruptcy. When *The Times* of London was censored in the Emirates for criticizing the royal family, there was no political response. Other European countries too scrambled for investment. Paris and the French Riviera were real estate hunting grounds for the wealthy from the Gulf. Germany attracted interest in its manufacturing sectors. Qatar, for instance, bought for US$7 billion shares in the German car builder Porsche. As tensions with Washington grew and as the transatlantic partnership eroded, Europe fell short of becoming an independent international actor. As a military power, it remained feeble. As a normative power, it was unconvincing.

Checkbook

Europe and the United States were increasingly at loggerheads about the importance of international organizations. Washington's penchant for unilateralism became visible, for example, with regard to the International Criminal Court and conventions on arms limitations. At the same time, it hesitated to support the reform of international financial institutions. The reputation of the International Monetary Fund and the World Bank was tainted by the financial crises in Mexico, Russia, and Asia. They became seen as an instrument to rescue Western investors, rather than to stabilize countries. The moral hazard was also recognized by American officials: as long as governments rescued speculators when their self-created bubbles imploded, private investors would take larger risks.

To many, the erosion of American financial leadership had already started in the 1960s, when Washington had to ask its allies, for the first time, to support the dollar as the global reserve currency, and it was further expedited by the decision in the early 1970s to stop backing the dollar with a fixed amount of gold. The crumbling continued in the 1980s, when the United States started running trade deficits, and in the 1990s, when these trade deficits were allowed to grow rapidly. Until then, however, there were no rivals to the dollar as the American reserve currency or to the most important international financial institutions. That changed. If at the beginning of the decade the American leadership of the global financial order was mostly criticized, some first steps were now taken to end it.

The world's most important financial institution was still the American Treasury, responsible for the finance of the world's biggest market. The Treasury could leverage its power through three important international organizations: the International Monetary Fund, the World Bank, and the Inter-American Development Bank. In all cases, the United States provided a small part of the capital, between 16 and 30 percent, while the numerous other members delivered the bulk. Still, it retained political control. In the World Bank and the International Monetary Fund, for instance, the board of governors can only make a decision with 85 percent of the votes. The United States held above 16 percent of the voting rights and thus could veto decisions. But the Fund and the Bank lost influence.

Even support from the United States was lukewarm. When the Clinton administration asked for additional capital to allow the International Monetary Fund to respond to the financial instability in Asia, he came under criticism from Congress. A report to Congress described the Fund as slow, costly, and prone to poor judgment in its habit of spending much on emerging powers like China. It proposed that the Fund's activities be scaled back. The Treasury disagreed and said it would "weaken the international financial institutions' capacity to promote central U.S. interests."[33] The Americans also clashed with some of their allies. In 2000, it ignored calls from Canada to allow the International Monetary Fund to reduce the negative impact of globalization and to involve civil society. It also refused to consider Europe's candidate for a new managing director position and suggested that European countries were overrepresented.

A broad movement now took issue with the policies of the Fund and the Bank. What stoked their anger was the decision of the World Bank to censor an internal study, the Kandur Report, that proposed to shift the focus from promoting growth to social corrections. To activists, it confirmed the bank's intransigence. A year earlier, its chief economist was forced to resign because of his criticism of the Washington Consensus. His colleagues retorted that the proposal for more social care was like peddling snake oil.[34] The G-77, a movement of the world's poorest countries, stated that the West was using the financial institutions for security purposes, in Iraq, and in the war against terror, not to alleviate debt and poverty.[35] "The centrifugal force in the IMF will become increasingly strong," warned a Chinese policy advisor. "The emergence of a tripartite world economic structure is inevitable."[36]

Washington promised reform, yet with the objective of minimizing it. The Treasury vowed that East Asian countries would get a greater say in the Fund.[37] At the same time, however, it stated that rather than giving more authority to China, the Fund had the responsibility to make such countries stop devaluing their currency. Showcasing the tensions inside the Fund, its analysts released a report that found the overpricing of the dollar and growing American external debt to be a bigger problem than the undervaluing of the Chinese yuan. It claimed that the Fund had to get back to its core mission of preserving financial stability. Still, the poverty reduction and growth mission were upgraded with a policy support instrument that guided the poorest countries' economic policy. Some developing countries were allowed to increase their voting rights, but this change was merely cosmetic.

The adjustment of the Bretton Woods institutions stalled. But the world moved on. While the external debt of the West grew, Thailand paid its loans back to the International Monetary Fund, ahead of schedule. Indonesia, Brazil, Argentina, and Russia followed. Some of these countries had benefited from surging commodity prices. There were also alternative lenders. By 2005, several emerging countries were hoarding huge reserves of dollars and euros. These foreign exchange reserves could be accumulated because they exported more to the West than they imported. Islamic investment funds, for instance, were worth US$800 billion by 2009. While the external debt of countries like the United States and the United Kingdom surged, China's net foreign international investment position grew from US$146 billion in 2000 to US$1.7 trillion in 2009 (figure 8.1). The World Bank and the International Monetary Fund combined had a portfolio of around US$400 billion. By 2006, the China Development Bank had lent more abroad than the World Bank.

One of the instant consequences was that Angola severed its cooperation with these institutions soon after it inked a multibillion credit scheme with China. Contrarily to the traditional Western demands for economic liberalization, China offered loans with mostly commercial strings attached: Chinese credit to buy Chinese products. Apart from demanding that borrowers sever ties with Taiwan, political demands with regard to human rights were absent. After the outbreak of the financial crisis of 2009, China offered affected European countries like Greece a lifeline. "We will continue to provide aid and help certain countries overcome their difficulties," said the Chinese prime minister.

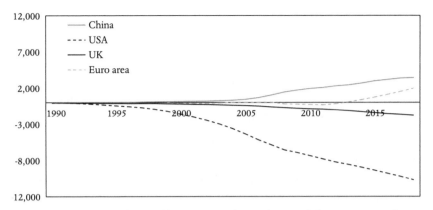

Figure 8.1 Lenders and borrowers: The evolution of the international investment position of the US, China, the UK, and the Eurozone (US$ tn)
Source: WDI.

The United States understood the challenge and upped the game. It asked its partners to triple the resources of the International Monetary Fund and committed US$100 billion itself. The Fund survived and was set to continue to play an important role as a lender of last resort. Still, again, China became crucially important as a quiet buyer of government bonds. As a large developing country, it reasoned, it could contribute only modestly to the International Monetary Fund. But it also felt that it had the responsibility to urge on behalf of weaker countries for adjustment: "The global financial architecture should represent the changing economic geography."[38] Beijing proposed that the dollar should be replaced by a basket of currencies, of which the Chinese yuan would be a part. China showed itself ready to support the reform of international financial institutions, if the United States gave up its leadership. Taking for granted that this would not yet happen inside the institutions, China kept stepping up its own financial engagement outside the institutions and pledged billions of dollars of credit to other countries. China's checkbook diplomacy quietly altered the global balance of power.

World trade

The intervention in Iraq, American unilateralism, the rift between the United States and the European Union, and the unwillingness to reform the world's financial architecture despite the steady loss of economic power all contributed to the discrediting of the West and the resentment in other parts of the world. It was not always clear what instigated the intransigence, especially from the side of the United States. The refusal to reform international financial institutions could be considered an attempt to defend global leadership and to preserve the position of the dollar as reserve currency. But this leadership was put more at risk by America's growing external debt, the incapacity to prevent internal financial crises, and the ineffective response to Western speculators on the global market. The leadership of the West was challenged primarily by its own policies. The same was true for trade policy. The focus of the United States and the European Union appeared to be to gain access to developing markets, to cheap goods and energy, and not to create a market space that encouraged their companies to invest in a more innovative and sustainable economy at home. Hence the chasm between the emphasis put on environment and labor rights in official discourses and the reluctance to tie them to trade rules in practice.

For developing countries like South Korea and China, the purpose of economic policy was clear: to raise incomes and to do so by growing a strong, productive manufacturing sector. In the short term, basic industries like textiles and the assembling of electronics would allow millions of workers to be employed. In the long run, the idea was to use cheap labor, raw materials, and capital to build advanced production chains. The production of basic goods, like textile and household electronics, would pave the way for advanced systems, like machines and planes, and onwards toward even more advanced components, like computer chips, or business services. This was in essence what Japan had achieved in the 1980s and Western countries had earlier on.

Other developing countries were less explicit in their goals. India, for instance, still had high hopes for its information technology. China could do the manufacturing, India the services. Developed countries were at an even greater loss about the future of their economies. Large companies often chose to build their factories in China, others to limit their activity in the West to complex components, design, scientific research, and marketing. Consider branded sports shoes: labor in Asia represented less than 5 percent of their price; design and marketing over 30 percent. In the international supply chains, many thought it was sufficient for the West to preserve the lucrative parts.

This had important consequences for global trade. The newly industrializing East Asian economies had one firm interest: to be able to export industrial goods to the rich Western markets. If they wanted the West to keep their markets open for goods, the Asian manufacturers themselves were reluctant to open theirs. In manufacturing sectors where they stood strong, borders slowly opened. But in sectors where they felt weak, foreign investors were forced to share their technology, to accept minority positions in joint ventures, to tolerate financial support for domestic competitors, and to see those same domestic firms receive privileged treatment in government procurement. In strategic sectors, like finance and telecommunications, the access to foreign providers was kept to a minimum. Opening up was acceptable, but only when domestic firms were competitive enough. Other developing countries tried to follow that example. In Africa, for instance, countries now more frequently demanded raw materials to be produced domestically. India and Brazil also had plans to nurture domestic industrial giants.

For Western countries, the United States and the United Kingdom to the fore, defending the domestic industrial sector was less a priority. Instead, the most important objectives in terms of trade were still the liberalization of services, investment, information technology, as well as the protection of intellectual property. This was in line with what the tech-multinationals from around the San Francisco Bay area or Munich had in mind. Sectors like steel, textiles, and furniture were protected occasionally, but became perceived by many policy makers as sunset industries, old industries that had to be replaced by other activities, like services. Neither were Western trade officials fond of agriculture. That sector, however, remained politically too important to ignore. The fixation of the West with technology, services, and consumption, and the preoccupation of China with export and industry, seemed a perfect fit. If the developing countries in between could grow their niches, like energy, agribusiness, and some services, world trade could only continue to grow. It was like the old ideal of David Ricardo becoming reality: to advance trade and progress through a mutually beneficial division of labor.

To do so, the world needed a new multilateral trade pact. A hopeful signal was that China had joined the World Trade Organization in 2001. For Beijing, it meant access; the West could explain it as China's readiness to embrace trade liberalization. Still, more was to happen. "Too much of this century was marked by force and coercion," explained the Director–General of the World Trade Organization. "Our dream must be a world managed by persuasion, the rule of law, the settlement of differences peacefully within the law and cooperation." In Washington, it was said that a new multilateral trade system was the only right answer to the terrorist attack on freedom and on unbridled bilateralism.[39] Even the Cuban leader Fidel Castro proclaimed that a stronger World Trade Organization could be "an instrument of the struggle for a more just and better world."[40] And so the world prepared for important negotiations. The Doha Round started in 2001, but important fault lines became clear: the developing world found that the West had to go further in dismantling support for agriculture, which hurt their farmers. The West was displeased with the lack of willingness of developing countries to sign up to intellectual property rights protection and services liberalization. In follow-up meetings in Cancun, Paris, and Geneva, talks collapsed, were revived, and collapsed yet again.

Strikingly modest in this Doha Round was the attention to environmental and social standards. The United States and the European Union did suggest integrating environmental and social standards into trade rules. Both in Washington and in Brussels there was interest in enforcing the standards of the International Labour Organization, ILO. These related to the freedom of association, the abolition of child labor, and the elimination of discrimination at work. Yet, compared to the liberalization of services, these issues were less important. That, in combination with skepticism among developing countries, meant that the discussions were delegated by the ministers to technical working groups, where they faded.

Officials at the World Trade Organization, as well as developing countries, argued that such social and environmental rules could lead to protectionism. The WTO had criticized initiatives of Western countries to introduce a social label for products, judging that it could be a technical barrier.[41] Previously the organization also ruled that trade trumped environmental concerns. The European Union, for example, was faulted for banning beef treated with growth hormones. The United States was condemned for banning tuna that was caught with fishing nets that also unintentionally caught dolphins, and for banning shrimps caught in a way that endangered sea turtles. Each time, the explanation was that such measures were discriminating.

In the international negotiations about trade, an alliance of developing countries and multinationals successfully resisted efforts to tie trade rules to social and environmental standards. The Western countries preferred not to let world trade negotiations be derailed over these issues. They did, however, pursue the linking of trade and different standards in bilateral agreements. In 2000, for instance, the European Union agreed with African and Caribbean countries, the so-called ACP group, to recognize key labor standards in a cooperation agreement. The United States did the same in agreements with Chile, Singapore, and Peru. They provided sanctions should a party not respect the rights at work of the International Labour Organization. In 2006, the European Union negotiated an agreement with several Caribbean states that included the participation of civil society to verify the respect of labor standards. In 2007, the Democratic and Republican parties endorsed a bill that required all pending free trade agreements to include enforceable labor and environmental standards.

This combative approach, however, masked a more complicated reality. The United States did indeed pressure partners to include social and environmental standards in trade agreements, but also insisted on a dispute settlement mechanism of the World Trade Organization that had frequently favored American investors when they filed a complaint against local environmental and social regulations that affected their profits. So, on the one hand, politicians claimed that they wanted to protect the American market from social and environmental dumping. On the other hand, the clauses on investment protection and dispute settlement deterred poor countries from issuing measures to protect the environment and social safety.

America wanted to have it both ways. Moreover, the advanced free trade agreements, which included the social and environmental clauses, were not signed with the main trade partners, like China and India. The majority of the ambitious treaties were signed with countries that had only modest trade relations with the West. The situation could become even more controversial. In 2006, China started revising its labor law. The draft law limited the use of temporary contract workers and also wanted the labor unions to have a bigger say. Walmart, Ikea, Nike, and many other multinationals fiercely lobbied against this law. They threatened to relocate their production to other countries.

As world trade negotiations ground to a halt, the debate about trade and the environment rekindled. In 2009, a bill was proposed in the American Congress to impose green border taxes. The European Commission, supported by member states like France, also proposed a carbon tax on imports from countries that did not have similar restrictions on carbon emissions. There were two important motivations for carbon border taxes. A first reason was that globalization could not be truly efficient if the price of products and services did not account for external costs like pollution. What was the use of cheap products if the whole world faced massive indirect costs from global warming? Another reason was that lax carbon emission laws gave an unfair advantage. As long as cheap yet polluting products and services were allowed, companies would not have an incentive to become greener. For now, however, the debate did not lead to concrete measures. In the case of the United States, it was difficult to reconcile carbon taxes on the border with its refusal to ratify the Kyoto Protocol. In the case of the European Union, the proposal caused internal division, including inside the European Commission. The Trade Commissioner explained that carbon taxes could lead to trade disputes.

Inconsistency characterized the Western position during the global trade talks. Throughout, countries like India and Brazil had led a large group of developing countries against the West. China, for now not really interested in agriculture and services, preferred to remain in the background. It also kept a middle ground between developed and developing countries. At certain moments, it insisted that the West had to come forward. "We already made a lot of compromises to join the World Trade Organization," a Chinese official stated. "It is up to the developed countries now to show goodwill."[42] At other moments, it differentiated itself from the poor ones: "The World Trade Organization is very important in getting access for our manufacturers to important export markets," a Chinese official of the Ministry of Commerce explained. "We do not want to give an advantage to our competitors from the developing world. Imagine that countries like India or Vietnam are allowed to protect their industries while we are not. That would be a threat to our development. We are happy with the rules as they exist."[43]

During the Doha Round, China had been targeted by trade measures from the United States, the European Union, India, and different other countries. It was accused of currency manipulation and dumping. Still, the existing state of world trade allowed it to realize its goals. Since the start of the Doha Round, Chinese exports to the West have grown threefold. Its share in the total imports of the West grew from 10 to 22 percent. It became the third largest manufacturing power, just after the United States. China, too, got it both ways. While it restricted access to foreign investors and forced them to share technology, it had almost unlimited access to Western markets. The West saw this imbalance and lack of reciprocity. The American government restated its hope for China to become a responsible stakeholder in the international trade system, but refrained from confrontation. A document from the European Commission from 2006 criticized China's intellectual property rights policies, the investment climate and forced technology transfer, but remained hopeful that those issues could be settled through dialogue.[44] During the crisis of 2009, China even tried to transform its image of rogue trader into an image of benefactor. In February 2009, its commerce minister took off for a so-called buying mission to Germany, Spain, and the UK, with hundreds of businessmen in his wake.

Cookie cutter

Asked by a journalist why human rights were highlighted in the relations with Cuba and not with China, Secretary of State Madeleine Albright explained: "We do not have a cookie-cutter approach to policy." She continued: "China is a huge and vastly important country and will be even more so to the United States."[45] It was a clear recognition of the double standards in American foreign policy. The neoconservatives in the administration of George W. Bush presented the defense of democracy as a sacred task and insisted that the United States had to preserve the power to defend its values. Like with the Clinton administration, though, there was a chasm between words and deeds. It was visible in the Middle East. In the wake of another invasion of Iraq, Washington granted unprecedented aid to authoritarian countries. Consider Saudi Arabia. The State Department reported human rights abuses, impunity on the part of the religious police, denial of public trials, and the lack of freedom of speech.[46] Despite all these issues, the United States remained the most important security provider to the regime in Riyadh.

Or consider China. The Bush administration expressed its hope for China to become a responsible stakeholder. This implied that the country would pursue economic openness and gradual democratization, which would have been in line with Beijing's commitment when joining the WTO. "Chinese leaders have decided that their success depends on being networked with the modern world," it was stated.[47] In terms of trade, however, it became clear that China's interpretation of being networked with the world implied Chinese companies controlling the networks and the state playing an important role in making that happen. China thus became part of the international community, but not integrated. In terms of political reform, the State Department was clear. "The government's human rights record remained poor, and the government continued to commit numerous and serious abuses," it reported. "There was a trend toward increased harassment, detention, and imprisonment by government and security authorities of those perceived as threatening to government authority."[48] The European institutions, too, remained critical of China's human rights record, suggesting that the United States and the EU converged in their assessment of China's defiant attitude.

In the 1990s, it became clear that Western partnerships with authoritarian countries mostly strengthened the position of the latter, and hardly resulted in progress regarding political reform. During the subsequent decade, these partnerships became more unbalanced. For the corporate world, however, the lure of doing business was too powerful. Said the CEO of General Electric: "When I am talking to GE managers, I talk China, China, China, China, China. You need to be there. You need to change the way people talk about it and how they get there. I am a nut on China." He continued: "Every discussion today has to center on China. The cost basis is extremely attractive. You can take an 18 cubic foot refrigerator, make it in China, land it in the United States, and land it for less than we can make an 18 cubic foot refrigerator today, ourselves."[49] Hence, the West continued to make authoritarian countries strong, weakening its own position. Between 2000 and 2009, the share of authoritarian countries in Western imports grew from 29 to 45 percent. Imports from China contributed the most to this shift, followed by growing imports of energy from the Middle East.

CHAPTER 9

GLOBALIZATION AND THE RETURN OF POWER POLITICS

THE PERIOD BETWEEN 2000 AND 2009 WAS THE HIGH AGE OF globalization. Globalization meant the growth of trade, capital movements, migration, and the exchange of knowledge. Despite the financial crises of the late 1990s and the subsequent Dotcom bubble burst, trade grew and tariffs fell. It confirmed optimists in their conviction that the page of protectionism and nationalism was turned at last. It was a thin line, however, between confidence and, as we saw in the previous chapter, recklessness. Exactly this golden age of global commerce exposed the flaws of several optimistic assumptions. If globalization was expected to lead to cooperation, unilateralism peaked. Strategic distrust and nationalism remained rampant.

Against the decrease of trade tariffs stood various other forms of economic nationalism, like aggressive export promotion and industrial policy. Globalization was said to be a driver of democratization, but authoritarian countries often profited the most and showed no desire to liberalize their political system. Globalization was also reckoned to reduce poverty. Yet, compared to the high growth in trade and production, the reduction of poverty was modest, especially in Africa and South Asia. There was progress, to be sure, but many regions remained much more fragile than in many growth miracle stories.

A first theme in this chapter remains this continuation of the slow sinking of the West. In 2006, in the sidelines of a UN conference, four large countries held a separate meeting. They pledged to a more democratic world order. Democracy in this case was a synonym for multipolarity and thus for ending the unipolar moment of the West. This establishment of BRIC, an abbreviation for Brazil, Russia, India, and China, also confirmed the slow shift in the balance of power. The West, the United States to the fore, remained the largest military spender. Its share in global military spending was 63 percent in 2000 and it was still 63 percent at the end of the decade. The West also remained the largest consumer market, but its share decreased from 61 percent in 2000 to 56 in 2009. Consumption and military spending, though, were less supported by a strong economy. The share of the West in global manufacturing dropped from 50 percent to 43 percent, its share in global exports from 24 to 21 percent. As the West weakened, resentment against it became more vocal. At the Global Millennium Summit in 2000, for example, the West was pilloried for ignoring the poorest countries and failing to show global leadership, and at the World Conference Against Racism in 2001, the West was lambasted for a continuation of colonialism and racism.

The flipside of the weakening of the West concerns the rise of China. BRIC, despite the hype, was largely a raw materials annex to China's industrial ambitions. China's economy grew twice as fast as the others. While China strengthened its industry, the economic role of the other three was confined to the supply of soy, gas, and minerals. China trod carefully. Its aim was not to bluntly attack Western-led globalization; its aim was to exploit globalization in order to catch up with the West. It steadily enmeshed the rest of Asia into a new sphere of influence. China's rise emboldened Russia and India as regional powers, and encouraged many other countries to revise their relations with the West.

A second important theme was the failure to stabilize the Global South. Soaring demand for raw materials brought wealth to developing countries but seldom strengthened their economies for the long run. Meanwhile, population growth remained high, environmental degradation struck hard, and actors from pirates to terrorists exploited this political fragility. In many ways, the decade between 2000 and 2009 was marked by overconfidence about the benefits of globalization. Globalization brought poverty relief, yet not necessarily to the countries that were the most liberal or democratic.

China

On April 1, 2001, an American EP-3 spy plane took off from Okinawa, Japan. Its mission was to gather intelligence above the East China Sea. Mid-air, a Chinese interceptor aircraft passed by at high speed, its pilot rendering a salute to the American visitors. It returned for a second close pass; on a third pass, it slammed into the American plane, and broke into two pieces.[1] Its pilot died. The American patrol aircraft made an emergency landing in China. On the tarmac, its crew frenetically destroyed sensitive material until they were detained. Beijing demanded an apology, which the American government initially refused. Only after ten days did Washington send a letter to apologize for the death of the pilot and for entering into Chinese airspace. It became known as the letter of the two sorries. The American crew was allowed to leave and the patrol aircraft, completely disassembled by Chinese engineers, was returned. The incident confirmed how the relations between China and the West were changing.

At the fundaments of that evolution was China's economic growth. In the 1990s, the Chinese economy expanded by 9 percent annually and that remained so in the following decade. In 2001, China was allowed to enter the World Trade Organization and that made it more appealing to foreign investors. Between 2000 and 2009, China attracted 60 percent of all foreign investment in Asia. Several factors powered the economic miracle. Its population continued to expand and to urbanize. China had hundreds of millions of cheap workers at its disposal. A clever investment strategy attracted foreign technology and tied foreign companies to its economy. The government, too, unleashed a tsunami of investment. At its peak, Chinese investment in infrastructure and machinery grew 30 percent per year. The financial system encouraged families to hoard massive amounts of savings in state banks at low interest rates. This capital was used to build the ports, bridges, factories, and research centers that had to make the economy more productive. It was state capitalism on an unprecedented scale. Finally, China had no peer rivals. Other large developing countries, like India, offered, as we will see, no alternative.

So, when the paramount leader, Jiang Zemin, met with a group of journalists, he showed himself relaxed and confident. He said that there would always be diplomatic tensions, but that China and other countries, despite being thousands of miles apart, could learn to enjoy the beauty of the moon they shared. "People part and meet, they have sorrow and joy, just like the moon that wanes and waxes," he said, quoting an ancient poet. Countries, he continued, had to appreciate differences.[2] China would continue to reform, but adopting Western democracy was not possible. "Should China apply the parliamentary democracy of the Western world," he said, "the result will be great chaos and should that happen it will not be conducive to world peace and stability."[3] Asked why China was banning an American newspaper, he responded that opening up also brought some unhealthy things, that he could not answer the question in detail, but that he thought the paper in question to be "very good." Either way, he added, the West had to try to understand his country better. Jiang's interview showed that China had learned to say "no" politely, to resist without being confrontational.

Jiang spoke of a strategic window of opportunity: the world was open to business with China and made no efforts to check its rise. That window of opportunity had to be fully utilized. China remained a fragile giant and needed more growth. Youngsters no longer wanted to toil like their parents. Citizens demanded cleaner air, more comfortable cities, safer food, and less corruption. Surveys showed that, at the beginning of the decade, only half of the Chinese were satisfied with the economic situation. In 2003, the fourth generation of leaders stepped into the limelight. President Hu Jintao and Premier Wen Jiabao envisioned for their country a harmonious society, or, more equality, innovative industries, sustainable development, and wealth to improve the quality of life.

For the world, the fourth generation of Hu and Wen proclaimed a policy of peaceful development. On the one hand, it held that core interests needed to be articulated: sovereignty, the preservation of the political monopoly of the Communist Party, and the incorporation of lost territory, including Taiwan, the South China Sea, the East China Sea, and some parts on the border with India. On the other hand, it promised to settle conflicts peacefully, to nurture mutually beneficial partnerships, to work through the United Nations, and not to become belligerent. The new foreign policy chief elucidated that the idea of peaceful development showed that the very nature of international politics had changed and that major powers would no longer operate as arrogantly as in the past. Before the United Nations General Assembly, President Hu proposed to create a harmonious world.[4]

That optimism was not entirely genuine. The peaceful development doctrine was riddled with inconsistencies. China presented itself as a satisfied power. Instead of seeking to overthrow the international system, it would seek to change it from inside. At the same time, though, some of its expectations clearly expressed revisionism. Its vision of a multipolar order implied the ending of American dominance and an assault on the bedrock principle in American strategy: security through preponderance. Its expectation that it would make a country of over one billion people rich while all other large developing countries lagged behind implied that China would emerge at least as a hegemon in Asia, eclipsing Japan and others. Despite its discourse, China was a revisionist power by default.

In policy documents, there was also a gap between the stated ideal world of peaceful development and the observation that power politics prevailed in the real world. This ambivalence was exhibited in several ways. After China joined the World Trade Organization, it benefited from the open trade in goods. Its trade surplus with the United States and the European Union alone increased from around US$100 billion in 2000 to over US$500 billion in 2009. The export of goods to the West contributed to its growth. But it refused to liberalize its services market, its government procurement, and its investment rules. China had it both ways: full access to Western markets without giving full access to its own market. It had free trade in its official discourse, economic nationalism in practice.

When win–win cooperation was promised, China wanted to win more, more revenues, more technology transfer, and more market share for its companies. Relative gains trumped absolute gains. As Jiang Zemin had highlighted in the 1990s, the government still wanted to reduce China's dependence on foreign companies and to nurture national champions. Economic liberalization had to remain selective. "Globalization is a double-edged sword," asserted a scholar.[5] In 2005, for instance, it decreed that at least 70 percent of the parts of wind turbines had to be made internally and hence forced European producers to relocate to China. In 2006, the government issued a long-term plan that prioritized indigenous innovation.

In 2007, it changed the rules for the telecom sector so that European companies rapidly lost market share to Chinese competitors. "If there had been no government policy to protect us, we would no longer exist," the founder of the largest telecom company avowed.[6] The outside of China's foreign policy became soft, but inside it remained guided by realist calculations.

A similar ambivalence was displayed in territorial disputes, like about the South China Sea, the East China Sea, and the border with India. China proposed that Japan, India, Vietnam, and the Philippines should shelve territorial disputes and focus on commercial cooperation. While broadening trade relations, it slowly expanded its military presence in contested territory. Thanks to its growing economy, it could afford to invest in modern weaponry. Between 2000 and 2009, China's defense budget grew threefold and became about as large as the defense budget of Japan, South Korea, India, and Taiwan combined. The first modern navy ships and submarines were commissioned. Advanced combat aircraft like the J-10 became operational. China did not refrain from using military force. In 2005, Chinese ships fired on Vietnamese fishing vessels in the South China Sea. Navy ships also started venturing far into the Pacific Ocean and an admiral proposed to the United States that the Pacific be divided into two spheres of influence.

The harmonious world that Hu spoke of was also difficult to reconcile with China's nationalism. In 2005, Beijing issued an anti-secession law that signaled the readiness to use force should Taiwan resist reunification or aim at independence. The same year, the government tolerated an outburst of riots aimed at Japanese companies. Tokyo had approved a textbook that did not acknowledge the Japanese war crimes against China in the early twentieth century. In 2008, China boycotted French companies. French flags were burned. The French government, so it was seen, had shown sympathy to the Tibetan minority and allowed protesters to tarnish the Olympic Games in Beijing when the Olympic torch was walked through Paris. That same year, a military crackdown was launched in Tibet and the year afterwards on the Uyghurs in Xinjiang. "China stand up!" a viral video clip bellowed. A new Cold War rages against China:

Finally, we remind us of Chairman Mao's famous words: the imperialism will never abandon its intention to destroy us . . . After its attack on

Chinese financial institutions, foreign capital begins to control our economy. Foreign hot money rampaged our stock market, drove up the prices, and lured common people to invest. And then it withdrew, and the share prices collapsed. Inflation grew. We work as usual, but our labour was devalued, down to the situation that even pork meat became a luxury. They act evilly in collusion with each other, compelling us to appreciate the renminbi. They buy over dignitaries as their agents, to enslave the Chinese. By money war, they pursue an invisible colonial rob. We provide them with cheap "Made in China" goods, but our people still have a rough time. The buffoon from the southeast [Taiwan] still clamours to separate from China, disregarding its own corruption and China's sense of honour. But the whole world knows who is his employer. Other splittist forces spread [. . .] Obviously, there is a cabal, a cold war against China. Stand up![7]

Bit by bit, China used its economic might to condition partnerships. Poorer countries were promised investment if they shifted diplomatic recognition from Taiwan to the Mainland, opened their market to Chinese goods, and gave access to their raw materials. When the Eurozone crisis started, it pressured weak countries to abandon critical statements about human rights. Beijing also expected them to make a more forceful call in European meetings to end the arms embargo that was still in place since the Tiananmen crackdown. It wanted countries like Greece and Italy to urge the European Commission, responsible for trade, to recognize China as a market economy, so that it would be more difficult to impose trade defense policies. "China makes its power felt," observed a European Commissioner. "If this is only a preview of what pressure we will experience when it gets really powerful; we have a reason to be concerned."[8]

Still, the West kept repeating that it wanted to work with China. "Change is coming," President Bush persisted.[9] The American government pledged to make China a so-called responsible stakeholder, its rising power being tamed by a web of institutions and norms. The European Union insisted on constructive engagement. But how was this tenacity to be reconciled with China's defiance regarding democracy and complete free trade? Its military was still weak and dependent on Russian equipment, but how would it behave in the long run? In 2006, a Chinese submarine surfaced very close to an American aircraft carrier. In March 2009, about eight years after the EP-3 incident, an American surveillance ship was harassed in the East China Sea. These dilemmas were understood. Intelligence services kept writing about the risks. But they were ignored. Trade will keep China a status quo power, an American diplomat maintained in a cable.[10]

Velvet glove imperialism

While China was not yet a global power, it did come forth as Asia's leading power. It replaced Japan as the region's largest investor and overtook Japan as the largest economy (figure 9.1). Beijing responded forcefully to the nationalist policy of the Japanese Prime Minister Junichiro Koizumi, inciting anti-Japanese protests and boycotting Japanese products. In light of China's growing influence, Koizumi had called for an end to some of the limitations on Japan's armed forces that were imposed after World War II. He deployed troops in Iraq and changed the name of the "Defense Agency" to "Ministry of Defense." He agreed to rewrite the constitution so that Japan could deploy its military, now still formally called "Self-Defense Forces," more flexibly. He also allowed the United States to deploy new radar to detect missiles from North Korea and China. His successor, Shinzo Abe, changed track. He highlighted that China had become Japan's

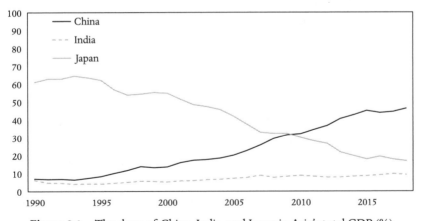

Figure 9.1   The share of China, India, and Japan in Asia's total GDP (%)
Source: WDI.

foremost trading partner, paid his first official visit to China, and urged pragmatism. Abe also considered Chinese support vital to hold North Korea back from developing nuclear weapons. In 2005, Pyongyang proclaimed that it possessed nuclear weapons, conducted a first nuclear test in 2006, and blackmailed the international community to extract aid and recognition. China did facilitate the Six-Party Talks, including also Japan, South Korea, Russia, and the United States. But North Korea held on to its weapons.

The power shift was particularly felt in Southeast Asia. China played the divisions between the countries in the contested South China Sea. Cambodia and Laos became so reliant on Chinese investment, that they served as proxies in the meetings of the Association of Southeast Asian Nations, ASEAN. In 2002, China accepted a code of conduct for the South China Sea. But it was not binding. China alternately disputed with Vietnam and the Philippines, modernized its navy base in Hainan, and made sure that relations with the largest country, Indonesia, remained friendly. A first achievement was thus to grow stronger in the South China Sea without provoking armed conflict. A second success was to grow its economy at the expense of its neighbors, while still preserving access to their markets. For decades, Japan was the largest investor in this region. Now, roads, railways, and pipelines slowly spread out from China's southern provinces like tentacles of commerce, across the borders with Vietnam, Laos, and Myanmar. Manufactured goods were sent out, raw materials brought back.

In 2000, China proposed a trade agreement to ASEAN. China overcame the opposition to the deal. While presenting it as an agreement with ASEAN as a whole, it negotiated with countries individually, granted concessions to their farmers, and agreed to open its own market earlier. This so-called early harvest offer was a diplomatic masterstroke: it was presented as an act of magnanimity, but its practical effect on the exports of the small countries was negligible. After the deal entered into force in 2003, China's trade surplus with the region expanded and it continued to divert foreign investment away to its own market. China managed to proffer competition as cooperation. The regional order was redrawn. Laos and Cambodia became very dependent on China. To other countries, the competition with China came on top of internal challenges. The Philippines was plagued by corruption scandals. In Thailand, a populist prime minister was toppled by a military coup. In Myanmar, the junta faced large uprisings. Indonesia remained stable, but suffered from the economic competition with China in its industrial sector. Such instability affirmed China's position as Asia's new center of power.

India was left behind too. In 2000, the Indian Prime Minister Atal Vajpayee asked for patience. While he believed freedom to be the strongest base for prosperity, democracy also meant that his government had to listen to the people and that economic reform would therefore be slower.[11] But the clock was ticking. India's labor force grew by 13 million workers annually. Each year seven million Indians migrated from the countryside to cities. Abject poverty, drought, the high cost of fertilizer, and the depletion of the soil as a result of the excessive use of it drove thousands of farmers to suicide. Each election, political power also became more fragmented and the ragtag of local parties made it more difficult to reform. While the two main parties, the Hindu-nationalist BJP and the social-nationalist Congress Party, had become sworn rivals, they both promised economic liberalization with compassion for the poor. Prime Minister Atal Vajpayee's advisors spoke of reforming without making it look like reform, a continuation of his predecessor's stealth reform. Prime Minister Manmohan Singh, elected in 2004, proposed inclusive growth. Singh, for example, lowered trade tariffs, but spent heavily on subsidies for farmers. India was a vast country, but would it also shine and become a major power?

The relationship between China and India was like that of the tale of the hare and the tortoise, but in this case, the hare was winning. Both Congress and the BJP promised ten million additional jobs each year. On average, only slightly more than two million were realized. Both parties also promised more foreign investment and Western countries pledged to set up shop in India. By the end of the decade, however, foreign investment had merely increased. The two parties promised to boost manufacturing, yet Indian manufacturing remained eight times smaller than China's. India's celebrated information technology companies invested more abroad than in their home country.

India saw China racing ahead and this had consequences for the balance of power.[12] While India was considered a demographic and democratic hedge against China, the security establishment warned that it was not keeping pace with China's military modernization along the border and that the Chinese Navy was making forays into the Indian Ocean.[13] China also became more present in Nepal and Sri Lanka. The government downplayed that fear, proposed to work with China to secure energy supply, to grow bilateral trade, and to attract US$50 billion of Chinese investment by the end of the decade. Politicians spoke of "Chindia," a partnership between equals in which India would specialize in services and China in manufacturing. By 2009, Chinese investment in India was only US$2 billion, though, and India ran a growing trade deficit with China. India was not standing up to China; it was mollified by China, bedazzled like so many others by the promise of trade. Hence, between 2000 and 2009, China became Asia's number one. The other two powers, India and Japan, could not keep pace with its growth and the rest of the continent was too divided to restore the balance of power.

Kaliningrad

In 2000, the Russian President Boris Yeltsin made way for a veteran intelligence officer: Vladimir Putin. When the new president paid his first visit to Western countries, he swore that the Cold War would not come back, that his country had to be considered a part of Europe, and that it preferred multilateral cooperation.[14] His message was effective. "I looked the man in the eye," said his American counterpart, concluding that a constructive relationship with Russia was possible. Putin indeed did want Russia to be a prosperous European country, but on his terms. If he first assumed that he could build stable relations with the West, this changed rapidly. After 9/11, for instance, the United States promised that its military presence in Central Asia would be temporary. Two years later, however, Washington changed its mind: "You know what? It turns out we really need this base, like, permanently."[15]

Putin proposed that his country had to stop copying from Western textbooks, that liberalism was not fit for Russia, and that a strong state had to be built.[16] Economic power and independence were key. While preserving democracy, Russian prosperity would be best served by a forceful executive government. He referred to the United States and Japan as rivals. He called the collapse of the Soviet Union the greatest geopolitical catastrophe of the century. So, while Putin remained diplomatic on the international stage, his message to his compatriots was clear: Russia would no longer be played with. After the Russians had passed through economic hardship, the West expanded its influence to Russia's detriment, and Russia had been ignored during the crisis in the Balkans, a new dawning arrived.

Putin brandished his determination. Just before becoming president, he masterminded a large military exercise that simulated the use of tactical nuclear weapons to counter an invasion by the West. The 2000 Military Doctrine spelled out the readiness to use nuclear weapons in response to conventional attacks. Putin blasted the American decision to leave the Anti-Ballistic Missile Treaty and threatened retaliation. He waged a ruthless military campaign against separatists and Islamists in the Caucasian state Chechnya. His war forced the separatists underground. But by 2002, Moscow declared victory. The same year, Russia and ten neighboring countries replaced the Collective Security Treaty of 1992 with a formal alliance, the Collective Security Treaty Organization, CSTO, a response to NATO enlargement. In 2003, Moscow offered to liberalize trade with Ukraine, Belarus, and Kazakhstan and to establish a common currency in a Eurasian Economic Space.

After America ignored Russia in the war on terror, new disappointments added to Russian nationalism. First there was America's unilateral decision to attack Iraq. During the Iraqi invasion, the Russians provided intelligence about the American troops to Saddam Hussein. The United States supported the democratic uprisings in Georgia, Ukraine, and Kyrgyzstan, the Color Revolutions. The Kremlin started referring to Ukraine as Little Russia. While Putin clearly sought to restore a Russian sphere of influence, the Western interference in these three countries was seen as a countermove. The reluctance of the European Union to relax visa requirements also made it plain that Russia was still not welcome in the European house.[17]

Distrust continued to grow. When several former Soviet countries joined NATO and the European Union in 2004, the new entrants, including Poland and the Baltic States, instantly pushed for a stronger policy to check Russia.

Putin, however, would not be stopped. That year, he won the presidential elections with a large majority. His inauguration ceremony marked that Russia had changed. State television showed hundreds of dignitaries waiting in the newly refurbished gilded halls of the Kremlin for the president-elect, Putin arriving in a convoy of limousines with black tinted windows, striding under the crystal chandeliers to a stage where he was welcomed by the chairman of the constitutional court, the president of the parliament, and the head of the Russian Orthodox Church.

A power grab followed. Responsibilities were taken back from local governments and loyalists appointed governor.[18] The president clipped the wings of the parliament, the State Duma. Wealthy businessmen critical of Putin's rule could choose: pack, prison, or support. Independent media were curtailed and foreign nongovernmental organizations obliged to register so as to halt foreign meddling. Economic assets, like the energy sector, were brought under state control. Foreign policy toughened as well. Russia reasserted its claim in a dispute with Japan over the Kuril Islands. It called on China to do something about the illegal migration of its citizens into Russia.

What allowed the Kremlin to recover was its skillful manipulation of the weakness of the West and the rise of Asia. As a result of the economic growth of China, energy prices had been soaring. Russian incomes from energy exports increased from around US$60 billion in 2000 to around US$200 billion by the end of the decade. The treasury filled up and by 2006 Russia could repay all its debt to the West.[19] Relations with China were not easy. Russia was critical of the unbalanced trade relations, Chinese migration, as we have seen, and growing Chinese influence in Central Asia. Still, Russia expected to sell more energy to China and pushed to settle a minor border issue. The relationship was also useful to open a joint front against American interventionism and Western liberalism. In 2005, the two signed a joint statement on the world order, in which they demanded that sovereignty be respected, interference in other countries stopped, and American unilateralism make way for multilateral cooperation. "The world should not be divided into a leading camp and a subordinate camp."[20]

At the same time, the Kremlin saw Europe becoming more and more dependent on its gas. Germany was a major importer. Chancellor Gerhard

Schröder allowed the Russian company Gazprom to become the majority shareholder in a new pipeline, called Nord Stream, guaranteed the payment of its construction – and started to work for Gazprom from the moment he stepped down from public office. With another pipeline, South Stream, Russia linked up to Bulgaria, Greece, and Italy. The Italian Prime Minister, Silvio Berlusconi, was pictured wearing a sweatshirt with the Russian double-headed eagle. The divisions inside the West became apparent during the brief Russo-Georgian War of 2008.

Moscow had been stoking unrest between Georgia and two breakaway regions, Abkhazia and South Ossetia. When South Ossetian rebels attacked Georgian troops, Russia intervened. The United States accused Russia of bullying and invading a sovereign nation and the Polish Prime Minister travelled to Tbilisi to show his support. The Italian government warned against an anti-Russian coalition. Paris, Madrid, and Berlin blocked a proposal to let Georgia join NATO. The same was true with regard to Ukraine. Tensions between Russia and Ukraine had been rising, over the latter's shift to the West, threats to revise the Russian Navy's access to its port in Crimea, and unpaid energy bills. "We consider NATO as a father and the EU as a mother," Kiev said. But Berlin, Paris, and other member states did not want Ukraine in the EU or NATO.[21] "Russia becomes more aggressive when it is isolated," said Paris. Another reason to show restraint was the promise of opportunities for aircraft and defense manufacturers, and, not the least, the supply of gas.[22]

Whether it was advisable or not to allow Ukraine and Georgia to join the EU and NATO, its European opponents were guided more by opportunism than by strategy. Relations hardened and Putin told the West to stop "poking its snotty noses" into others business.[23] He gave the United States a "taste of its own medicine." In 2008, Moscow falsely claimed to have received a letter from a critical senator requesting a financial contribution to his presidential campaign. Russia could afford relations to harden, thanks to the growing energy exports to Europe. During the decade, its economy grew 5 percent annually, its defense spending 20 percent. In 2007, Russia withdrew from the Treaty on Conventional Armed Forces in Europe, a treaty that limited the deployment of conventional weapon systems, like artillery, tanks, and attack helicopters, in Europe.

A new generation of long-range nuclear missiles was deployed and it would be fitted with multiple warheads. When the United States proposed putting missile defense systems in Central Europe, Russia threatened to withdraw from the Intermediate Nuclear Force (INF) Treaty and to deploy short-range missiles in the Baltic enclave of Kaliningrad. While said to be conventional, these Iskander missiles could also carry nuclear warheads. Its military exercises on the Western border became larger and larger. The more Russia pushed back, the more its European neighbors called for countermeasures. But the West had become a useful adversary. Putin was riding on a wave of anti-Western resentment. After the elections of 2008, he switched positions with his ally Dmitry Medvedev and became prime minister. The first measure of the new government: to extend the presidential term to six years.

Russia's assertiveness was instilled by a decade of troubled relations with the West. It was made possible by China's rise and dysfunctional European energy policy. China contributed to high energy prices; Europe bought Russian energy at these high prices. Still, China clearly left Russia behind, as also happened to Japan and India. It became a giant among lesser giants. With each new railway built across its border, each new pipeline financed, and each new commercial delegation dispatched, China slowly redrew the Eurasian order. In the east, Beijing started to end the traditional maritime dominance of the United States and Japan in its adjacent seas. Further to the south, Southeast Asia was too divided and India too dysfunctional to restore the balance. As the West was pulled deeper into the quagmires of Iraq and Afghanistan, China arrived as a new important partner in Central Asia and the Middle East. Further west, European countries fell for its charm, enticed by business opportunities and the prospect also of a multipolar order that would check American arrogance. The financial crisis that started in 2009 would only expedite that power shift. This power shift, the next sections explain, was also felt in Africa and Latin America.

African renaissance aborted

In June 2003, a team of American elite forces landed on the outskirts of Monrovia, the capital of Liberia. Operation Shining Express, it was called.

Its mission was to protect the American embassy. As rebels closed in on the capital, desperate Liberians piled mutilated corpses before the embassy compound and begged the American government to intervene. Atrocious violence had spread over West Africa: in Sierra Leone, where armed rival gangs fought over blood diamonds; in Ivory Coast, where strife was aggravated by migration from neighboring countries and dwindling cocoa prices. In Nigeria, fighting raged on in the coastal area and in the impoverished north. Rival gangs competed over oil smuggling, politicians in the capital over billions of taxes from foreign oil companies. West African war was a cocktail of ethnic division, criminal economy, migration, excruciating poverty, and the proliferation of small arms.

The largest tragedy unfolded in the heart of Africa. The Second Congo War (1998–2003) cost around four million lives. In the forested east of Congo, violent battles raged between dozens of armed factions over small mines in which children worked as slaves, over smuggling routes, taxation points, diamonds, precious timber, bush meat, and so forth. At a higher echelon, warlords fought for political power in Kinshasa and hence access to the large lucrative mines of copper, cobalt, coltan, and other precious minerals. The surging global sales of mobile phones and laptops caused prices of these metals to skyrocket. The Second Congo War was also a regional conflict during which neighboring countries fought for influence in the country: Rwanda, Uganda, Zimbabwe, Angola, and so forth. Rwanda said it interfered because rebels from its genocide were hiding in the Congolese forest, and financed other rebel groups to hunt them down, smuggling being a lucrative side activity. Uganda, too, had its proxies. Beyond, the Second Congo War was also a global conflict, with China and the United States wrestling over the critical minerals, and Europe trying to hold its ground.

Around 2003, a peculiar mood of optimism returned to the African continent. More countries held free elections. Newspapers spoke of a coming African miracle and investors returned. An important explanation was the commodity boom. Chinese and multinational companies scrambled to secure the supply of resources. War fatigue and international pressure also paved the way for peace agreements, in the Democratic Republic of Congo, for instance, in Liberia and in Ivory Coast. As a result, violence subsided somewhat. If there were around 50,000 battle deaths in 2003, this dropped to around 28,000 in 2009.[24] During the United Nations Millennium Summit of 2000, international donors had pledged to give special attention to Africa. In 2001, the leaders of the eight largest economies, the G8, signed a compact for African recovery. African countries themselves established the African Union in 2003. Like the European Union, it had its own parliament, a commission, and a court of justice. Donors vowed to help it to stamp out new conflicts, like in Sudan, where oil money emboldened the president to crack down on minorities in Darfur Province. ECOWAS, the Common Market for Eastern and Southern Africa (COMESA), and the Southern African Development Community (SADC) also promised to open up regional markets to trade. Experts celebrated the fact that new factories were being erected in countries like Kenya and Ethiopia.

Africa enjoyed economic growth. Roads and railways were built. The arrival of cheap Chinese goods, like mobile phones, benefited households and entrepreneurs. Nurses in the rural countryside could now summon ambulances to distant clinics, and farmers were able to follow the commodity prices on the stock market. Compared to digital connectivity, however, traditional infrastructure, like roads, remained inadequate. Farmers could now follow the prices, but storing and transporting their goods remained a challenge. Hence, the majority of Africans roamed in an economic no-man's land, amidst the mega mines, the mega farms, and mega ports: a land of slums, informal work, and destitution. The share of the urban population living in slums decreased less: from 62 percent in 2000 to 57 percent in 2009. In 2009, only 28 percent thought the economic situation was good. Trust in democracy also receded.[25]

The fundaments of the boom were not solid either. Financially, the region still spent more on imported consumer goods and equipment than it earned from exports. Between 2000 and 2009, Africa had an average annual trade deficit of US$7 billion. It spent on average US$23 billion per year on servicing external debt and it lost about US$35 billion per year from capital flight, often to tax havens.[26] What emerged was an economy of the taking. Large mines, oilfields, and mega farms were opened. They were connected, by means of transport infrastructure built by foreign workers

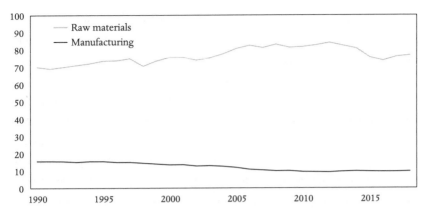

Figure 9.2   Africa's commodity trap: Raw materials as a share of Africa's total exports and manufacturing as a share of Africa's total GDP (%)
Source: WDI and UNCTAD Stats.

who used foreign materials, to ports that were operated by foreign shipping companies. In theory, local governments could redistribute the revenues, but corruption was widespread. In theory, also, the commodity boom, the newly built roads, and the arrival of investors could help entrepreneurs to spearhead growth into sectors like manufacturing, but Africa's market was flooded with Chinese manufactured goods, its share in global manufacturing remained well below 2 percent, and its exports dangerously dependent on oil and minerals (figure 9.2).

Striking in this context was the resilience of these poor, their ingenuity to survive. To some, surviving meant taking up arms: for subsistence farmers or cattle raisers to defend their land, for others to extract small amounts from their toil, and so forth. For hundreds of thousands of African men, the Kalashnikov became their most important source of income. In Nigeria, they were attracted by a new movement, Boko Haram. It preached a holy war against the government, which allegedly discriminated against the predominantly Muslim population in the north, and, thanks to funding from the Gulf States, it could offer its young combatants a handful of dollars and pride. It started a terror campaign, burning churches and killing children. Other such movements were Al-Qaeda in the Islamic Maghreb, operating from the south of Algeria and Mali, and Al-Shabaab in the Horn of Africa. At the end of the decade, these groups had thousands of fighters in the belt of desert and savannah between, operating in jeeps and on motor bikes. Besides financing from the Gulf, they profited from human trafficking, ransoms, and drug smuggling.

As a part of the war on terror, the United States established an Africa Command in 2007. France, too, deployed troops. China sent peacekeepers to Congo and Sudan, two countries where it had invested. In 2008, it deployed three navy ships to the coast of Somalia to protect its merchant ships against piracy; Japan and other countries followed suit. Russia was approached by the Somali government to restore security. So, on top of the many internal Africa challenges, great power politics asserted itself once more, merely a decade after the joust between the Soviet Union and the United States had ended. China competed with the United States over strategic minerals in Congo and with almost all other large economies for oil, construction contracts, fishing grounds, and so forth. While China and Russia vetoed sanctions against Sudan and Zimbabwe in the Security Council, France and the United States tried to bolster privileged ties with various other authoritarian leaders.

In the 1990s, Africa suffered from neglect and slow growth. During this decade, between 2000 and 2009, international interest in Africa returned. More precisely, the interest in its raw materials increased. Growth accelerated. The downside of this renaissance was neglect of sectors other than manufacturing and disappointing results in the fight against poverty. Africans were now more connected by means of Chinese railways and mobile phones, but the majority of Africans remained marginalized by globalization. The most destabilizing trend was thus still not reversed: a growing mass of destitute Africans. Between 2000 and 2009, the absolute number of Africans living in extreme poverty grew by 14 million. A second destabilizing trend concerned the return of power politics. Africa became another arena of the global contest for power. Countries like the United States, China, France, and Russia scrambled to gain or preserve their influence.

Medellin

These economic forces were also at work in Latin America. Latin American countries enjoyed higher living standards and more security than African countries. Like in other parts of the world, China's demand for raw materials created growth opportunities. In Brazil, rainforest gave way to soy production. Bulk ports were expanded to ship it to China. In Chile, copper mines were opened and shipping lines to China expanded. Whether it concerned the Brazilian Port Santos or the Chilean Port Angamos, the trade pattern was such that bulk carriers were loaded and full Chinese containers offloaded. The Brazilian President Ignacio Lula cautioned about the risks of such unbalanced trade and called for a robust industrial policy. "We want to be a more industrialized country," he said. "Iron ore and oil, these are things that run out, so if you are not careful, soon you exhaust the supply and then you are orphaned."[27]

But Brazil and most other countries failed to avoid the commodity dependency trap. In 2000, 40 percent of Brazilian exports consisted of raw materials, 60 percent in 2009. Latin America's share in global manufacturing remained flat at around 6 percent. Few countries used the commodity boom to invest in public infrastructure. The fragility prompted local investors to flee to safe havens abroad. In the case of Argentina, the average annual capital flight was US$20 billion.[28] Fragility also meant that governments paid high interest rates on their debt, so that speculative capital again flowed in.[29] Latin American growth was far from solid.

What also characterized the situation in the region was the persistence of violence. Economic growth, as we saw, was unbalanced, but did contribute to a reduction in poverty. Extreme poverty declined in the region, from 14 percent in 2000 to 8 percent in 2009. The share of urban residents living in slums also decreased from 30 percent in 2000 to 22 percent in 2009. Despite this improvement, the violence-related death rate did not decrease. In countries like El Salvador, Venezuela, and Honduras, the violence-related death rate was higher than in conflict countries like Iraq and Afghanistan. Overall, the violence-related death rate in Latin America was higher than in Africa. There were several reasons for this: the availability of arms, the continued appeal of narcotic crime, poverty, and the inclination of governments to respond to the problem by sending more criminals to crammed prisons or heavy-handed police purges, instead of strengthening civil society, education, and prevention. The failure of that strategy was especially highlighted by the few success stories in the region: in cities like Medellin and Bogota in Colombia, a mix of economic reform, integration schemes, public infrastructure, education, and social participation projects reversed the trend of growing crime and violence. These remained exceptions, though.

Here, too, power politics returned. It returned behind the back of the United States. Since the 1990s, Washington's interest in the region had been modest and the terrorist attacks of 2001 made it reorient its attention to other corners of the world. The United States did spend growing amounts of money on programs to counter the drugs trade, like the Andean Counterdrug Initiative and Plan Colombia. It also allowed armed contractors to fight drug producers and traffickers. Nevertheless, this campaign merely made narcotics production relocate from Colombia to other countries. It also confirmed countries in their perception that Washington only minded its own narrow security interests, not the long-term stability and prosperity of the region. It hardly invested in Latin America, except in mines in Chile and Brazil. Its refusal to help bail out Argentina at times of financial turbulence caused anger; the government blamed American vulture funds for speculating on the country's problems and turned to China for relief. So did its tacit support for an uprising and attempted coup against the nationalist Venezuelan leader Hugo Chávez in 2002 and reports about the poor treatment of Latin American immigrants. Ignacio Lula, the popular leftist president who came to power in 2003, proclaimed that the United States and the other G7 nations no longer spoke for the world. Russia contested Washington by sending warships to Cuba and Venezuela, and China elicited American distrust by investing in strategic assets like the Panama Canal, the main American choke point between the Atlantic and the Pacific.

Valley of the Wolves

Greed, the pursuit of economic gains, grievance, anger about discrimination and poverty, were considered important factors contributing to the civil wars in Africa. "Wasting in idleness and attendant resentments," an academic described the attraction of the war economy. "Most of the men were motivated by the opportunity to drink, loot, murder, and enjoy higher living standards than they were previously accustomed to."[30] If, on top, the environmental conditions deteriorated, instability became almost inevitable. All these ingredients remained present in the Global South. So too in the Middle East.

The Middle East faced up to a considerable youth bulge. In many countries, poverty and drought undermined subsistence farming, the small-scale farming on which millions of people depended. In 2000, for instance, drought reduced the cereal output in Iraq by 40 percent. Irrigation farms in Syria experienced chronic water shortage. In Egypt, the fertile land of the Nile valley was abraded on the one side by fast urbanization, on the other by the rising level of the Mediterranean Sea. Social tensions were rife, yet repressed most of the time by brutal authoritarianism. The situation here was complicated further by the political abuse of religion, ill-judged intervention, and the concentration of heavily armed, ambitious regional powers.

The invasion of Iraq in 2003 was justified as an attempt to stop the proliferation of weapons of mass destruction, to restore democracy, and to combat terrorism. The opposite was achieved. In Iraq, tyranny was replaced by anarchy. Elsewhere in the region, authoritarian regimes were further empowered, like in Egypt, Kuwait, Saudi Arabia, Qatar, and the United Arab Emirates. Western countries bought more of their oil and gas. Energy exports to Europe and the United States grew from US$35 billion in 2000 to US$105 billion in 2009. In exchange, Western countries annually supplied around US$20 billion of arms, riot control gear, and solutions to censor the internet. Moreover, the West was still expected to provide military protection against Iran.

While the presence of the United States in the Gulf was often said to serve their energy interests, a more important objective was to preserve the balance of power between the authoritarian regimes on the Western side of the Gulf and the authoritarian regime in Iran, and to preserve the political status quo. In Egypt, strongman Hosni Mubarak, one of the main recipients of American military aid, was reconfirmed president during an election in which only 23 percent of the eligible voters participated, and cracked down mercilessly on a protest for judiciary independence. Hundreds of Egyptian dissidents were put in prison or disappeared. Saudi Arabia continued to jail political activists. And the same happened in most other countries. The war in Iraq was followed by an affirmation of authoritarianism instead of the propagation of democracy.

These authoritarian regimes were loath to respond to requests to help fight international terrorism. While the terrorist attacks of 2001 were widely denounced, formal mechanisms were set up to oversee financial flows, and officials openly expressed their gratitude, confidential cables revealed that the engagement was a failure. A secret document from 2009, drafted by the American State Department, eight years after 9/11, left nothing to the imagination. "It has been an ongoing challenge to persuade Saudi officials to treat terrorist financing emanating from Saudi Arabia as a strategic priority," it observed. "Donors in Saudi Arabia constitute the most significant source of funding to Sunni terrorist groups worldwide."[31] Qatar, where the United States and the United Kingdom had significant military presence, was considered the "worst in the region" regarding efforts to fight terrorism. "Although Qatar's security services have the capability to deal with direct threats," it was noted, "they have been hesitant to act against known terrorists out of concern for appearing to be aligned with the U.S." The Emirates was described as a global financial center with weak oversight; Kuwait as a source of funds and a transit point for terrorists. Polls also showed that there was widespread popular support in the region for Al-Qaeda. "Those governments that don't feel the pulse of their people and respond to it will suffer the fate of the Shah of Iran," the Saudi crown prince explained.[32]

The Iranian government was still led by the pragmatic Prime Minister Mohammad Khatami and during its last year, the Clinton administration made new diplomatic overtures. In 2000, Clinton and Khatami had a close encounter at the United Nations headquarters. Staff members had orchestrated a hallway handshake that had to look spur-of-the-moment. But Prime Minister Khatami changed his mind, afraid that hardliners would criticize the photo of the handshake. He hid in a bathroom until the American party left the hallway.

Iran had already purified plutonium and was close to finalizing facilities to enrich uranium. The nuclear program had become a symbol of pride and sovereignty, so that it could no longer be abandoned. At the same time, the position of Iran's rivals hardened. The newly elected American President, George W. Bush, imagined Iran, alongside Iraq and North Korea, to be part of an axis of evil. The newly elected Israeli premier, Ariel Sharon, proposed to Washington that after Iraq, Iran should be next. Israel complained bitterly about Iran supplying the Hezbollah in neighboring Lebanon with new missiles. In 2003, Mohammad Khatami proposed an ultimate grand bargain. He offered full transparency of its nuclear program and termination of support for Hamas and Hezbollah in exchange for security guarantees. The proposal was refused. In 2005, Iran proposed a new deal to the European Union, but that was turned down too. Iran was ready to offer openness and religious leader Ali Khamenei issued a fatwa that forbid nuclear weapons.

The stumbling block was that Iran did not want to halt the enrichment of uranium for civilian purposes, a core demand of the West. That year, the country elected a hardline president, Mahmoud Ahmadinejad. The gloves were off. Ahmadinejad called for the destruction of Israel and threatened shipping through the Strait of Hormuz with small missile boats. New sanctions followed, until, in 2009, Iran, the UK, France, Russia, and the European Union agreed that Iran was allowed to enrich uranium, yet only to the point that it could not be used for weapons and that weapons-grade uranium would be sent abroad. That deal too collapsed and it prompted countries like Saudi Arabia to threaten that they also would build nuclear weapons if Iran was not checked.[33]

For many decades, the United States approached the Middle East partially through the prism of Israel's security interests. From the viewpoint of Tel Aviv, security was threatened by Hezbollah in Lebanon, by Syria, by expanding Iranian influence, by Palestinian armed movements, and by unreliable autocrats in the Gulf. The opposite point of view was that it was Israeli revisionism that caused instability. Israel itself continued to modernize its nuclear weapons. In 2000, for instance, it test-fired a nuclear-capable missile into the Mediterranean Sea, which splashed down not far from an American warship. It was Israel also that violated sovereignty and bombed neighboring countries, like Syria and Lebanon. It was Israel that violated international agreements by annexing Palestinian territory on the West

Bank with a newly built wall and ignored even the calls of its main sponsor, the United States, for the recognition of two states.

The result was a vicious circle in which Israeli assertiveness sparked retaliations, which in turn caused a harsher Israeli response. The visit of Prime Minister Sharon to the Temple Mount in 2000 provoked a large uprising: the Second Intifada. The Temple Mount is a plateau in the City of Jerusalem. The plateau itself is home to several important Muslim shrines, including the Dome of the Rock; but its walls are a holy place where Jews come to pray. The election victory of the radical armed movement Hamas in Gaza in 2006 was followed by financial sanctions and military reprisals. Hamas was a security threat, but also a politically useful bogeyman. In a leaked cable, an intelligence chief avowed: "If Hamas managed to take complete control then the Israel Defense Forces would be able to relate to Gaza as a hostile territory."[34] The United States could take stock of these policies, criticize them, but Israel, under two hardline prime ministers, showed itself defiant. It had the military clout to act and enough support in Washington to get away with it.

Turkey was a recalcitrant ally as well. Turkey had started reaching out to Greece and officially became a candidate to join the European Union, but slowly turned away from the West. Against the backdrop of a new economic crisis and disillusionment with the reforms prescribed by the International Monetary Fund, Recep Tayyip Erdoğan founded the conservative Justice and Development Party, the AKP. He won election after election and became prime minister in 2003. Turkey was furious at the invasion of Iraq, America's lack of concern for the interests of neighboring countries, and the opportunity it would create for the Kurds to seize power in the region. The Kurdish people straddled the borders with Turkey, Iraq, Syria, and Iran. They could become a powerful actor and incite secessionism. Ankara refused access to American troops, despite Washington's threat to cut financial aid.

Anti-Americanism became rampant. News media compared President Bush to Hitler and called him the worst enemy of Islam.[35] *Valley of the Wolves*, a popular movie, showed American soldiers using Iraqi children as a human shield, attacking a wedding party, and committing torture. In the novel *Metal Storm*, Turkish and American troops wage war in Iraq. Erdoğan made some compromises with the United States and stressed his desire to join the European Union. Still, the rift widened. The Iranian President Mahmoud Ahmadinejad was received in Istanbul by crowds singing "Death to America." Ankara threatened to invade Northern Iraq, opposed American military muscle flexing in the Black Sea after Russia's intervention in Georgia, and staged a military exercise with Syria.[36] Instead of aligning itself with the West, Ankara opted for a broad effort to establish ties with neighboring countries as well as powers like Russia and China. "Rolls Royce ambitions with Rover resources," an American diplomat mocked.[37]

Made in the West

The ingredients of globalization were the prosperity and technology of the West, the labor force of China, and the raw materials of the rest of the world. They were bound together by more and more complex chains of production and trade. However tight the global production chains, the political relations remained tense. Even among close trade partners, strategic tensions built up. The best examples were China, Japan, and the United States. China's accession to the World Trade Organization was celebrated as a turning point. Yet, it did not mean the end of Chinese economic nationalism. The more China diverted trade and industry to its economy, the more it grew, the more it tried to repulse American and Japanese presence. Neither did China's increasingly central position in global trade flows make it less interested in territorial control, like over the South China Sea or parts of the disputed border with India. Other examples were Russia and Turkey, two countries which, despite their enormous economic dependence on the West, also remained suspicious of the West and more assertively tried to check its influence.

Rather than advancing democracy, the high age of globalization contributed to a revival of authoritarianism. Authoritarian Gulf States benefited from record oil prices, but made no significant steps toward democratization, and remained defiant toward Western requests to stop sponsoring Islamic extremism. In Russia, growing gas exports to Europe permitted Vladimir Putin to grow his power domestically and to push back on the West externally. Russia started running large trade surpluses, which not only allowed it to repay its loans to the West, but also to invest in energy networks that expanded its influence.

Consider China. The West outsourced a significant part of its manufacturing to China. A former American defense secretary summarized it: "The de facto economic relationship we have with China is that we give up skilled jobs in exchange for cheap goods made in China – which we buy with money borrowed from China."[38] China in turn needed to invest in raw materials overseas, which came with political influence. The computers and mobile phones that it assembled in vast quantities for Western consumers, for instance, required rare metals. This prompted China to venture deeper into Africa, where it emerged as a strategic competitor with the West. The large trade surpluses earned from exporting to Western consumers were transferred into strategic credit lines of state banks, with which China financed infrastructure projects overseas – and gained more influence. The technology that Western countries shared with China allowed the latter to grow its industrial power and also to modernize its armed forces. The rise of China was in the West, at least to some extent.

The ascent of China had as a consequence that several other powers seized it as an opportunity to revise their relations with the West. Even poor countries in Africa, South Asia, and elsewhere now had an opportunity to resist the West and its conditions. As they played their old and new partners off against one another, the elites in the Global South grew rich, the rest of their society less so. Poverty and the failure to become less dependent on raw materials cast a shadow over their future. Poverty rates dropped significantly, but in absolute terms, close to 750 million people still earned less than US$1.9 per day. To some, that formed the next large reservoir of labor, the next frontier of globalization. To others, it remained a source of great uncertainty.

ACT 3 (2010–2020)

CHAPTER 10

WHAT THE HELL HAPPENED?

AFTER THE FINANCIAL CRISIS, STABILITY NEVER RETURNED IN THE West. During the second term of President Barack Obama, new racist murders by police officers triggered race protests. The installation of Donald Trump was a milestone in American politics. Never before had an American president thrown so much oil on the flames of partisan politics. He upset the political system, to the point that it led to rebellion of the deep state, of judges, generals, and corporate leaders. Against the backdrop of growing protest against racism, the president called the Democratic Party a mob and incited agitation on the right. At the end of his presidency, he incited his followers to storm the parliament building on Capitol Hill.

In Europe, social unrest continued to flare up, including protests in Greece, and the anti-government protests of the Yellow Vests in France. Nationalism challenged European unity more than ever before. Eurosceptic parties became dominant in Hungary, Poland, and Italy. In January 2020, the United Kingdom left the European Union. All over the West, the lack of courage and vigor of center politicians, their litany of broken promises, contributed to the longing of citizens for more outspoken leadership. Despite new alarm signals, however, the center still failed to address the causes of discontent.

Reforms of the capitalist system remained limited. While many citizens – around 60 percent of Americans and over 80 percent of Europeans – supported a green new deal that provided innovative industries and quality jobs at home, few politicians were ready to explain that this also implied the need for them to change their own behavior[1] – by ceasing to reward social and environmental dumping whenever they went shopping, for instance. As a result, investment in new environment-friendly industries remained underwhelming; the dependency of mass consumption on cheaply imported goods and raw materials immense. Instead of an economic transformation, many countries continued to incur large trade deficits, growing external debt, and vast flows of money to overheated stock markets and real estate.

The same was true for the response to social fragmentation. Under President Barack Obama, racial tensions grew.[2] Expectations were very high just after his election, but his restraint on racial matters led to disappointment among African-Americans. At the same time, a perceived lack of empathy bred anger inside the white rural underclass. European governments added to the discontent by welcoming refugees and immigrants without an adequate policy to give them a proper place or addressing the reservations of the indigenous population. As flimsy as many of the policies of pragmatic politicians were, just as flimsy was the nationalism of the rightist politician. He called for a fortress in which to sustain a mellow lifestyle and often even to mask the fact that they sold their country out as much as many center politicians had done. Both ends of the political spectrum made the mistake of confirming the society in its passiveness or trying to preserve the status quo instead of mustering citizens to change. The period between 2010 and 2020 was yet another opportunity missed.

American atrophy

Barack Obama (2009–17) campaigned by highlighting the audacity of hope. When he became president, Obama inherited a country in shambles. The financial crisis had just struck, society had become immensely polarized, and the nation was embroiled in two wars. Obama recognized these challenges. He criticized the greed that ruled Wall Street, the tribal tendencies of politics, the nagging fear that the next generation had to lower its sights. Still, satisfaction with the way things were going in the country, polls showed, merely recovered during his two terms. Political trust sank further (see figure 7.2). Distrust between Republicans and Democrats was unprecedented. Thanks to his courteousness and moderate foreign policy, Obama became more popular abroad than at home. What explained this situation? Polls revealed that the primary concern remained the state of the economy, including the affordability of healthcare and education. The second cause of anger was the state of politics, the impact of lobbyists and specific interest groups.

In the wake of the financial crisis, the Federal Reserve began a campaign of quantitative easing. Quantitative easing meant that money was injected into the economy by letting the Federal Reserve buy troubled debt products from financial institutions. By bringing relief to financial institutions, the Fed tried to keep interest rates low. Low interest rates discouraged companies and households from saving and encouraged them to spend. The Obama administration cut taxes and increased public spending. Households and companies also benefited from a sharp decrease in energy prices as a result of growing domestic oil production. At the end of Obama's presidency, the United States had recovered faster from the economic crisis than other Western economies. It achieved near full employment. Stock markets broke records.

Obama's successor, Donald Trump, went all out to assert that the growth was *his* merit, that *he* was making America great again. But recovery was flawed and citizens sensed it. Public debt grew. On December 22, 2018, the American federal government shut down. A conflict between Congress and President Trump over the budget meant that many government agencies remained closed for almost a month. One million public servants were no longer paid. The government proposed that they offer their services to their landlords in exchange for partial rent relief. Coastguards were advised to babysit or walk pets. Hundreds of thousands of families of civil servants turned to food banks. The shutdown exposed America's slump in the most blatant manner.

Consumer confidence remained lower than during the long period of growth in the 1990s. Real disposable income grew slowly and stagnated in the poorest segments of society. Net worth of families, so assets minus liabilities, remained lower than in the previous decade. The poor now had zero family wealth and the lower middle class saw its wealth stagnate.[3]

Income inequality increased. Citizens complained about the high cost of healthcare, housing, and education.[4] Between 2010 and 2020, family healthcare spending grew by 20 percent, spending on housing by 15 percent. Americans worked longer days and often farther from home. So, while the United States had warded off a catastrophic financial meltdown and growth rebounded, growth figures were unconvincing to many Americans.

Citizens grew particularly bitter about economic justice.[5] A majority of Americans believed that the bonuses in the financial sector were disproportionate and thought lobbyists stayed too powerful.[6] Still, bonuses for bankers and stock market traders remained higher than ever before.[7] Spending on corporate lobbyists remained above the levels of previous administrations. For every dollar spent on lobbying by labor unions and public-interest groups, large companies and their associations spent 30 times more.[8] During his first election campaign, Barack Obama's fundraising had broken all records. One third of his sponsoring came from the financial sector, one third from other large companies.[9] Goldman Sachs, Google, and Microsoft topped the list. After the election campaign, senior officials were recruited from the very companies whose investment policies helped trigger the financial crisis. "Indispensable expertise," it was claimed in justification. A former director of Lehman Brothers, for instance, became assistant for legislative affairs to the secretary of the Treasury. An executive of Fannie Mae was appointed assistant secretary of the Treasury. A senior Citigroup executive became assistant to the president. One of the first main decisions of Obama was to support the bailout of Citigroup. In the eyes of the average American, an immense gap existed between promise and practice. There was general disillusionment given that the president had campaigned on hope and justice. The lack of ethics in government was identified by citizens as one of the most pressing problems under President Obama and it remained so under Donald Trump.[10]

Economic policy also did not repair the structural flaws of American capitalism. Despite the fact that quantitative easing made it cheap to borrow capital, investment in public infrastructure and manufacturing did not grow faster. As a share of the total economy, investment in infrastructure plunged below 20 percent. Never in American history had it been so low. Government spending on research and development remained stagnant.[11]

Like in the previous decades, capital was available, and now also extremely cheap, but it was insufficiently used to strengthen the economy in the long run. What did grow, once again, was household consumption. Especially the high-income earners spent more. More capital was also poured into the stock market, despite signals that it was overvalued.

The financial situation of the country did not improve. Despite low interest rates, the depreciation of the dollar, and the fact that the exploitation of shale oil reserves allowed the United States to become more self-sufficient in terms of energy, the current account deficit did not decrease. There was indeed a decrease in oil imports. But the imports of other goods, like smartphones, cars, laptops, televisions, furniture, toys, and textiles grew. America's net external debt hence continued to surge: from US$2.7 trillion in 2010 to US$12 trillion in 2020.[12] Foreigners still bought a lot of Treasury bonds. The foreign holdings of American government debt increased by another US$3.5 trillion between 2010 and 2020. "The most significant threat to our security is our national debt," observed the highest ranking military officer. The stock market attracted US$4 trillion of foreign capital. At the same time, American foreign investment in tax havens increased by US$2.3 trillion, investment in overseas manufacturing by US$350 billion (figure 4.1). A new record. The American economy attracted a torrent of capital, but it did not lead to a significant increase of investment in infrastructure, education, and other matters that strengthen an economy.

Economic policy put a brake on the greening of American industry. The majority of American citizens supported a green industrial deal, or the pursuit of more sustainable home-grown jobs.[13] President Barack Obama rolled out measures to reduce pollution and subscribed to international caps on greenhouse gas emissions. The explosion of an oil rig in the Gulf of Mexico, in 2010, added momentum. Still, domestic oil production surged and energy prices decreased, so that investment in alternatives was dissuaded. In fact, the oil cluster was one of the few industrial sectors that recorded a significant increase in investment. The tendency to import more consumer goods, and thus to outsource a part of the pollution, was a second important impediment for industries to channel capital into cleaner products, to cut external costs, and, hence, to boost productivity. America's total energy consumption, including domestically used energy and energy needed for the imported goods, increased steadily. When Donald Trump arrived in the White House, he rolled back dozens of environmental rules and abandoned climate change goals altogether. Despite scientists and even the military stating the opposite, Trump downplayed global warming as a challenge. He chose protectionism instead. Yet, the trade deficit that he hoped to reduce became larger during his presidency.

Amazon

One of the companies that epitomized this situation was Amazon. In 2015, the sales of the online store surpassed Walmart's. President Barack Obama praised the company for rebuilding the American middle class and gave a speech in one of its warehouses. Amazon became immensely popular among younger families and teenagers. In 2019, teenagers spent over US$40 billion at Amazon.[14] Amazon brought impulse buying to a new level, bringing the shop to the front door and offering a device that allowed customers to make online purchases via spoken commands. It had a name: Alexa. The company congratulated itself on paying its workers more than the minimum salary, around US$15 per hour.

Yet, working conditions were dismal. "We are machines, we are robots, we plug our scanner in, we're holding it, but we might as well be plugging it into ourselves."[15] Flex drivers had to pay for their fuel and female drivers said they were under such pressure that they needed to keep buckets to go to the bathroom. Amazon paid almost no income tax. Its effect on local shops was devastating. While it was denied access to the Chinese consumer market, the bulk of its sales to American consumers were Chinese products offered by Chinese online sellers. Forty percent of Amazon's sellers were based in China. Each year, it imported at least 100,000 containers from China. After the corona crisis broke out, the closure of traditional shops and the devastating impact of the pandemic on household incomes, online retailers like Amazon broke new records. It was deliberate policy to bring the American consumer as close to Chinese producers as possible. That gave the company a price advantage. Goods indeed became outrageously cheap. But the indirect costs for the American economy, the jobs lost elsewhere, and its discouraging effect on rebuilding sustainable local industries were hardly considered.

It confirmed the contradictory situation that already emerged in the previous decade. Many citizens became critical of capitalism, the demise of local communities, the closure of small, local shops, the decay of identity, and the influence of mega companies like Amazon. Yet they themselves behaved like mini-capitalists. During the corona crisis, Amazon became more trusted than the government.[16] As much as the rich sought to maximize their wealth in a way that often weakened the economy, the poor tried to maximize their wealth power by spending it on the very companies that banked on social and environmental dumping. Rich Americans exploited poor Americans; poor Americans exploited even poorer workers elsewhere. Research showed that the less satisfied Americans were and the lower their confidence about the future, the more they were inclined to consumerism and impulse buying.[17] This was a vicious circle.

Citizens were bombarded by advertisements, even the youngest ones. Research revealed that toddlers' screen time had doubled since the 1990s, partially as a consequence of digital babysitting. An average American was estimated to be exposed to over 4,000 advertisements per day.[18] Amazon was the third largest spender, using its online platforms to profile customers, to understand their personalities, and to tie interests to opportunities to spend: from war games for the bored teenager to a Nietzsche e-book for the critical university student. For each inner need, Amazon had an external solution. More than any other company, Amazon materialized personal identity, turning the search for identity and originality into a search for shopping.

Amazon forged a partnership with the internet companies Google and Facebook to advance in artificial intelligence, and hence the power to identify and shape needs. The first and second largest spenders on advertisements were both media and telecommunication companies. Connectivity was a business on its own. The more connected citizens were, the more persistently and the more precisely they could be targeted. The need for digital connectivity was cultivated through cute advertising campaigns. Google's most successful campaign, for instance, was called "Friends Furever" and was shared over six million times. It featured friendships between cats, dogs, orangutans, and dolphins even. Behind the mellow images, indeed, was a bone-hard business model.

Advertising is about programming lifestyles, propagating role models, and shaping desires for products. To influence what individuals want to *be*, one influences what they want to *have*. In 2019, US$240 billion was spent on advertisements in the United States. This was about ten times more than the budget for critical thinking and citizenship at school and almost as much as the salary of all secondary school teachers combined.[19] New tests confirmed the finding in previous decades that youngsters performed badly in civic knowledge and skills.[20] Government spending on critical education and citizenship at school did not increase. The focus shifted to the sciences and math instead of ethics and history.[21] Less than 20 percent of liberal arts colleges offered mandatory courses in history and society.[22] Experts once again sounded the alarm bell: "When our schools and our colleges and universities fail to set the kind of requirements that ensure that the students who leave their halls will be ready for engaged citizenship, they're really letting the nation down."[23] It was in vain.

More than ever, education became the burning point of partisan tension. Conservative Republicans became harsher in their criticism of the role of the federal government. Like Ronald Reagan, Donald Trump proposed to abolish the department of education. During his term, an attack was launched against common core requisites for schools and federal education spending. "Get rid of the common core," Trump advocated, "and keep education local."[24] This mirrored the aversion of conservative Republicans to state intervention, the interest in enlarging the scope for conservative faith-based schools, and the fact that the white upper middle class was satisfied with the quality of education for its children in better-funded, predominantly white schools. President Barack Obama had tried to use the increased federal government spending in the wake of the financial crisis to make states invest more in inclusion and quality standards, but to gain Republican support for his Every Students Succeeds Act, he actually gave states more power in deciding the curriculum and assessment. His proposal to provide universal preschool education was blocked and most of his other programs only had small budgets. In the partisan battle, the interests of American schoolkids were trampled.

Despite the robust economic recovery, real education spending between 2010 and 2019 did not increase. As a share of the total economy, spending decreased from 6 percent in 2010 to 5 percent in 2019. The salary gap between private-sector workers and teachers widened so that more schools ended up with underqualified staff, especially non-white schools. These non-white schools had on average 16 percent less funding per student than white schools.[25] In 2017, the Trump administration abolished a grant program to help districts with socioeconomically diverse student populations. Racial inequality still haunted American schools, together with the long-lasting problem of inequality. In 2020, one out of nine pupils arrived at school hungry.

These were the extreme cases, but a significant proportion of lower middle-class children suffered from the stress of their parents combining more than one job.[26] The education gap between rich and poor, black and white remained enormous. It led to persistently low results of the United States in international education rankings. The problem became so alarming that the military considered investments in high-quality education a matter of national security.[27] In 2020, three quarters of young Americans were unfit to serve: too fat or too stupid.[28] This was still a nation in reckless consumption mode, much more than a nation waking up to the many challenges.

The weaker American society became, the more angry, cynical, and selfish citizens grew. Whether one compared this to Barack Obama's call for hope or Donald Trump's rallying cry to make America great again, patriotism became flimsier. Americans lost hope, felt powerless, and worried that the future would be worse. Trust in fellow citizens decreased. Fewer citizens were making an effort to turn the tide through social engagement. Fewer Americans volunteered or supported charity.[29] Fewer followed the news.[30]

This was particularly the case for youngsters. Youngsters became somewhat more permissive, regarding issues like same-sex marriage and migration, for instance, but not more engaged. They were concerned about the state of the society, about the environment. Yet, they were less involved in household tasks, spent less time socializing, became less interested in developing a meaningful philosophy of life, and became less altruistic.[31] Middle-class youngsters were often spoiled, finding it perfectly normal to go online, order something produced by underpaid adult factory workers in developing countries and having it instantly delivered to their room by underpaid adult flex couriers. Teens were influenced by social media idols. The teen idealized by such media was a spoiled teen.[32]

Enter the life of Nicolette Gray, also known as Beverly Hills Brat, a teenager from Los Angeles. She was rapped over the knuckles in a television show for demanding too much pocket money from her mother and being spoiled. "I don't want a job, it's so much work." It was an orchestration, most likely, but she became an instant idol. Her social media channels turned into an advertisement channel with hundreds of thousands of youngsters following. Other teenagers competed to become Beverly Hills Brat for one day. Snobbery and waste became an ideal. Take the following conversation from an online video clip watched over 1.5 million times:

Girl: "Hi, I have to break some news to you . . ."

Mother: "What?"

Girl: "So, I broke my iPhone, so I need you to go to the Apple store to fix it for me today."

Mother: "Again!?"

Girl: "It's right here. It doesn't work. I don't know my own password, but I promise you the phone doesn't work."

Mother: ". . . How many times have you broken . . .? She has three phones, maybe four now. I don't even know . . . But that's OK as a loving mother."[33]

Tribalism

Frustration about the state of society did not bring Americans closer. It made them more selfish; it divided them and widened the partisan gap. Never before had Republicans been so negative toward the Democratic president, and vice versa. Many other tensions heightened. Trust in politics was especially low among African-Americans. In 2008, 90 percent of African-Americans voted for Barack Obama. Initially, they drew hope from his election victory. Incidents like the shooting of a young black citizen in the City of Ferguson, in 2014, however, led them to the conclusion that even an African-American president could not tackle the problem of racial inequality. An investigation revealed that the Ferguson killing was the result of racism and the fact that the police were pressured by local governments to generate incomes from fines.[34] African-Americans traditionally favored the Democratic Party. Yet, under Barack Obama, political trust inside this group suffered a dramatic drop. Young African-Americans in particular turned their backs on the Democrats – and politics at large.

The countryside became rebellious as well.[35] The more poverty afflicted the rural communities, the more economic self-sufficiency and independence became a source of pride. Independence meant the limitation of political interference, such as the objective of the Obama administration to reform health insurance, or laws related to abortion and same-sex marriage. Independence was idealized as the capacity to defend one's family and hence the permission to own guns. Independence also implied that the rural way of life, tradition, and race needed to be defended against migration. It certainly meant to stand up against the urban elite and remarks like those made by Barack Obama. "They get bitter," he said. "They cling to guns or religion or antipathy to people who aren't like them." Economic struggle became an identity struggle. This was not new, but the more rural communities were cornered, the more radical some of them became. Meanwhile, their say in politics became larger. Typical white rural Americans became a minority, but rural states delegate a large number of senators to Capitol Hill. Compared to its demographic weight, the aggrieved countryside wielded disproportionate electoral strength.[36]

News media exacerbated the polarization. "The media is not the enemy of the people," a former Chief of Staff for Donald Trump avowed. "But if you only watch Fox News, because it's reinforcing what you believe, you are not an informed citizen."[37] Social media allowed for even greater tribalization of the information landscape. If partisan lines were dominant before, a colorful variety of social media prophets stepped into the limelight. Even Donald Trump, who had thrived on the torrent of frustration that gushed through Facebook and Twitter, lost control. When the corona pandemic broke out and the American government ordered a lockdown, erstwhile supporters first turned into digital mobs, berating the federal government for curtailing their freedom, then used social media to mobilize street protests against the lockdown, and later organized heavily armed private militia to secure those street protests. Donald Trump had first called for a revolution in Washington, DC; now that he had conquered Washington, the mob and his revolution turned against him.

In between the factions, a growing number of Americans considered themselves independent. Their turnout during elections was extremely low, but they identified the ability of Republicans and Democrats to work together as one of the main challenges. This was also the sobering observation of retired marine general James Mattis. Mattis, versed in the ancient Greek and Roman literature about politics, had just resigned as Secretary of Defense. "What concerns me most as a military man is not our external adversaries; it is our internal divisiveness," he said. "We are dividing into hostile tribes cheering against each other, fueled by emotion and a mutual disdain that jeopardizes our future, instead of rediscovering our common ground and finding solutions."[38] Intellectuals like Mattis saw the specter of demagogy, of the rule of the mob, and all other political vices that the founders of the United States had sought to prevent. "The difficulty," they asserted, "is to constantly impose on the national rulers the necessity of a spirit of accommodation to reasonable expectations of their constituents."[39] Donald Trump expelled what was left of that spirit from Washington's vestiges of power. Tribalism threatened American democracy.

When former Republican President George W. Bush was asked about his opinion of Donald Trump's inauguration, he answered: "That was some weird shit." Donald Trump was a disturbing person. It was difficult to imagine anybody more alien to the virtues of a statesman that America's Founding Fathers had in mind. The Manhattan property developer who bragged about his gilded apartment, mentioned in chapter 2: that was Donald Trump. Trump swanked that his net worth was US$10 billion. He made discourteousness and disrespect his trademark. During the campaign, for instance, he mocked his Democratic rival, Hillary Clinton, about the affair of her husband, Bill Clinton. "If Hillary Clinton can't satisfy her husband, what makes her think she can satisfy America?" He sneered at his main Republican critic, a highly decorated veteran, for having been a prisoner of war during the Vietnam War. He is not a war hero, he said, war heroes are not captured. Once elected president, Trump openly sympathized with dictators. "He is a strong head," he commented about the North Korean leader Kim Jong-un. "He speaks and his people sit up at attention. I want my people to do the same." He praised the Chinese president for having abolished a two-terms limitation. He said, with some irony though: "He was able to do that. I think it is great. Maybe we will give that a shot someday." American intelligence services also confirmed that Donald Trump had been favored by the Russian government in the run-up to the 2016 elections; Chinese officials considered Trump their favored candidate for the elections of 2020.

As Donald Trump ranted and rambled, the old political elite mourned. In 2018, at the funeral of a prominent Republican Senator, former Democratic Vice-President Joe Biden spoke of the passing of a generation. "They look at him as if John came from another age, that lived by a different code, an ancient, antiquated code where honor, courage, character, integrity, duty were admired," he eulogized. "All we do today is attack the oppositions of both parties, their motives, not the substance of their argument."[40] Biden was of course right, but it was also his generation that was unable to use several decades of power to prevent some of the problems from growing worse, to no longer repeat errors, to match the virtue in its discourse with virtue in its deeds, to restrain powerful interest groups, to make difficult adjustments instead of letting imbalances grow further.

The two American presidents of that decade, Obama and Trump, were two manifestations of the same impasse. While Barack Obama had courtesy, he did not always have the courage to act. He fought for a new healthcare system, but sidestepped a lot of other, more fundamental battles: against the growing detachment of multinational companies, for instance, and even against the growing racial polarization. While Trump lacked the courtesy, he did show courage, reckless courage, in addressing the debt-based economic model and the weakening of America's industrial base. He slapped tariffs on Chinese imports, promised more investment in infrastructure, made the rebuilding of industries a key point in his agenda, and took companies like Amazon head-on. In most of his efforts, however, Trump was not successful and he had to backtrack on many policies. Despite his bragging that he would quickly control the corona pandemic and reopen the economy soon, his response was a disaster. Some of the departments established to fight pandemics, abolished by Trump after his election, were severely missed. The poor state of the medical sector became fully visible. Both presidents were like a Messiah to about half of the American population and a demon to the other half. In their final months as president, Trump had an average approval of around 44 percent, Obama 48 percent. Both presidents failed to heal the nation. Both presidencies ended in more disappointment and anger.

European firewall

In the autumn of 2019, a European Commissioner shared a provocative observation with a group of officials and policy advisors. The spirit of the American Founding Fathers has moved to Europe, he said. These Founding Fathers had in mind a political system in which the tendencies toward populism and mob rule were neutralized by various checks and balances. Hence, if one American state were to become a rotten apple, the whole basket of apples would not be affected. "This is how European democracy works today. We have the spirit of the American federalists in Brussels, mob rule in Washington," the official reasoned. "There are rotten apples, but they cannot destabilize the whole European project, which will continue to advance steadily."[41] Compromise and political dilution as a democratic advantage.

The former Council President, Herman Van Rompuy, echoed that idea. He spoke of European integration as a pragmatic project, which, thanks to its scale and checks and balances, together with its common institutions, would steer clear of destabilizing emotional politics.[42] He also posited that setbacks like the Eurozone crisis forced the member states each time to make the European Union stronger. The European institutions, the assemblies of ministers, heads of state, parliamentarians, the multinational European bureaucracy functioned as a firewall against populism. The idea became widespread in European policy circles. But was it also valid?

Optimists had several arguments. Consider the impact of the Eurozone crisis. While some countries were in pain, others recorded high growth figures. Or consider the rise of political extremism. In Hungary, the rightist Viktor Orbán became prime minister in 2010. In Poland, the rightist

Law and Justice Party of Jarosław Kaczyński remained influential. Rightist parties joined the national government of Austria and Italy. But elsewhere pragmatic politicians held their ground. In the 2019 elections for the European Parliament, the Eurosceptic formation failed to break through. Yes, there was the Brexit referendum of 2016, that led the UK to leave the European Union. But, at the same time, new steps were taken toward integration. Citizens' attitudes, despite different crises, hardly changed. Slightly more than half of Europeans found that their country benefited from the European Union. Support for the common currency, the euro, did not decrease. Constancy throughout crisis: that appeared to characterize Europe.

Or was it crisis through constancy? Were pragmatic European leaders perhaps too self-congratulating? Had just keeping the European project afloat become the benchmark of success? About half of Europeans were supportive of preserving the union, but that also implied that still about half remained less convinced. Ten years after the crisis, and even before the outbreak of the corona pandemic, about half of Europeans considered the economic situation bad. There were families in countries like Greece that had lost over 30 percent of their income and saw their country engulfed by refugees. There were families in Italy that lost 5–10 percent of their income and also experienced how thousands of destitute Africans, many illegal immigrants, tried to survive in their impoverished city quarters and villages. There were the millions of retired people in small towns and villages in Eastern Europe, often cut off from relatives that had migrated to the cities or Western Europe, who still felt in no way connected to the European project. There were the millions of working poor in Germany and the Netherlands, bitter about governments that celebrated high economic growth yet ignored the fact that the cost of living was rapidly becoming higher. European integration to them still meant that they needed to share the work floor with hard-working colleagues whose language they did not speak.

Skepticism simmered. The challengers remained defiant. In Poland, the Eurosceptic government defied a ruling of the European Court of Justice and went ahead with a law that forced Polish judges to retire. In Hungary, the Orbán administration kept pushing for a new administrative court, overseen by the government, that was to handle electoral and corruption issues. The separation between executive and judicial power was hence abandoned. These were attacks against the core principles and values of the European Union. In France, the pro-European president, Emmanuel Macron, known for his numerous initiatives to deepen European integration and to reform his country's economy, became more unpopular than most of his predecessors. He was referred to as the world champion in falling flat. French citizens also became increasingly skeptical of the European project. The German economy, in spite of its massive exports, lost traction. The Brexit negotiations absorbed immense political and human resources, both in the United Kingdom and the rest of Europe. Most of all, European leaders collectively failed to deliver on three important objectives: the strengthening of the Eurozone and the internal market, an effective approach toward refugees and immigrants, and the rebalancing of the European project between economic openness and the search for identity and security. Let us take a closer look at these three issues.

Morals and markets

The Eurozone crisis affected all countries: both borrowers and lenders. Surplus countries, like the Netherlands and Germany, fumbled at the bad management of deficit countries. But because Dutch and German banks were so invested in countries like Italy, they could not afford for them to go bankrupt. What followed was a political achievement. In 2010, the Eurozone countries established two financial stabilization mechanisms with a combined worth of US$1 trillion. These mechanisms lent money to afflicted countries like Greece, Ireland, and Portugal. This helped reassure international investors, and consequently to lower interest rates for the crisis-stricken countries, and to stabilize the whole Eurozone. In addition, the European Central Bank carried out quantitative easing by buying the troubled debt products of private banks. In the following years, markets stabilized. From an accountant's viewpoint, the Eurozone, and the European Union more broadly, were in better shape than the United States. Its public debt remained smaller, its international investment position improved, and its external trade deficit made way for a small surplus.

But, like the United States, the European Union did not seize the crisis to lay the basis for a new stage of progress. Central banks swamped the market with money. Employers could profit from decreasing wages in countries like Greece, and taxes were cut. Everything was present for a relaunch. It did not happen. Economic growth remained anemic. European countries invested more in factories outside Europe than at home.[43] Spending on research and development remained flat. Public infrastructure investment decreased. Money again started to flow more to the real estate sector, where the financial crisis partially began.

This was peculiar, because the European institutions had promised to unleash a fourth industrial revolution, factories that were more sustainable. It vowed to spearhead a circular economy that kept precious materials in use, and product designs that permitted components to be reused instead of being thrown away. Europe also showed ambition to become a leader in clean energy. So, the capital was available, production costs were repressed, and the ambitions declared. The circumstances for a relaunch seemed perfect. The idea was powerful: rebuilding industries, making them greener, growing wealth at home, generating jobs, driving innovation, and halting the geopolitical debacle of making authoritarian competitors strong.

Why then was this relaunch so disappointing? There are a few explanations. Exigent standards could force companies to innovate and hence to strengthen their leadership in the long run. But why would they invest in new production capacity if the existing infrastructure was not fully utilized? Europe could be perfectly served by existing production capacity. Several sectors, from farming to manufacturing, suffered from overcapacity. Alternative markets beckoned, like Asia, with faster growth and fewer rules. Those cheaper and laxer countries could serve the European market, especially because low energy prices had also reduced global transportation costs. Some shipping companies offered to transport a full container from China to Europe for a few hundred dollars. Large European multinationals, like the car industry, also had a greater interest in benefiting from overseas markets. Volkswagen, for instance, produced almost twice as many cars in Asia as in Europe. Some companies and governments were opposed to ambitious internal social and environmental standards, because it would make them less competitive against imports that were not held to these rules: the playing field was not level. This was an understandable concern.

So, why were these *internal* standards not tied to *external* trade? The European Union was interested in a new sustainable industrial revolution and it could be a way out of its economic impasse. The case for also impos- ing environmental standards on imports was strong. But Europe even failed to include enforceable and ambitious standards in trade agreements with like-minded countries such as Japan and Canada.[44] What kept Europe from doing so was inconsistent neoliberal ideology. Officials asserted that such import measures would be green protectionism. Yet, protectionism implies discrimination, that foreign companies are treated differently compared to domestic companies. This was not the case, as rules would apply to both of them. The protectionism argument was thus not valid.

Another argument was that such unilateral measures would undermine the World Trade Organization and cause others to retaliate. But other trade partners were already undermining the World Trade Organization, as we have seen, by manipulating trade in different ways. This second argument was thus also flawed. Some reasoned that green import measures would go against free trade. Yet, trade was never entirely free and the founders of economic liberalism, like Adam Smith, had always insisted that a market cannot be disconnected from morals. Liberalism holds that a market must be free, but that it also is a means to strengthen societies, to make private initiative contribute to the common good. The markets hence must mirror morals. All great economic revolutions coincided with moral revolutions. Some bureaucrats were just scared, scared of retaliation from China and the United States against big European companies. "We cannot afford impor- tant Germany industries to pay the price," testified one German official.[45]

Despite the fact that many European politicians and officials presented themselves as innovators and trailblazers of a greener society, inconsistent neoliberal prescriptions justified the continuation of the standstill. Local European producers could benefit from elevating the marketplace to a new level of ambitions, norms, and standards. It would reward them for contrib- uting innovative solutions and for boosting productivity in new materials, product design, and business models. For multinational producers, how- ever, the situation was different. For them, the European Union was only one of many markets. They were often pressured by governments outside, like China and the United States, to help prevent the European Union from tying more demanding standards to trade. Large German companies in particular lobbied frenetically against conditioning trade. Even when the corona pandemic damaged their supply chains in China, their first priority seemed to be to re-establish them, not to relocate them back to Europe.

By the end of the decade, the situation was such that many associations of smaller companies had become convinced that tying internal standards to external trade had become the only way to respond to social and environmental dumping practices. The corona pandemic created new momentum for the advocates of reinforcing manufacturing in Europe and reducing dependence on distant producers like China. The European Commission, and member states like France and the Netherlands, pressed for a green new deal, but made little progress. Berlin continued to block the proposal for a European border tax on polluting companies. Large multinationals were better organized and the political leadership still lacked the courage to make a decision. The interest of the few trumped the interest of the many.

The result of this inconsistency was harmful. Capital was available, but hardly helped grow new industries, cleaner cities, and better housing. It was like this in the early 1990s and it remained like this 30 years later. Companies that did try were seldom rewarded. In the Netherlands, for instance, a steel company tried a very clean blast furnace, but could not compete against cheap imported steel. Parts of the chemical sector forayed into bioplastics, but they were discouraged by the fact that the shale energy boom in the United States made traditional polymers cheaper. Textile producers that wanted to shift to sustainable fibers only saw cheap retailers taking over.

Like the United States, the European economy was a leaking casket. Between 2010 and 2019, despite low energy prices, its annual imports of oil and gas cost US$350 billion, its annual imports of cheap consumer goods from Asia US$200 billion. What compensated for this import bill was vast exports of cars, mostly German luxury brands, aircraft, and chemical products. From a short-term macroeconomic viewpoint, it was balanced, more balanced than American trade. From a long-term perspective, it was uncertain whether Europe could retain its leading edge in these core sectors, as other important economies also advanced in car building, aeronautics, and advanced chemicals. From a social viewpoint, it prevented the European Union from putting its social and environmental ambitions into practice, and taking the lead in a new socioeconomic revolution.

The recovery of the European Union, following the crisis of 2009, was slow and sloppy. It was sloppy because the capital made available through quantitative easing or the austerity measures did not make the economy stronger. This was the case for the Eurozone, but also for countries like the United Kingdom. A complete economic meltdown was averted, but that was about it. Another moment of uncertainty, another opportunity to repair the economy at its fundaments, was lost. If growth somewhat recovered, the real disposable income in most European countries remained flat. Adjusted for inflation, wages in Greece, Italy, Portugal, Spain, and the United Kingdom did not fully recover between 2010 and 2019. Private-sector employment in the European Union in 2019 was still 2 percent below the pre-crisis level. Poverty rates slightly increased. Even in countries with strong economies, like the Netherlands, citizens hardly benefited from booming exports and production.

Then came corona. For months, fragile countries, like Italy, sank into mayhem. Entire regions had to be cordoned off to stop the spread of the virus. Export champions too came to discover their vulnerability as global demand crashed. Without any prospect of a new economic relaunch, a green new deal, Europe stuck to its policy of saturating the market with money. In the fall of 2020, leaders took great pride in the fact that European institutions could now directly borrow money, a step forward in more financial cooperation. But at the same time, they continued to surrender the market, its entrepreneurs, and its workers to competitors that turned pollution and dumping into an advantage. Many of the measures on paper proved modest in practice. Most of Europe's advanced trade agreements, which included some rather weak social and environmental standards, were with like-minded countries, still not with the main economic competitors such as China and the United States. This all discredited the idea of harnessing a socially equitable market, the third way, as a force to preserve peace, democracy, and cooperation in Europe. Polls showed that most Europeans were dedicated to European cooperation and democracy but found that neither the European market nor democracy properly delivered.

Lesbos

In 2015, close to two million people crossed Europe's borders illegally. For more than a year, European citizens kept reading about refugees from Syria, Iraq, and Libya that arrived in shabby lifeboats on the outer islands of Greece and Italy. The shores of the Greek island of Lesbos were awash with orange life jackets and shards of black rubber. From there, long lines of fortune seekers forged north, some taking the train to Budapest, Hungary, some walking hundreds of kilometers. In the summer of 2015, hundreds of refugees started to walk from Budapest to Vienna. The images were dramatic.

Many citizens, we saw in previous chapters, found that the integration of immigrants had been a failure in the past, feared that European enlargement would lead to a larger influx, and looked warily toward a new inflow of refugees from Muslim countries.[46] If citizens were preoccupied by the Eurozone crisis between 2009 and 2014, migration became the most important concern in the following years. About 40 percent of Europeans thought immigration a problem, 40 percent were ambivalent, and 20 percent saw immigration as an opportunity.[47] A minority of Europeans assumed that immigrants were a burden on the welfare system and worsened crime.[48] In most countries, about 15–20 percent had a clear inclination against migration and particularly against Muslim immigrants. A smaller minority were optimistic.[49]

The majority of Europeans were hesitant. The aversion of the minority, however, revealed several underlying problems, like loneliness and insecurity. Answering the question of how many immigrants from countries outside Europe should be allowed, 24 percent of less-educated European citizens but 10 percent of the highly educated said none; 24 percent of the poorest income quintile but 11 percent of the highest income quintile would say none; 40 percent of lonely citizens but 15 percent of those with frequent social contacts would say none; 21 percent of those finding traditions important said none compared with 14 percent of those finding traditions unimportant.[50]

Hesitation rather than widespread xenophobia dominated Europe's views about migration. Yet, fears did grow that this was only the beginning of a larger exodus. European citizens also became concerned that radicalized

Islamic fighters were among Syrian refugees and those fears were exacerbated by the Islamic terrorist campaigns in 2015 and 2016, and a horrendous wave of sexual assaults in Germany, mainly committed by North African immigrants and asylum seekers. Many Europeans felt under attack.[51] What followed was a toxic political clash. On the one hand, rightists blamed the moderates for being weak and claimed that they would better control the migration flows if they came to power. The leader of the French far right compared the migrant crisis to the barbarian invasions that precipitated the fall of the Roman Empire: "Without action by the French people, the migrant invasion that we face will be nothing compared to that of the fourth century and will perhaps have the same consequences."[52]

On the other hand, moderate politicians blamed the far right and claimed to be in control of the refugee and migration challenge. In 2015, the German Chancellor Angela Merkel stirred animosity by stating that the refugee crisis was under control: "Wir schaffen das." Politicians like Merkel had valid points. Europe was bound by international law to accept refugees from war zones and most citizens did not oppose that. Furthermore, as a percentage of the total European population, the number of refugees that arrived between 2010 and 2020 remained below 1 percent. The idea that there would be many terrorists among the refugees, as some suggested, also had to be put into perspective.[53]

But these valid arguments could not mask the fact that the pragmatic politicians failed to take control. In Southern Europe, Greece and Italy were not at all in control. The image became more like "Wir schaffen das nicht." By 2020, for instance, there were still over 100,000 people of concern in overcrowded camps in Greece. Along the way, most countries hardened their policies. In 2015, still 52 percent of asylum applications were accepted; in 2020, it was 36 percent. By 2020, there were no indications of peace returning to Syria, to the point that refugees in Europe could safely return. This meant that many of the refugees could start to consider applying for citizenship, which in most European countries was possible after five years. Yet, efforts to integrate the refugees were insufficient. Internal reports of the European Commission hinted at a widespread lack of good language education, insufficient measures to prepare them for the labor market, a lack of policy of local governments, but also of abuse, sexual exploitation, and racism.[54]

It emerged that many refugees would stay in Europe. Still, national governments did not properly prepare for the moment at which hundreds of thousands of refugees might apply for citizenship. Countries also grappled with large numbers of illegal immigrants. In 2020, over 600,000 illegal immigrants, mostly asylum seekers whose requests had been turned down, were in the European Union. Thousands more did not apply for asylum on the continent but tried to reach England. For years, they loitered in railway stations and along the northern coast of France. The result was growing anger on both sides: native Europeans complaining, but also refugees becoming disillusioned, angry, and, albeit a small minority, radicalized. In several European countries, the sentiment of segregation and polarization increased further, with Islamic schools and Islamic political parties being established, and the far right responding to that more forcefully.

Hence, while the pragmatic political elite in many European countries put itself on a pedestal for being humane toward refugees and immigrants, their policy was dysfunctional and added to the tensions that were rising inside European societies. However much they loathed the far right, this failure at times confirmed the warning of the far right that Europe was unable to accommodate the new refugees and immigrants. Governments did not have a reassuring strategy to deal with the instability in Europe's southern neighborhood either. They paid countries like Turkey and Algeria to stop refugees and immigrants from reaching Europe, very much, indeed, like the decaying Roman Empire did with the *foederati*. The European Commission, the German government of Angela Merkel, the French government of Emmanuel Macron, and many others vowed to invest in North Africa so as to help mitigate the migration pressure, but financial efforts remained cosmetic at best.

Symbolizing the lack of vision of these pragmatic politicians was their response to European citizens that went to fight in Syria and Iraq, and were caught in various camps in the region, often with women and children. There were thousands of them. As these were European citizens, the demand from local governments and even from the United States was to repatriate them to Europe, to investigate their contribution to war crimes, and, if needed, to put them on trial. It took years for the capitals to respond and even then, their police services and courts were often not properly equipped. Hence, as much as the center politicians tried to clench a fist against the far right, they failed to neutralize the causes of concern that led citizens to vote for the far right.

The response to the refugee and migration crisis shows again how the pragmatic politicians continued their elastic run, their campaign for openness without being truly inclusive, openness without having a plan. Citizens that somewhat followed the news knew all too well that migration pressure would not subside. Citizens that were skeptical about the idea that migration helped advance economic growth also had a point. Only 58 percent of the refugees were employed, 45 percent were proficient in the language of the host country, and less than 20 percent had enjoyed higher education.[55] The lack of an efficient integration policy once more posed a challenge to social cohesion. Besides these rational concerns, there were also emotions at work, of elderly people that were isolated and saw their communities disappear, of poor people who felt the openness to migration as confirmation of disrespect by their leaders, and of the many others that were disturbed by the remarkable cohesion of the Islamic community in light of the erosion of their own society.

But however dysfunctional and short-sighted the pragmatic politicians were, the far-right alternative was equally problematic. The return to nation states would make security much more expensive compared to the protection of one common border. Neither did the nationalists have an answer to the long-term security threats in the South. Fences might halt a few million immigrants, but they would never be effective if tens of millions of people sought to escape violence, repression, poverty, and climate change. How could one expect to push refugees back to countries like Tunisia and Algeria if these countries too were about to succumb to instability? The fence fetish of the nationalists was as problematic as the inconsistent migration policy of the moderates, as naive also as the initial assumption of some of the left that migration would contribute to a happy multicultural society. As a proposal to make Europe more secure, the rightist isolationism was another delusion.

The nationalists' promise to defend European liberty and to keep it strong was also in stark contrast with their sympathy for authoritarian countries. Russia had sponsored rightist parties as a way to divide Europe.

Victor Orbán signed a security agreement with the United Arab Emirates, a country known as a safe haven for sponsors of radical Islam. Orbán used his campaign against Islam, refugees, and the European Union to consolidate his personal power, nationalism as a guise for corruption and the enriching of his family. The nationalist leader of the Conservatives, Boris Johnson, called Qatar, a country that intelligence services reported to be reluctant to crack down on the financing of terrorist movements, a partner in the fight against terrorism.

Moreover, while the nationalists blamed immigrants for undermining social security and taking jobs, some reached out to China, an economy that kept unleashing damaging trade policies at Europe. While they blamed immigrants for imperiling local culture, nationalist politicians encouraged cheap international brands to set up shop in their cities. "I want that too in Antwerp," said a Flemish nationalist mayor about Primark, a chain notorious for its low-quality standards and social dumping. Immigrants had to adjust to the local rules, but nationalists kept going further in adjusting local standards to large foreign multinationals.

Middle class

This all added up to another form of flimsy patriotism: tough in form, spiritless in substance. Most of all, the shift to the right and the blaming of others – the immigrants, other regions, and other countries – gave European citizens a pretext to remain idle. Nationalists did explain how immigration challenged local values and cohesion, but they did not explain how citizens could help uphold values and cohesion. They allowed citizens to retreat into cynicism and selfishness, to hide in fenced villas and large cars, to continue to fall for consumerism.

The rich spent fortunes on expensive cars. Sales of luxury car brands in Europe expanded by 40 percent between 2010 and 2019. The young middle class flocked to cheap retail chains like Ikea and Primark, and became angry if those chains did not set up shop nearby. The poor tried to keep up, albeit with smaller cars and cheaper stores.

For the young, average European, perfect life was to own a detached house in the suburbs, to drive a fancy German car to one of these stores, to have a latte at a franchise of an American coffee chain, and to end the day watching American soaps on a South Korean flat screen television – muttering about the dismal state of the world. It was this garage-parking-garage-existence, a society of consumer-citizens that the moderates had allowed to grow and that the rightists now promised to defend.

Soldiers were literally deployed to guard the consumerist lifestyle of Europeans, patrolled shopping malls, stood guard before large fashion stores where hordes of teenagers came to shop for fashionable pre-ripped jeans, and kept an eye on the masses of city trippers at airports. It was security populism. Similar to President George W. Bush calling on his compatriots to continue shopping after 9/11, European politicians wanted to give their citizens the impression that life could continue. Soldiers were patrolling in shopping streets: everything that could make security visible. Out of sight, however, intelligence services often kept lacking resources to keep track of radicalizing. Prevention by means of an integration strategy, care for left-behind minority areas, and dedicated education programs also attracted limited concern.

No politician explained to the shoppers that they were in fact exacerbating the challenges of terrorism and migration. Consider again the fast-fashion retailer Primark. Fast fashion meant that vast volumes of textiles ended up in garbage bins after only being used a few times. Precious commodities, like cotton, were treated like waste. Cotton, however, is grown in precarious regions like West Africa. In West Africa, the cotton that fast-fashion consumers so easily discarded required enormous amounts of farmland and water. Cotton production in the Sahel hence challenged hundreds of thousands of small farmers. It contributed to migration, first to African cities, then to North Africa. It also made terrorist movements attractive as they offered an economic alternative. This was security populism in its most perverse form: While some soldiers guarded the fast-fashion shops in European cities, other soldiers were sent to fight the security challenges that this consumerism contributed to.

The corona crisis did not change this. Instead of trying to come to grips with the downside of a globalization of mass consumption, politicians in different countries urged citizens to resume shopping. Shopping became a declaration of confidence almost. "People should shop, and shop with confidence," the British Prime Minister said while visiting a shopping mall.[56] The Italian prime minister made a similar call.[57]

With a vicious interplay of short-sighted pragmatic politicians and equally short-sighted rightist policies, Europe was brewing its own clash of civilizations, exacerbating the divisive forces inside its societies. For now, this polarization seemed manageable. Radicalism was limited to the fringes. Yet, for the longer term, no solutions were offered for the social uncertainty that gripped many citizens, the weakening of Europe's southern frontier, including countries like Greece and Italy, the loneliness among millions of seniors, and the craving for some sense of belonging.

Against the backdrop of social polarization, some governments, finally, started to introduce courses of citizenship at school, but usually confined to only one hour a week or some extra activities. Even universities, which often placed themselves on the moral high ground, reprimanding populism, often tried to maximize their student registrations, without investing in the skills and attitude critical for the leaders of tomorrow to keep their democracy alive. The pragmatic and progressive parties showed a great interest in securing the vote of minority groups and, most of the time right-fully, criticized racism and discrimination. But they offered few solutions to the growing segregation and were slow in insisting that building a society required some basic common values and an effort from all sides. Morals became extremely selective: in all corners of society. Social engagement, meanwhile, kept falling. Around half of European youngsters did not par-ticipate in any organization whatsoever and only 30 percent did voluntary work.[58] Average civic knowledge of students in European countries was below the level of Russia.[59] Social media were considered as a means to bring politics closer to youngsters, but only around 5 percent posted com-ments on social or political issues on a weekly basis.[60]

The pragmatic politicians hence continued to undermine the European project: by wasting another decade to repair the flaws of the Eurozone and unfair trade, by wasting another crisis to formulate a comprehensive answer to the relentless pressure of migration and segregation, and by not offering an alternative to the nationalism of corruption and effrontery as pioneered by politicians like Viktor Orbán. The dilemma in this regard was thus not so different from America's political tension between the unmannerly muscle of Donald Trump and the inconsistent moralism of Barack Obama. In other countries, rightist politicians waved their banners, but behind the banner was often only emptiness: no vision of rebuilding economic strength, no vision of replacing materialism with morals, no vision of strengthening cohesion. It was façade politics. Both sides made Europe weaker.

CHAPTER 11

ABDICATION

I N THE SPRING OF 2015, A COMPANY OF OFFICIALS FROM A COUNTRY IN THE Middle East, some experts, and European officials dined in a hotel in Brussels. The discussion touched on issues from terrorism to cyber security, but what the delegates from the Gulf were really interested in concerned the capability of European countries to handle the instability in the Middle East. "The American leadership turns its sight to Asia. But what does Europe do? It sticks its head in the sand," one delegate carped. "Countries in the region no longer think that Europe can look after its own interests, let alone look after the Middle East."[1] The visitors from the Gulf had already formed their conclusion.

During a private breakfast meeting in the winter of 2016, in Rome, a billionaire from Lebanon stated: "Do not think that the world will let you retire safely behind the Mediterranean Sea. You Europeans will sell everything. There has never been honesty in your conduct, but now there is even no pride anymore."[2] The gentleman had a point. In 2016, the government of Malta sold citizenship to Zhongtian Liu, a Chinese billionaire. Liu received a golden passport in exchange for investing in a villa. A few years later, the tycoon was charged with tax evasion and other crimes. Malta and other countries sold hundreds of these visas to oligarchs from Russia, China, and the Middle East. European citizenship was for sale. It was symptomatic of the main evolution studied in this chapter: the accelerating decline of Western influence.

The financial crisis of 2009 undermined the position of the West as the global economic center. The British prime minister uttered: "The old systems of economic co-operation are over."[3] In the wake of the crisis, China promised to buy more government bonds from the United States and the European Union, yet also suggested reforming the International Monetary Fund and questioned laissez-faire capitalism. "You were my teacher," a Chinese official said to the American Treasury secretary. "But now here I am in my teacher's domain and look at your system. We aren't sure we should be learning from you anymore."[4] Other Chinese officials were less subtle: "Europe's labour laws make workers lazy."[5] Vladimir Putin called the United States a parasite on the global economy. The Russian ambassador in Brussels said: "Europe presents itself as a shining temple on top of the hill, but in reality, it becomes a backyard of globalization."[6] These critiques were also increasingly heard at meetings of the BRIC countries, Brazil, Russia, India, and China.

Western countries did consider reforming global economic governance, but changed track. The United States first tried to salvage its economic primacy by negotiating trade agreements with like-minded countries. These trade deals collapsed. Meanwhile, however, it had allowed the World Trade Organization to weaken and angered trade partners. President Donald Trump resorted to protectionism. By the end of the decade, the United States had almost entirely destroyed its own system of governance and created nothing in its place. The corona pandemic of 2020 magnified the fissures across the Atlantic. Western countries struggled to recover and the pandemic exposed their reliance on supplies from China. European countries were more hesitant than the American government to confront China. While China also accused Europe of a misinformation campaign about the causes and impact of the corona pandemic, the European institutions gave in to Chinese pressure and censured one of its own critical assessments of the situation. The 27 European ambassadors to China tolerated the censoring of a collective article they wrote for a Chinese newspaper. We will need more trade and investment on both sides, they insisted. The Italian government begged China for support. The King of Belgium pleaded for support from his "friend," the founder of the Chinese online store, Alibaba. The European Union also preferred to work with

China to salvage the World Trade Organization. It kept blowing hot and cold.

The West, as this chapter clarifies, further undercut its position by enriching authoritarian countries through energy imports. The German *Energiewende*, a policy that phased out nuclear power plants, and the absence of a common energy policy caused European countries to rely on imports more than in previous decades. The West also betrayed the call for democracy resulting from the Arab Spring and fell back into its habit of sponsoring dictators as a quick fix for instability. The migration and refugee crisis around 2015 had made authoritarian countries emerge as gatekeepers that needed to be paid to hold some of the fortune seekers away. The rise of the Islamic State led to an inconsistent military response that repressed the insecurity in the Middle East and prompted the West to bestow honor on the leaders of countries like Saudi Arabia for their combat against terrorism, while, in many cases, their country was still a sanctuary for the financing of radical Islam. Whatever influence the West had in the Middle East, it dwindled fast.

The military limitations were also visible in encountering Russia and China. Both countries deployed missiles and other systems to deny access to their neighborhood. NATO and the United States developed different strategies in response. But, this chapter clarifies, they were not solid. A last theme examined is multilateralism. While the election of Donald Trump exacerbated the tensions between the two sides of the Atlantic, other powers were taking the initiative to shape the agenda of international organizations – from the International Telecommunication Union to the World Health Organization.

Paper tiger

During a meeting in Brussels in 2010, a European official gave a glum update of the partnership with China: "The situation today is that we permit China to compete with our companies in an unfair way, that its trade surplus keeps growing by billions each year, and that we now have to ask China to lend us money. This situation must change."[7] At about the same time, President Obama questioned his advisors about whether China's accession to the World Trade Organization in 2001 had truly prompted it to open up: "Did you guys give away too much?"[8] A few years later, he said: "It is not fair when foreign manufacturers have a leg up on ours only because they are heavily subsidized."[9] Western governments once more acknowledged that trade relations with China were unbalanced.

But no one wanted to risk a confrontation at this point. The American government was lobbied to be patient, by tech companies, retail chains, and so forth. The European institutions experienced the same pressure, for instance from the car industry in Germany and the aviation industry in France. Chinese loans and the import of affordable consumer goods were deemed indispensable in the wake of the financial crisis of 2009.[10] The policy response, hence, was inconsistent. On the one hand, a plea was made to China to invest more in Europe and the United States. New dialogues were established to engage China and to persuade it of the need for reform. On the other hand, and this was the most innovative response, the United States and the European Union started to negotiate advanced trade agreements around China.

The rationale of the agreements was straightforward. The promotion of trade between countries that respected social and environmental standards would encourage China to improve its own standards. It was a continuation of constructive engagement by different means. The attempt, however, remained unsuccessful. The European Union brokered an advanced trade agreement with countries like Canada, South Korea, Japan, and Vietnam, but the impact on the trade imbalance with China was minimal. Trade negotiations with other important Asian markets, like India and ASEAN, broke down.

An important vehicle of choice for Washington was the Trans-Pacific Partnership (TPP), a trade block including Japan, Mexico, Canada, Australia, and Vietnam. The agreement, officially signed in 2016, was believed to have more effect on China than an aircraft carrier.[11] The deal would include environmental standards, oblige countries to protect endangered animals, fight illegal fishing, and protect forests. Countries committed to ban child labor and to allow labor unions. Even if such rules were never applied to so many countries before, they were still only minimum rules. TPP did not provide, for example, rules to limit carbon emissions and would most likely boost American exports of shale oil. The very complexity of the deal meant that it risked favoring large companies that could afford an army of lawyers in trade disputes. Leftist Democrats and protectionist Republicans were united in their fear that TPP would destroy more manufacturing jobs. TPP would elevate the economic playing field only a little. In 2018, the trade deal was scrapped by President Trump.

There was another trade scheme that was intended to handle growing competition from China: the Transatlantic Trade and Investment Partnership (TTIP), between the European Union and the United States. Most assessments expected TTIP to spark a boost in trade. Yet, while TPP at least required some developing countries to elevate their social and environmental standards, the TTIP would most likely force Europe to adjust to the less demanding standards of the United States. The trade zone would give American exporters the advantage of cheap shale oil, laxer social regulation, fewer restrictions on pesticides, and so forth. From the American viewpoint, however, fears existed that the market would be glutted by German cars, pharmaceutical goods, and machinery. Europe had a clear manufacturing advantage. "There are already too many German cars in the streets of Manhattan," it argued.[12] In 2018, TTIP was also abandoned. The attempt to put in place advanced trade agreements to spread Western standards and to check China was unsuccessful.

Efforts to confront China directly were not effective either. There were three such attempts. In 2013, the European Trade Commissioner took the initiative to start two important dumping investigations. "China can try to put pressure on member states," he said, "but they will waste their time trying to do so with me."[13] A few months after he spoke these words, the commissioner was forced by the member states to drop an anti-dumping case against Chinese solar panels. Another year later, he was also pressured by Germany and France to abandon an investigation against dumping practices by Chinese telecom companies. His successor took a softer line on China and prioritized an investment agreement instead. In 2019, the European Commission issued a paper in which it labeled China a trade competitor, a systemic rival even.[14] It was a paper tiger, though. Key officials refused to consider unilateral trade measures and the member states backtracked. Almost at the same moment that the paper came out, Italy decided to formally join China's Belt and Road Initiative. The initiative was announced by China in 2013 and involved weaving a web of ports, airports, and railways. The European Union was talking tough, but acting weak. The corona crisis did not change this situation. The opposite even. In 2020, a senior European official declared that China was no longer a systemic rival. In the final week of that year, the German government pressured the European institutions to sign an investment deal with China.

A second example of failed muscular trade policy concerns President Trump. In 2018, he unilaterally slapped unprecedented tariffs on Chinese imports. "We cannot allow China to keep raping this country," he said. Still, the deficit with China barely narrowed. During his first three years, it remained larger than during the term of Barack Obama. In 2020, the Trump administration signed an initial agreement in which the United States promised to refrain from levying new tariffs and China to buy American agricultural goods. In other words, the deal, presented by the White House as a victory, gave China what it wanted: access to raw materials and access to American consumers to keep exporting industrial goods. Trump's protectionism was turned into a diplomatic victory for China. The Trump administration was successful in persuading other countries to bar the Chinese telecom company Huawei from their 5G networks, but most American partners remained reluctant to go any further and even the Trump administration finally agreed to allow American technology to be supplied to Huawei for systems other than 5G.

Between 2010 and 2020, the West tried thus two extremes: a constructive attempt to make the market more open and more sustainable through advanced trade agreements, and a confrontational attempt to sanction unfair competition by limiting access to the market. Both were half-hearted; both failed. The damage was significant. The combined trade deficit of the United States and the European Union with China grew from US$350 billion in 2010 to US$495 billion in 2020.

Some of these earnings were used by China to grow influence inside Europe. Greece, Italy, and Portugal opened strategic sectors like ports and energy to Chinese investors. Eastern European countries established their own cooperation platform with China, the 16+1, later, with Greece on board, 17+1. The President of Hungary, Viktor Orbán, praised China's development model. Belgium and the Netherlands competed to attract Chinese shipping companies to their ports. Germany and France rushed to sell aircraft, machinery, and so forth. Germany in particular came to value its partnership with China as special and critical. The Chancellor's office refused the wider distribution of an intelligence report that warned of China's growing influence on German politics and business.[15] The United Kingdom went all out to secure a trade deal with China in anticipation of Brexit. "They were very rude," the Queen was caught saying, but Buckingham Palace and the government did not have much room for maneuver. In 2019, the British defense secretary was fired for having released a critical assessment of the telecom company Huawei. The European Commission was left dealing with the question of unfair competition. It made one think of the words of the orator Demosthenes, who observed the Greek city states giving in to Macedonia's influence: They traded away their liberty with begging cups.

There was another consequence. While countries were absorbed by the TTIP and TPP negotiations, traditional multilateral bodies like the World Trade Organization and the World Bank weakened. A last important attempt to strengthen the World Trade Organization, in Geneva in 2008, did not succeed. The very idea of cementing two large trade agreements signaled that the United States subsequently lost confidence in trade multilateralism. Yet, China was still able to exploit the unbalanced framework of the WTO. While it benefited from the obligation to open countries to trade in goods, it kept delaying talks in specialized committees about opening trade in services, about the ability of foreign companies to secure government contracts, and about investment liberalization. The United States turned against the WTO, but gave China another decade to profit from its imbalanced trade rules.

At the same time, China started coaxing Western countries into its own trade projects. The Belt and Road Initiative attracted several European countries. The Asian Infrastructure Investment Bank, established in 2016 to help finance Belt and Road projects, also attracted European countries. Their explanation was that it would allow them to "shape" the objectives of the Belt and Road Initiative. What happened, however, was that China kept negotiating most of the projects bilaterally, supported by its own state banks. The World Bank, at the same time, was attacked by American administrators for becoming irrelevant and "flying bureaucrats on a first-class ticket to give advice to governments."[16] Even its new president agreed the bank was becoming irrelevant with regard to new creditors.[17] By 2019, the China Development Bank had lent US$333 billion to other countries, the World Bank US$44 billion. Failed trade policy helped China to grow stronger, added to the internal divisions of the West, and drove Western politicians and corporate leaders to be even more desperate to do business with China. This phenomenon, however, was not limited to China.

Pipeline addicts

"Liar!" the French President Nicolas Sarkozy slung at the Russian foreign minister, and grabbed him by his suit.[18] The Russian politician had just flatly denied that there were Russian troops in Georgia, whereas intelligence reports told differently. Relations with Russia were tense and confused. The Russian government stated that a post-American world had dawned, that the West did not have to try to put it behind an iron curtain again, and that it could send its energy eastward, to China, if the West kept criticizing it. In 2009, the Russian gas monopoly Gazprom halted almost all exports to Europe, sharply increasing prices. At that time, it also became clear that the Russian government was behind the poisoning of a former spy and dissident in London.[19] The West did not know how to react. At that point, the moderate Dmitry Medvedev was still president, but it was all too clear that the hardliner Vladimir Putin was the real leader and would again become president in 2012. "He plays Robin to Putin's Batman," a cable concluded.[20]

The American Secretary of State offered a red reset button to her Russian counterpart and invited him to start on a new page. The European Union proposed a partnership for modernization. The president of the European Council stated that Europe was ready to support Dmitry Medvedev to promote democratic values, to build an open economy, and to empower civil society.[21] Europe's priority, though, was to secure Russian gas. Germany had started closing its nuclear power plants and needed more Russian energy. Former chancellor Gerhard Schröder began to work for Gazprom. In 2011, Nord Stream I, a gas pipeline through the Baltic Sea, was opened. Never mind that diplomats described Putin as an alpha dog who allows a venal elite of corrupt officials to siphon off cash from energy sales.[22] In 2012, Russia was allowed into the World Trade Organization.

Russian billionaire oligarchs became important investors in Paris and London. "It is only a four-hour flight from Moscow, schools and shopping are good."[23] Russian oligarchs were among the prominent guests at fund-raising parties of the ruling British Conservative Party. The Conservatives also had a Russia friendship group. The French government went as far as selling two large amphibious assault ships to the Russian Navy. Local politicians in fancy French ski resorts like Courchevel rolled out the red carpet for Russian oligarchs to buy property. A Russian official was quoted: "You have no idea how extensive these networks are. Russia has penetrated media organizations, lobbying firms, political parties, governments and militaries in all of these places."[24]

Between 2010 and 2012, European energy imports from Russia still surged. It is in this context that Vladimir Putin returned as president. He resorted to a combative foreign policy, sending bombers as far as Alaska, deploying missiles in Kaliningrad, and cracking down ruthlessly on dissidents. The short-lived reset was reset. In 2014, Putin ordered his troops to invade Ukraine and annexed Crimea. A civilian airline, flight MH17, that had taken off from Amsterdam, was shot down by a Russian air defense missile. Almost 300 passengers died.

The West imposed sanctions. But they barely had any impact as it kept importing around US$120 billion of energy each year. Not even a year after the Dutch government had organized a dramatic funeral ceremony for the casualities of the flight MH17 incident, the energy company Royal Dutch Shell agreed with Gazprom to double Nord Stream's capacity. "We do not want to get involved in politics," it said.[25] In the following year, a Dutch company was selected by Gazprom to build another pipeline between the Black Sea and Greece, Turkish Stream. By 2019, all European countries were desperate to normalize relations with Russia, despite continued Russian military pressure and repression of Russian dissidents. "Putin is talking pride

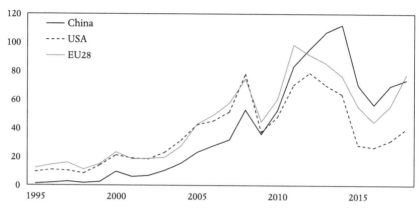

Figure 11.1   Middle East fuel exports (US$ bn)
Source: UNCTAD Stats.

and power; we are talking profit and became pipeline addicts," a former Dutch foreign minister summarized.[26]

The West itself once more embraced authoritarian regimes and kept helping other regional powers become stronger and stronger. This was also the case with the Gulf States. Between 2010 and 2019, annual energy imports from the Gulf totaled US$85 billion (see figure 11.1). The European Union became the region's largest export market. The Gulf States were keen on showing the world that they no longer supported terrorism and were bent on reform. Saudi Arabia and the United Arab Emirates, however, used Al-Qaeda as a proxy when they intervened in Yemen in 2017 and provided it with American weapons. Qatar financed Al-Shabaab in Somalia and armed terrorist groups in Libya with French weapons.[27] The Gulf States were fanning the flames in Europe's backyard.

This did not prevent the Europeans from continuing to deliver weapons. Together with the United States, they annually sold US$12 billion of weapons to the region. Arms companies sometimes joked that countries like Saudi Arabia were too backward to learn to use the weapons and would never be a threat to the West. A French defense minister was more cynical. "We do not support the Saudis; we support French companies that create jobs," he said. "I was minister of defense not minister of ethics."[28] If the terrorist proxy wars in Yemen and Somalia were remote, attacks in Paris and Brussels brought terrorism to the heart of Europe. German intelligence reports provided evidence of ongoing Saudi and Qatari support for extremist preachers.[29] A British report estimated Saudi spending on the worldwide promotion of Wahhabism to have increased, to around US$4 billion.[30] In 2019, a French study documented how Qatar Charity was still injecting extremism into the French suburbs.[31] The US State Department complained that terrorist financiers still operated inside the countries.[32] Bling bling conservatism was very much alive.

In 2018, President Donald Trump received the Saudi crown prince in the White House. In the Oval Office, the two briefed the press. The president smiled and had brought two cardboard charts. Here is what he had to say:

> Saudi Arabia has been a great friend and a big purchaser of equipment and lots of other things, and one of the[ir] biggest investments in the US . . . is buying stock in companies . . . and creating jobs. We have become very good friends . . . and we are bringing back hundreds of billions of dollars into the United States . . . Some of the things that have been approved and are currently under construction and will be delivered to Saudi Arabia very soon . . . If you look in terms of dollars: 3 billion dollars, 533 million dollars, 525 million dollars – that's peanuts for you, we should have increased it – 880 million dollars, 645 million dollars, 6 billion dollars – that's for frigates . . .[33]

Oil and gas went in one direction, weapons in the other. As the European Union was paralyzed by stagnation and the decision to abandon the European Union caused economic uncertainty in Britain, the Gulf States were more than ever seen as potential investors. Former Prime Minister Tony Blair offered his services as a lobbyist to Riyadh and took a US$10 million reward for his Tony Blair Institute.[34] Despite the deadly attacks in Paris being masterminded by a young terrorist who was affected by Saudi-backed Salafi preachers, it was no more than a year before the French prime minister visited the Saudi king in pursuit of business agreements. He was kept waiting for an hour.[35] The visiting Saudi crown prince was awarded the Légion d'Honneur, France's highest honor, for his fight against terror. The French trade promotion agency called Saudi Arabia the promised land for investors.[36] Another former politician lobbying for

Saudi Arabia was Jacques Attali, a former senior advisor to several French presidents. Germany, too, was attracted by the financial power of the Gulf. After the murder of the dissident journalist Jamal Khashoggi, Germany imposed a short-lived restriction on arms exports to Saudi Arabia, but as France, Italy, and the United Kingdom kept selling weapons, Berlin relaxed its own sanctions. The German government criticized its own intelligence service for being critical of the Saudi foreign policy. In 2019, the Saudi government hired hundreds of Western social media influencers to join a dance festival with Western disc jockeys. "That a journalist gets killed is of course terrible," responded one of these influencers to criticism, "but these things happen everywhere and Saudi Arabia is changing very fast in the right direction."[37]

Of the large European countries, the United Kingdom was the most forthcoming. Qatar remained London's largest real estate property owner. Between 2010 and 2020, it invested over US$35 billion in the city, acquiring landmark buildings like the Shard, Harrods, and Camden Market.[38] It became an important shareholder in British Airways and key sea ports. When Britain decided to leave the European Union, Qatar pledged US$6 billion of additional investment. Officials thanked its new sponsor for its "sense of commitment and confidence."[39] The Conservative Brexit front man, Boris Johnson, had called it "a partner in the fight against terrorism" and praised the relationship "going from strength to strength."[40] Off the record, however, diplomats described the Emir of Qatar's frequent visits to London as a landlord visiting his estate. What was more, evidence kept coming out that Qatar was not fighting extremism but still supporting it. The Qatari Al Rayan Bank was found servicing organizations linked to terrorism in Britain.

In the spring of 2018, the crown prince of Saudi Arabia paid a state visit to Britain, a visit celebrated as "a clear demonstration of the strong international confidence in our economy."[41] The crown prince pledged US$70 billion of investment. A stream of reports about Saudi Arabia's continued support for terrorists and the above-mentioned brutal murder of a dissident journalist did not prevent the British government from lobbying relentlessly to have the oil company Aramco listed on the London stock market. It showed how desperate Britain was to attract investors. In 2017, a strategy paper from the Foreign Office was withheld amid concerns over angering London's capital providers. Europe's energy import addiction and its incapacity to roll out a green new deal caused it to lose hundreds of billions to authoritarian countries, which in turn made the weakened European countries humble themselves before these regimes and turn a blind eye to the various ways in which these regimes undermined European security.

Twenty tons of tear gas

China, Russia, and the Gulf States grew their influence through the demand of the West for energy, for cheap goods, and, magnified by the economic uncertainty, for investment capital. Authoritarian regimes in the Middle East and Africa benefited from the Western tilt toward isolationism. European countries in particular wanted to limit the inflow of migrants and to ward off terrorism, but did not want to make an effort to foster stable governance in the long term. They ended up paying strongmen all around the southern frontier.

What brought this opportunism to a new climax was the Arab Spring, a surge of protest and rebellion in North Africa and the Middle East. In December 2010, a poor street vendor in Tunisia burned himself to death. He could no longer stand the corruption and arbitrariness. The event sparked riots, first throughout the country, then throughout the Middle East. First, Western countries did not know how to respond. Sometimes, intelligence services concluded that the longing for democracy would help fight religious extremism and terrorism.[42] Other times, they thought the protest could destabilize the region.

Like in the intelligence estimates, the contradictions in policy could not be starker. With regard to the uprising in Tunisia, France first tried to salvage the regime of Zine al-Abidine Ben Ali. The French minister of defense had offered to support the Tunisian riot police.[43] Emblematic of the close ties, she spent her Christmas vacation in Tunisia using the private jet of a businessman close to the regime. Other ministers had stressed that Ben Ali had done a lot for his country and that his dictatorship was not "unequivocal."[44]

Only when the protests seemed unstoppable did Paris switch camps. Its foreign minister put it thus: "For too long, we have brandished the

Islamist threat as a pretext for justifying to an extent turning a blind eye on governments which were flouting freedom and curbing their country's development."[45] In the following years, Europe sympathized with democratic movements and offered a privileged partnership to some countries. But investments and trade remained stagnant throughout the decade. European development assistance jumped from US$400 million in 2010 to US$520 million in 2011, but fell back below US$400 million in the following years.

In Libya, a Western military intervention in 2011 helped overthrow Muammar Gaddafi. Gaddafi was a brutal leader, but had long been a European partner. Italy provided financial support. In exchange, the Libyan Navy intercepted migrants. But Gaddafi wanted more. In 2010, he traveled to Rome. First, he had his embassy hire 200 Italian catwalk models to be lectured for an hour about the merits of converting to Islam. Afterwards, he threatened that Europe would receive a flood of immigrants if it did not pay US$6 billion annually.[46] "Tomorrow Europe might no longer be European, and even black, as there are millions who want to come in," he said. "We do not know if Europe will remain an advanced continent or if it will be destroyed, as happened with the barbarian invasions."[47] About one year later, Gaddafi was killed in an uprising.

After the intervention, the West left Libya at the mercy of warlords and terrorists. A civil war broke out and more refugees left Libya for Europe. Italy and most other European countries threw their weight behind a new government in Tripoli and paid hundreds of millions of dollars to intercept refugees. France, however, supported a warlord that operated from the eastern part of the country, directly by means of special forces and arms deliveries, and indirectly via the United Arab Emirates. To France, the warlord was a partner to fight armed groups in the Sahel. French and Italian energy companies also competed over oil interests. "It would be very serious if France for economic or commercial reasons," an Italian deputy prime minister warned, "supported a party that is fighting."[48] Another politician put it thus: "France above all has never stopped colonising dozens of African countries." Yet, Italy too, had economic interests and not only in oil. The Libyan foreign investment company, the largest in Africa, had channeled billions into Italian companies. Acting opportunistically, Italy also reached out to the rebels in the east to broker a fishery agreement and to discuss oil interests when its military campaign closed in on Tripoli in 2018. In 2012, the Belgian government suggested releasing some of the frozen funds of Gaddafi, if the transitional government could make some outstanding payments to Belgian companies, and allowed the transfer of large amounts of profits on the frozen Libyan capital to a bank in the United Arab Emirates, a country supporting the rebels.[49]

In Egypt, protesters called for the dismissal of President Hosni Mubarak. "We are on your side," the British prime minister assured the protesters. Yet, the protesters were first repelled with British tear gas. Another delivery of twenty tons of tear gas canisters arrived from the United States while protesters occupied the central square of Cairo. Mubarak stepped down. When a narrow majority of Egyptians elected a candidate from the Muslim Brotherhood to replace him, the American Secretary of State stated: "These guys are wacko." The aversion to the Muslim Brotherhood was inculcated by Saudi Arabia, which considered the movement a threat to its influence and its more puritanical interpretation of Islam.[50] One year later, in 2014, the president was replaced by a general, Abdel Fattah el-Sisi. "It was reassuring that Egypt would not fall into a civil war," was the government line in Washington.[51] In subsequent years, el-Sisi became another partner of Europe to control migration. The president himself spoke of five million refugees who were being taken care of in the country. "This is a partner which is taking its responsibility seriously," praised the president of the European Council.[52] Internal tensions, however, kept flaring up. In 2018, new protests broke out, which were repressed ruthlessly. Thousands of dissidents were jailed. Torture became rampant. Polls showed that a majority of Egyptians found the situation in the country to have deteriorated.[53]

In Syria, protestors demanded that President Bashar al-Assad step down. They escalated into civil war. The West first echoed the calls for al-Assad to resign, but it refused to intervene. The American president drew a red line and threatened retaliation if the regime used chemical weapons against defiant cities. The bluff was called. In 2012, an attack with sarin gas by Assad's troops killed over a thousand people. Western retaliation remained limited to a pinprick operation with cruise missiles. In the subsequent years, Iran and Russia helped stamp out the rebellion. The United States and different

European countries supported Kurdish fighters, with their stronghold in the east of the country.

By 2016, the Obama administration concluded that the world would have to learn to live with the Assad regime. In 2019, Donald Trump ordered the withdrawal of the last American soldiers that buffered the Kurds from the Syrian government in the west of the country and the Turkish government in the north. President Assad was once more in control; around seven million Syrians had fled their country. It made one think about the knack for brinkmanship of the father of President Assad, as described by Henry Kissinger: "He was the only one who would actually jump off the precipice, hoping that on his way down he could break his fall by grabbing a tree he knew to be there."[54]

Most of the Syrian refugees transited via Turkey. Turkey was also an important transit country for refugees and migrants from other countries. In 2016, the European Union sealed a deal with the Turkish government of President Erdoğan in which it promised US$6.6 billion to Ankara if it prevented migrants from reaching Greece and permitted Greece to send rejected asylum seekers to Turkey. When Turkish politicians demanded that European countries take back their citizens who had previously joined terrorist movements in Syria and Iraq, so-called foreign fighters, the European countries first expected them to be tried by countries in the Middle East and only reluctantly returned some of them. Europe was outsourcing its refugee and terrorism problem to a government that had grown increasingly hostile to the West and pitiless in censoring domestic critics.

Tensions continued to rise. European countries made it clear that Turkey would never become a member of the European Union. President Erdoğan himself loathed the lack of interest from Washington in the Turkish viewpoint about Syria and Iraq, American cooperation with the Kurds, and Washington's refusal to extradite Fethullah Gülen, whose movement Ankara believed to be behind an attempted coup in 2016. Erdoğan threatened to send millions of refugees to Europe and to open the floodgates. In 2019, after Turkey invaded Syria, some European countries demanded that he retreat, but had no idea how to pressure him.

The Arab Spring, the refugee and migration crisis, and terrorism made Europe more reluctant to engage in the Arab region. Its response was not to support democratic transition, but to support dictators. That was also true for the United States. The West had been preaching democracy for decades in the Middle East. Now, several societies embraced democracy and they were betrayed. Dictatorship is like a pressure cooker. Corruption, discrimination, and state monopolies fuel anger. The more the heat is stoked up, the harder dictators try to keep the lid on the pot. The cooker has a safety valve that releases some steam: the readiness of democratic countries to take some dissidents. When also that safety valve gets blocked, it is a matter of time before the lid blows off. This explains the flaw of supporting dictatorship: it is the vain hope that the lid holds a while longer, but the result of supporting repression without addressing the internal pressure is that the explosion only becomes more devastating. Supporting dictatorship is about postponing crises, repressing the sources of insecurity, not solving them.

Europe turned its eyes away from the misery in its backyard. There was no common policy. While the German chancellor said "Wir schaffen das" and called for a humane treatment of refugees, the prime minister of Hungary said that the refugees looked like an army threatening Christian Europe. Europe's tendency was to hide behind the Mediterranean and to build fences elsewhere. Countries that were already plagued by instability were asked to take more refugees, to set up camps to hold them, and to cooperate in pushing back migration flows from sub-Saharan Africa. Thousands of fortune seekers drowned in the Mediterranean Sea, thousands more died in the Sahara Desert. One key question in this regard was never answered: What would happen if the neighboring states on which Europe relied for the pushback succumbed themselves to new instability?

Fig leaf operations

So far in this chapter, we have seen the West continue to make competitors rich. We studied how Europe made no effort to use the Arab Spring as an opportunity to support stable democracies in the Arab region. Instead, it financed authoritarian regimes as door guards, to ward off migration and terrorism. Equally myopic was the war on terror.

In 2010, the West had 180,000 soldiers in Iraq and Afghanistan. After a decade of fighting, it prepared to exit. The rise of the Islamic State, IS, and various other terrorist organizations, however, pulled the West back into these sandbox wars. The result was a new stage in the remote-control interventions. Western countries wanted instant retaliation against terrorism, but no longer showed resolve to drain the breeding grounds of terrorism in the long run. Governments wanted to show their voters that they acted forcefully, but at the lowest price. Hence, victory became impossible. With the West signaling that its main objective was to get out, all the terrorists had to do was to wait it out, while the population in countries like Iraq, disillusioned about the prospect of democracy and the rule of law, had to accept political factionalism, armed groups, and terrorist movements as a new fact of life.

From the outset, intelligence reports were not optimistic about the prospect of stabilization. They warned that the Sunnite minority in Iraq had become increasingly bitter about the alleged discrimination by the predominately Shia government, that Al-Qaeda was trying to profit from their grief, and that Iran was growing its influence by means of Shia militias. Classified cables also warned that anger among Iraqis was stoked by the failure to investigate torture, rape, and murder by Iraqi police, Western soldiers, and private contractors.[55] The leader of Al-Qaeda, Osama Bin Laden, was killed, but Western troops could not defeat the Taliban in Afghanistan decisively as its fighters kept hiding in Pakistan. As one secret cable revealed: "We spent a lot of time, money, blood, and treasure on going after Taliban leaders, but it did not have a great deal of effect because the Taliban is not hierarchical."[56]

Still, President Barack Obama accelerated the withdrawal. "We are leaving behind a sovereign, stable and self-reliant Iraq," he said.[57] In December 2011, the last soldiers left Iraq under cover of night. Four days after their departure, a series of bombings rocked Baghdad and various other cities in Iraq. A new insurgency had started, led by hardened Al-Qaeda fighters, joined by thousands of soldiers from the former army of Saddam Hussein, and supported by tens of thousands of angry Sunnites. As the Sunnites in neighboring Syria had also taken up arms to fight their government, the whole Mesopotamian plain, from the Zagros Mountains to the Mediterranean, became a battlefield. Out of this battle grew IS, the Islamic State. Established in 2014, IS was terrorism at its worst. It committed mass killings and its sophisticated digital propaganda inspired lone fighters throughout the world. At almost the same time, the Taliban started a counteroffensive in Afghanistan and took the northern city of Kunduz.

It created a dilemma. The West was tired of the war on terrorism, but with the rise of IS, terrorism became more frightening. Western journalists and aid workers were beheaded on camera, a Jordanian pilot burned alive in an iron cage. New remote-control intervention was the response. It was aimed at IS in the Middle East, the Taliban, and various other terrorist groups, mostly in Africa. Air power remained crucial. Between 2014 and 2019, Western armies conducted around 35,000 air strikes in the Middle East. A growing number of these strikes were carried out by unmanned aerial vehicles, or drones. A second weapon that became more important was special forces. Instead of sending in large numbers of soldiers, special forces work in very small teams. They guide local soldiers to their target, provide training, and limit their direct role mostly to the capturing of senior terrorist leaders. They work, in a way, like financial hedge funds: you invest a limited amount of your own resources, borrow a lot from others, and hence try to generate maximal gains. Between 2010 and 2019, the number of American special forces grew from around 23,000 to 70,000. European countries followed. A third instrument concerned military financing. "Advise and assist," it was called: to help unstable countries fight their own terrorists. A fourth tool was proxies: warlords and armed groups that were supplied with weapons to do a part of the fighting.

The climax of this way of war was the Battle of Mosul in 2017. It was the biggest urban battle since World War II. Mosul was the bastion of IS, who had dug in there for years. Around the city, it had a first ring of fortified villages. The second ring consisted of the suburbs whose main roads were mined. In the Old City, the center, it had developed a maze of tunnels, a thick barrier of improvised explosives, sniper dens, and bunkers. There were about 8,000 IS troops, now surrounded by 100,000 Iraqi soldiers who were guided by around 1,000 Western troops. They provided air strikes, intelligence, and electronic warfare support, mostly from the rear. Iraqi units modeled themselves on the Western forces, taking names like scorpion unit, tiger unit, and thunder unit. But they often lacked training and equipment. After nine months of fighting, Mosul fell. The battle was won, but not the war. A young citizen of Mosul testified:

> The terrorist groups will not be eliminated from Iraq. The reason is that the state does not provide in basic needs. Nothing has changed here, two years after the liberation. When the government decided on the 2019 budget, Mosul got one percent. Young people have two choices when they graduate from college. Two paths. Either they emigrate and leave Iraq. Or they stay and work hard without any benefits. So, they join gangs and terrorist groups. How can they live if the state does not take care of them? We are like zombies. The living dead.[58]

Leading from behind had its limits, it became clear. The international community hoped to rebuild and restabilize the city through the local government, but the government was incapable of doing so. Moreover, the predominantly Sunni population became bitter over the fact that Shia seemed to be benefiting the most from the money that came in via Baghdad. Moreover, less than a year after the fall of Mosul, IS was regrouping in the mountains south of Mosul, from where they organized targeted killings of village leaders, ambushes on Iraqi security forces, abductions, and ransom operations. The mountains were their hideaway; night offered cover.

These new remote-control wars eliminated thousands of terrorists, destroyed safe houses, and killed senior leaders. They did not, however, address the causes of global terrorism. In Iraq and Syria, for instance, IS was defeated as a territorial power, but not as an idea. The Sunni group in both countries remained angry with the government and Western presence. Whether it concerned the Middle East or Africa, drones, special forces, and military instructors thrust deeply into hostile ground; the political reforms and the economic investment often did not follow.

The new stage in the global war against terror repressed the anger; it did not solve the problems at their origins. The fight interrupted the criminal networks that financed terrorism; it did not solve the problem of Gulf States spending oil money on radical preachers and millions of poor men being willing to fight for a fistful of dollars. The fight interrupted propaganda channels; it did not stop ideas from spreading. Bullets do not kill ideas. It was like fighting a killer virus with surgical operations. The special forces prided themselves on being far ahead, but they were far ahead alone. Their small operations often became fig leaf operations. They permitted politicians to demonstrate that they fought terrorists at a low cost. Politically sustainable warfare, it was called. In reality, though, they masked a tendency toward isolationism and reduced willingness to engage comprehensively, to invest in long-term stability and strong partnerships. The special forces had an aura of adventure, courage, and sacrifice: qualities that Western society had lost.

Western society wanted to retreat, to hide. It sealed its defeat. For decades, it had declared that dictators were bad, it had mobilized citizens in Iraq and Afghanistan to vote at the risk of their lives, it had praised, albeit reluctantly, the courage of demonstrators during the Arab Spring. But all the people now felt was betrayal. The prospect of democracy seemed more distant. In Iraq, two thirds believed their country had moved in the wrong direction and one third found the situation worse than under Saddam Hussein.[59] Two years after the Arab Spring, more people in Tunisia and Algeria came to believe that democracy was the best possible system, yet that their country was not ready for it.[60] Cynicism and distrust were the most common responses. Hatred and opportunism kept driving people into the arms of thugs and terrorists. In many Muslim countries, a small yet sizable minority of around 10 percent showed sympathy toward terrorist movements.[61] "Even if one out of a thousand Muslims would consider joining a terrorist movement," said a special forces colonel, "that would still create an army of half a million fighters."[62]

The fig leaf operations created a false sense of security. They confirmed the idea that a society could retreat and secure its environment with a minimum of investment.[63] There were several more consequences. The global war on terror kept overstretching military forces. The American special forces commanders repeated again and again that their troops could not keep up with the operational tempo and that their capabilities were fraying. European countries struggled to deploy larger conventional units in the Middle East or the Sahel. Even for the small teams of special forces, they struggled to guarantee enough qualified soldiers, medical support, intelligence capacity, transport aircraft, or fire support. Western military force was wearing thinner and thinner. Troops became less confident. Polls showed, for instance, that the majority of American troops wanted to end the war in Iraq as soon as possible. Demoralization struck, particularly when President Trump ordered his troops to turn their backs on the Syrian fighters, on whose side they had fought IS and Al-Qaeda. "I am ashamed," was now widely heard among soldiers.

Another consequence was more security populism. Citizens remained concerned, particularly about terrorism and migration, but were less keen on investing in security and addressing the root causes in countries overseas. Hence, it became more rewarding for politicians to show off, by means of walls and border fences, by means of fig leaf operations, and by means, particularly in Europe, of heavily armed soldiers patrolling the streets of European cities. Meanwhile, the challenges kept growing. The disengagement, finally, created a power vacuum. Many countries in the Middle East now saw countries like China as more reliable partners than the West.[64] With the West pulling back, countries like Russia, Turkey, and Saudi Arabia also started competing more blatantly against one another, thus complicating the situation in the region even more.

Bluffing around the battlefield

Between 2001 and 2020, the global war on terror cost the United States alone around US$6 trillion. It was the most expensive operation since World War II. Not only the special forces, as we saw in the previous section, suffered from overstretch. The whole military was overburdened. In 2020, despite the promise of President Donald Trump to diminish overseas engagement, the West still had troops fighting terrorism in more than 18 countries. The operational rhythm was so high that soldiers could barely rest. The United States diverted aircraft from the Pacific to the Middle East, had sailors from ships of the Pacific Fleet fight in the Iraqi desert. A structural shortage of funds and budgetary crises meant that maintenance was not carried out and that crews were insufficiently trained.[65] Crews were exhausted. In January of 2017, an American guided-missile cruiser ran aground just outside Tokyo, Japan. That same year, an American destroyer crashed into a cargo ship, also near Japan, and another destroyer drifted into an oil tanker. The Air Force struggled. The number of flight mishaps doubled between 2007 and 2018.[66]

Europe too was in bad shape. Countries like France, Italy, and Belgium used soldiers to support the police force at home. More than in the United States, armed forces struggled to recruit. Greece proposed crowd funding to finance its navy. Less than a third of Germany's fighter jets could fly. "No matter where you look, there is dysfunction," testified a general.[67] The British Public Accounts Committee reported that US$27 billion was needed to compensate for a long period of underinvestment.[68] France was at pains to continue its missions to fight terrorist movements in Africa. "We are in an extremely critical situation," said a French general. "We will soon be exhausted and we are no longer capable of conducting sustained operations."[69] In 2015, Paris invoked Article 42.7 of the Maastricht Treaty – a mutual defense clause in the treaty – to get other European countries to join the fight against terrorism. In 2018, it proposed a European intervention capacity, which was greeted with skepticism in other capitals. Europe found it difficult to muster enough capabilities for small operations, to sustain operation Atlanta, meant to protect merchant ships against piracy in the Indian Ocean, or Operation Sophia, which was put in place to patrol the Mediterranean. The number of modern ships, submarines, fighter jets, and other important systems in Europe had fallen to the point that it could no longer independently conduct medium to large operations. This was confirmed once more during the intervention in Libya in 2011, during which Europe lacked precision-guided munitions, aerial refuel capacity, and satellite intelligence.

If the wars in the southern neighborhood of Europe exposed its military weakness, two other developments did so too: Russia's military modernization and America's shift to the Pacific. Russia became a challenge that was at least as large as the instability in the south. Thanks to the revenues from selling energy to Europe, it could accelerate the modernization of its navy fleet, tank units, aircraft, and so forth. Besides its intervention in Ukraine and the annexation of Crimea in 2014, it deployed highly capable missiles along its Western border: air defense missiles, anti-ship missiles, and surface-to-surface missiles. These missiles covered its own territory, but also the territory of European countries, as well as most of the Baltic and Black seas. European countries joined large America-led exercises in the

Baltic Sea, but while navy ships gathered in the north, it sometimes implied that there were more Russian Navy ships deployed in the south, in the Mediterranean, than European warships. Various incidents also showed that European countries were incapable of tracking Russian submarines in the Atlantic or in the Mediterranean.

After the annexation of Crimea, European countries deployed soldiers in bases in Poland and the three Baltic countries, but they were incapable of stopping any Russian campaign without American support. Some member states provided support to Ukrainian troops fighting Russian proxies in the east of their country, but in practice accepted that Crimea was lost and that the Black Sea slowly turned into a Russian lake. Internal reviews showed that European armed forces were incapable of countering this so-called anti-access and area denial capacity, or A2AD. At NATO meetings, European leaders promised to invest in the modernization of their armed forces, but defense spending hardly increased between 2010 and 2020. The balance of power shifted to Europe's detriment.

Europe's response to Russia's military rejuvenation was symbolic. It did not resolve on regaining the advantage on the battlefield. Instead, it was bluffing around the battlefield. European countries joined NATO exercises in the Baltic Sea and in Eastern Europe. European air forces often brandished photographs of jets intercepting Russian military aircraft. In reality, however, air force commanders avowed that their jets would be extremely vulnerable to Russian missiles. Few European navies had ships with a chance of surviving Russia's high-end coastal defense. When the Germans had to deliver 44 tanks to a NATO high readiness taskforce, it could only send nine. Throughout Europe, ammunition stocks were dangerously small. In private, American officers also acknowledged that providing quick relief across the Atlantic would not be evident with China looming in the Pacific. The West showed the flag, but was not certain to attain victory should it come to fighting. The United States became critical of this attitude and the Trump administration warned that the lack of effort could undermine the future of NATO.

Still, in a way, the United States was bluffing around the battlefield too: in Asia, where it had great difficulty in responding to China's military rise. In 2010, the Obama administration announced its intention to rebalance to Asia. The rebalance held that the United States deployed 60 percent of is military capabilities in the region. An aircraft carrier was homeported in Japan, for instance, and its bases in Guam, an American island close to the Philippines, were expanded. In addition, the navy deployed into the South China Sea to insist on freedom of navigation.

The rebalance, however, had limited effect. Consider the military balance. Between the announcement of the rebalance in 2012 and 2019, the United States added one extra submarine to its fleet in the Pacific, whereas China built 21 new ones. In the same period, the United States deployed five additional large navy ships in the Pacific, while China commissioned 40 new ones. Washington sent one squadron of 12 F-35 combat aircraft to Japan; China built around 350 new modern fighter jets. As a result, Beijing remained underwhelmed. It kept reclaiming land in the South China Sea and ignored an international tribunal that judged in 2016 that its claims were not justified.

The most important problem with the rebalance to Asia was that, even if a larger share of its military capacity was shifted to Asia, America's overall capacity decreased. The end result on the ground, hence, was minimal. Area commanders relayed to Washington that both checking the rise of China and watching North Korea required more resources. They did so in vain.[70] Washington forced local commanders to provide ships despite warnings that they were not ready. President Barack Obama trivialized the risk. When he was asked about the state of the armed forces in the Pacific, he answered: "You mention the Navy, for example, and that we have fewer ships than we did in 1916. Well, we also have fewer horses and bayonets."[71] The rebalance to Asia and the freedom of navigation operations in the South China Sea, called FONOPS, were symbolic.

This overstretch became embarrassingly clear during a crisis with North Korea in 2017 and 2018. The White House threatened to send a powerful armada in response to North Korea's test of a nuclear warhead and missiles. But the destroyer squadron commander in Yokosuka replied that no ships were ready. In 2017, as North Korea prepared for a missile launch, two B-1 bombers stationed at Guam were called on for a show of force, but only one was capable of taking off.[72] The three aircraft carriers that were said to be deployed as a show of force were not combat-ready and remained thousands of miles away from the Korean Peninsula.

The Navy stated that the rise of China and Russia required at least 66 attack submarines and the ability to deploy 34 ships at short notice. The Pacific Commander spoke of an overall erosion in his forces' operational readiness: "We are at risk of overstressing the force."[73] President Donald Trump promised to spend more on the armed forces, but not sufficient to allow the armed forces to acquire the equipment it needed to preserve its dominance. When the United States faced the Soviet Union as a peer rival, it deployed around 500 ships, compared to around 270 in 2020 and 355 ships foreseen by the year 2030. The number of attack and fighter aircraft dropped from over 3,000 during the Cold War to around 1,250 in 2020.

Numbers matter. As China, like Russia, lined its coast with missiles, electronic warfare capabilities, air force bases, and increasingly advanced warships, it started to undermine America's dominance. War games showed that China's anti-access and area denial capabilities made it risky for the United States to intervene in a conflict around Taiwan. In other words, the century-old strategy of checking the military might of continental Asian rivals and preserving a line of defense as close as possible to the Eurasian landmass was being contested. Moreover, as a result of the relative decline, Washington quietly abandoned the long-standing goal of being capable of fighting and winning two large wars at the same time, which was an implicit recognition of the fact that it was not capable of standing up to Russia and China simultaneously.[74] American planners and experts tried to come up with new approaches, like the AirSea Battle concept and the AirLand Battle doctrine.[75] These concepts sounded dramatic, but often were not backed by capabilities and hinted at a continuation of the remote-control warfare – now applied to a much more formidable rival.

They increasingly focused on long-range precision attacks or standoff operations, fighting China from a greater distance, for instance, by launching missiles from ships or strikes from aircraft carriers in the Pacific Ocean instead of nearing the Chinese coast. The problem with this concept was that even standoff operations would demand a very large number of ships and aircraft. Moreover, China was also developing weapons to destroy carriers at such large distance. The Dong Feng 21-D missile was built to take out carriers as far away as 1,500 kilometers.

A second strategy was to avoid the main battlefield and to strike China elsewhere, its vulnerable supply lines in the Indian Ocean, for example. This was referred to using concepts like horizontal escalation, distributed lethality, and mosaic warfare. This approach appeared to be a recognition, not a contestation, of China's dominance in and around the South and East China seas. It has several obvious weaknesses. China, for example, has already taken various measures to reduce its vulnerability beyond its immediate sphere of influence, by diversifying its supply lines, for example, or by building up strategic reserves of indispensable commodities. Dispersion is also expensive. It requires more bases and a more complex logistical chain.

A third approach concerned the Third Offset: an attempt to find new and creative technologies "to sustain advantages in times of limited resources."[76] Central was the objective to develop a killer web of unmanned and autonomous platforms, including missile launch containers on the sea floor, anti-ship or air defense missile launchers that are also hidden under water and rise to the surface in case of war, long-range unmanned aerial combat vehicles, and so forth, unmanned undersea vehicles that are capable of launching missiles and torpedoes. But the deployment of these platforms would take time and it was not clear whether the United States would achieve the upper hand in these unmanned weapons systems. China too advanced rapidly.

None of the three concepts gave a proper response to the key question: how could China be stopped, driven back, and defeated if it were to occupy Taiwan by force, for instance? President Donald Trump vowed to rebuild the armed forces and increased the military budget. That increase, though, fell short of addressing these deficiencies. It was grandstanding rather than strengthening that characterized his defense policy: a form of security populism.

Multilateralism

The contest that the West kept losing was the contest for influence in international organizations. The United States had a more ambivalent relation with international rules and organizations, but at least assumed them to serve its interests some of the time. The European Union had embraced multilateralism as the heart of its foreign policy. Its 2003 security strategy pledged to promote effective multilateralism and expected a multipolar world order to become more conducive to multilateral cooperation.

None of that materialized. Global economic organizations, like the World Bank and the International Monetary Fund, were increasingly bypassed. The United States lost interest in them and new creditors like China used their own banks. The World Trade Organization made way for bilateral and plurilateral trade agreements, with the difference that the TPP broke down, while China successfully enmeshed ASEAN countries further into its sphere of influence. By the end of 2019, the situation of the World Trade Organization was that if the West insisted on including the liberalization of investment, services, and government procurement, it would lose the support of developing countries like China, whereas if the developing countries continued to be able to protect these domains, the World Trade Organization would become irrelevant to the West. American officials made that point forcefully. Only Europe continued to entertain an obstinate hope of reviving the World Trade Organization and to consider itself a leader inside the institution.[77]

If the initial hope was to use international organizations to socialize non-Western countries and to make them embrace Western norms, non-Western countries now assertively used international organizations to advance their interests and norms. Consider Interpol. The organization not only became led by a Chinese official; it also started to serve as an instrument for authoritarian countries to hunt down dissidents. After the coup attempt of 2016, Turkey issued tens of thousands of so-called red notices to track members of the political opposition. Russia and China followed suit. In 2016, China, Russia, Saudi Arabia, and other countries used a discrete committee, Study Group 20, inside the International Telecommunication Union, the ITU, to champion a so-called digital object architecture. This would make it possible to trace digital information to its owner. China used the World Health Organization to recognize traditional medicine as well as its specific research protocols for medicines.

In 2019, China surpassed Japan as the second largest contributor to the budget of the United Nations. Senior UN officials started to praise China's role in the world and endorsed projects like its new Silk Road, the Belt and

Road Initiative. After the United States left the UN Human Rights Council in 2018, China upped its game to shape the debate and to deflect criticism about the detention of hundreds of thousands of members of the Uyghur ethnic minority. Only now, the alarm bells started to ring. After the United States had long ignored and scorned the United Nations, it issued a critical paper in 2019. "Chinese leaders at INTERPOL, the International Telecommunications Union (ITU), and the International Civil Aviation Organization (ICAO) have demonstrated a bias towards Chinese foreign policy and a lack of transparency and accountability," it stated. "This is in keeping with public statements by a senior Chinese official that Chinese nationals working in international organizations are expected to align with Chinese policy without question."[78] The concerns were laughed away by the majority of developing countries, and a few weeks after the paper was released a Chinese official was chosen to lead the Food and Agriculture Organization (FAO).

The shifting balance of power was also reflected in the realm of arms control. As China deployed growing numbers of increasingly advanced land-based intermediate-range missiles, with a range between 500 and 5,000 kilometers, followed by Russia and Iran, the United States decided that it was enough. In 2019, it abandoned the Intermediate Nuclear Force Treaty. This INF treaty, signed during the Cold War, was never ratified by China. Neither was Beijing interested in joining the United States and Russia to talk about the Strategic Arms Reduction Treaty. START limited the number of missiles and bombers that can deliver nuclear warheads. China was not a party to this treaty either. Given its growing nuclear arsenal, China's absence was considered by Washington and Russia a reason to abandon the hope for a new deal. The Outer Space Treaty, another Cold War document, was ignored by the major powers. In 2015, Russia re-established its space forces, followed by the United States and India in 2018, and France in 2019. The decay of global frameworks to limit arms did not prompt the West to close ranks. Divisions inside NATO grew. Especially after the election of Donald Trump, European allies became frustrated with America's insistence on higher defense budgets, its unilateral policy toward Russia and Iran, as well as its insistence on having a NATO approach toward China.

Whether it concerned economic affairs, telecommunications, human rights, or arms control, in all these areas, the multilateral framework crumbled and the West steadily lost its leadership. The very positive comments of the World Health Organization about China's handling of the corona crisis were the last straw. It made Washington leave the organization and emboldened it in its skepticism. In a speech during a visit to Brussels in 2018, the Secretary of State proposed to a flabbergasted European audience that Europe ought to pursue principled realism. That certainly marked a milestone in American foreign policy:

> After the Cold War ended, we allowed this liberal order to begin to corrode. It failed us in some places, and sometimes it failed you and the rest of the world. Multilateralism has too often become viewed as an end unto itself. The more treaties we sign, the safer we supposedly are. The more bureaucrats we have, the better the job gets done. Was that ever really true? The central question that we face is that – is the question of whether the system as currently configured, as it exists today, and as the world exists today – does it work? Does it work for all the people of the world?
>
> Today at the United Nations, peacekeeping missions drag on for decades, no closer to peace. The UN's climate-related treaties are viewed by some nations as simply a vehicle to redistribute wealth. Anti-Israel bias has been institutionalized. Regional powers collude to vote the likes of Cuba and Venezuela onto the Human Rights Council. The UN was founded as an organization that welcomed peace-loving nations. I ask: Today, does it continue to serve its mission faithfully? . . . Our mission is to reassert our sovereignty, reform the liberal international order, and we want our friends to help us and to exert their sovereignty as well. We aspire to make the international order serve our citizens – not to control them."[79]

Struggle

Between 2010 and 2019, Western military power declined significantly. The missions in Afghanistan and Iraq had worn out the armed forces, their equipment, and their personnel. As troops were pulled out of these countries, it became clear that the war on terror had brought defeat and that the campaign to bring democracy had become a fiasco. In an attempt to limit damage, it kept resorting to remote-control operations, by means of unmanned armed vehicles, or drones, special forces, and military financing. After a decade of hubris, now followed a decade of restraint. The share of the West in global defense spending dropped from 62 to 50 percent. Despite growing security threats, defense budgets remained stagnant. An intervention in Libya confirmed that European countries were no longer capable of conducting relatively small military operations independently. The United States struggled to respond to the military modernization of China and Russia. It abandoned the objective of being capable to fight two major wars simultaneously.

While the military modernization of China and Russia was recognized as a growing threat, the West kept growing the wealth of rivals. Russia still benefited immensely from its energy exports to Europe. After it annexed Crimea and shot down a passenger aircraft, the West imposed sanctions, but European countries' gas imports continued to sponsor the Kremlin. China's trade surplus with the West grew rapidly, despite it being clear that these incomes were used to expand its political influence and that technology transfers from the West were critical for its military modernization. The same for the Gulf States. Intelligence services kept writing that many of these countries remained safe havens for financers of extremist and terrorist movements, but they too kept exporting to Europe and received red-carpet treatment as investors. It was no surprise then that Europe and the United States also lost power in international organizations, the capacity to shape the agenda of existing organizations, and to build new ones. The West was abdicating from international leadership.

CHAPTER 12

FRAGMENTED AND TURBULENT

AFTER 30 YEARS OF PEACE IN THE WEST, THE FRAGILITY OF THAT PEACE became manifest throughout the world. This occurred not least, as we witnessed, in the West itself. Democracy was lackluster, the economy fragile, and citizens uncertain about the future. Three other important changes came to define the world order. A first concerned the institution of a new large Eurasian power: China. History never entirely repeats itself. Compared to the Soviet Union, for instance, China traded intensively with the West. It struck a careful balance between integration into the international community and efforts to revise it. China was determined to avoid the overstretch that contributed to the downfall of the Soviets. It also had a larger economy and was thus better placed to compete for dominance.

Yet, there were also commonalities with the Cold War. Similar to the Soviet Union, China contested the supremacy of the United States. China was a revisionist power, bent on reshaping world politics. Indeed, China agreed to participate in international organizations. But instead of accepting the agenda, the rules, and the standards, it was now bent on reshaping them. The acceptance of a superficial status quo did not end the deeper revisionism. China, we saw before, was a revisionist power by default. The size of its territory, its position in the middle of Asia, its large population, and its growth made it predestined to become a leader, certainly when the other regional powers failed to keep pace.

Like during the Cold War, the United States faced a continental power that sought to repel Western influence along the fringes of Eurasia and increasingly into the adjacent seas. Similar to the Cold War, both major powers attempted to avoid direct military conflict, yet spent heavily on military modernization. They vied for technological leadership. There was also an ideological tussle, with Beijing assertively discrediting Western liberalism and proposing its model of authoritarianism and state capitalism to the rest of the world.

A second change concerns the ebbing of the optimism in the Global South. Regional powers like India, South Africa, Nigeria, and Brazil failed to strengthen their economies. They, as well as numerous smaller countries, were confirmed in a role of commodity supplier and remained a backwater in the global economy. It made them very prone to setbacks in the commodity market, political instability, nationalism, violence, and interference by the major powers. Demographic pressure was immense. In absolute numbers, the population in the Global South expanded by 62 million annually. The area was scourged by climate change and problems in the agricultural sector. While food production per capita grew quickly in East Asia, it was stagnant in Africa. Migration and refugee flows kept breaking records. So, while the West weakened, massive forces built up: a rising China in the East and a demographic bulge in the South. The two combined implied the return of power plays in a southern arc of hardship.

A third change concerns the spreading of hard hedging. With the West on the defense and China on the march, regional powers showed a tendency to maximize their autonomy, their leverage, and their commercial chances by playing both camps. One example was Russia, which kept earning hundreds of billions from energy exports to Europe and spent a part of those incomes to advance its influence over the West. The annexation of Crimea was the culmination of this policy. At the same time, it started building pipelines to China. Turkey, Saudi Arabia, Egypt, Israel, and several others followed this example and tried to have it both ways: resisting the West, its values, and its influence, yet continuing to profit from it in different ways, at the same time reaching out to China as an alternative partner and showing affinity with its state capitalism. The absence of a balance against the main new rising power reinforced the tendency of Eurasian countries to wriggle from underneath America's sway and China's further propagation of its influence.

Belt and Road

An important assumption in international relations thinking is that the rise of a new power causes other countries to balance. The emergence of a strong country instills fear about its intentions and hence an effort among other countries to reinforce their own position. China grew its power spectacularly, its nationalism was obvious, and its military progress remarkable. Between 2010 and 2020, China became the second largest economy in the world and grew its share in Asia's economic production from around 32 percent to 49 percent. In 2020, China's economy was much larger than Japan's, India's, and South Korea's combined. China flaunted its economic prowess. There were the Olympic Games in 2008, the Shanghai World Expo in 2010, the landing on the moon in 2013, and so forth.

Its military budget also became bigger than its neighbors' combined. In the autumn of 2019, the Chinese government staged a military parade to celebrate the 70th anniversary of the People's Republic, a parade larger than any before. New hypersonic missiles, drones, and tanks were put on display. China was back as Asia's leading power, back, some would say, as a middle kingdom. The power shift was obvious. Still, there was surprisingly little balancing from its neighborhood. The situation can be summarized as follows: China grew and as the neighbors accommodated it, China was not hampered by expensive conflicts and could keep that growth going.

What accounted for this situation, was, of course, the ability of the Chinese leadership to keep its growth on track. It is important to recognize that this was no smooth visionary policy. The economic approach was still more akin to groping for stones to cross the river. In the 1990s, Jiang Zemin had decided that China relied too much on foreign investors. He started to grow national champions to replace them. This policy put new Chinese equivalents next to the factories built by foreign companies and contributed to overcapacity. Production exceeded demand. Hence, a central objective of the next generation of leaders became to channel that overcapacity to foreign markets, to boost exports, by keeping the currency low, and to lend capital to foreign consumers. That saddled China with massive overseas credit, which the generation of Xi Jinping wanted to use more strategically, by launching the Belt and Road Initiative.

These steps are a simplification, but testament to China's pragmatism. Oftentimes, the leadership struggled to deliver. Already in 2006, the government found that the economy depended too much on investment and promised to shift toward consumption. By 2020, that rebalancing remained disappointing. One of the reasons was Beijing's estimation that investing in infrastructure, technology, and manufacturing was the only way to build a rich nation. Another explanation was that state banks had lent thousands of billions of dollars to large companies that were not competitive, so that a decrease in investment would cause bankruptcies and social unrest. The leadership kept stressing the need for more sacrifices to become an affluent industrialized country.

In a way, the government took an enormous gamble with the money that Chinese households had saved in state banks, by transferring it to large companies and infrastructure projects that were not always profitable. The Chinese economy was thus fragile. For now, however, it worked. It worked because Beijing bent fragility into an opportunity. Take the fact that China's population became older: It prompted investments in automation and healthcare solutions. Consider the environmental challenges: They emboldened China to become a leader in renewable energy and electrical cars. Take the overcapacity: China produced too many goods compared to its domestic consumption and had to export a lot, but the euros and dollars earned from the exports helped it buy technology, acquire ports, and make other governments compete for Chinese investment.

What was initially a form of economic fragility was transformed into an opportunity to grow political influence, to conduct checkbook diplomacy that replaced the image of China as an emerging military power with the image of China as a preferred business partner. It made companies forget about the security dimension altogether. By 2020, a large part of the Chinese Navy was running on French turbines or German submarine engines; its drones were stuffed with other European and South Korean technology, its military computers with American chip technology. Take Japan. Despite tensions in the East China Sea, Japanese investment in China increased by

US$74 billion between 2010 and 2020. American investment in China (including Hong Kong) grew by US$100 billion. Never mind the calls of the White House to repatriate production. Even after the corona crisis, multinationals like Walmart, Tesla, Volkswagen, and Toyota pledged billions of dollars of new investment in China.

Hence, one of the reasons why China's rise triggered limited counter-moves was its cunning statecraft. The Belt and Road Initiative, announced in 2013 by Xi Jinping, was a masterstroke. The initiative was a continuation of previous policies to penetrate foreign markets, to boost exports, and to support the expansion of service providers in construction, telecoms, and so forth. The new publicity around it, the combination of a romantic view of the ancient Silk Road with modern technology, made it irresistible to many countries.

Consider the Philippines. For years, the Philippine government had clenched a fist against China's growing presence in the South China Sea. In 2016, China proposed a package deal, including loans to build ports, energy infrastructure, and so forth. It was a diplomatic triumph. Manila turned against the United States. At the same time, the deal meant business for Chinese companies and the loans would have to be repaid anyhow. Economic and political interests went hand in hand. The same happened to Russia. In the Russian parliament, politicians became critical of Chinese smuggling in the Far East. As soon as Vladimir Putin returned as president, in 2012, Beijing offered him more investment in this remote area. After the annexation of Crimea, China threw a financial lifeline, which made it gain political goodwill in the Kremlin and access to energy.

The Chinese government engaged in dialogue with numerous countries. They allowed China to buy time, to extend unequal trade relations, and to grow its power without making substantial compromises. The mollification of foreign governments and elites was also pursued by organizing prestigious summit meetings, high-level visits, student exchanges, business fairs, and so forth. While critical voices were ignored, pro-China voices were pampered with funding and travel opportunities. While manufacturers abroad suffered, retail companies, ports, and real estate developers were cajoled with cheap Chinese goods and generous investment. Xi's Belt and Road Initiative added momentum to China's pursuit of economic influence and the attempt to capitalize on the short-sighted policies of other countries.

China kept weaving a sphere of influence in Asia. The response of other countries defied a central proposition in international relations thinking: namely that the rise of a power triggers balancing behavior, that it prompts others to resist it, especially when they are close to the new pretender and share a history of conflict with it. First, many Asian states reckoned that they could go on working with the rising power as long as the United States remained militarily preponderant. This hedging behavior allowed China to continue to grow its power. As that happened, the calculus changed, from expecting the United States to keep a check on China, to accepting Chinese dominance. Instead of proximity leading neighbors to organize themselves against China, they came to the conclusion that it was useless to resist it. As one Cambodian spectator formulated it: "China is so big that it can do what it wants to do."[1] Another key politician remarked: "The reality is that we have to accept suzerainty."[2]

The hardening of influence

China did not rest on its laurels. "The United States shows a clear shift toward containment and wants to maintain its dominance," explained an influential advisor. "This is a new Cold War in the making."[3] This was echoed in an official document in 2019. "The Cold War mentality of encirclement, constraint, confrontation and threat is resurfacing," it concluded, and warned of a new arms race and war.[4] Tensions were also growing internally. Minority regions like Tibet and Xinjiang remained restive. Factory workers rioted more frequently against their working conditions. Citizens protested about pollution. In Hong Kong, an electoral reform in 2010 was followed by protests in defense of democracy.

"We are only half way on our journey to becoming an affluent society," clarified another policy advisor. "We have to preserve unity, because otherwise we will fragment before we are strong."[5] Whereas Hu Jintao and Wen Jiabao still experimented with grass-roots and intra-party democracy, Xi Jinping resorted to harsh authoritarianism. In 2013, an internal document instructed Communist Party members to fight seven false ideological trends, including democracy, civil society, freedom of the press, and judicial independence.[6] Embassies, foreign news media, and nongovernmental organizations, it argued, were spreading Western ideas to undermine the government. If, in 2010, academics still praised democracy as a good thing and economic liberalization as indispensable for innovation, universities subsequently replaced vows on academic freedom with allegiance to the Party.

Xi Jinping dashed into the limelight with exceptional ambition. With an anti-corruption campaign, he silenced opponents inside the Party. Several top leaders were sent to an elite prison. He established small leading groups to shape the policy agenda, bypassing ministers and government departments. Xi reinforced propaganda, increased censorship, and imposed a social credit system. Supported by smart cameras, internet surveillance, a network of public security volunteers, and intelligence services, it monitored citizens and punished them if they did not follow the Party ideology. Dictatorship went high-tech. More private companies were forced to accept Party commissars and to adopt a corporate credit system. In 2018, Xi removed the two-term limit as president. He warned opponents of "crushed bodies and shattered bones," called the Party to show fighting spirit, to be ready for struggle, and not to take the great rejuvenation of the country for granted.[7] Xi's offer to the people of China was stability, growth, and a better livelihood, in exchange for loyalty, patriotism, and obedience. China was still a fragile power and its leadership was aware of that. "China's growth is one of the most important events of our times," explained one of his close officials. "We still have a long way to go. Our economy is not yet strong; our unity cannot be taken for granted. If we relax too much, accidents will happen."[8]

China had its weaknesses, but so too did its neighbors. What followed was a tightrope between restraint and assertiveness. The Chinese leadership understood that it could not afford hubris, yet sensed that its influence was growing. President Hu Jintao already suggested the country should move from keeping a low profile to "trying actively to accomplish something," a statement that was affirmed in the so-called confidence doctrine of Xi Jinping. Along the way, the peaceful development idea of Hu Jintao also became more conditional. As one official put it: "Even though we have pledged ourselves to a path of peaceful development, we will not do so at the expense of our national interests."[9] Or: "The key premise is that the outside world respects our core interests." These core interests included the defense of the position of the Communist Party, but also the sovereignty over Taiwan and the contested seas. A military strategist pointed out that loving peace is not the same as weakness and that China needed to keep its sword sharp.[10]

In the past, China had already tied economic cooperation to the readiness of countries to sever diplomatic relations with Taiwan. New was that China increasingly advanced interests at the expense of others, knowing that they could not retaliate. It diverted water from international rivers, like the Mekong, the Brahmaputra, and the Ili, menacing farmers on the other side of the border, and it did so with impunity. It illegally fished in the seas of poor countries who could no longer stand up to China. There was illegal emigration to and illicit trade with almost all neighboring countries, again without serious consequences.

Conversely, China more readily retaliated whenever its interests were harmed, like in 2010, when Norwegian salmon was left to rot after a Nobel Peace Prize went to a political dissident; in 2012, when customs slowed the screening of imported bananas after the Philippines irked Beijing in the South China Sea; in 2016, when taxes on the border with Mongolia increased after the latter received the Tibetan leader, the Dalai Lama; or in 2017, when about a dozen South Korean shopping malls in China were closed for fire safety reasons, after Seoul agreed to participate in an American missile defense system.[11] China's influence hardened.

Growing economic presence was followed by military presence. This was the case around its continental border. On the Tibetan plateau, China built railways, roads, and airports, which helped alter the military balance along the contested border with India. The passes across the Himalayas were lined with modern military bases, missile launch facilities, airstrips, and so forth. China also sought to protect its interests beyond the border. Its navy was permanently deployed in the Indian Ocean. In 2011, it persuaded Laos and Myanmar to have joint patrols on the Mekong River. In 2016, the government of Tajikistan agreed to let China police the Wakhan Corridor to Afghanistan via its territory and to build a military base on its soil. In 2017, it opened a large military base in Djibouti to support its navy in the region as well as land operations in Africa and the Middle East. Next to that base, a Chinese-built railway and water pipeline reached all the way to Ethiopia. China had peacekeepers patrolling nearby oilfields owned by its companies in South Sudan.

While China's overseas presence was dwarfed by Western countries, it slowly but surely adjusted its traditional doctrine of not interfering militarily in other countries toward an acceptance of the use of military force to protect interests abroad. Think tank experts stated that China could not go on to withdraw each time expatriates or economic assets were threatened. A 2019 defense document highlighted that overseas interests were a crucial part of China's national interests.[12] In Chinese cinemas, blockbusters showed Chinese special forces hunting down pirates and terrorists around the Red Sea, and the Chinese Navy launching strikes against targets in distant nations. The doctrine changed, the attitude toward foreign operations changed, and the military acquired the means to carry out those operations, like large transport aircraft and amphibious ships. Civilian ships of companies like COSCO Shipping were built with thick beams between the decks, so that they could carry tanks and other equipment whenever needed.

An even more dramatic change took place in the China seas. China first of all asserted its claim by imposing rules for fishing in the adjacent seas and a zone above the East China Sea in which all aircraft had to identify themselves. Important was the fortification of islands in the South China Sea. Islands, initially only strips of coral, became maritime fortresses. They allowed China to monitor the seas around and to affirm its territorial claim. In the contested waters, China deployed swarms of small fishing boats, trained to act like a maritime militia, a mob at sea, whenever they faced ships of other states. Next came the coastguard, whose fleet became larger than those of all the neighboring maritime countries together. The biggest coastguard ship had the same tonnage as the whole Vietnamese coastguard combined and was five times as large as the whole coastguard of the Philippines. Furthermore, China invested in different systems to monitor its seas: long-range radars, drones, satellites, undersea sensors, and so forth. A following layer consisted of missiles: around 2,000 short- and medium-range ballistic missiles that could destroy bases in Japan and Taiwan, among others, but also land-based missiles against ships and aircraft. One type of missile was developed to destroy aircraft carriers up to 1,500 kilometers away. China also expanded its navy fleet, adding 15 new warships a year, compared to three in Japan and nine in the United States.

These different layers permitted China to assert its influence in a measured way. Often, it started with diplomatic and economic signals, then sent in the coastguard, and finally had the military instruments at hand – from a flyover to large navy exercises. As Liu Huaqing had proposed with his famous map, China changed the military balance inside the first island chain, reclaimed land around contested islands, deployed ships in contested seas, and ignored international arbitration rulings about the matter. Yet the only responses were statements of indignation and flag waving. Warships were deployed by countries like Japan and the United States to insist on freedom of navigation, but nothing was done to stop China's power grab.

The situation made one think of one of the descriptions in the records of the ancient Han emperors. "Overawed by military strength and attracted by wealth," it was written, "they bared their heads and kneeled down towards the east to pay homage to the Son of Heaven."[13] Contrary to the assumption of growing power instilling fear, it made other countries want to be part of it. The opportunism of rich Western countries disillusioned the reformist voices inside China. Commenting on Europe's response to China's hardening policy, Ai Weiwei, China's most famous contemporary artist, put it thus: "Germany is leading the whole [of] Europe, they are so ambitious, they want to be leader but morally they are collapsed."[14] China's rise remained a remarkable feat and even more noteworthy was that this rise elicited such limited contestation from its neighbors. China was now, no doubt, Asia's leading power.

As it advanced its military might into the Pacific, it became the first power since the Cold War to challenge a pillar of American grand strategy: to preserve dominance in the oceans. It was a classic security dilemma, a zero-sum game almost: the more China's military gained prominence in the Pacific, the less capable the United States would be of preserving its security through dominance. The apparent success of its authoritarianism and state capitalism also challenged the Western liberal canon and further discredited the United States as a role model. Despite the lack of balancing, a clash between the two titans appeared inescapable. China's economy was already strong, but the ambition to make Chinese national industries more competitive would stretch Washington's tolerance of such state capitalism further. China's military was fearsome to its neighbors, but its advancing beyond the first island chain would also push America's strategic patience and tolerance to the limits. The new tournament for world dominance only now started in earnest.

The crowded waiting room of globalization

South Asia remained the waiting room of globalization, but its people became more impatient. If one departed from the port of Tokyo, most of the East Asian coast was now lined with container terminals and modern skyscraper cities. Onwards to Southeast Asia, most ports and cities became smaller. Once past the Malacca Strait, the coast of the Indian Ocean remained primarily inhabited by farmers and fishermen in small villages. The first megacities along the shores of the Indian Ocean, Dhaka and Kolkata, had a quarter of their population living in slums. The average production per capita also decreased: from around US$40,000 in Japan, US$10,000 in China, US$4,000 in Southeast Asia, to US$2,000 in South Asia. The imposing container ships that plied the Indian Ocean were only passing by, connecting the factories of East Asia with European consumers. Almost all large fishing boats originated from East Asia and Europe, and so did the growing number of surveillance ships that scanned the ocean floor for precious minerals.

In the global economy, South Asia remained a transit zone rather than a participant. The Indian Ocean was a freeway between continents, with few locals profiting. Between 2010 and 2020, total foreign direct investment, manufacturing, and exports of East Asian countries was 12 times larger than in South Asia. Nothing in this regard had changed compared to the previous decade. Between 2010 and 2020, extreme poverty in South Asia declined, but more slowly than in the previous decade. Meanwhile, the region was also scourged by record numbers of heat waves and anomalies in the monsoon rains.

The greatest disappointment came once more from India. Prime Minister Manmohan Singh was lauded by the international community as an honest leader. At home, he encouraged girls to go to school, guaranteed minimum employment in the destitute countryside, and handed out mobile phones to the poor. His coalition, however, did not have a majority and that caused economic reforms to fall flat. The initial optimism was replaced by criticism. At the end of his rule, Singh was referred to as a fallen angel, an underachiever, and a tragic figure.

In 2014, Narendra Modi was elected prime minister with another pledge to reform. As the leader of the State of Gujarat he had built up some credentials in that regard, but also a reputation for stoking hatred between Hindus and Muslims. International investors responded enthusiastically to Modi's arrival, but a few years later, foreign investment inflows almost fell flat. They were deterred still by bad infrastructure and stories about Modi blackmailing companies to support his policies. India was in no position to keep up with China. In 2020, its economy was seven times smaller than China's. Despite much higher wages, China also kept attracting four times more European and American investment than India. India never escaped from large government and trade deficits.

The situation was similar in other South Asian countries, including Pakistan, Sri Lanka, and Bangladesh. Bangladesh received some interest from the global market as Asia's sweatshop, with underpaid workers stitching clothing and shoes in dismal conditions. In 2013, over a thousand workers were killed when a factory collapsed in Dhaka. Multinationals promised to improve working conditions, yet continued to rely on informal suppliers and modern slavery. Despite these sacrifices, Bangladesh was stuck in poverty, trade deficits, bad governance, and huge environmental problems.

South Asia remained an ephemeral promise. As a first consequence, the region became overshadowed by China. The United States and the European Union remained the most important export market for South Asia. China, however, cultivated expectations as an investor. In Myanmar, China completed a pipeline from its southernmost province to the Gulf of Bengal, and showed interest in developing a railway and a port. In Bangladesh, it proposed a large industrial park where cheaper Bengali workers could produce for China's middle class. In Pakistan, it completed the port of Gwadar, and various energy projects, and started modernizing roads through the Karakoram Pass. By 2020, China had disbursed around US$38 billion of loans to South Asia.[15] The region's trade deficit with China grew from US$2 billion in 2000 to US$30 billion in 2010 and US$92 billion in 2020. This mirrored

China's habit of gaining a lot from trade and transferring a small part back in the form of investment.

India also embraced China as a potential investor, especially after trade talks with Europe and the United States broke down. The Indian president put it: "Chinese companies with inherent strengths in infrastructure and manufacturing can look towards India as an important destination in their Going Global strategy."[16] The ministry of industry affirmed: "Chinese companies have shown significant interest to invest in India in a wide range of sectors since the launch of *Make in India* campaign."[17] During the corona crisis in 2020, India hoped to lure some companies away from China. Yet, at the same time, Delhi took two loans from Chinese-backed development banks. As a token of goodwill, the Indian government curtailed the activities of Tibetan refugees in the country. A few months into the corona crisis, Indian and Chinese soldiers had a deadly clash on the border. The brawl was clearly caused by an assertive Chinese display of power.

Was South Asia becoming China's Mexico? A low-wage neighborhood? Indian officials insisted that they could still deter China by means of nuclear weapons and threaten China's long maritime trade routes through the Indian Ocean. In reality, however, the Indian Navy suffered from poor maintenance, a lack of ammunition, and various other problems. In 2019, it was reportedly only capable of permanently deploying six large warships in the Indian Ocean. Underneath India's nuclear umbrella, China steadily gained ground.

A second consequence of South Asia's enduring marginalization was instability. A long-lasting civil war in Sri Lanka officially ended in 2009 and tourists returned to its pristine beaches. Elsewhere in South Asia, the situation was less positive. What changed the outlook decisively was the election of Narendra Modi as India's prime minister. As a prime minister, Modi profiled himself, like his predecessor, as a trailblazer of good governance, a fighter of corruption, and an economic reformer. As the latter failed and poverty grew again, Modi had no other option but to give sway to radical Hindu forces.[18] The Hindu youth group Bajrang Dal saw its membership soar and intimidated Muslim cattle traders in the name of protecting cows. It incited so-called Hindu lions to attack interfaith couples. Muslims were the main target, but Christians were not spared either.

In 2016, Hindu nationalists caught a pastor, shaved his head, and paraded him through town on a donkey. A BJP parliamentarian called the murderer of the resistance leader Mahatma Gandhi a patriot. Her statement was echoed by hundreds of thousands via social media. Between 2010 and 2019, there were more terrorist incidents in India than in the decade before. Stoking the flames of nationalism, Modi scrapped the autonomy of the predominantly Muslim state Jammu and Kashmir, in 2019, and launched an air attack against alleged terrorist camps in the Pakistani part of Kashmir. For a few days, the two countries were on the brink of war. Corporate leaders decried the climate of fear that had taken control of India, and the fact that Hindu nationalism masked the problem of bad governance and poverty. India had drifted further away from the ideal of an inclusive state and the instability made it less likely that it would catch up with China as a regional power.

Harsh Hindu nationalism was a blessing for the Pakistani military. Rivalry with India had always been the military's most important justification for its central position in society and the renewed tensions over Kashmir affirmed that argument. For a brief moment, the military was defied by Prime Minister Nawaz Sharif. He tried to limit defense spending, the role of the armed forces in the economy, and their influence on foreign policy. When the nation went to the ballot box in 2018, Sharif, embroiled in corruption scandals, had no chance. His opponent, the popular former cricket player Imran Khan, was supported by the military. Khan promised a new Pakistan. Still, ordinary citizens remained devastated by inflation and unemployment. Military spending rebounded. Generals offered businessmen impunity in corruption investigations in exchange for support. Dissidents were prosecuted or killed. News media were censored.

Repression hardened, but could not prevent the fragility from being laid bare by mass protests, terrorist attacks, and persistent violence in provinces like Balochistan and the border area with Afghanistan. The Pakistani population kept growing by about four million each year while drought knocked down food production. A former American defense minister referred to Pakistan as the most dangerous country. Security officials warned that while Pakistan was now still a sanctuary for terrorists from Afghanistan, Afghanistan could become a sanctuary for resistance movements from

Pakistan as soon as Western troops left.[19] Against this backdrop of instability, the Pakistani military kept testing new nuclear weapons, and it built two nuclear power plants with the help of China.

Throughout the region, new barriers emerged. Pakistan and India installed fences and alarm systems along the border. India erected over 3,000 kilometers of barbed wire to stop migration from Bangladesh. The tragedy of these barriers was that they stopped economic exchanges, but not the proliferation of violence. India accused Pakistan of using drones to airdrop weapons to insurgents on its side of the border and of training terrorists in deep sea diving to be capable of carrying out strikes. Indian rebels found new ways to cross the border with Bangladesh and used neighboring Myanmar as a hideaway. As the region remained gripped by political instability, the large container ships from China kept mostly passing by. South Asia was on its way to become a security black hole. It remained a restless and crowded backwater of globalization, but with at least two hundred million more mouths to feed each passing decade.

Neocolonialism

On the northern board of the Indian Ocean, South Asia remained stuck. On the other side of the Indian Ocean, Africa suffered from a hangover. As expected, the commodity boom of the previous decade had not strengthened the African economy. After the euphoria, the reality of economic marginalization asserted itself. Despite upbeat reports about factories in Nigeria and Ethiopia, Africa's share in global manufacturing remained below 2 percent. By 2020, 80 percent of African exports consisted of raw materials. The continent was caught in a commodity trap. As global raw material prices collapsed, the value of African exports stagnated.

At the same time African imports of consumer goods and machinery increased, so that the region evolved from a trade surplus at the beginning of the decade to a large trade deficit by the end, and, inevitably, growing external debt. Between 2010 and 2020, African external debt increased by US$30 billion annually. While foreign loans increased, capital flight continued. In the 1990s, annual capital flight from Africa was about US$16 billion; in the 2000s it was US$21 billion; in the subsequent decade US$63 billion.[20]

Capital flight was twice as large as the inflow of investment. The same African elites that committed their country to repaying large Chinese loans, burdening the next generation, took fortunes out of the continent. For private citizens, the decade of stagnation meant that incomes hardly increased, that still two thirds of them existed on less than US$3 per day, and that the prevalence of undernourishment was again emergent. Between 2010 and 2020, the number of African poor increased by 120 million; the number of Africans suffering from famine by almost 60 million.

Africa's soil, its seas, and its trees were of interest to the global economy; its people less so. If one approached Africa from the Indian Ocean, one found fishing fleets from Asia poaching in the seas around the continent, depriving hundreds of thousands of local fishermen of an important source of revenue. Some of them turned to piracy instead. African countries could not stop it. Along the whole East African coast there were five patrol boats. China deployed warships in the Gulf of Aden, near Somalia, to combat the problem of piracy that its illegal fishing boats had helped to create.

The ports in East Africa saw bulk carriers transporting minerals to China and container ships transporting finished goods to Africa. In Port Sudan, China operated a large oil terminal. In Djibouti, it developed a port, guarded by a military base, next to bases of France, Japan, and the United States. China was the dominant player in the Port of Mombasa, Kenya. The port's imports were ten times larger than its exports. In 2020, the local government was about to lose control over the port to China because it could not repay its loans. In Dar es Salaam, Tanzania, port imports were six times larger than exports and China once more emerged as the main trader. From these ports, railways, built by Chinese contractors and financed with Chinese loans, connected the hinterland. The new railway between Djibouti and Ethiopia channeled a flood of Chinese goods. Their value was ten times larger than what African countries exported. "The old train had so much importance for the city. Passengers used our restaurants and hotels, all services. But this time such things won't happen," said a local trader. "The new train is simply passing through."[21]

This was also the situation in the hinterland of Africa. Consider Sudan. The country exported around US$10 billion of oil each year. Most of the oil was found in the south. That led to a split between Sudan and South Sudan in 2011. "The focus is peace, peace, peace," said an official from the newly established South Sudan.[22] But in 2013, a civil war erupted, primarily over the control of oil. Since then, four million citizens have been displaced. South Sudan exported around US$3 billion of oil per year and still poverty increased. Its national oil company paid at least US$80 million per year to war-related activities.[23]

Neighboring Ethiopia was considered a poster child of progress. Chinese companies set up some factories and Dutch companies planted flowers for export. In 2018 the country brokered a peace agreement with Eritrea. It earned the prime minister the 2019 Nobel Peace Prize. Yet, by 2019, manufacturing contributed less than 5 percent of the total economy. Six percent of Ethiopians had a formal job, and the country ran a large trade deficit. Flower farms were attacked by mobs and violence increased among ethnic groups like the Oromo, the Amhara, and the Tigray, whom the Nobel-laureate prime minister described as daytime hyenas. In 2020, tensions in the Tigray region escalated into full-blown war. Unprecedented numbers of people tried to flee East Africa, via the treacherous corridors of the Sahara Desert, and an even more risky journey across the Mediterranean.

Another example of such economic distress was the Democratic Republic of Congo. "The population is very, very young. It's almost a time bomb," said President Joseph Kabila. "You have to make sure those young men and young women are employed; otherwise you'll have social upheaval."[24] The mining sector of Congo generated around US$10 billion in exports, whereas annual fiscal revenues from the sector were only US$1.4 billion, and around a third of that was embezzled.[25] In 2020, ten years after Kabila's statement, 2.5 percent of the Congolese population had a formal job. Kabila himself retired to a large farm outside Kinshasa, "Ferme Espoir," the farm of hope. His family kept cropping up in investigations about tax havens. In Nigeria, Goodluck Jonathan won the 2010 presidential elections with a promise to combat corruption. Mr. Honesty, he was called, but in 2011, Shell and Eni reportedly paid US$1 billion in bribes for an oil license. In 2019, Jonathan called corruption "no more than common stealing."[26] Globalization was not generous to Africa and African strongmen fought for the crumbs.

The state was a vehicle for looting on a massive scale. Both local leaders and foreign actors were complicit. Most Africans endured this lost decade in silence, with a sense of powerlessness and resignation. "Africans live longer," stated an activist, "but an African life still has not much value in this world."[27] Indeed, life expectancy increased, but more Africans were scourged by violence, sexual abuse, crime, and political instability. There were now more gleaming office buildings in cities like Lagos and new Chinese railroads. But the problems of overpopulation, environmental distress, disease, migration pressure, the erosion of states, and the empowerment of private armies were still prevalent.

Yes, young protesters had expedited the downfall of authoritarian regimes in Ethiopia, Sudan, and Angola, but overall, Africa did not become more democratic. Africans became more supportive of democracy but also more disillusioned about its viability.[28] African citizens also found that corruption increased and one third reported having had to pay a bribe in the past year.[29] There were as many political coups as during the previous decades. Important countries were beset by political polarization and nepotism, like South Africa after the death of Nelson Mandela in 2013. Botswana and Ghana, once bright stars of governance, lost their luster. In international organizations, like the African Union, heads of state patted each other on the back, but the organization remained toothless in combating corruption and insecurity. The number of countries in armed conflicts did not decrease and citizens were more exposed to non-state violence from terrorist groups, criminal gangs, factions fighting for land, rioters, and, most of the time, a combination of them.[30]

The Democratic Republic of Congo remained an epicenter of such violence. The number of displaced people increased from two million in 2010 to five million in 2020. "I do not think the wars here will ever stop," testified a former fighter.[31] Warring factions, around 120 in total, held sway in the east of the country. They competed over mines, pastureland, profit from extortion, and ransom. Alliances and frontlines between these factions shifted perpetually. Some maintained networks across borders, with Rwanda, Uganda, and elsewhere. Radical Islam became increasingly used as a justification for loot and terror. "He came back from Saudi Arabia ready to die for Islam," said a fighter about his leader.[32] Eastern Congo offered a sanctuary to rebels from South Sudan, Uganda, and the Central African Republic.

In East Africa, Somalia was the center of fighting, with the terrorist movement Al-Shabaab spreading its tentacles into Kenya, Tanzania, Ethiopia, and

South Sudan. The UN peacekeepers were powerless and were frequently attacked. In West Africa, too, the security situation deteriorated. Consider Nigeria. The terrorist movement Boko Haram gained ground in the north of the country. The campaign of Boko Haram, which began in 2009, has cost around 38,000 lives. The more the Nigerian regular army fought it, the more the movement splintered into small cells. Thousands more were killed by gangs of farmer bandits or Fulani herdsmen militia.[33] "Cattle herders were known to carry sticks and machetes," it was said, "but these ones are carrying Kalashnikovs."[34] In the southern cities, violence increased between natives and immigrants from neighboring countries. Along its coast, piracy proliferated, threatening the offshore oil industry.

North of Nigeria, the whole Sahel region destabilized. Boko Haram expanded into Cameroon, Chad, and Niger. In 2010, a coup was staged in Niger, in 2012, one in Mali. There were many fault lines. Traditionally, the Tuareg nomads in the north competed with the pastoralists in the Sahel, among whom the Fulani are the most important ethnic group, over water and trade routes. The pastoralists competed for grazing land with the farmers further south.[35] Tensions also existed between the inhabitants of the southern tropical strip, along the Gulf of Guinea, and northern immigrants. These traditional tensions were aggravated by population growth, climate change, and, again, the fact that the revenues from the energy business, cash crops like cotton and cocoa, seldom benefited the society.

Inside these belts, hundreds of factions competed, Tuaregs against Tuaregs, Fulani against Fulani, and so forth. This anarchy offered a perfect sanctuary for terrorist groups. "Now it is eternal war," said a woman from Niger.[36] In the Sahel, from the Red Sea over Lake Chad to the Atlantic Ocean, there were close to ten million people displaced in 2020: five million more than in 2010. This internal migration caused a xenophobic backlash. An Algerian politician spoke of diseases invading the streets. In South Africa, Nigerian and Zimbabwean immigrants were attacked and accused of being criminals. In Kenya, far-right politicians called for the expulsion of Tanzanians and Ugandans: "Enough is enough."

What European countries saw was a demographic explosion on their doorstep. The African population grew by 30 million people each year and is set to surpass two billion by 2040. What the United States perceived was a persistent terrorist threat. France and the United States were in the frontline of a fight against terrorism. In 2013, France ordered special forces to protect the uranium mines in Niger. Most other countries were hesitant to engage and/or cynical about the chance of success. "The French want us to exert pressure on the border between Niger and Mali," said a military officer. "But if we move north, we leave the border between Niger and Nigeria to armed groups, and before you know, you have a new corridor of terrorism here. You press at some point, and the problem just relocates."[37] Despite promises of a Marshall Plan for Africa, Western aid and investment in Africa stagnated.[38] Without a plan for lasting development, military operations were like desperate firefighting.

At the same time, other powers stepped into the void. China emerged as the largest provider of credit and also increasingly sought to secure its interests by growing its military presence. China imported a lot of raw materials from Africa, but still exported more, so that it had a trade surplus with the continent. Africa lost capital on the trade balance and received loans instead, which allowed China to claim infrastructure, mines, or land if countries could not repay them. The Congolese President Joseph Kabila explained China's growing footprint as follows:

What is the Chinese deal? We said we had five priorities: infrastructure, health, education, water and electricity, and housing. Now, how do we deal with these priorities? We need money, a lot of money. Not US$100 million from the World Bank or 300 from the International Monetary Fund. No, a lot of money, and especially that we're still servicing a debt of close to 12 billion dollars, and it's 50 to 60 million dollars per month, which is huge ... We talked to everybody. Americans, do you have the money? No, not for now. The European Union, do you have three or four billion for these priorities? No, we have our own priorities. Then we said: why not talk to other people, the Chinese? So, we said, do you have the money? And they said, well, we can discuss. So, we discussed.[39]

Africans saw China as an alternative partner and development model.[40] By 2019, Brazil, India, Russia, and Turkey had all announced their return to Africa and organized large political summits. "We cannot allow the revival of neocolonialism, a predatory attitude toward African resources," stated the chairman of the Russian parliament during a summit with African leaders.[41] Still, Russian companies were aggressively trying to get hold of oil, diamonds, and uranium, dispatching mercenaries to at least ten countries to provide protection to the incumbent elite. Russia opened an airbase in the south of Libya. It sent mercenaries to the Central African Republic and Sudan. Turkey agreed on a maritime corridor with Libya, sent weapons and mercenaries to the Libyan government, and started searching for uranium in Niger. African politicians often thought that they were playing the external powers; but more often they were being played. African intellectuals were critical and spoke of neocolonialism and new dependency.[42] The new partners, one opinion leader posited, cared no more about the Africans than European colonial powers did at the Berlin Conference in 1884.[43] Foreign countries were interested in Africa's soil, not in the people living on it. The enduring hardship made 40 percent of its people want to emigrate.[44]

Hangover

Latin America, too, suffered from a painful hangover from its commodity boom. Consider the Chilean Port Angamos. The port continued to send out the same volume of copper as in the previous decade, but at much lower prices. The value of Chilean copper exports climbed from US$5 billion in 2000 to US$30 billion in 2011, but then shrank back to US$15 billion. It was the same situation on the other side of the continent, in the Brazilian port Santos. In 2020, the port sent 25 million tons of soybeans to overseas markets. All along the Amazon River, precious tropical forest was burned to grow soy. Trucks transported it via dirt tracks to small ports on the river, small ships forwarded it to the mega ports, and they loaded it onto bulk carriers to China and Europe. The value of soy in 2020, however, was less than half its value in 2012.

During the boom, Latin America, despite the pledges of political leaders, was not able to reduce its economic dependence on these raw materials. Moreover, while the commodity boom brought about a temporary wave of optimism and relief for the poor, most countries did not seize the opportunity to carry out structural measures to improve infrastructure, education, security, and governance. The elite continued to send a lot of capital to offshore tax havens; the middle class to spend it on imported consumer goods. Corruption was rampant. A dramatic example: a Brazilian construction conglomerate was discovered to have spent US$780 million in bribes in Latin America to secure US$3.3 billion in contracts. Between 2010 and 2019, poverty rates did not decrease at all, and spiked in 2020, as a consequence of corona. The price paid for this wasted momentum was colossal.

Latin America remained stuck in its swamp of violence. Colombia was one of the rare places where the homicide rate decreased. Throughout the region, around 1.6 million people were murdered between 2010 and 2019.[45] This would be twice as many as the number of civilian deaths during the civil wars in Syria and Iraq. This structural criminal violence was now exacerbated by growing political violence. In 2019, unrest escalated in Chile. The trigger was a hike in public transport tariffs. The deeper cause was the fact that millions of poor had progressed slowly thanks to the commodity boom and were thrown back into uncertainty. The economic setback exposed the high inequality and the lack of empathy of the elite. When the first protesters were shot, the president was seen taking his family to the capital's most expensive pizzeria. This gesture was the modern Chilean equivalent of Marie Antoinette's "Let them eat cake!" The same dynamics were at work in Ecuador. When the economic slowdown forced the government to trim fuel subsidies, the strikes by bus and taxi drivers detonated a powder keg of anger among marginalized indigenous groups. In Bolivia, riots broke out after the president tried to change the constitution to hold on to power. In Peru, unrest erupted after a bribery scandal with a Brazilian construction company, a money laundering complaint against the main opposition leader, and the nascent expropriation of hundreds of small farmers for a mining project. In Paraguay, protests also followed an attempt of the president to have an unlawful third term. Asked how he would respond, he answered: "Rubber bullets."[46]

Violence advanced; democracy retreated. The majority of citizens in Latin America became disillusioned with democracy. The support for authoritarianism was again on the rise. In 2018, the Brazilians elected a former army captain who had promised to combat crime with an iron fist. Jair Bolsonaro had scorned parliament, referred to the opposition as a party of dicks and faggots, to immigrants as scum, and to Human Rights Day as the day of losers. The same year, the Mexicans also elected a president, Andrés Obrador, who had made scorn of parliament, criticism of the supreme court, and militarism his trademark.

Venezuela was the epicenter of unrest in Latin America. It was also the country in which the forces of great power rivalry were most visibly at work. Thousands of citizens were killed by regular government troops and death squads. The unrest started in 2014. Students rallied against rape incidents on their campus. After they were brutally beaten by the police, the demonstrations grew like wildfire, propelled by frustration about insecurity, corruption, and hyperinflation. For a long time, the country had been led by a leftist populist regime, first under Hugo Chavez, and, after his death in 2012, under Nicolas Maduro. The regime had founded its power on the oil sector. Between 2013 and 2016, however, oil exports almost halved. What followed was a social crisis, mixed with a constitutional crisis, and an international stalemate. The United States and many other countries opposed President Maduro, but China and Russia supported him. In 2018, Moscow deployed fighter jets and 100 soldiers to signal Washington to back off. The crisis in Venezuela made about one million people flee.

Like in Africa, pessimism surged after the missed momentum. While the Inter-American Development Bank announced the 2010s as the Latin American decade, polls showed that, by the end of the decade, one third of the Latin American population wanted to emigrate.

Hard hedging

So far, we have studied the rise of China and the weakening of the Global South. The third focal point of this chapter concerns the return of hard hedging. Hedging means that countries refuse to take sides between the major powers.[47] It is typical of a multipolar order in which no major power is capable of commanding obedience. Hard hedging implies that they actively play the protagonists against one another and assertively advance their interests abroad. A preference for hedging was already visible in the 1990s. At that stage, though, the unipolar moment left no options to the regional powers but to nurture ties with the West and to respect the United States as a global leader, despite the humiliation that several regional powers felt. In the subsequent decade, especially in the wake of the invasion of Iraq, this frustration was more openly expressed and regional powers started cultivating ties with China. Now, as a result of Western military overstretch, its isolationist tendency, and its economic weakening, the hard hedging became brazen. Regional powers created alternative security partnerships and actively resisted Western values. Hard hedging became more articulate as a result of the rise of China, which permitted countries to temper the traditional influence of the West. It became also more manifest as a result of the weakening of the South, which elicited opportunistic attempts to exploit this fragility, particularly as the influence of Western powers diminished.

Important hedgers were found at the crossroads between West, East, and the global south: Russia, Turkey, Iran, Saudi Arabia, and Israel. These countries had sizable economies, yet still smaller than those of China, the United States, and, if considered as a single market, the European Union. With the exception of Israel, they all drifted into rough economic weather and recorded scarcely any growth between 2010 and 2020. It was partly as a remedy against socioeconomic uncertainty that governments resorted to aggressive nationalism and harsh authoritarianism. Vladimir Putin referred to the West as a decadent society. "The liberal idea has become obsolete. It has come into conflict with the interests of the overwhelming majority of the population."[48] Tayyip Erdoğan called Europe a sick man and Benjamin Netanyahu labeled Europe ignorant. They all invested in partnerships with the East, partnerships that were primarily economic but also maturing in political and military terms. They started to pursue a foreign policy of unilateralism, marked by shifting partnerships with each other, the assertive use of military power, interference in other countries, and disregard for the West. Their military strategy was a combination of traditional warfighting and guerrilla tactics, also called hybrid warfare. In the slipstream of these regional powers trailed lesser powers, such as Qatar, the United Arab Emirates, and Egypt.

Russia consolidated its position as a regional power. It invaded Ukraine, interfered in Western internal politics, flexed its muscle all around Europe, rebuilt its military power in the Baltic and Black seas, and did so almost with impunity. For a country with an economy smaller than Germany's, this was a remarkable achievement. Russian commentators called it payback time for the embarrassment of the 1990s. There were several other factors that emboldened Russia. Between 2009 and 2013, the Russian economy grew strongly. Thanks to the partnership with China, Moscow could push back against Western liberalism. Russia thus entered the new decade with some confidence, but also saw its frustration toward the West confirmed on various occasions. Russia resented the arrival of American missile defense systems in Poland in 2010, the Western intervention in Libya in 2011, the conclusion of free trade negotiations between the European Union and Ukraine in 2012, and Western sympathy for anti-government protests in Moscow. In 2012, Vladimir Putin returned as president and judged that the West was in decline and that it was time for a forceful counteroffensive.[49]

The most dramatic campaign concerned the war with Ukraine and the annexation of Crimea. It was a cunning combination of intimidation, surprise, and playing on the weaknesses of the adversary. President Putin first pressured the Ukrainian government to abrogate the trade deal with the European Union. When mass protests in Kiev broke out against the U-turn, Russia supported rebellion in the eastern region of Donbass and in Crimea. In January 2014, a lawmaker from Crimea urged Putin to send Russian forces to protect Ukraine from Western secret agents. In a national security council meeting in February 2014, Putin concluded: "We must start working on returning the Crimea to Russia." In the following days, elite soldiers were sent in, without the Russian flag on their shoulder patches. They were called little green men. Under the protection of "Crimean self-defense forces" a referendum was held, asking: "Do you support the reunification of Crimea with Russia?" Ninety-seven percent voted for reunification. Russia had just staged an annexation through a referendum. More Russian troops poured into Ukraine. While Russia fortified its position on Crimea, it intervened in the exhausting civil war between Kiev and Donbass. The instant response of other frontline countries in Eastern Europe was to lie low, fearing that they would follow Ukraine's fate. With the annexation of Crimea, Vladimir Putin scored the biggest military victory of his time.

By the end of the decade, Russia had regained influence over Moldova and Belarus, so that they fulfilled the function that the Kremlin had in mind for them: that of buffer states. Russian soldiers were also present in the Caucasus, in Armenia, in two breakaway regions of Georgia, Abkhazia and South Ossetia, and in Central Asian countries like Tajikistan. The Kremlin restored a significant part of its old sphere of influence. It was at the height of the tensions in Ukraine that Russia launched a campaign to influence the presidential elections in the United States.[50]

NATO responded to Russia's offensive by deploying troops in Poland and in the Baltic countries, but analysts privately avowed that this deployment was largely symbolic. Russia, after all, had rapidly developed weapons that could deter the United States from replenishing these forward troops in case of conflict. It deployed advanced radar systems to monitor the situation around its borders, over 350 S-400 anti-aircraft missiles with a range of 250 kilometers, hundreds of Kalibr anti-ship missiles with a range of over 660 kilometers, over 400 new fighter aircraft, mobile platforms for electronic warfare, and so forth. For Vladimir Putin this was only the beginning:

In the near future, the Russian Armed Forces will receive new hypersonic-speed, high-precision weapons that can hit targets at intercontinental distance and adjust their altitude and course as they travel. No country in the world today has such arms in their military arsenal. Why did we do all this? As you can see, we made no secret of our plans and spoke openly about them, primarily to encourage our partners to hold talks. Let me repeat, this was in 2004. It is actually surprising that despite all the problems with the economy, finances and the defence industry, Russia has remained a major nuclear power. No, nobody really wanted to talk to us about the core of the problem, and nobody wanted to listen to us. So, listen to us now.[51]

In Ukraine, Russia intervened in an unconventional manner, deploying green men and supporting rebels; around the Mediterranean, it showed that it could also fight in a conventional way. Occasionally, Russian submarines would disappear and then surface near to NATO warships, as if they wanted to say: "Got you!" Between 2015 and 2019, the Russian air force, navy, and special forces were decisive in restoring the regime of Bashar al-Assad in the Syrian civil war. Russia used the crisis to rebuild its presence in the strategically located sea port of Tartus and literally took over some of the bases that the Americans had abandoned in Syria. If the West had lost its military campaigns in the Middle East, Russia scored a second important victory in Syria. With the port of Tartus, Moscow reinforced its staging point in the Mediterranean. From Syria, Russia supported a military intervention in Libya, where it supported the warlord in control of the east of the country, and staged exercises with Egypt and Algeria. Russia was consolidating its influence in the Southern Mediterranean, Europe's soft underbelly.

While Russian energy exports to Europe remained steady, pipelines were built to China. In 2015, Russia obtained a US$25 billion Chinese credit line to help its companies overcome Western financial sanctions. "We are grateful to the people of China, whose leaders have always considered the situation in Ukraine and Crimea taking into account the full historical and political context," said Vladimir Putin.[52] Whereas Russia kept Europe dependent on its energy, it reduced its own dependence, in the energy sector, as well as in the financial domain, where it developed an alternative for the clearing mechanism Swift and Visa credit cards, and in the domain of information technology, where it worked toward a Russian internet, disconnected, if need be, from the global internet. Putin's hard hedging had not made the country stronger at home, for economic production in 2019 was at about the same level as in 2010. Yet, he made Russia a power that was again taken seriously and he succeeded in convincing many Russian citizens of an important idea: that there was no alternative to the president and his new authoritarianism. "Old geopolitical frontlines have returned," clarified a government advisor. "Yet, Europe is so weak that there cannot be a return to the Cold War. In a way, the situation is ideal. Eastern Europe member states stir enough animosity for the president to have an external adversary, yet Europe also calms down United States and faithfully pays its energy bills."[53]

Exemplary of the new power politics in the region were the relations between Russia and Turkey. Turkey was concerned about Russian military modernization and the fact that Russian soldiers occasionally fought alongside Kurdish rebels in Syria. Turkey in turn provided support to the IS terrorists that were fought by Russia. In 2015, Turkey shot down a Russian fighter jet that crossed its border. Turkey and Russia also supported opposing camps in the Libyan civil war. Tensions built up. Both sides, however, tried to avoid a breakdown. In 2016, when President Erdoğan faced a coup attempt, Vladimir Putin was one of the first to offer his support. A while later Turkey agreed to build a gas pipeline with Russia, TurkStream, and to order Russian air defense missiles. The latter was a clear provocation toward the West.

Erdoğan became increasingly critical of Europe. "Stop leading us by the nose," he told Brussels with regard to possible Turkish membership. "We do not need EU membership anymore." He went further:

> My brothers and sisters in the European Union are not honest. Recently, the European member states met at the Vatican. These developments recall something. What's up? Why did you meet in the Vatican? Why did you meet in front of the pope? When did the pope become a member of the European Union? Ah, the Alliance of Crusaders has shown itself in the end. Indeed: You do not accept Turkey to the European Union because Turkey is Muslim.[54]

To the Turks in Europe he said: "Make not three, but five children. Because you are the future of Europe. That will be the best response to the injustices against you."[55] Ankara kept criticizing the United States for supporting the Kurds and creating chaos in the Middle East. The Turkish military moved into Syria from the moment that the United States evacuated most of its troops in 2019. Turkey kept quiet about the incarceration of the hundreds of thousands of Turkic Muslims in China, the Uyghurs, and preferred to celebrate the arrival of Chinese trains and trade instead. The vitriol against the West was partially meant to distract attention from the poor economic state of the country and came on top of hidden repression of dissidents. Between 2016 and 2020, 292,000 people were arrested; 70 newspapers closed. Like Russia, Turkey lived through a decade of stagnation and rising inflation. Contrarily to Putin, however, Erdoğan had no energy reserves. Erdoğan's internal approval rating was also lower than Putin's. Turkey was a combination of a strong leader and a fragile country, slowly drifting away from the West.

Ankara forcefully asserted its claims over a large part of the Mediterranean, called the Blue Motherland. Turkey wanted to build itself a maritime sphere of influence, like most other powers, and to exploit offshore energy reserves to reduce its import dependence. Ankara sealed a maritime agreement with Northern Cyprus and started sending research ships into the latter's adjacent seas. It brokered a deal with Libya that provided for a joint maritime zone, a corridor between Anatolia and Africa. Between 2010 and 2020, Turkey built 25 navy ships. With the help of Spain, it commissioned its first light aircraft carrier. Turkey strengthened its presence in Africa. It supported the Libyan government, by means of mercenaries recruited in Syria and drone campaigns. It set up a small military facility in Somalia – Camp Turksom – an interesting project also in terms of neo-Ottoman architecture.

Russia and Turkey were militarily resurgent, yet economically stagnant. This was also true for Iran, another regional power that pursued hedging. The replacement of the hardliner president Ahmadinejad with Hassan Rouhani (2013–21) helped prepare the ground for a breakthrough in the negotiations about the country's nuclear program. In 2013, direct talks with the American government took place. They led to an agreement in which Iran promised to limit its stock of enriched uranium, to send everything in excess of 300 kilograms to Russia, and to allow monitoring of its facilities. The deal permitted the government to stick to its right to pursue the civilian use of nuclear power and the international community to put checks on the development of nuclear weapons.

But this only eliminated one dilemma. Iran continued to support proxies throughout the region, and bolstered Hezbollah in Lebanon and armed groups in Syria against Israel, rebels in Yemen against Saudi Arabia, and various actors in Iraq against the United States. And it built more advanced missiles. Washington, like in the past, saw the moderate president Rouhani as a façade for the conservative religious regime which considered the United States and Israel as demons. The century-old geopolitical conundrum of Persian influence toward the Levant colliding with the ambitions of other powers in the West was still alive.

Hence the decision of the American President Donald Trump in 2017 to cancel the action plan and to impose massive new sanctions. Iran felt betrayed, by the United States primarily, but also by the Europeans for not standing up to Washington. The American sanctions crippled the economy, helped trigger protests against rising prices, yet also affirmed most Iranians in their anti-Westernism.

Diplomatically, Iran was cornered. It reached out to China, but Beijing did not think Iran important enough to confront the United States. It reached out to Europe, but potential European investors did not want to risk American retaliation either. Iran did not have many weapons to strike back. In Iraq, efforts to stoke instability backfired. A drone and missile strike against a large Saudi Arabian oil facility in 2019 did not have much effect either. In 2020, Iran's most influential general was killed by an American air strike. Tehran backpedaled. It still carried out small guerrilla strikes. It quietly fortified its position in the border zone of Iraq, along transport corridors between Iraq and Syria, inside Syria, and in Lebanon. For now, the objective was consolidation without confrontation.

This was in stark contrast with Saudi Arabia's confidence. In 2020, Saudi Arabia spent almost as much on military power as all other countries in the Middle East put together. Riyadh showed itself ready to use it. In 2011, it deployed its armed forces to repress unrest in Bahrain. In 2013, it started arming militants in Syria to fight Iranian-backed factions. In 2015, it intervened in Yemen, once more, to combat armed groups that were supported by Iran. Its intervention was marked by brutal air strikes and support for terrorist movements, including Al-Qaeda and the Yemeni branch of the Islamic State. Internally, Crown Prince Mohammad bin Salman, who became the principal leader in 2017, combined promises for reform and modernization, with a zealous purge of opponents. Hundreds of princes were sent into luxury confinement. While Riyadh charmed the world with news about women being allowed to drive, female activists were jailed and tortured. A secret death squad was assembled to intimidate, kidnap, and kill dissidents, like the journalist Jamal Khashoggi who was suffocated and cut into pieces in the Saudi consulate in Istanbul. Just a few months later, bin Salman was rehabilitated by the announcement that Saudi Arabia would host a G-20 summit. Relations with the United States and Europe remained close. Still, Riyadh showed great appetite for sending more energy to Asia. It invited China to help build drones, ballistic missiles, and cyber security systems. Like Turkey, it kept silent about the imprisonment of members of the Muslim minority in China. "We support China's rights to take counter-terrorism measures," the crown prince explained.[56]

In Riyadh's relations with regional powers, pragmatism, rather than religion or ideology, prevailed. With Turkey, Saudi Arabia clashed over Libya and Egypt. While Riyadh supported el-Sisi, Erdoğan called him a tyrant. Saudi Arabia opposed Russia's support for al-Assad in Syria, but worked with Russia in matters such as energy. Ties warmed with Israel, with whom Saudi Arabia shared the rivalry with Iran. One of the most conservative Islamic countries, Saudi Arabia had closer relations with the two non-Muslim regional powers than with the two main Muslim regional powers.

The nimblest hedger was Israel. Each year, Israel received over US$3 billion in aid from the American government. Still, Prime Minister Benjamin Netanyahu declined American calls to stop the construction of new Israeli settlements in Palestinian areas, spoke of American criticism as a shameful anti-Israel ambush, and, at some point, declined to meet President Barack Obama. About Europe, Netanyahu uttered that it would shrivel and disappear. Israel could afford the provocations, because of its traditional inroads in American politics, by remaining an indispensable intelligence partner for Washington in the Middle East, and by exploiting the antagonism with Iran. During the Trump presidency, Israel wrested from the United States the recognition of Jerusalem as its capital and almost complete silence regarding its construction of new settlements.

At the same time, Israel passed sensitive missile and optical technology to China. It independently developed its relations with Saudi Arabia, the United Arab Emirates, and Egypt. Once again exploiting the rivalry with Iran, its aim was a non-aggression pact with the Gulf-Arab countries. Relations with Turkey remained tense, which prompted Israel to work more closely with Russia. Tel Aviv played the regional animosity with virtuosity, setting religion and historical distrust aside, to work pragmatically with the Gulf States and others. In 2020, it signed a peace deal with Bahrain and the United Arab Emirates. The world became multipolar and Israel acted accordingly. This maneuvering, persistent American support, European impotence, and superior hard military power allowed Israel to bomb targets in Sudan, Syria, Iraq, Lebanon, and the Egyptian Sinai Desert with impunity.

The United States had always been an unpopular overlord in the region. Now, countries flagrantly ignored it. Europe hardly appeared on their radar screens. The focus on the West made way for diversification. The partnership with China became important and even more so the nervous relationships with other powers in the region. The Eurasian crossroads between the Black Sea and the Gulf of Aden became an arena of restless regional power politics. The tussle was about influence and status, much more than religion. Thanks to its position in Syria and its readiness to sell advanced weapons, Russia developed pragmatic relations with all countries, from Turkey, over Iran, to Saudi Arabia. Russia, to be sure, was critical of Turkey's interference in Syria, disliked Iran's nuclear program, and loathed the support of Saudi Arabia for terrorists. Nevertheless, Vladimir Putin reached out to all of them. With Israel, it agreed not to sell advanced weapons to Iran in exchange for a halt of Israeli arms deliveries to Georgia. Israel, together with Saudi Arabia and the Emirates, proposed that the West accept Russia's claims in Ukraine in exchange for more cooperation in Syria. Iran and Saudi Arabia remained key rivals, but avoided all-out war.

A quartet consisting of Bahrain, Egypt, Saudi Arabia, and the Emirates imposed sanctions on Iran. Yet, the Emirates did not follow Riyadh's hard line and quickly tried to mend relations with Iran through secret diplomacy. Qatar in turn reached out to Russia for energy projects and security cooperation, as well as to Turkey, which opened a military base housing 4,000 soldiers in the country. Even with Israel, an increasingly important partner of the Saudis, Qatar agreed to coordinate regarding the humanitarian aid it provided to the Palestinians and offered to mediate between Israel and Lebanon. Israel continued to refer to Qatar as a sponsor of terrorism the whole time. In this arena of power politics, there seemed to be three certainties: the rivalry between Iran and Israel, the rivalry between Iran and Saudi Arabia, and the animosity between Saudi Arabia and Turkey. The rest was in a permanent state of flux. The Middle East was a restless arena of power politics. There was anarchy between states, and anarchy inside states. Or, as one Iraqi taxi driver testified: "Saddam Hussein hanged my brother, but things since his death are worse. Now there are many Saddams all fighting for money. There is no rest."[57]

Fragmented and turbulent

The new world order that emerged from the three decades after the Cold War was by no means more democratic or stable. This chapter has identified three important evolutions. One concerned the affirmation of China as a regional power with global ambitions. The return of China as a protagonist inevitably meant the advancing of authoritarianism and state capitalism at the expense of democracy and free trade, with the difference that Chinese leaders made both features of their regime increasingly sophisticated. The Chinese president, Xi Jinping, saw no problem in propagating free trade on the international scene while sticking to economic nationalism at home and launching an unequaled state-financed push for exports: the Belt and Road Initiative. China's rise also brought back the long-lasting quandary of a large Eurasian power that challenged American preponderance. This was especially so because China had no regional peer-rival and most other Eurasian countries were reluctant to counterbalance it. China was a rising power unchecked. Even the United States was mollified. When tensions peaked during Donald Trump's presidency, Beijing offered to buy more American oil and soy. These were goods that China needed anyhow and did not compromise its industrial goals, but still permitted it to prevent a confrontation. Nevertheless, this was a new major security dilemma in the making.

A second feature was the failure of the Global South: South Asia, Africa, and Latin America. This, too, challenged the ideal of trade advancing prosperity and stability. Armed conflict, crime, and migration in this part of the world remained rampant. In many countries, citizens grew disillusioned with the feasibility of democracy. What was left of the confidence in the Washington Consensus, if any, vanished entirely. The instability in the South, the immense migration pressure, loomed as a second important security challenge to the West. This quagmire was the scene of new power politics, between China and the United States, and also involving other regional powers like Russia and Saudi Arabia. The isolationist tendency of the West, its diplomatic divisions, and its inability to turn economic clout into political influence created security dilemmas that were filled by other protagonists. Russia again symbolically sent soldiers to Latin America, while China got hold of mines and ports in America's backyard. The same was true in Africa, where Russian mercenaries added to the instability in different countries and China actively tried to undermine Europe's remaining influence.

With Western influence dissipating and China rising, regional powers commenced to hedge their bets. That is the third change. The Eurasian interface between West and East became a theater of restless power politics. Russia, Iran, Saudi Arabia, Turkey, Israel, and others relentlessly tried to maximize their influence with a mixture of conflict and cooperation, and permanently shifting relationships. The hubris and unilateralism of the sole superpower was replaced by the hubris and unilateralism of many regional powers. As a result, the world became more fragmented and turbulent.

WATERSHED

THIRTY YEARS IS A RIPPLE. BUT THIS RIPPLE IN WORLD POLITICS WAS THE drama of our time. And it took a disturbing turn. The drama, as we have seen, is about one part of the world that missed an opportunity to reinvent its strength, another part of the world that seized the opportunity to gain strength with both hands, and a third part of the world that did not get much of a chance to grow stronger. It consisted of three acts.

The first act was the charade of liberal humanitarianism. The West exited the Cold War as the most powerful region. The unipolar order left other countries no alternative partner, investor, or security provider. The roots of discord, however, were already present. The West ignored them. Officials proclaimed moral superiority and vowed to change the morals of other countries through trade. "We stand tall and we see further than other countries," it was said. Trade was soon all that mattered. Engagement, with its diplomatic dialogues and its summit meetings, was superficially preserved. But the commitment to advance freedom disappeared. The priority of the West was not to revitalize democracy and the free market, or to empower citizens and entrepreneurs; its main priority was to empower consumption and corporate giants, whatever the consequences in terms of financial instability, pollution, and geopolitics. Leaders like Bill Clinton and Tony Blair were masterful communicators, highlighting human rights and social justice. Their main merit, though, was to give opportunism a friendly face. China and the Gulf States showed that all they needed to do was to

somewhat conceal their distrust of the West, to keep the charade of engagement going, and to exploit its greed to grow stronger.

The second act was a travesty of globalization. In 2001, the Western
world faced four important reality checks: the Dotcom bubble burst, the
terrorist attacks of 9/11, the EP-3 spy plane incident between the United
States and China, and the European Commission's warnings that the newly
established currency, the euro, was imperiled by large government deficits.
In the case of the Dotcom bubble burst, nothing was done to stop capital
from creating new bubbles and to turn the savings glut into an opportunity for building a sustainable, humane economy at home. In the case of
9/11, the Bush administration embarked on a crusade, started two massive
ill-conceived military campaigns, tightened its relations with authoritarian
leaders in the Gulf, and stoked more anger in the Muslim world. In the
case of the EP-3 incident, it wrote a letter to say sorry and continued its
stunted engagement. In the case of the European Union, despite many indications of design flaws in the Eurozone and skepticism about enlargement,
center parties continued their elastic run. What allowed them to ignore the
warning lights was a period of growth and surging trade. Globalization,
hence, came to be seen by some as a given, borders as a relict. This was
the period of the large E-Class container ships, the double-decked Airbus
380, the first iPhone. During this time, though, economic globalization no
longer coincided with the spreading of democracy. As a European official
said: "Whenever we see countries like China remove barriers, they instantly
erect more subtle ones instead."[1] Throughout the world, a new generation
of strong leaders took the helm, happy to send more oil and other goods to
the West, yet increasingly determined to restrict its influence. The Global
South surfed on a wave of high commodity prices, and Chinese capital
empowered authoritarian leaders. At the same time, more cracks appeared
inside the Western world.

The third act can be titled "retribution and retreat." Between 2010 and
2020, the West faced the consequences of 20 years of hubris and complacency.
Cosmopolitan forces were confronted with the advance of rightist nationalists. The neglect of the Global South, the false euphoria about the commodity
boom, and the devastating impact of environmental distress evolved into the
spreading of political instability, the propagation of terrorism, and migration

pressure on societies that felt no longer confident. As a result of 20 years of opportunism toward China, the latter saw the chance to start a push-back, economically and militarily. The rise of China and the weakening of Western influence emboldened other regional powers: Russia, Turkey, and Saudi Arabia. They eagerly filled the power vacuum left by the West. The refusal to retaliate against the Syrian government after having crossed the red line of using chemical weapons against civilians was a milestone in that regard, and so were the frail responses to Russia's annexation of Crimea, the withdrawal of American troops from Afghanistan after a humiliating treaty with the Taliban, and the lack of protest against the incarceration of millions of Chinese Muslims in so-called re-education camps. The return of rude geopolitics and the growing appeal of strong leadership made politicians try to keep up appearances instead of calling on citizens to support genuine reforms. Money was poured into the economy, but it hardly contributed to a new industrial revolution. Leaders spoke tough against China and Russia, but kept enriching them. They spoke about sustainability, but kept accepting pollution if it could be turned into a competitive advantage. Migrations were pushed back to unstable countries. Politicians behaved like anesthetists, keeping their society in a state of lethargy. Then came Brexit and President Donald Trump, who formally declared the end of the era of globalization:

Americans know that in a world where others seek conquest and domina-tion, our nation must be strong in wealth, in might, and in spirit. That is why the United States vigorously defends the traditions and customs that have made us who we are.

Like my beloved country, each nation represented in this hall has a cher-ished history, culture, and heritage that is worth defending and celebrating, and which gives us our singular potential and strength. The free world must embrace its national foundations. It must not attempt to erase them or replace them.

Looking around and all over this large, magnificent planet, the truth is plain to see: If you want freedom, take pride in your country. If you want democracy, hold on to your sovereignty. And if you want peace, love your nation. Wise leaders always put the good of their own people and their own country first.

The future does not belong to globalists. The future belongs to patriots. The future belongs to sovereign and independent nations who protect their citizens, respect their neighbors, and honor the differences that make each country special and unique.[2]

Thirty years is a ripple, but as the flow of political events has become restless, we wonder what comes around the next bend. Can we hear the roar of a cataract? Or is this just a rapid that will again give way to a wide open plain? Speeches like President Trump's hint at a dramatic moment, an era in which the gathering forces will cause more havoc. We cannot make a prediction, but we can draw conclusions about the nature of the recent changes in world politics.

Gathering forces

One of the forces building up concerns the disappointment in the Global South. Globalization is often conceived as a frontier: it started in the West and moved on to East Asia. Furthermore, it was meant to bring prosperity to the South. The reality is different. While East Asia still benefited from labor-intensive industries to employ people in the cities, industrial growth has become less labor-intensive. The traditional prospect of urbanization through industrialization has become uncertain. Coincidentally, the environmental circumstances in large parts of the Global South became more precarious. Consider the absence of the combination of temperate climate and thick layers of fertile soil. That precarious environment is hit very hard by climate change, changing patterns in rainfall, and so forth. Economic and environmental distress are on the rise. It is in this context that a sustained population boom has taken place. Between 1990 and 2020, the population in Africa, South Asia, and Latin America grew by around 55 million per year. It is set to grow just as fast in the next decade. Despite the exceptional resilience and entrepreneurialism of its people, the Global South remains a security black hole that brews violence, organized crime, extremism, and mass migration. A growing number of countries have drifted toward authoritarianism, xenophobia, and religious polarization. Instability in the region is inevitable, but it will not be confined to this arc of hardship. The question, for instance, is not whether the migration flows will become larger, but how large they will be. The question is not whether anger will grow against the West keeping its doors closed and financing dictators as its doorkeepers, but how that anger will manifest itself in the remainder of this century, around what leader, ideology, or rallying cry it will organize itself. The question is not even whether some of that anger will become violent, but *how* it will affect the rest of the world and react with the growing extremism that looms elsewhere.

Another force that gathered concerns the mistrust and the military build-up across the Pacific. The conflict between the United States and China reached a turning point. China has come to challenge the main premise of American security: to remain the strongest. The whole policy establishment in Washington has concluded that constructive engagement has not worked. Beijing for its part has never stopped distrusting the United States. Since the 1990s, it kept criticizing America's hegemonic pretenses and its so-called Cold War spirit. Reluctantly, the United States tried to push back. This is a typical power transition: the leader defending its position against a pretender. It is a geopolitical zero-sum game, because whatever advance China makes in the Pacific, it is perceived by America as a menace. Conversely, China considers American attempts to preserve its Pacific sphere of influence a threat. The conflict is also about economic strength. China, as we observed, has always sought to reduce its reliance on the West and to grow a strong national industry. While the United States has benefited for decades from China's cheap labor, it has reached the conclusion that growing a consumerist and indebted economy dependent on a geopolitical rival is not a good idea. Finally, the conflict provides both governments with a useful political adversary. In times of internal uncertainty, it helps divert attention from internal trouble. Rivalry has become inescapable. This is Sparta versus Athens – on a global scale. The conflict already simmers across a broad battlefield: from ideology, over technology, to space. The main uncertainty is how violent it will ultimately be. Even if one of the protagonists were to falter, faltering powers can be as aggressive as steadily rising powers. Not all imperial projects die as gently as the Soviet Union did.

The West, meanwhile, became beset by self-inflicted frustration that stems from self-inflicted decline. Most of the region is caught in a decadence trap. It has specialized in consumption, in lawyers, restaurants, and shops, insufficiently invested in productivity, and piled up debt. The West does include strong trading states, like the Netherlands, but their exports largely go to other Western deficit countries. Economic demagogy has characterized 30 years of center politics. The same was true in security matters. Center politicians hardly invested in security. All around Europe, they paid unstable countries to keep refugees, terrorists, and criminals at a distance, hence creating another false sense of security. While there were wakeup calls, the center politician tranquilized the situation by means of quantitative easing, importing cheap goods, and outsourcing security to dictators. The moderate political leader prided himself on his mild manner and disparaged the extremist, but this courteousness without courage was often nothing more than expediency.

Citizens lost confidence, and that allowed moderate demagogues to be challenged by extremist demagogues. The extremist demagogue, despite his flair and courage, often continued to confirm citizens in their passiveness. They did not call citizens to take their responsibility, but put the responsibility on others. They presented borders as a shield, while everything inside the borders, the civics, the economy, weakened. The extremist demagogue in that regard is as much a coward as the moderate demagogue: both lack the courage to call for the sacrifice needed to repair the economy, to protect values, and to preserve security. The result: as new empires are in the making, the West gets consumed by anger and political tribalism. It becomes an empty fortress. Or, as the Roman statesman Scipio was quoted as saying: "No society is fortunate when its walls are standing while its morals are in ruins."[3]

The presidential election of 2020, which replaced Donald Trump with the cautious Democrat Joe Biden, did not change that situation. It inflamed anger and sparked violent protests. If Biden promised to heal the nation and genuinely understood the anger as a result of his long political career and friendships across the partisan divide, this was much less the case with his entourage and other key personalities in the Democratic Party. The young urban elite, which gathered for Democrat rallies in their parents' fancy Volvo SUVs, seemed totally estranged from white angry America, and vice versa, of course. The world heaved a sigh of relief when Donald

Trump failed to be re-elected to the White House. Recent history was looked back at, even in Europe, as a bad dream. It was not. The experience was real: the power shift, the erosion of Western might, the fear this incited, the assertiveness of other powers. In the long run, the relapse into self-congratulation of the pragmatic politicians and its misplaced sense of moral superiority is perhaps as big a threat to political stability as the recklessness of the Trump administration.

The weakening of the West and the rise of China gave way to wrecking centrifugal forces throughout Eurasia. The power vacuum left by the dwindling influence of the West and the commercial opportunities presented by China allowed a multitude of regional powers to play off both sides, to maximize their freedom of action, and to interfere in other countries. Hard hedging, we called it. In 2003, the United States was scorned for its unilateral intervention in Iraq. In the decades that followed, unilateral interventionism became the rule. The new Eurasian anarchy consists of a layer of major power politics. The United States and China are set for a long contest along Eurasia's littorals and the Eurasian Sea. Countries like China, Russia, and Iran seek to reduce America's capacity to project power onto the land mass and to deny access to its surrounding seas. The United States tries to find new ways to overcome that resistance. A second layer concerns the wrangling between regional powers. If China and Washington see Eurasia as a giant chessboard, South Korea and Japan compete in Northeast Asia. Southeast Asian countries, despite ASEAN, failed to overcome their divisions and to unite against the major powers. In South Asia, the situation remains tense between India and Pakistan. Rivalry between Iran, Saudi Arabia, Israel, and Turkey has become fiercer in the Middle East, the Levant and Iraq being important battlegrounds. Russia has built a maximum of presence with a minimum of resources from Murmansk to the Sahara. The European Union, notwithstanding the promise to advance a common geopolitical vision and its immense market, remains a playground much more than a player. Besides the anarchy between states, there is growing anarchy inside states: throughout Eurasia, both democracies and authoritarian governments struggle to preserve cohesion and legitimacy. With the largest concentration of regional powers, Eurasia remains the world's primary arena of power politics.

The world has also noticed the power of proximity. If Hollywood has spread, most of the screen time throughout the world is still taken up by local programming. Travel has become more affordable. But even in borderless Europe, hardly 11 percent of the people go on holiday abroad.[4] The global elite reads the *Financial Times*, *The New York Times*, and the *Wall Street Journal*, but these media reach less than 1 percent of the global newspaper readership. We have social media, but less than 10 percent of Facebook friendships are international.[5] Cosmopolitanism has always been a minority experience. In addition, the abstract global themes are less pressing than local concerns. Even major common threats, like terrorism and climate change, are interpreted differently depending on the country that one lives in. Citizens accept openness as long as they feel secure. The default alternative to insecurity is entrenchment. In the last decade, that entrenchment has taken the form of nationalism. In many countries, one already sees that nationalism equals regionalism: giving up the state project for smaller political projects. Think of Spain, Belgium, the United Kingdom. In the United States, the conservative nationalism of Donald Trump was overruled by even more extreme factionalism. Or consider the many city mayors, who pretend to be cosmopolitan leaders, yet even fail to engage their immediate neighborhood. State-based nationalism seems to be a prelude to further fragmenting, to tribalism. The main tension might therefore not be between states, but between tribalism and new projects of empire building: of major powers, existing or new ones, exploiting tribal tendencies, their petty quarrels, their disdain for discipline, their selfishness without vision.

The flipside of the power of proximity was the fraying of global governance. Might is right. Global governance in the past decades was largely a reflection of the power of the West. "The Charter of the United Nations is our kind of Charter," summarized an American scholar-diplomat. "It embodies the concept of an open world society of independent states which stands at the opposite extreme from the Communist pattern of standardization and coercion."[6] Or, as another scholar put it: Politics is not merely a struggle for power, but also a contest for legitimacy.[7] The balance between unilateralism and multilateralism has always been an awkward one. Consider the tendency toward trade protectionism, the reluctance of the senate to ratify treaties, and the unilateralist proclivity of the neocon-servatives of the administration of George W. Bush. A vicious cycle has come to exist in which the reluctance to invest in global governance was exploited by other rising powers to advance their interests, which in turn confirmed the unilateralists in their skepticism. Attacking multilateralism became a trademark of Donald Trump. The other main power, China, pursued a subtler strategy of paying lip service to international institutions, yet bypassing them with its own diplomatic initiatives or economic pro-jects. Consider the Belt and Road Initiative, the emerging of its state banks as international lenders. Other powers followed that example on a smaller scale. By 2020, many of the traditional Western-dominated institutions, like the International Monetary Fund and the World Bank, and the institutional embodiment of economic globalization, the World Trade Organization, had become marginalized. More dangerous still was the failure to reinforce the arms control framework of the Cold War. A new military showdown was in the making, but there were not even basic rules of the game. With President Joe Biden, dedication to multilateralism returned, but America's power and legitimacy had slipped, so that it would remain difficult to truly rebuild multilateral leadership.

Another important force that we saw at work concerns the growing environmental distress of nature. Environmental distress is an enduring theme in world politics, from *stenochoria*, or the lack of land in ancient times, to Thomas Malthus. "The power of population," he wrote, "is indefinitely greater than the power in the earth to produce subsistence for man." In the early 1990s, new environmental activism saw the light and gathered strength. Yet, most forms of pollution increased. Rich countries were reluctant to make their economies more sustainable. They out-sourced polluting activities to poor countries. Poor countries themselves started to damage nature more as a result of economic and demographic growth. Since 1990, for instance, CO_2 emissions have grown by 40 percent, the volume of plastic waste trebled. Technology brought limited relief. Environmental disasters became more common: hurricanes, heatwaves, fires, flooding, desertification, fish migrations, and pandemics. There are many political consequences: water conflicts, a new scramble for farmland, and social instability.

We could also add to this the resistance of human nature against a society in which commodification and anonymization prevail. As Francis Fukuyama warned, humans need security, but also daring, imagination, a sense of belonging, a sense of purpose. Some respond positively to the challenge, like artists and creative entrepreneurs. Others indulge in extreme consumption, or seek to live a virtual life of gaming. It leads to wealth diseases, depression, and so forth. The craving for some sense of belonging, the existential crisis, and need for recognition contribute to political extremism, radicalism. "We are like zombies," a young adult from Iraq summarized it. "The living dead." Similar cries, fears of becoming a zombie generation, are heard in East Asia. How remote this is from the prospect of humans becoming demigods. If people have no cause to fight for, they will invent new ones, some bright, some dark.

A final "force" concerns the limits of learning. The historian Barbara Tuchman spoke of the march of folly. That march moves on. Consider Western diplomatic injudiciousness despite warnings of its consequences. China's continued indebting of poor countries, despite seeing the growing repayment problems, the reluctance to respond to climate change. And even if leaders at some point vowed to change track, changes were modest. In 2019, the Speaker of the American House of Representatives acknowledged the opportunism in three decades of China policy: "It was always about the money."[8] Other politicians made similar remarks. Yet, the American government kept pursuing a good business "deal" with China. The same happened in Europe with regard to China, but also with regard to other states. "The outrage isn't if there is interference," concluded a British intelligence committee about Russia's meddling with domestic politics. "The outrage is no one wanted to know if there was interference."[9] Still, the Prime Minister flatly denied the problem. Folly dominated other domains. Despite scientists painting somber scenarios, governments remain reluctant to take action on climate change. Despite economists warning of unbalanced growth, governments kept pumping money into their economies without guidance to make them more productive or sustainable. Or take the weakening of citizenship and democracy. Politicians promised more civic education, but it remained marginal. Universities claimed the moral high ground in making students more critical, but kept turning classrooms

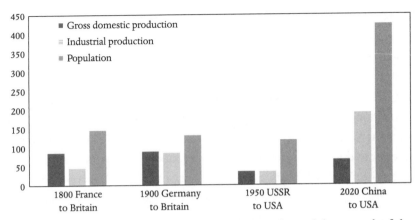

Figure 13.1   The strength of the rising powers as a share of the strength of the
incumbent power (%)

Source: Angus Maddisson, 2008. *Historical Statistics of the World Economy.*
Groningen: Groningen University.

China's quest to become a rich country could inflame nationalism and make it more belligerent. Rising powers become dangerous when they suddenly falter. Consider it the cornered cat syndrome.

External policies of containment are also unlikely to become effective when the Western world continues to be guided by short-term business interests. Advisors of the newly elected president Joe Biden vowed to continue to compete with China, yet reassured the business community that their supply chains would not be harmed. Strategic competition would be made business-friendly. The same was true in Europe. The investment deal, signed in 2020, showed how much China policy remained a continuation of the interests of large corporate interest groups that had become dependent on China, such as the German car industry. Asked what he thought about the Chinese government imprisoning hundreds of thousands of Uyghurs in re-education camps, the head of Volkswagen cynically said: "I don't know what you are referring to. I am not aware of it."[10] Chancellor Angela Merkel too remarked that mass imprisonment and forced labor among the Uyghurs were not serious enough to justify forsaking the investment treaty.

Fragmentation also hampers the West to stand up to the challenges. This fragmenting relates to its diplomatic cohesion. Whether one considers

China's propaganda offensive during the corona crisis or its crackdown in Hong Kong, both failed to bring the Western countries together. While the United States slapped sanctions on Beijing, the European Union uttered a faint condemnation. "We will continue discussing," its chief diplomat said.[11] The divide between European countries and the United States, and even among European countries, remained immense. The fragmenting also concerns Western society. During the Cold War, the Western model was superior to the Soviet system in terms of economy, innovation, and governance. The West still holds advantages, but is debilitated. As one does not erect strong defenses around a weakened society, a pressing question is whether the West can reinvent itself.

The best way to restore the balance of power is not to try to stop China, but for the West to push its prosperity to a higher level and to help partners do the same. This restrained balancing can be considered a growing together. Restrained balancing implies turning the China challenge into an incentive to push the Western development model, its economy, and its other attributes of power to a higher level. Such balancing depends on the capacity to set clear ambitions, and to cultivate the ethics to achieve them. It entails that, while the ultimate outward manifestation of power is hard military coercion, it is soft at the core. Power depends on qualities like integrity, inquisitiveness, civic responsibility, and the cherishing of deployment of individual talents for collective improvement. This is civilization: the combination of social refinement with power. The ultimate inward manifestation of power is thus not for a politician to make citizens vote, but to make them preserve or change their behavior according to these values. This is what many ancient political thinkers had in mind when they highlighted virtue. True political power is to make a society virtuous.

In that regard, the capacity of declining societies for self-deception has proved endless. There is a tacit recognition in the West that virtue depends on its capacity to make growth more humane, sustainable, and responsible toward the next generations. In 2020, the president of the European Commission, for example, announced hundreds of billions of euros in investments to prepare for the next generation. She reiterated the need for a green deal. Yet, only a small part of the funds was tied to sustainability, and the European Commission remains reluctant to apply its internal social and environmental standards to external trade. It is a continuation of the policy that started decades ago, of flooding Western markets with money, yet with only a few measures to make it benefit positive entrepreneurship, to advance innovation, and to ward off social and environmental dumping. Think of the French President Emmanuel Macron. During his campaigns, he brilliantly made a case for the need for cohesion and identity, for positive patriotism. Yet, he paid one of his first company visits to a mammoth warehouse owned by Amazon. The German Chancellor Angela Merkel kept profiling herself as a role model of moderation and sober-minded statecraft, dedicated to the European project. Yet, her government kept blocking various initiatives to tie values to trade and shaped its policies with the overseas interests of large German companies in mind more often than with the interim strengthening of Europe. "What goes for Volkswagen goes for Germany," a senior official summarized cynically. "What goes for Germany goes for Europe."[12] It is quite likely that the passion of such leaders for building a stronger European society was sincere, but that they did not have the courage or the imagination to act upon it, to accept the challenge of escape from the decadence trap.

Rightist demagogues also kept polarizing and weakening Western societies. The American President Donald Trump was the best example. When racial riots broke out, when four police officers suffocated an African-American citizen, in the spring of 2020, he threw oil on the flames by threatening to send in the National Guard. He kept rolling back the environmental regulation of previous administrations, and to trim federal spending on education. He intimidated European countries, yet still remained an example for European nationalists. While European rightists embraced Trump's anti-China policy, they kept celebrating the authoritarianism of the Russian strongman Vladimir Putin, and some even to accept financial support from the Kremlin. In countries where they came to power, like Hungary and Poland, nationalism continued to be a pretext for hollowing out the constitution. The West appears to be set for slow, grinding auto-destruction.

There is no evidence that possible partners will become stronger either. Balancing China could perfectly match with an effort to empower the Global South, to present a new cooperation model to developing countries that focuses more on local industry and sustainable farming, instead of just buying their raw materials. It could imply an effort to support struggling democracies, such as India. India hoped to profit from the trade war between China and the United States and to attract more foreign investment. In 2019, however, China still received over twice as much foreign investment from Japan and the United States. The corona crisis and the uncertainty in the global markets make it unlikely that India will soon find a strategic window of opportunity similar to the one China benefited from between the 1990s and today. The damage done by religious extremism will be felt many years into the future. Other Asian countries, meanwhile, prioritize relations with a close neighbor above a distant friend. Many of them try to preserve relations with both China and the United States.

There is little chance of restrained balancing, that the world will respond to China's rise by setting its own bar higher and holding the line. Hard balancing by the United States has become the likeliest scenario. Even while China's economic growth is set to slow as a result of the corona crisis, the size of its economy will still inch closer to that of the United States. The dilemma remains. In the run-up to the presidential elections in 2020, Donald Trump seized on the tensions with China to shore up his credentials as a strong leader. At the same time, the school of war imposes hard new lessons on the pretender. Trump's ban on transferring technology strengthened the desire to become technologically independent. American sympathy with the uprisings in Hong Kong magnified the fixation with sovereignty. American patrols and military exercises added impetus to the effort to undermine Washington's military preponderance in the Pacific. At the same time, China also learned that this strife can be won by non-military means. The fact that Europe remained so obsessed with Chinese investment and that Asia remained so divided seemed to support the old imperial stratagem: to pit barbarians against barbarians.

The shift in the balance of power will cause more turbulence. Nothing, from proxy wars to direct major wars, can be excluded. At the same time, the combination of the weakening of the West and the weakness of the Global South morphs into an ever-growing power vacuum. In 2020, Russia opened a new airbase in Libya and started expanding its facilities in Syria. France and other European countries struggled to fight the Islamic extremists in the Sahel, as the United States reduced its military presence. Many

African and South Asian countries were at pains to repay their loans to China. Sri Lanka, already heavily indebted to Beijing, asked for new loans, and Pakistan needed to postpone the repayment of Chinese loans. The corona pandemic made the situation more precarious.

Charles V

Let us reconnect these final conclusions with some of the guiding themes that were laid out in the introduction, starting with the power shift. Since ancient times, philosophers have insisted that dominance portends exuberance, complacency, and decline. As this wheel of fortune rolls through history, powers rise and fall. As the political scientist Hans Morgenthau put it: "Underneath the chaos of international politics, there are perennial forces that shape social life."[13] The power shift that came to the fore in this book is thus no new phenomenon. More surprising is the spectrum of instruments and arguments with which the decaying society has kept itself in a state of denial. Consider the economic policies of printing money, encouraging strategic adversaries to sustain cheap exports, and of increasing external debt. What makes these instruments particularly devastating is that they are often invisible for most citizens, and that they create a false sense of prosperity.

Sure, we have seen empires sink into debt and deficits before. Think of the late Roman Republic debt crisis or the massive debt piled up by the Habsburg Emperor Charles V. But seldom did it happen with such a sophistication of financial trickery. Or what to think of the self-congratulating Western diplomacy that claimed the number of summit meetings and dialogues was a benchmark of success and influence, even when they were undeniably just allowing adversaries to buy time? Or the many forms of military grandstanding, that masked failure and retreat on the ground? What ingenuity the West has displayed to cover up its problems. So, while the rising powers cause instability, the flipside is that the stagnation of the incumbent powers contributes as much to this conundrum. William Pitt the Younger summarized it somewhat dramatically: Weakness and improvidence are to be the forerunners of war.[14]

Hubris is another phenomenon that alters the fate of mighty societies. Hubris knew many forms in post-Cold War history. One example concerned the claim that trade was to change the norms and principles of trade partners. Another example concerned the recklessness with which the West, especially the United States, engaged in military operations, operations that were ill-conceived and had no exit plan. The attacks on Al-Qaeda and the Taliban in Afghanistan following 9/11, the global war on terror, was perfectly understandable, but its mission creep and its expansion to Iraq was one of the costliest military blunders in the last centuries. In 2020, it still carried on in the form of fig leaf operations and remote-control war. It gave competitors the opportunity to exploit the consequent anger and exhaustion.

Another important lesson, related to the first two, is that three decades of liberalism had as one of its main achievements that it made authoritarianism strong. Liberalism, free trade, and interventionism are usually characteristic of dominance, much more than of dedication to the principles of enlightenment. Openness becomes essential for companies of the leading societies to enlarge their markets, to celebrate their competitiveness on a global scale. But without an effort to keep pushing that competitiveness to a higher level at home, domestic markets soon become saturated, so that companies search for growth elsewhere, disconnect from the home market, and become more fixated on well-organized countries that offer cheap labor and the prospect of new consumer markets. In the last 30 years, that has been China. So, liberalism in international politics has little to do with enlightenment, with the pursuit of a society of emancipated citizens, and more to do with profit and power. Astute authoritarian states have been quick to exploit that inconsistency.

We also noticed that liberal harmony never had a lot of legitimacy throughout the world, not even inside Western societies. Throughout the high age of globalization, there were signals, from the left and the right, from progressive to conservative, that while the scale of markets, connectivity, and politics became larger and larger, many people felt lost and doubtful. Views from non-Western societies were not negative about democracy and human rights per se, but about the double standards that the West used, and about the fact that openness was advanced as a justification for interference, for introducing flows of hot investment capital without attempts to preserve long-term financial stability, for advancing conditions without serious engagement, for military interventions and regime change without attempts to build stable societies. Authoritarian adversaries like China and Russia plotted a pushback; millions of protesters, entrepreneurs, and ordinary families that once embraced the spirit of enlightenment angrily turned their back on the West, as it was seen to be supporting their oppressors. Those resisting liberalism were empowered; those welcoming it were estranged.

The school of strife left a much larger impression on world politics than the school of peace. If the West was distrusted from the start, Western hubris and interventionism taught its competitors how to resist it. From operation Desert Storm, countries like Russia and China studied how the West fought its high-tech wars, and how it could be efficiently repelled. They saw how technology and the dominance over channels of communication, from the internet to satellites, were vital not only to compete economically, but also to win militarily. First, they started to apply their newly gained insights predominantly through asymmetric warfare, including cheap missiles; later they organized it into an intimidating wall of missiles, warships, fighter jets, electronic warfare, and so forth. Also learning were the various terrorist groups. They knew that the West had no commitment to stay in the dusty battlefields of the Middle East and Iraq; they knew also that it had weak spots at home. And so, they kept striking, little pinpricks often, yet with devastating effects.

So, the stream of world events continues to flow: at times calmly, at times turbulently. The forces remain the same, but the circumstances change, perpetually. Perhaps the most important cause of today's uncertainty is that these forces were hardly recognized, that foreign policy was misused, trivialized even in some cases. This does not mean that we should become fatalistic, that conflicts cannot be avoided, and that we cannot strive toward human improvement. The key, however, is to remain humble. That goes for states, but also for leaders in diplomacy, in the public debate, and in the corporate world. Because, like with the hubris of states, the aura of influence, the prestige of summit meetings, the badge, the title, the exclusiveness of classified sources, also bring a risk of losing touch, of losing touch with the deep forces of world politics – and with the people we serve. The knowledge of our recent diplomatic history in that regard can hopefully be a moderating force.

ACKNOWLEDGEMENTS

This book benefited from the kind contribution of the Belgian tax payer and the support of different funds along the way. Many impressions and insights were collected while I worked for official institutions. Numerous people and occasions have inspired me. While I cannot name them all, I am immensely grateful for the experiences and encounters.

This book was written primarily for my students. They commented on earlier drafts of the manuscripts. I don't think we can overestimate the importance of investing in these future leaders and challenging them to explore the world in all its aspects. The book benefited from the feedback of He Baogang, Bruno De Cordier, Amitai Etzioni, Zsuzsa Anna Ferenczy, Sumit Ganguly, Sergey Karaganov, K.C. Lin, Astrid Pepermans, Paul Scheffer, Mark Thys, Yan Xuetong, and four anonymous reviewers. Finally, I would like to thank the Polity team, Louise Knight, Ian Tuttle, Inès Boxman and Evie Deavall.

NOTES

The pendulum

1 Jenny Erpenbeck, Thomas Brussig, Kathrin Schmidt, David Wagner, and Sabine Rennefanz, 2019. Watching the fall of the Berlin Wall. *The Guardian*, November 9.

2 Thomas Friedman, 2005. *The World Is Flat*. New York: Farrar, Straus and Giroux; Martin Wolf, 2005. *Why Globalization Works*. New Haven, CT: Yale University Press; Jagdish Bhagwati, 2004. *In Defense of Globalization*. New York: Oxford University Press.

3 Richard Baldwin, 2016. *The Great Convergence*. Cambridge, MA: Harvard University Press.

4 Barry Buzan, Ole Waever, and Jaap de Wilde, 1998. *Security: A New Framework for Analysis*. London: Lynne Rienner; Scott Barrett, 2007. *Why Cooperate? The Incentive to Supply Global Public Goods*. New York: Oxford University Press.

5 *Time*'s cover of October 10, 1995 ran the following title: "Black Renaissance"; *The Economist* of December 3, 2010 was titled "Africa Rising".

6 "Africa Rising," *The Economist*, December 3, 2011.

7 Conversation with former South Korean minister, Singapore, March 24, 2018.

8 Lord Bolingbroke. Quoted in: Per Maurseth, 1964. Balance-of-power thinking from the Renaissance to the French Revolution. *Journal of Peace Research*, 1(2), 120–36.

9 Sustainable Development Solutions Network, 2019. *World Happiness Report*. Available at: https://worldhappiness.report/ed/2019/changing-world-happiness/

10 Abhijit Banerjee, and Esther Duflo, 2011. *Poor Economics: A Radical Rethinking of the Way to Fight Global Poverty*. New York: Public Affairs.

11 Kenneth Waltz, 1959. *Man, the State, and War*. New York: Columbia University Press.

12 Linda Weiss, 1998. *The Myth of the Powerless State*. Ithaca, NY: Cornell University Press; John Dunning (ed.), 1999. *Governments, Globalization, and International Business*. Oxford: Oxford University Press; David Smith, Dorothy Solinger, and Steven Topic, 1999. *States and Sovereignty in the Global Economy*. New York: Routledge.

13 John G. Ruggie, 1992. Multilateralism: The anatomy of an institution. *International Organization*, 46(3), 561–98; John Mearsheimer, 1994. The false promise of international institutions. *International Security*, 19(3), 5–49.

14 Neither war nor peace. *The Economist*, January 25, 2018; Rory Cormac, and Richard Aldrich, 2018. Grey is the new black. *International Affairs*, 94(3), 477–94.

15 Conversation with military officers, Brussels, January 11, 2018.

16 Anatoliy Gruzd, and Ksenia Tsyganova, 2015. Information wars and online activism during the 2013/2014 crisis in Ukraine. *Policy and Internet*, April 27, 2015.

17 Thomas Piketty, 2014. *Capital in the Twentieth Century*. Cambridge, MA: Belknap.

18 Quoted in: Michel Crozier, Samuel Huntington, and Joji Watanuki, 1975. *The Crisis of Democracy*. New York: New York University Press. This report also discusses the dismal state of Western democracy.

19 Francis Fukuyama, 2014. *Political Order and Political Decay: From the Industrial Revolution to the Globalization of Democracy*. New York: Farrar, Straus and Giroux; Francis Fukuyama, 2018. *Identity: The Demand for Dignity and the Politics of Resentment*. New York: Farrar, Straus and Giroux; Patrick Deneen, 2019. *Why Liberalism Failed*. New Haven, CT: Yale University Press; Steven Levitsky, and Daniel Ziblatt, 2018. *How Democracies Die*. London: Crown.

20 Daron Acemoglu, and James Robinson, 2013. *Why Nations Fail: The Origins of Power, Prosperity, and Poverty*. New York: Crown Business.

Chapter 1: Progress

1 Steven Pinker, 2018. *Enlightenment Now*. London: Penguin.

2 Hans Rosling, 2018. *Factfulness*. New York: Flatiron.

3 Yuval Noah Harari, 2016. *Homo Deus*. New York: Penguin.

4 C-Span, 1990. Earth Day 1990 Rally, April 22. Available at: https://www.c-span.org/video/?14203-1/earth-day-1990-rally

5 Cesare Marchetti, 1989. How to solve the CO_2 problem without tears. *International Journal of Hydrogen Energy*, 14(8), 493–506.

Chapter 2: A doubtful victory

1 William Safire, 1991. The new, new world order. *The New York Times*, January 17.

2 John Campbell, 2011. *The Iron Lady*. London: Penguin, p. 48.

3 Concerns triadic patents.

4 The North Atlantic Treaty, Washington, April 4, 1949.

5 See the declaration of US–EC relations, December 1, 1990.

6 Kenneth Newton, and Pippa Norris, 1999. Confidence in public institutions: Faith, culture or performance? Paper for presentation at the Annual Meeting of the American Political Science Association, Atlanta, September 1–5.

7 Ze'ev Chafets, 1990. The tragedy of Detroit. *The New York Times*, July 29.

8 Gordon Brown, 1989. Thatcherism. *London Review of Books*, 11(3), 3–4.

9 OECD: Gross fixed capital formation in constant prices between 1981 and 1990.

10 Ronald Shelp, 1987. Giving the services economy a bum rap. *The New York Times*, May 17.

11 Barry Bluestone, 1984. *The Deindustrialization of America*. New York: Basic Books.

12 Rick Rogers (ed.), 1989. *Education and Social Class*. Lewes: Falmer; Stephen Ball, 1990. Markets, inequality, and urban schooling. *The Urban Review*, 22(2), 85–99.

13 For instance: Diane Ravitch, 1990. Education in the 1980's: A concern for "quality." *Education Week*, January.

14 Jonathan Kozol, 1991. *Savage Inequalities*. New York: HarperPerennial.

15 Brian Dumaine, 1993. Illegal child labor comes back. *Fortune Magazine*, April 5.

16 Kozol, *Savage Inequalities*, p. 25.

17 Louise Menand, 1988. The triumph of Trumpery. *The New Republic*, February 1.

18 Trade deficits may be good for U.S., *Los Angeles Times*, January 11, 1988.

19 Marshall Robinson, 1989. America's not-so-troubling debts and deficits. *Harvard Business Review*, July.

20 Jeffrey Sachs, 1988. Global adjustments to a global trade deficit. *NBER Papers on Economic Activity*, 2, 639–74.

21 Peter Peterson, 1987. The morning after. *The Atlantic*, October, p. 44.

22 James Madison, Alexander Hamilton, and John Jay, 1987. *The Federalist Papers* (Isaac Kramick, ed.). London: Penguin, p. 483.

23 Theodore Roosevelt, 2008. *Letters and Speeches*. New York: Library of America, p. 786.

24 Saint Augustine, 2003. *Concerning the City of God Against the Pagans* (Henry Bettenson, trans.). London: Penguin, p. 96.

25 Richard Rosecrance, 1990. *America's Economic Resurgence*. New York: Harper and Row.

26 Paul Kennedy, 1989. Can the US remain number one? *New York Review of Books*, March.

27 John Kenneth Galbraith, 1958. *The Affluent Society*. Boston, MA: Mariner Books, p. 259.

28 National Assessment of Educational Progress (NAEP) Report Card in Civics.

29 Allan Bloom, 1987. *The Closing of the American Mind*. New York: Simon & Schuster.

30 Francis Fukuyama, 1989. The end of history. *The National Interest*, Summer, pp. 3–4.

31 José Ortega y Gasset, 1958. *Man and Crisis* (Mildred Adams, trans.). New York: W.W. Norton, p. 145.

32 Fukuyama, The end of history, p. 17.

33 MEXIQUE: la fin du voyage du pape Jean-Paul II définit une troisième voie entre marxisme et capitalisme, *Le Monde*, May 15, 1990.

34 Pierre De Gasquet, 1993. Exception culturelle: François Mitterrand réplique fermement à Bill Clinton. *Les Echos*, October 18.

35 Irving Kristol, 1995. *Neoconservatism: The Autobiography of an Idea*. New York: The Free Press, p. 134.

36 Seymour Martin Lipset, 1993. Waves of democracy often get reversed. Address before the 88th annual meeting of the American Sociological Association, Miami, November 8.

37 Wallace Peterson, 1995. *Silent Depression: Twenty-Five Years of Wage Squeeze and Middle-Class Decline*. New York: W.W. Norton. Also: Herbert Gans, 1995. *The War Against the Poor*. New York: Basic Books.

38 George F. Will, 1990. "Who will stoke the fires?" *Newsweek*, April 9, p. 78.

39 Peter Davis, 1995. *If You Came This Way*. New York: John Wiley & Sons.

40 William Henry, 1990. Beyond the melting pot. *Time*, April 9; National Research Council, 1989. *A Common Destiny: Blacks and American Society*. Washington, DC: National Research Council.

41 Daniel Pipes, 1990. The Muslims are coming! *National Review*, November 19.

42 Robert Pear, 1986. New restrictions on immigration gain public support. *The New York Times*, July 1; Nona Mayer, and Pascal Pirrineau, 1992. Why do they vote for Le Pen? *European Journal of Political Research*, 22(1), 123–41.

43 Bernard Lewis, 1990. The roots of Muslim rage. *The Atlantic*, September.

44 For instance: David Pearce, 1988. Economics, equity and sustainable development. *Futures*, 20(6), 598–605; Harry Broadman, 1986. The social cost of imported oil. *Energy Policy*, 14(4), 242–52.

45 Alexander King, and Bertrand Schneider, 1991. *The First Global Revolution*. New York: Simon and Schuster.

46 Times Mirror Center for the People & The Press, 1993. *America's Place in the World*. Washington, DC: Times Mirror Center for the People & the Press.

47 Joseph Nye, 1990. *Bound To Lead*. New York: Basic Books.

48 Charles Krauthammer, 1990. The unipolar moment. *Foreign Affairs*, 70(1), 26.

49 Richard Rosecrance, 1990. *America's Economic Resurgence*. New York: Harper and Row.

50 OECD, 1992. *Long-term Prospects for the World Economy*. Paris: OECD, p. 4.

51 Michael Porter, 1990. The competitive advantage of nations. *Harvard Business Review*, March–April; Dale Jorgenson, and Koji Nomura, 2005. The industry origins of Japanese economic growth. *Journal of the Japanese and International Economies*, 19(4), 482–542.

52 Andrew Moravcsik, 1991. Negotiating the Single European Act: National interests and conventional statecraft in the European Community. *International Organization*, 45(1), 19–40.

53 Alexander Wendt, 1992. Anarchy is what states make of it: The social construction of power politics. *International Organization*, 46(1), 391–425.

54 Richard Spielman, 1990. The emerging unipolar world. *The New York Times*, August 21.

55 Senate Select Committee of Intelligence, 1991. *Hearings on the Nomination of Robert Gates as Director of CIA*, September 20.

56 Patrick Tyler, 1992. US strategy plan calls for insuring no rivals develop. *The New York Times*, March 8.

57 Samuel Huntington, 1988. The US – Decline or renewal? *Foreign Affairs*, 67(4), 95.

58 Immanuel Wallerstein, 1987. The United States and the world crisis. In Terry Boswell, and Albert Bergesen (eds.), *America's Changing Role*. New York: Praeger, p. 17.

59 Lester Thurow, 1985. *The Zero-Sum Solution*. New York: Simon & Schuster, p. 67; Is America a global power in decline? *Boston Globe*, March 20, 1988, p. A22.

Chapter 3: The new order seen from elsewhere

1   Richard Felix Staar, 1991. *Foreign Policies of the Soviet Union*. Stanford, CA: Stanford University Press, p. 179.

2   Mark Kramer, 2011. The decline in Soviet arms transfers to the Third World. In Artemy Kalinovsky and Sergey Radchenko (eds.), *The End of the Cold War and the Third World*. New York: Routledge, p. 47

3   Sayyid Ruhallah Musawi Khomeini, 1993. *The Great Leader of the Islamic Revolution and Founder of the Islamic Republic of Iran To President Mikhail Gorbachev, Leader of the Soviet Union*. Tehran: Institute for Compilation and Publication of Imam Khomeini's Works, p. 3.

4   Anatoly Chernyaev, 1989. *The Diary of Anatoly S. Chernyaev* (Anna Melyakova, trans.). Washington, DC: National Security Archive, p. 29.

5   Ibid., p. 45.

6   Ibid., p. 50.

7   Mikhail Gorbachev, 1992. Address at the Sorbonne, Paris, April 22.

8   Sam McFarland, Vladimir Ageyev, and Marina Abalakina-Paap, 1992. Authoritarianism in the former Soviet Union. *Journal of Personality and Social Psychology*, 63(6), 1004–10.

9   Bill Keller, 1991. Collapse of an empire; Soviet politicians agree the Union is dying but there is no accord on what's ahead. *The New York Times*, August 27.

10 Peter Rutland, 1999. Mission impossible? *Review of International Studies*, 25(2), 201.

11 Fiona Hill, and Clifford Gaddy, 2015. *Mr. Putin: Operative in the Kremlin*. Washington, DC: Brookings Institution Press, p. 115.

12 Václav Havel, 1990. *Disturbing the Peace* (Paul Wilson, trans.). New York: Knopf.

13 Timothy Garton Ash, 1990. *The Magic Lantern*. London: Penguin, p. 301.

14 Good revolutionaries tend to make bad rulers. *The Economist*, September 22, 1990.

15 Serge Schmemann, 1990. Evolution in Europe. *The New York Times*, September 30.

16 Gavriil Popov, 1990. Dangers of democracy. *New York Review of Books*, August.

17 China: Background to Military Situation, https://en.wikisource.org/wiki/UK _cable_on_Tiananmen_Square_Massacre

18 Secretary of Defense, 1994. Memorandum on the US–China Military Relationship, August, p. 3.

19 Yan Xuetong and Li Zhongcheng, 1995. Zhanwang xia shiji chu guoji zhengzhi [Prospects for international politics at the beginning of next century]. *Xiandai guoji guanxi*, June, p. 7.

20 Song Ping, 1991. Zai quanguo zuzhi buzhang huiyi shang de jianghual. In Zhonggong Zhongyang (ed.), Wenxian yanjiushi [Speech at the national meeting of organization department heads] *Important Documents Since the Thirteenth Party Congress of the Chinese Communist Party. Volume 2*. Beijing: Zhongyang Wenxian Publishing, pp. 566–77.

21 Robert Ash, 1991. Quarterly chronicle and documentation. *The China Quarterly*, 127(2), 668.

22 Willy Lo-Lap Lam, 1999. *The Era of Jiang Zemin*. New York: Prentice-Hall, p. 83.

23 Xin Peihe, 1991. Foundation stone for new world order: Brief analysis on Baker's Europe–Atlantic integration, *Shijie zhishi* [*World Knowledge*], August 16, in FBIS-China, September 5, p. 7.

24 https://dengxiaopingworks.wordpress.com/2013/03/18/the-international-situation-and-economic-problems/

25 Wang Jisi, 1994. Pragmatic nationalism: China seeks a new role in world affairs. *Oxford International Review*, Winter, 29.

26 Jiang, Zemin, 1992. Political report to the 14th Party Congress, Beijing, October 20, pp. 15–16.

27 Peter Nolan, 2001. *China and the Global Economy*. Basingstoke: Palgrave, p. 17.

28 Dennis Kux, 1991. *Estranged Democracies*. Washington, DC: NDU Press, p. 39.

29 Nani Ardeshir Palkhivala, 1990. *Forty-three Years of Independence*. Cambridge: Cambridge Trust.

30 Stuart Gold, 1989. The costs of privatization: Turkey in the 1980s. *The Multinational Monitor*, 10(1), 10.

31 Ziya Öni, 2004. Turgut Özal and his economic legacy: Turkish neo-liberalism in critical perspective. *Middle Eastern Studies*, 40(4), 113–34.

32 Central Intelligence Agency, 1985. *Turkish Economy Under Ozal*. March 29.

33 George H.W. Bush, 1991. *Address to the Nation on the Invasion of Iraq*. White House, January 16.

34 Naguib Mahfouz, 1992. *The Journey of Ibn Fattouma*. London: Doubleday.

35 Quoted in: Harvey Sindima, 2006. *Major Issues in Islam*. Lanham, MD: Hamilton Books, p. 355.

36 Michael Chege, 1991. Remembering Africa. *Foreign Affairs*, 71(1), 146–63, p. 156.

37   Rufin Batota-Mpeho, 2014. *From Political Monolithism to Multiparty Autocracy.* London: Lulu Publishing, p. 153.

38   Beko Ransome-Kuti, quoted by Lee Kuan Yew. Speech by Lee Kuan Yew on the African Leadership Forum, November 8, 1993.

39   Paul Lewis, 1990. Nyerere and Tanzania. *Associated Press,* October 24.

40   Russell Chandler, 1990. Apartheid is "on way out." *The Los Angeles Times,* May 20.

41   George Ayittey, 1989. Africa's injustices aren't all to the south. *The Christian Science Monitor,* January 26.

42   Axelle Kabou, 1991. *Et si l'Afrique refusait le développement?* Paris: L'Harmattan.

43   Chinua Achebe, 1958. *Things Fall Apart.* Oxford: Heinemann, p. 132.

44   Wole Soyinka, 1992. Culture, memory and development. In Ismail Serageldin and June Taboroff (eds.), *Culture and Development in Africa.* Washington, DC: World Bank, p. 209.

45   Penélope Pacheco-López, and A. P. Thirlwall, 2004. *Trade Liberalisation in Mexico: Rhetoric and Reality.* Studies in Economics, School of Economics, University of Kent.

46   Abraham Lowenthal, 1988. The United States and South America. *Current History,* 87(525), 1–4.

47   Alan Riding, 1998. Latins want Bush to help on debts. *The New York Times,* November 29.

48   Tim Golden, 1992. After the Cold War: Views from Latin America. *The New York Times,* May 30.

49   Ibid.

50   Juan Cruz, 1989. Yo no soy un reaccionario. *El Pais,* June 25.

51   Octavio Paz, 1990. *Nobel Lecture,* Stockholm, December 8.

52   James Brooke, 1993. Conversations/Jair Bolsonaro; A soldier turned politician wants to give Brazil back to army rule. *The New York Times,* July 25.

53   Henry Kamm, 1992. After the Cold War: Views from Vietnam; Vietnam, now master of its own house, tries to mend neighborhood fences. *The New York Times,* June 19.

54   John Taylor, 1991. *Indonesia's Forgotten War.* London: Zed Books.

55   Nanak Kakwani, Elene Makonnen, and Jacques van der Gaag, 1990. *Structural Adjustment and Living Conditions in Developing Countries.* Washington, DC: World Bank; K. Subbarao, Jeanine Braithwaite, and Jyotsna Jalan, 1995. *Protecting the Poor During Adjustment and Transitions.* Washington, DC: World Bank. Also: G. W. Helleiner, 1992. The IMF, the World Bank and Africa's adjustment and external debt problems: An unofficial view. *World Development,* 20(6), 779–92;

Roger Plant, 1993. *Labour Standards and Structural Adjustment in Mexico*. Geneva: ILO.

56 Giovanni Cornia, Richard Jolly, and Frances Stewart, 1987. *Adjustment with a Human Face*. New York: Clarendon Press for UNICEF.

Chapter 4: Missed opportunities

1 Sandra Black, and Donald Morgan, 1998. *Risk and the Democratization of Credit Cards*. New York: Federal Reserve Bank of New York.

2 OECD, 2000. *OECD Information Technology Outlook*. OECD: Paris, pp. 31–2.

3 US Census Bureau, 2001. *People and Families in Poverty by Selected Characteristics*. Washington, DC: US Census Bureau.

4 Cynthia Duncan, 2002. *Worlds Apart: Why Poverty Persists in Rural America*. New Haven, CT: Yale University Press.

5 No single problem dominates Americans' concerns today, Gallup, May 2, 1998.

6 Dena Kleinman, 1990. In a time of too little time, dinner is the time for family. *The New York Times*, December 5; KFF, 1994. *National Survey of Public Knowledge of Welfare Reform and the Federal Budget*. Washington, DC: KFF; Times Mirror Center for the People & the Press, 1993. *America's Place in the World*. Washington, DC: Times Mirror Center for the People & the Press.

7 Roger Wilkins, 1996. *Are We Taking Care of Our Democracy?* University of Maryland, March 7.

8 Jeffrey Mirel Daedalus, 2002. The decline of civic education. *On Education*, 131(3), 49–55.

9 E.D. Hirsh, 1999. *The Schools We Need: And Why We Don't Have Them*. New York: Anchor.

10 Diane Ravitch, 2000. *Left Back: A Century of Failed School Reforms*. New York: Simon and Schuster, p. 462.

11 National Constitution Center, 1997. *Startling Lack of Constitutional Knowledge Revealed in First-Ever National Poll*. Washington, DC: National Constitution Center; National Assessment of Educational Progress, 1998. *Report Card in Civics*. Washington, DC: NAEP.

12 Barbara Schneider, and David Stevenson, 1999. *The Ambitious Generation*. New Haven, CT: Yale University Press.

13 Jonathan Franzen, 2001. *The Corrections*. New York: Fourth Estate, p. 228.

14 Christine Ockrent, 1995. François Mitterrand parle. *L'Express*, July 7.

15 R. Von Leick, and M. Schreiver, 1991. Wir müssen Grossmacht werden, *Der Spiegel*, October 14.

16 In-country regional inequalities in many countries increased. For instance: Florence Bouvet, 2010. Dynamics of regional income inequality in Europe and impact of EU regional policy and EMU. *Journal of Economic Inequality*, 8(1), 323–44.

17 John Dunford, and Clyde Chitty (eds.), 1999. *State Schools: New Labour and the Conservative Legacy*. Abingdon: Routledge; Alwyn Turner, 2013. *A Classless Society: Britain in the 1990s*. London: Aurum.

18 John Ezard, 2000. 18 to 24: The dumber generation. *The Guardian*, October 28.

19 Ron Fraser, 2000. Britain's final decline. *The Trumpet*, September–October.

20 Andrew Roberts, 1995. *The Aachen Memorandum*. London: Weidenfeld, p. 275. Note: The memorandum is in fact a political novel.

21 Tony Judt, 1996. Europe: The grand illusion. *New York Review of Books*, July 11.

Chapter 5: Reluctance to lead

1   Renato Ruggiero, 1996. Statement before the Argentinian Council on Foreign Relations. Buenos Aires, September 10.

2   Treaty on European Union, C 191/1, Maastricht, February 7, 1992, Article J.1.

3   European Council, 1992. Conclusions of the Presidency of the European Council in Lisbon. Brussels: European Council, June 27, p. 26.

4   White House, 1990. *National Security Strategy 1990*. Washington, DC: White House, p. 1; White House, 1991. *National Security Strategy 1991*. Washington, DC: White House, pp. 3–4.

5   White House, 1994. *A National Security Strategy of Engagement and Enlargement*. Washington, DC: White House, p. 6.

6   White House, 1993. *National Security Strategy 1993*. Washington, DC: White House, p. 1.

7   White House, 1994. *National Security Strategy*. Washington, DC: White House, p. 2.

8   Andrew Kohut, and Robert Toth, 1994. *Trade and the Public*. Washington, DC: Times Mirror Center for the People & the Press; Hearing Before the Committee on Finance of the US Senate, March 9, 1993, p. 11.

9   Kohut and Toth, *Trade and the Public*.

10   Ibid, p. 2.

11   For instance: *The Charlie Rose Show*, November 15, 1994. Also: James Goldsmith, 1993. *The Trap*. New York: Carroll & Graf Publishers.

12   ILO Director-general urges parallel commitment to labour standards and trade liberalization, ILO, March 6, 1996.

13   For instance: Mochtar Riady, John Huang, Walmart's Sam Walton, Goldman Sachs.

14   John Smidt, 2015. How we created the WTO. *Wilson Quarterly*, Summer.

15   Mickey Kantor, 1997. US trade negotiations: Lessons learned, lessons applied. Council on Foreign Relations, Working Paper, November.

16   Andrew Bacevich, 2002. *American Empire*. Cambridge, MA: Harvard University Press, p. 85.

17   Department of Commerce, 1997. *Framework for Global Electronic Commerce*. Washington, DC: Department of Commerce, July 1.

18   William Clinton, 2000. *Public Papers of the Presidents of the United States: William J. Clinton: 2000–2001*. Washington, DC: White House, p. 135.

19   Sherry Jones, 1999. The crash. *PBS Frontline*, June 29.

20   For example: Robert Rubin, 2003. *Uncertain World*. New York: Random House.

21   Department of the Treasury, 1998. *National Treatment Study*. Washington, DC: Department of the Treasury.

22   Ravi Ramamurti, 1992. Why are developing countries privatizing? *Journal of International Business Studies*, 23(2), 225–49.

23   Harry Dexter White and others.

24   Steven Mufson, and David Hoffman, 1998. Russian crash shows globalization's risks. *The Washington Post*, November 8.

25   Charles W. Calomiris, 1998. The IMF's moral hazard, American Enterprise Institute, August 5.

26   Quoted in: Fund managers in a Surrey state, *The Times*, December 5, 1997.

27   Stanley Fischer, 1997. Capital account liberalization and the role of the IMF. Paper for IMF Seminar, September 19.

28   Lawrence Summers, 1997. Commentary. In Ricardo Hausmann and Liliana Rojas-Suares (eds.), *Volatile Capital Flows*. Washington, DC: Inter-American Development Bank, p. 55.

29   An overview of 1999 survey data: Steven Kull, 2001. *Culture Wars? How Americans and Europeans View Globalization*. Brookings Institution, September 1.

30   Jack Ludwig, 1999. Economic status: Americans assess opportunity, fairness, and responsibility. *Global Policy Forum*, April.

31 Department of Defense Appropriations of the US Congress, 1991. *Hearings Before a Subcommittee of the Committee on Appropriations. Part 1*. Washington, DC: US Government Printing Offices, pp. 44–55.

32 Tim Weiner, 1994. Proposal cuts back on some weapons to spend more on personnel. *The New York Times*, February 8.

33 Fred Kaplan, 1991. Powell: The US is running out of demons. *The Seattle Times*, April 9.

34 Lydia Saad, 1999. Americans support active role for US in world affairs. Gallup, April 1.

35 George Will, 1995. A dog in that fight. *Newsweek*, November 6.

36 https://www.youtube.com/watch?v=idf_sdeVpO4&ab_channel=zivstepa

37 Ivo Daalder, 1998. *Decision to Intervene: How the War in Bosnia Ended*. Brookings Institution, December 1.

38 Steve Collinson, 2016. Clinton and Blair's secret conversations revealed. *CNN*, January 8.

39 Patrick Cockburn, 1994. US foreign policy: Post-Cold War world defeats Clinton. *The Independent*, May 30.

40 Quoted in Anne Devroy, and Jeffrey Smith, 1993. Clinton re-examines foreign policy under siege. *The Washington Post*, October 17.

41 Joint Chiefs of Staff, 2010. Joint vision, 2010. Washington, DC: US Government Printing Office.

42 United Nations Secretariat, 1998. *Unilateral Economic Measures as a Means of Political and Economic Coercion against Developing Countries*. New York: United Nations.

43 United States General Accounting Office, 1992. *Economic Sanctions: Effectiveness as Tools of Foreign Policy. Report to the Chairman of the Committee on Foreign Relations*, US Senate, February 19. See also Lynn Bragg, et al., 1998. *Overview and Analysis of Current US Unilateral Economic Sanctions*. Washington, DC: US International Trade Commission.

44 Pew Research Center, 1995. *Public Opinion of the UN*. Washington, DC: Pew.

45 Interview with Madeleine K. Albright, *NBC The Today Show*, February 19, 1998.

Chapter 6: Making rivals rich

1 Tom Raum, 1990. Bush says Saddam even worse than Hitler. *AP*, November 1.

2 Hearing before the Committee on Finance of the US Senate, March 9, 1993, p. 53.

3 George H. W. Bush, and Brent Scowcroft, 1998. *A World Transformed*. New York: Vintage, p. 102.

4 Secretary of Defense, 1994. *Memorandum on the US–China Military Relationship*. Washington, DC: Office of the Secretary of Defense, August, p. 3.

5 George H.W. Bush, 1991. Remarks at the Yale University Commencement Ceremony in New Haven, Connecticut, May 27.

6 James Baker, 1991. America in Asia: Emerging architecture for a Pacific community. *Foreign Affairs*, 70(5), 1–18, p. 16.

7 Susumu Awanohara, and Tai Ming Cheung, 1991. Abusive treatment, *Far Eastern Economic Review*, January 3.

8 In Kohl's China visit, business comes first. *Chicago Tribune*, November 17, 1993.

9 Caving in to China, *International Herald Tribune*, April 14, 1997.

10 David Sanger, 1997. Boeing and other concerns lobby Congress for China. *The New York Times*, April 29.

11 Yan Xuetong, 1993. 当前我国外交面临的挑战和任务 [*Challenges and Tasks Currently Facing Our Diplomacy*]. Beijing: Tsinghua University.

12 Richard Baum, 2000. Jiang takes command. In Hung-mao Tien and Yunhan Zhu (eds.), *China under Jiang Zemin*. London: Lynne Rienner, p. 20.

13 Speech by Jiang Zemin for the America China Society, New York, October 30, 1997.

14 Gordon Williams, 1989. Spinning their wheels in China. *The New York Times*, November 19; Jim Mann, 1989. *Beijing Jeep: The Short, Unhappy Romance of American Business in China*. New York: Simon & Schuster.

15 Barton Gellman, 1998. US and China nearly came to blows in '96. *The Washington Post*, June 21.

16 NSC, 1993. Declassified Report of the Principals Committee Meeting on China, Washington, November 10, 1993.

17 Director of Central Intelligence, 1995. *China: Short-Term Implications of Deng Xiaoping's Death*. Declassified National Intelligence Estimate, February.

18 Andrew Nathan, 2002. *Soldiers, Statecraft, and History*. Westport, CT: Praeger, p. 119.

19 David Finkelstein, 2007. China's national military strategy. In Roy Kamphausen and Andrew Scobell (eds.), *Right Sizing the People's Liberation Army: Exploring the Contours of China's Military*. Carlisle, PA: Army War College Press, p. 103.

20 National Security Council, 1993. NSC Principals Meeting on China, November 10.

21 European Parliament, 1997. *Resolution on the Commission Communication.* Brussels: European Parliament, June 30.

22 European Economic and Social Committee, 1997. Opinion on Relations between the European Union and China. *Official Journal of the European Communities*, May 26.

23 Remarks by Samuel Berger, Assistant to the President for National Security Affairs to the National Press Club, Washington, DC, January 6, 2000.

24 Press Briefing by National Security Advisor Sandy Berger, Treasury Secretary Bob Rubin, and Director of the National Economic Council Gene Sperling, June 17, 1998.

25 Paul Orzulak, 2000. Draft President William Jefferson Clinton remarks to Johns Hopkins University School of Advanced International Studies on China, March 7.

26 Warren Christopher, 2001. *Chances of a Lifetime.* New York: Lisa Drew, p. 240.

27 Human Rights Watch, 2002. *We Have No Orders To Save You.* Washington, DC: Human Rights Watch, p. 46.

28 Suzanne Goldenberg, 1999. India close to declaring all-out war in Kashmir. *The Guardian*, June 16.

29 Department of State Information Center, 2000. *Afghanistan: Bin Laden for the Long Run.* Confidential Discussion Paper, State Department, October 12.

30 Bruce Riedel, 1999. *American Diplomacy and the 1999 Kargil Summit at Blair House.* University of Pennsylvania: Center for the Advanced Study of India.

31 Lee Kuan Yew, 2000. *From Third World to First.* New York: HarperCollins, p. 339.

32 Bangkok Summit Declaration of 1995. Bangkok, December 14–15, 1995.

33 Martin Wolf, 1998. Let lenders beware. *Financial Times*, January 3.

34 An open government saved US: Ramos, *The Straits Times*, June 16, 1988.

35 Peter Katzenstein, 2000. Regionalism and Asia. *New Political Economy*, 5(3), 353–68, p. 361.

36 Thailand's financial dilemma. *Nation* (Bangkok), June 10, 2000.

37 Speech by Goh Chok Tong, Prime Minister of Singapore, Asia House, New York, September 7, 2000.

38 Wolf, Let lenders beware.

39 ASEAN–China Expert Group on Economic Cooperation, 2001. *Forging Closer ASEAN–China Relations.* October.

40 David Shambaugh, 2004. China engages Asia, reshaping the regional order. *International Security*, 29(3), 64–99, p. 69.

41 https://www.sciencespo.fr/ceri/sites/sciencespo.fr.ceri/files/artnp.pdf

42 White House, 1993. *Public Papers of the Presidents of the United States, 1992–93. Book 1.* Washington, DC: US Government Printing Office, p. 181.

43 Ibid., p. 522.

44 White House, 1993. *Memorandum of Conversation: Working Dinner with President Boris Yeltsin.* Vancouver, April 3.

45 Note: between 1992 and 1997, 7% of EU aid was spent on governance: European Commission, 1998. EU-Relations. Internal memo 98/5, January 27, 1998.

46 Charles Dick, 1999. *Russia's 1999 Draft Military Doctrine.* Sandhurst: Royal Military Academy, November 16, p. 4.

47 White House, 1995. Summary report on the one-on-one meeting between Presidents Clinton and Yeltsin, May 10.

48 Ibid.

49 Niall Fergusson, 2004. *Colossus.* London: Penguin, p. 211.

50 Excerpts from Iraqi document on meeting with US envoy. *The New York Times*, September 23, 1990.

51 Conversation with British diplomat, June 11, 2016.

52 Nachum Barnea, and Shimon Shifer, 1996. Not attacking them, strangling them. *Yediot Ahronot*, March 8.

53 https://wikileaks.org/plusd/cables/91CAIRO12383_a.html

54 Christian Chesnot, and George Malbrunot, 2019. *Qatar Papers. Comment l'émirat finance l'islam de France et d'Europe.* Paris: Lafon; Daveed Gartenstein-Ross, and Aaron Zelin, 2013. Uncharitable organizations. *Foreign Policy*, February 25.

55 Lina Kathib, 1993. Qatar's foreign policy: The limits of pragmatism. *International Affairs*, 89(2), 417–31.

56 Safar al-Hawali, 2000. *The Day of Wrath.* London: Kalamullah Books, pp. 17–18.

57 Documents released by Wikileaks: https://wikileaks.org/plusd/cables/97AD DISABABA2584_a.html and https://wikileaks.org/plusd/cables/92DOHA32 40_a.html

58 Ingrid Bakken, and Siri Aas Rustad, 2018. *Conflict Trends in Africa.* Oslo: Prio, p. 24.

59 Ibid.

60 US Department of Defense, 1995. *United States Security Strategy for Sub-Saharan Africa.* Washington, DC: US Department of Defense, Office of International Security Affairs, p. 3.

61 Robert Kaplan, 1994. The coming anarchy. *The Atlantic*, February.

62 Peter Sutherland, and John Sewell, 1998. Gather the nations to promote globalization. *The New York Times*, February 8.

Chapter 7: Disregard and decadence

1   Bubble bubble, *The Economist*, March 23, 2000.

2   Robert Schiller, 2000. *Irrational Exuberance*. Princeton, NJ: Princeton University Press.

3   *Boiler Room*. Released in 2000. Written and directed by Ben Younger.

4   David Kleinbard, 2000. The $1.7 trillion dot.com lesson. *CNN Money*, November 9.

5   Remarks by the President to Airline Employees, September 27, 2001.

6   Press Conference by the President, December 20, 2006.

7   Stuart Vyse, 2008. *Going Broke: Why Americans Can't Hold On To Their Money*. Oxford: Oxford University Press; Amy Novotney, 2008. What's behind American consumerism? *Monitor on Psychology*, 39(7), 40.

8   Erik Olin Wright, and Joel Rogers, 2015. *American Society: How It Really Works*. New York: W.W. Norton, p. 23.

9   George Carlin, 2005. Life is worth losing. Beacon Theater, New York City, November 5.

10 Gilles Slade, 2007. *Made to Break: Technology and Obsolescence in America*. Cambridge, MA: Harvard University Press; Claudio Luz, 2007. Waste couture: Environmental impact of the clothing industry. *Environmental Health Perspectives*, 115(9), 449–54.

11 Olin Wright and Rogers, *American Society*.

12 Charles Fishman, 2006. *The Walmart Effect*. New York: Penguin.

13 Anthony Dukes, Tansev Geylani, and Yunchuan Liu, 2010. Dominant retailers' incentives for product quality. Working Paper. Los Angeles, CA: University of Southern California.

14 Norman Ornstein, 2004. Outspoken, outgunned, outsourced. *The Washington Post*, February 22.

15 OECD, 2019. OECD Statistical Database. Fixed assets by activity and by asset, ISIC rev4: Computer Software and Database: American fixed assets decreased slightly, by 0.36 percent.

16 Bureau of Economic Analysis, National Data, Fixed Assets Account Tables. Table 2.3. Historical-Cost Net Stock of Private Fixed Assets, Equipment, Structures, and Intellectual Property Products by Type.

17 American Society of Civil Engineers, 2009. *Score Card for American Infrastructure*. Reston, VA: American Society of Civil Engineers, p. iii.

18 The United States of Entrepreneurs. *The Economist*, March 14, 2009.

19 Measured by GDP per capita in constant USs.

20 Jon Bakija, Adam Cole, and Bradley T. Heim, 2010. Jobs and income growth of top earners and the causes of changing income inequality: Evidence from US tax return data. Williams College, November.

21 Stefanie Cohen, 2009. Meet NY's hidden rich people. *New York Post*, October 25.

22 Concerns real disposable income.

23 https://www.census.gov/data/tables/time-series/demo/income-poverty/historical-poverty-people.html

24 Ron Suskind, 2004. Faith, certainty and the Presidency of George W. Bush. *The New York Times*, October 17.

25 Rakesh Khurana, and Nitin Nohria, 2008. It's time to make management a true profession. *Harvard Business Review*, October.

26 William Kristol, 2008. Let Palin be Palin. *The Washington Examiner*, September 8.

27 As a share of GDP. Judith Torney-Putra, Rainer Lehmann, Hans Oswald, and Wolfram Schulz, 2001. *Citizenship and Education in Twenty-eight Countries*. Amsterdam: International Association for the Evaluation of Educational Achievement; Wolfram Schulz, John Ainley, Julian Fraillon, David Kerr, and Bruno Losito, 2009. *ICCS 2009 International Report: Civic Knowledge, Attitudes, and Engagement among Lower Secondary School Students in 38 Countries*. Amsterdam: International Association for the Evaluation of Educational Achievement.

28 George Archibald, 2003. Ignorance of US history is called threat to security. *Washington Times*, April 14–20.

29 Sean Richey, 2011. Civic engagement and patriotism. *Social Science Quarterly*, 92(4), 1044–56.

30 Barack Obama, 2008. Election Victory Speech, Chicago, November 4.

31 Gallup, Obama job approval rating. Available at: https://news.gallup.com/poll/116479/barack-obama-presidential-job-approval.aspx

32 Ambrose Evans-Pritchard, 2004. Dutch want power returned to states from Brussels. *The Independent*, June 4, 2004.

33 Joschka Fischer, 2000. Speech at the Humboldt University, Berlin, May 12.

34 Pim Fortuyn, 2002. *De Puinhopen van Acht Jaar Paars*. Rotterdam: Karakter, p. 27.

35 Gallup, 2002. *Flash Eurobarometer 132-1*. Luxembourg: Eurobarometer, p. 8.

36 European Social Survey data for 2002, answering the question "Allow many or few immigrants from poorer countries in Europe?"

37 Eurobarometer, 2006. *The Future of Europe*. Luxembourg: Eurobarometer, p. 55.

38 Gunter Verheugen, 2001. Debate on EU enlargement in the European Parliament, September 4.

39 European Social Survey data 2002, responding to "Immigrants take jobs away in country or create new jobs." Also: European Social Survey data for 2002 and 2010, responding to the statement "Immigration bad or good for country's economy." Includes: Belgium, German, France, UK, Spain, Finland, Denmark, and the Netherlands.

40 Oliver Duff, 2007. Morrissey blames immigration for "disappearance" of British identity. *The Independent*, November 29.

41 Paul Scheffer, 2000. Het multiculturele drama. *NRC*, January 29.

42 Conversation with former Italian Prime Minister, Brussels, October 31, 2016.

43 Note: imported mass grew from 96 million tons to 113 million tons, value from US$16 billion to US$57 billion.

44 André Sapir, et al., 2003. *An Agenda for a Growing Europe: Report Submitted to the European Commission*, July 3.

45 Horst Kohler, 2001. *The Euro: An Emblem of the Successes and Challenges of European Integration. Remarks on the Occasion of the Informal Meeting of the ECOFIN Council*, Laken, December 14.

46 If export countries had kept the money and spent it on consumption, they would have imported more so that the trade imbalance disappeared.

47 VW-Chef Martin Winterkorn im Interview. *Autobild*, June 16, 2008.

48 Thomas Stewart, and Louise O'Brien, 2005. Transforming an industrial giant. *Harvard Business Review*, February.

49 Gary Herrigel, 2015. Globalization and the German industrial production model. *Journal for Labour Market Research*, 48(2), 133–49.

50 Karl Brenke, 2014. Eastern Germany still playing economic catch-up. *DIW Economic Bulletin*, November.

51 Berlusconi comments on WW2 death camps spark German anger, *BBC World News*, April 27, 2014.

52 John Hills, et al., 2010. *An Anatomy of Economic Inequality in the UK: Report of the National Equality Panel*. London: Government Equalities Office.

53 Slums in the sky: Dealing with Britain's decaying tower blocks will be both tricky and expensive. *The Economist*, September 29, 2005.

54 University and College Union, 2009. *Decline and Fall: How the UK is Being Left Behind in Education*. London: University and College Union; Jim Hall, et al., 2010. *Strategies for National Infrastructure Provision in Great Britain*. London: ITRC.

55 Antony Heath, 2013. Education under New Labour. *Oxford Review of Economic Policy*, 29(1), 227–47.

56 Sven-Olov Daunfelt, Oana Mihaescu, Helena Nilsson, and Niklas Rudholm, 2019. Spillover effects when IKEA enters: Do incumbent retailers win or lose? *Papers in Regional Science*, 98(6).

57 Liam O'Connell, 2018. Leading 5 purchasing countries of IKEA products from 2012 to 2016. Available at: https://www.statista.com/statistics/255586/leading-5-purchasing-countries-of-ikea-products/

58 Ikea Rail stelt capaciteit op spoor veilig. *Nieuwsblad Transport*, November 2001: Over 30 percent of Ikea's supplies are sourced from Asia.

59 Robert D. Hisrich, and Claudine Kearney, 2014. *Managing Innovation and Entrepreneurship*. Thousand Oaks, CA: Sage, p. 108.

60 Eurydice, 2005. *Citizenship Education at School in Europe*. Brussels: European Commission; César Birzea, et al., 2004. *All-European Study on Education for Democratic Citizenship Policies*. Strasbourg: Council of Europe; Wolfram Schulz, John Ainley, Julian Fraillon, Bruno Losito, Gabriella Agrusti, and Tim Friedman, 2016. *Becoming Citizens in a Changing World*. Amsterdam: International Association for the Evaluation of Educational Achievement.

61 Torney-Putra et al., *Citizenship and Education in Twenty-eight Countries*, p. 47.

62 Brian Wheeler, 2005. Is Big Brother really more popular than election? *BBC World*, May 31.

63 James Bowman, 2009. The reason why. *The New Criterion*, November 9.

Chapter 8: A foreign policy of recklessness

1 José Manuel Barroso, 2010. Europe's rising global role. *The Guardian*, January 3.

2 Benjamin Lambeth, 2005. *American Carrier Air Power at the Dawn of a New Century*. Santa Monica, CA: RAND, p. 20.

3 Nese DeBruyne, 2018. *American War and Military Operations Casualties: Lists and Statistics*. Washington, DC: Congressional Research Service, p. 7.

4 Mark Thompson, 2015. The true cost of the Afghanistan War may surprise you. *Time*, January 1.

5 In Bush's words: "Iraqi democracy will succeed." *The New York Times*, November 3, 2003.

6   Donald Rumsfeld, 2001. Memo to Paul Wolfowitz, December 17, 2001.

7   Kimberly Zisk Marten, 2002. Defending against anarchy: From war to peace-keeping in Afghanistan. *The Washington Quarterly*, 61(1), 35–52.

8   Donald Wright, et al., 2005. *A Different Kind of War*. Fort Leavenworth, KS: Combat Studies Institute Press.

9   Project for the New American Century, 1997. *Statement of Principles*. Washington, DC: Project for the New American Century; Project for the New American Century, 2000. *Rebuilding America's Defenses*. Washington, DC: Project for the New American Century.

10 Ron Suskind, 2004. Faith, certainty and the Presidency of George W. Bush. *The New York Times*, October 17.

11 Condoleezza Rice, 2011. *No Higher Honor*. New York: Broadway Paperbacks, p. 26.

12 White House, 2002. *The National Security Strategy of the United States of America*. Washington, DC: White House, p. 2.

13 Donald Rumsfeld, 2001. Working Paper on Iraq, July 27. Available at: https://nsarchive2.gwu.edu/NSAEBB/NSAEBB326/doc06.pdf

14 David Usborne, 2003. WMD just a convenient excuse for war, admits Wolfowitz. *The Independent*, May 30.

15 Brent Scowcroft, 2002. Don't attack Saddam. *The Wall Street Journal*, August 15.

16 Wolf Blitzer, 2003. Search for the smoking gun. *CNN*, January 10.

17 Dick Cheney, 2002. Vice President speaks at VFW 103rd National Convention. *White House Archives*, August 26.

18 Bush makes historic speech aboard warship. *CNN*, May 2, 2003.

19 Al Qaeda in Iraq becoming less foreign – US general. *Reuters*, November 18, 2019.

20 Joel Rayburn, and Frank Sobchack, 2019. *The US Army in the Iraq War*. Carlisle, PA: US Army War College Press.

21 David Petraeus, 2007. *Report to Congress on the Situation in Iraq*, September 10.

22 David Petraeus, 2008. *Multi-national Force – Iraq Commander's Counterinsurgency Guidance*. Baghdad: Headquarters Multi-National Force, June 21.

23 Lawrence Korb, Loren Thompson, and Caroline Wadhams, 2006. *Army Equipment After Iraq*. Washington, DC: Center for American Progress.

24 Robert Kagan, 2003. *Of Paradise and Power*. New York: Knopf.

25 Condoleezza Rice, 2000. Campaign 2000: Promoting the national interest. *Foreign Affairs*, 79(1), 45–62.

26 Jim Garamone, 2001. Bush announces ABM treaty withdrawal. *American Forces Press Service*, December 13.

27 John Bolton, 2005. There is no such thing as the United Nations. *The Times*, August 2.

28 EU High Representative, 2003. *A Secure Europe in a Better World*. Brussels: European Council.

29 European Commission, 2004. *Communication from the Commission: European Neighbourhood Policy*. Brussels: European Commission.

30 Tony Blair, 2005. Conference speech, September 27.

31 Louise Baring, 2005. Scandal of the sheikh and his £1bn shopping spree. *The Telegraph*, April 30.

32 David Leigh, and Rob Evans, 2007. How Blair put pressure on Goldsmith to end BAE investigation. *The Guardian*, December 21; Ben Russell, and Nigel Morris, 2011. Court condemns Blair for halting Saudi arms inquiry. *The Independent*, October 23.

33 Committee on Foreign Relations, 2000. The Meltzer Commission: The future of the IMF and World Bank. Senate Committee on Foreign Relations, May 23; Joint Economic Committee, 2000. Reform of the IMF and the World Bank. Hearing before the Joint Economic Committee, April 12.

34 David Dollar, and Aart Kraay, 2000. Growth is good for the poor. Development Research Group, World Bank, March; Kenneth Rogoff, 2002. An open letter to Joseph Stiglitz, IMF, July 2.

35 World Bank/IMF meetings fail to resolve debt issue. *Journal of the Group of 77*, Fall 2004, 17(2), 11.

36 Yongding Yu, 2002. IMF reform: A Chinese view. In Edwin Truman (ed.), *Reform the IMF for the 21st Century*. Washington, DC: Institute for International Economics, pp. 515–25.

37 John Snow, 2005. Statement by the Honorable John W. Snow, US Secretary of the Treasury, International Monetary and Financial Committee, April 15.

38 Mark Landler, 2009. Rising powers challenge US on role in IMF. *The New York Times*, March 30.

39 Robert Zoellick, 2001. In the next round. *The Washington Post*, July 21; Allan Greenspan, 2001. Testimony before the Committee on Banking, Housing and Urban Affairs, US Senate, September 20.

40 Fidel Castro, 1998. Speech at the Special Session Commemorating the 50th Anniversary of the Multilateral Trade System. Geneva, May 19.

41 For instance: WTO Committee on Technical Barriers, 2001. ASEAN concerns regarding the proposed Belgian Law for the promotion of socially responsible production, May 28.

42 Remarks during a seminar, Brussels, February 3, 2006.

43 Ibid.

44 European Commission, 2006. EU–China: Closer partners, growing responsibilities. Brussels: European Commission.

45 Secretary of State Madeleine K. Albright, interview on the *Diane Rehm Show*, March 27, 1997.

46 State Department Bureau of Democracy, Human Rights, and Labor, 2009. *2008 Country Report on Human Rights Practices: Saudi Arabia*. Washington, DC: State Department, February 25.

47 Department of State, 2005. *Deputy Secretary of State Robert Zoellick's keynote address to the National Committee on US–China Relations Members' Gala*, September 21.

48 State Department Bureau of Democracy, Human Rights, and Labor, 2006. *2005 Country Report on Human Rights Practices: Saudi Arabia*. Washington, DC: State Department, March 8.

49 US Congressional Record, Proceedings and Debates of the 111th Congress, Second Session, volume 156, part 14, December 2010, p. 10531.

Chapter 9: Globalization and the return of power politics

1 Department of the Navy and National Security Agency, 2001. *EO-3E Collision: Cryptologic Damage Assessment and Incident Review. Final Report*. Washington, DC: Department of the Navy, pp. 5–6.

2 In Jiang's Words, *The New York Times*, August 10, 2001.

3 Ibid.

4 Hu Jintao, 2005. Build towards a harmonious world of lasting peace and common prosperity. Statement at the United Nations Summit, New York, September 15.

5 Wang Yizhou, 2009. Transition of China's diplomacy and foreign relations. *China and World Economy*, 17(3), 93–102.

6 Jonathan Holslag, 2019. *The Silk Road Trap*. Cambridge: Polity.

7 Available at: https://www.youtube.com/watch?v=DGR64foVb8A. For a discussion: Evan Osnos, 2016. Angry youth. In David Shambaugh (ed.), *The China Reader*. Oxford: Oxford University Press, p. 196.

8 Conversation with European Commissioner, Brussels, March 3, 2008.

9 George W. Bush, 2002. Speech at Tsinghua University, Beijing, February 22.

10 Clark Randt, 2008. Prospects for US–China relations. Secret Cable, February 24.

11   Atal Vajpayee, 2000. *Speech for the Asia Society Annual Dinner*. New York, September 7.

12   Pranab Mukherjee, 2006. Indian foreign policy: A road map for the decade ahead. Speech at the 46th National Defence College Course, Delhi, November 15.

13   Ministry of Defence, India, 2000. *Annual Report 1999–2000*. New Delhi: Ministry of Defence, p. 5. This report underlined the PLA's restructuring "with a view to enhancing cross-border military capability". The 2000–2001 Report stressed the fact that "every Indian city [is] in range of Chinese missiles" and that despite preoccupation with growth, there is "not enough trust" (p. 8). The edition of 2003–2004 addresses China's military modernization, its nuclear and missile arsenals, and its maritime aspirations in the Indian Ocean (p. 16). The Annual Report of 2005–2006 remains suspicious about China's role in Pakistan and the military presence along the Sino-Indian border (p. 10).

14   Vladimir Putin, 2001. *Speech in the Bundestag of the Federal Republic of Germany*, Berlin, December 25. See also Government of Russia, 2000. *The Foreign Policy Concept of the Russian Federation. Approved by the President of the Russian Federation*. Moscow: Government of Russia; Robert Service, 2003. *Russia's Experiment with a People*. Cambridge: Cambridge University Press, p. 167.

15   Michail Zygar, 2016. *All the Kremlin's Men: Inside the Court of Vladimir Putin*. New York: Public Affairs, p. 34.

16   For example: Vladimir Putin, 1999. *Russia at the Turn of the Millennium*, December 30.

17   Russia and EU do not want "Schengen wall" to separate Europe. *Pravda*, May 31, 2005.

18   Andrew Konitzer, and Stephen K. Wegren, 2006. Federalism and political recentralization in the Russian Federation: United Russia as the party of power. *Publius*, 36(4), 503–22.

19   Peter Finn, 2006. Oil profits help Russia pay off Soviet-era debt. *The Washington Post*, August 22.

20   China–Russia Statement on New World Order, July 2, 2005.

21   Andrew Rettman, 2008. Germany and Russia threaten EU–Ukraine relations. *EU Observer*, August 28.

22   US Department of State, 2009. France grows closer to Russia: Opportunities for convergence and divergence with US interests. Washington, DC: US Department of State, November 24.

23   Clifford Levy, 2007. Putin accuses US of trying to discredit Russian vote. *The New York Times*, November 27.

24 Ingrid Bakken, and Siri Rustad, 2008. *Conflict Trends in Africa, 1989–2017*. Oslo: Prio, p. 3.

25 http://afrobarometer.org/online-data-analysis/analyse-online

26 James Boyce, and Léonce Ndikumana, 2012. *Capital Flight from Sub-Saharan African Countries: Updated Estimates, 1970–2010*. Amherst, MA: University of Massachusetts, pp. 7–8.

27 Interview transcript: President Luiz Inácio Lula da Silva, *Financial Times*, November 8, 2008.

28 Argentina's currency controls, *The Economist*, November 1, 2011.

29 Alejandro Jara, Ramon Moreno, and Camilo Tovar, 2009. The global crisis and Latin America: Financial impact and policy responses. *BIS Quarterly Review*, June, pp. 53–68.

30 Philip Gourevitch, 1998. *We Wish to Inform You that Tomorrow We Will Be Killed with Our Families: Stories from Rwanda*. New York: Farrar, Straus and Giroux, p. 93.

31 Secretary of State, 2009. *Terrorist Finance: Action Request for Senior Level Engagement on Terrorism Finance*. Secret cable, December 30.

32 James Dorsey, 2001. Saudi leader warns US Mideast policy may force kingdom to review relationship. *The Wall Street Journal*, October 29.

33 EO 12958 Decl: 01/27/2019. TAGS PARM, PREL, MARR, MNUC, IR, SA, RU. Subject: Saudi Exchange with Russian Ambassador on Iran's Nuclear Plans. Classified By: P/M Counselor Scott McGehee. Reasons 1.4 (b) (d).

34 Barak Ravid, 2010. Fatah asked Israel to help attack Hamas during Gaza coup. *Haaretz*, December 20.

35 The Middle East Research Institute, 2005. Anti-Americanism in the Turkish media. *The Middle East Research Institute Special Dispatch*, February 25.

36 https://wikileaks.org/plusd/cables/08ANKARA1567_a.html

37 What lies beneath Ankara's new foreign policy. Confidential cable, January 20, 2020. Available at: https://wikileaks.org/plusd/cables/10ANKARA87_a.html

38 Ash Carter, 2019. *Inside the Five-Sided Box*. New York: Penguin, p. 208.

Chapter 10: What the hell happened?

1 Robinson Meyer, 2019. It's younger and cooler than a carbon tax. *The Atlantic*, June 21; Eurobarometer, 2020. *Attitudes of European Citizens towards the Environment*. Brussels: European Commission.

2 Jennifer Agiesta, 2016. Most say race relations worsened under Obama, poll

finds. *CNN*, October 6; Giovanni Russonello, 2016. Race relations are at lowest point in Obama Presidency, poll finds. *The New York Times*, July 3; Kimberley Johnson, 2019. Swimming the multiple currents. In Wilbur Rich (ed.), *Looking Back on President Barack Obama's Legacy*. Cham: Palgrave, pp. 133–49.

3 Patricia Buckley, and Akrur Barua, 2018. Are we headed for a poorer United States? Growing wealth inequality by age puts younger households behind. Deloitte, March 12.

4 Lee Rainie, and Andrew Perrin, 2019. *Key Findings about Americans' Declining Trust in Government and Each Other*. Pew Research Center, July 22.

5 Ibid.

6 Martin Gillens, and Benjamin Page, 2014. Testing theories of American politics: Elites, interest groups, and average citizens. *Perspectives on Politics*, 12(3), 564–81.

7 Telis Demos, 2018. Wall Street bankers get biggest raise in four years. *The Wall Street Journal*, March 26.

8 Lee Drutman, 2015. *The Business of America is Lobbying: How Corporations Became Politicized and Politics Became More Corporate*. Oxford: Oxford University Press.

9 Dan Eggen, 2011. Obama campaign attracts Wall Street money. *The Washington Post*, July 22.

10 Lee and Perrin, *Key Findings*.

11 National Science Board, 2020. *Research and Development: US Trends and International Comparisons*. Washington, DC: National Science Board, p. 10.

12 Concerns net international investment position as reported by the Bureau of Economic Analysis.

13 Abel Gustafson, et al., 2019. Changes in awareness of and support for the Green New Deal: December 2018 to April 2019. The Yale Program on Climate Change Communication, May 8.

14 James Melton, 2019. US teenagers say Amazon is their favorite online shopping website. *Digital Commerce*, April 16.

15 BBC, 2013. The truth behind the click, *Panorama*, BBC One, November 25.

16 Joe Concha, 2020. Americans trust Amazon, Google more than the US government, news media. *The Hill*, January 14.

17 Sunyee Yoon, and Hyeongmin Christian Kim, 2016. Keeping the American dream alive: The interactive effect of perceived economic mobility and materialism on impulsive spending. *Journal of Marketing Research*, 53(5), 759–77.

18 Media Dynamics, 2014. *Media Usage Trends Report*. New York: Media Dynamics.

19 The program, called Effective Teaching and Learning for a Well-Rounded Education, had a budget around US$246 million.

20 National Assessment of Educational Progress (NAEP). Available at: https://www.nationsreportcard.gov/hgc_2014/#civics/scores

21 Rebecca Burgess, 2015. *Civic Education Professional Development: The Lay of the Land*. Washington, DC: American Enterprise Institute.

22 Ibid.

23 Ibid.

24 Cory Turner, 2016. Can a President Trump get rid of common core? *NPR*, November 10.

25 Ebuild, 2019. *$23 billion*. Washington, DC: Ebuild, p. 3.

26 Claire Miller, 2015. Class differences in child-rearing are on the rise. *The New York Times*, December 7.

27 Mission Readiness, 2009. *Ready, Willing, and Unable to Serve*. Washington, DC: Mission Readiness.

28 Thomas Spoehr and Bridget Handy, 2018. *The Looming National Security Crisis: Young Americans Unable to Serve in the Military*. Washington, DC: Heritage.

29 School of Public Policy, 2018. *Where Are America's Volunteers?* College Park, MD: University of Maryland.

30 https://news.gallup.com/poll/195749/number-americans-closely-following-politics-spikes.aspx

31 Manifest in the Freshman Survey, with most recent data in: Ellen Bara Stolzenberg, et al., 2019. *American Freshman: National Norms, Fall 2017*. Los Angeles, CA: Higher Education Research Institute; Tamar Kremer-Sadlik, Marilena Fatigante, and Carolina Izquierdo, 2010. Making meaning of everyday practices: Parents' attitudes toward children's extra-curricular activities in the United States and in Italy. *Anthropology & Education Quarterly*, 41(1), 35–54; Wendy Klein, and Antony Graesch, 2009. Children and chores: A mixed-methods study of children's household work in Los Angeles families. *Anthropology of Work Review*, 30(3), 98–109; Elisabeth Kolbert, 2012. Spoiled rotten. *The New Yorker*, June 25. See also: UCLA Freshmen Survey.

32 Anna Coates, Charlotte A. Hardman, Jason C.G. Halford, Paul Christiansen, and Emma J. Boyland, 2019. Social media influencer marketing and children's food intake: A randomized trial. *Pediatrics*, 114(5), 18–39; Hao Mingyi, 2018. Social media celebrity and the institutionalization of YouTube. *Convergence*, 25(3), 534–53.

33 https://www.youtube.com/watch?v=TOg8zUSHvfA

34 United States Department of Justice, Civil Rights Division, 2015. *Investigation of the Ferguson Police Department*. Washington, DC: United States Department of Justice.

35 Robert Wuthnow, 2018. *The Left Behind*. Princeton, NJ: Princeton University Press; Katherine Cramer, 2016. *The Politics of Resentment*. Chicago, IL: University of Chicago Press.

36 Jonathan Rodden, 2019. *Why Cities Lose*. New York: Basic Books.

37 Aris Folley, 2020. John Kelly says media is not the enemy of the people. *The Hill*, February 13.

38 Jim Mattis, 2019. Duty, democracy and the threat of tribalism. *Wall Street Journal*, August 28.

39 James Madison, Alexander Hamilton, and John Jay, 1987. *The Federalist Papers* (Isaac Kramick, ed.). Penguin: London, p. 92.

40 Joe Biden eulogizes John McCain, August 30, 2018: https://www.youtube.com/watch?v=nfjYggdO8q4

41 Informal conversation, Brussels, September 30, 2019.

42 Statement by Herman van Rompuy, Brussels, October 1, 2019.

43 Eurostat reports a net increase of outward foreign direct investment of €1.5 trillion between 2008 and 2017, versus an increase of €380 billion in European fixed assets in manufacturing (no data for Spain and Ireland).

44 Demy Van 't Wout, 2020. *The Enforceability of the Trade and Sustainable Development Chapters of the European Union's Free Trade Agreements*. Unpublished master's thesis, Vrije Universiteit Brussel, May.

45 Conversation with German official, Berlin, April 14, 2020.

46 In 2018, 40 percent thought integration was a failure. European Commission, 2018. *Special Eurobarometer 469*. Brussels: European Commission, p. 62.

47 European Social Survey data for 2016.

48 Ibid., p. 71.

49 European Social Survey 2014: Allow many or few Muslims to come and live in country; Allow many/few immigrants from poorer countries in Europe.

50 Results from the European Social Survey, 2018 edition. Loneliness defined as meetings with friends or relatives less than once a month.

51 Georg Mascolo, and Britta von de Heide, 2016. 1200 Frauen wurden Opfer von Silvester-Gewalt. *Süddeutsche Zeitung*, July 10.

52 Marine Le Pen compare l'afflux de migrants aux invasions barbares. *Le Point*, September 15, 2015.

53 Manni Crone, 2017. Europe's refugee crisis and the threat of terrorism. Copenhagen: Danish Institute for International Studies; Marina Eleftheriadou, 2018. Refugee radicalization/militarization in the age of the European refugee crisis: A composite model. *Terrorism and Political Violence*, 31(1), 1–22.

54 European Commission, 2016. *How Are Refugees Faring on the Labour Market in Europe?* Brussels: European Commission.

55 Ibid.

56 Andrew Brown, 2020. "Optimistic" Boris Johnson urges shoppers to return as he visits Westfield before stores reopen tomorrow. *The Sun*, June 14.

57 Giuseppe Conte, lo shopping del premier nei negozi di Roma. *Corriere del Umbria*, July 18, 2020.

58 Eurobarometer, 2017. *European Youth: Flash Eurobarometer.* Brussels: European Commission.

59 Wolfram Schulz, John Ainley, Julian Fraillon, Bruno Losito, and Gabriella Agrusti, 2018. *IEA International Civic and Citizenship Education Study 2016: International Report.* Amsterdam: IEA, p. 16.

60 Ibid, p. 76.

Chapter 11: Abdication

1 Informal round table meeting, Brussels, February 5, 2015.

2 Informal conversation, Rome, December 3, 2016.

3 Isaac Chotiner, 2020. Gordon Brown's case for global cooperation during the coronavirus pandemic. *The New Yorker*, April 18.

4 Hank Paulson, 2015. *Dealing with China.* London: Headline Publishing, p. 95.

5 Yin Liqun during a hearing in the European Parliament, May 10, 2013.

6 Vladimir Chizhov, 2019. Lecture at Ghent University, Ghent, November 20.

7 Policy meeting, European Commission, Brussels, November 6, 2010.

8 Mark Landler, 2012. Obama's evolution to a tougher line on China. *The New York Times*, September 20.

9 Ibid.

10 Jeff Bader, 2013. *Obama and China's Rise: An Insider's Account of America's Asia Strategy.* Washington, DC: Brookings Institution, p. 6.

11 Ash Carter, 2018. *Reflections on American Grand Strategy in Asia.* Cambridge, MA: Harvard Belfer Center.

12 US trade official, London, November 4, 2017.

13 EU trade chief: Won't yield to pressure from China on solar panels. *Reuters*, May 28, 2013.

14 European Commission, 2019. *EU–China: A Strategic Outlook.* Brussels: European Commission, p. 1.

15 Bethany Allen-Ebrahimian, 2020. Top German official hushed up report on China's influence. *Axios*, October 6.

16 Landon Thomas, 2018. The World Bank is remaking itself as a creature of Wall Street. *The New York Times*, January 25.

17 Ibid.

18 Jim Jarassé, 2010. Quand Sarkozy traitait un ministre russe de menteur. *Le Figaro*, December 2.

19 Jamie Doward, 2010. Russia was tracking killers of Alexander Litvinenko but UK warned it off. *The Guardian*, December 11.

20 https://wikileaks.org/plusd/cables/08MOSCOW3343_a.html

21 Herman Van Rompuy, 2010. Remarks by Herman Van Rompuy, President of the European Council, at the EU–Russia Summit, Rostov-on-Don, June 1.

22 https://wikileaks.org/plusd/cables/10MOSCOW272_a.html

23 Anna White, 2014. Russians pour money into London property. *The Telegraph*, March 22.

24 Ali Watkins, 2017. Obama team was warned in 2014 about Russian interference. *Politico*, August 14.

25 I like when people leave our gas stations with a smile, *Capital Ideas*, July–September 2014, pp. 28–31.

26 Conversation, The Hague, July 3, 2019.

27 Treasury designates Al-Qa'ida supporters in Qatar and Yemen, US Department of Treasury, December 18, 2013.

28 Gérard Longuet, Minister of Defence in a 2011 ARTE documentary: "On subventionne pas Saoudiens. On soubventionne entreprises françaises implantées sur place qui ont besoin de travail. Contribuer à développer nos territores. Accepter monde tel qu'il est. Conflicts existent avec ou sans nous. Chacun ses responsabilités. J'étais ministre de la défence pas ministre de la morale. Si j'étais abbé Pierre; je ferrais sans doute quelque chose différent": doc: Crimes de guerre au Yémen, quand les armes européennes tuent – Complicités européennes.

29 Saudis unterstützen deutsche Salafistenszene. *Süddeutsche Zeitung*, December 13, 2016.

30 Tom Wilson, 2017. *Foreign Funded Islamist Extremism in the UK*. London: The Henry Jackson Society.

31 Christian Chesnot, Georges Malbrunot, and Michel Lafon, 2019. *Qatar Papers. Comment l'émirat finance l'islam de France et d'Europe*. Paris: Michel Lafon.

32   Elisabeth Dickinson, 2014. The case against Qatar. *Foreign Policy*, September 30; US Department of State, 2018. *Country Reports on Terrorism*. Washington, DC: Department of State, p. 154.

33   Transcribed from a presentation given by President Trump, March 20, 2018. Available at: https://www.youtube.com/watch?v=PTM6yEDc1DE

34   Jim Pickard, 2018. Tony Blair Institute confirms donations from Saudi Arabia. *Financial Times*, September 5.

35   Fallait-il honorer un haut responsable d'un pays qui décapite sur les places publiques, et refuse aux femmes d'avoir les mêmes droits que les hommes?

36   L'Arabie Saoudite, terre d'opportunités pour l'offre française. *Business France*, October 15, 2019.

37   Remco Andersen, 2019. Influencers onder vuur na promoten Saoedi-Arabië. *Volkskrant*, December 23.

38   Jamie Robertson, 2017. Qatar: Buying Britain by the pound. *BBC World News*, June 9.

39   Mohammad Shoeb, 2018. Qatar's investment in the UK soars to over QR180bn. *The Peninsula*, September 23.

40   Jack Peat, 2019. UK's relationship with Qatar "going from strength to strength." *Evening Express*, September 20.

41   William James, 2018. UK's May defends Saudi ties as crown prince gets royal welcome in London. *Reuters*, March 6.

42   Michael Morell, 2015. *The Great War of Our Time*. New York: Twelve.

43   Tunisie: les propos "effrayants" d'Alliot-Marie suscitent la polémique. *Le Monde*, January 13, 2011.

44   Angelique Chrisafis, 2011. Sarkozy admits France made mistakes over Tunisia. *The Guardian*, January 24.

45   Alain Juppé, 2011. Closing speech by Alain Juppé, Ministre d'Etat at the Arab Spring symposium. Institut du Monde arabe, April 16.

46   Gaddafi wants EU cash to stop African migrants. *BBC World News*, August 31, 2010.

47   Ibid.

48   Ahmed Elumami, and Giselda Vagnoni, 2019. Libya fighting kills 56, European powers jostle over conflict. *Reuters*, April 11.

49   Giulia Paravicini, 2018. Millions flow from Gaddafi's "frozen funds" to unknown beneficiaries. *Politico*, February 8.

50   https://wikileaks.org/clinton-emails/emailid/12181

51 Patrick Kirkpatrick, 2018. The White House and the strongman. *The New York Times*, July 27.

52 Nikolaj Nielsen, 2018. EU promotes Egypt model to reduce migrant numbers. *EU Observer*, September 18.

53 Mark Habeeb, 2018. Poll reflects anxiety, frustration in the Arab world. *The Arab Weekly*, December 16.

54 Michael Kramer, 1983. Taking Syria seriously. *New York Magazine*, October 3, p. 35.

55 Nick Davies, Jonathan Steele, and David Leigh, 2010. Iraq war logs: Secret files show how US ignored torture. *The Guardian*, October 22.

56 https://wikileaks.org/wiki/Major_RAND_study_with_300_interviews:_Intelligence_Operations_and_Metrics_in_Iraq_and_Afghanistan,_Nov_2008

57 Barack Obama, 2011. Remarks by the President and First Lady on the end of the war in Iraq. White House, December 14.

58 Rebuilding Mosul, *HBO News Tonight*, December 5, 2018.

59 Kelly Kennedy, 2019. Iraqis' state of mind 16 years after US invasion. *The Arab Weekly*, April 14; NDI, 2019. *National Survey Findings: Improved Social Cohesion, but Iraqis Remain Dissatisfied with Government*. Baghdad: NDI, p. 4.

60 Zogby, 2018. *Middle East Public Opinion 2018*. Washington, DC: Zogby Research.

61 Alex Schmid, 2017. *Public Opinion Survey Data to Measure Sympathy and Support for Islamist Terrorism*. ICCT Research Paper.

62 Conversation, London, September 4, 2019.

63 Shibley Telhami, 2002. *Put Middle East Terror in Global Perspective*. Washington, DC: Brookings Institution, February 17.

64 Zogby, *Middle East Public Opinion 2018*, p. 15.

65 Christian Miller, Megan Rose, and Robert Faturechi, 2019. Fight the ship. *Pro Publica*, February 6.

66 James Geurts, Steven Rudder, and Scott Conn, 2019. Statement on the Department of the Navy Aviation Programs, Senate Armed Services Committee, April 10, p. 26. They appear to have dropped slightly in 2018. Tara Copp, 2019. Is military aviation getting any safer? New mishap data shows mixed results. *Military Times*, April 4.

67 Matthew Karnitschnig, 2019. Germany's soldiers of misfortune. *Politico*, February 15.

68 Public Accounts Committee, 2019. *Defence Equipment Plan 2018–28*. London: Public Accounts Committee.

69 Jacques Hubert-Rodier, and Anne Bauer, 2015. Au rythme actuel, l'armée française sera bientôt épuisée. *Les Echos*, October 26.

70 Ibid.

71 Amy Sorkin Davidson, 2010. Obama wins battleship – with bayonets. *The New Yorker*, October 23.

72 Stephen Losey, 2017. Growing readiness woes: Only 7 in 10 Air Force planes are ready to fly. *Air Force Times*, April 2.

73 Harry Harris, 2017. Statement on the US PACOM Posture. House Armed Services Committee, April 26, p. 23.

74 Jim Mitre, 2019. A eulogy for the two-war construct. *The Washington Quarterly*, 41(4), 7–30.

75 Jose Carreno, Thomas Culora, and George Caldorisi, 2010. What's new about the AirSea Battle concept. *Proceedings*, 136(8), 1–29; Ministry of Defense of the USA, 2011. Background Briefing on Air-Sea Battle by Defense Officials from the Pentagon. Ministry of Defense, November 9. See: http://www.defense.gov/Transcripts/Transcript.aspx?TranscriptID=4923

76 Chuck Hagel, 2014. Letter on the Defense Innovation Initiative, November 15.

77 Erkii Bahovski, 2019. The World Trade Organization is in crisis and must be reformed. *Diplomaatia*, November 22.

78 Vince Chadwick, 2019. Chinese candidate takes FAO top job amid US concerns. *Associated Press*, June 24.

79 Michael Pompeo, 2018. Statement at the Brussels Forum, Brussels, December 4.

Chapter 12: Fragmented and turbulent

1 Hannah Beech, 2019. A jungle airstrip stirs suspicions about China's plans for Cambodia. *The New York Times*, December 22.

2 Malaysian PM Mahatir, as quoted by a diplomat of a European member state, confidential private conversation, June 15, 2020.

3 Conversation with Chinese think tank expert, Brussels, March 22, 2019.

4 State Council Information Office, 2019. *China and the World in the New Era*. Beijing: State Council, p. 32.

5 Conversation, Singapore, September 19, 2017.

6 A notice from the Central Committee of the Communist Party of China's General Office, April 22, 2013, retrieved as a translation from the original Chinese document from http://www.chinafile.com/document-9-chinafile-translation

7   Xu Wei, 2019. Xi calls for fighting spirit in face of risks. *China Daily*, September 4.

8   Conversation, Bruges, April 1, 2014.

9   AFP, 2011. China seeks to dispel military build-up fears. *AFP*, September 7.

10 Qiao Liang, 2011. 战争主动权并非由挑衅者决定 中国有选择和回旋余地, Zhangzheng zhuding quan bingfei tiaoxin zhe jueding Zhongguo you xuanze he huixuanyudi, [War provocations do not leave China much choice to choose its response]. *Jiefang Ribao*, August 29.

11 Peter Harrell, Elizabeth Rosenberg, and Edoardo Saravalle, 2018. *China's Use of Coercive Economic Measures*. Washington, DC: Center for a New American Security.

12 State Council Information Office, 2019. *China's National Defense in the New Era*. Beijing: State Council, p. 6.

13 Yu Yingshih, 1986. Han foreign relations. In Denis Twitchett and Michael Loewe (eds.), *The Cambridge History of China. Volume 1*. Cambridge: Cambridge University Press, p. 413.

14 *La Repubblica*, June 1, 2020.

15 Myanmar: US$10 billion; Bangladesh: US$9 billion; Sri Lanka: US$8 billion; Pakistan: US$6.6 billion; Maldives: US$3.4, billion; and Nepal: US$300 million.

16 Pranab Mukherjee, 2016. Speech on the occasion of the India–China Business Forum, Guangzhou, May 25.

17 Press Information Bureau, 2017. *Chinese Investment under "Make in India"*. Government of India Ministry of Commerce & Industry, March 20.

18 T. V. Jayan, 2019. With no official data, India is in dark about poverty numbers. *The Hindu*, October 30; Pramit Bhattacharya, and Sriharsha Devulapalli, 2019. India's rural poverty has shot up. *Mint*, December 3.

19 Confidential briefing, Brussels, April 15, 2019.

20 Léonce Ndikumana, and James Boyce, 2018. *Capital Flight from Africa*. Amherst, MA: Political Economy Research Institute, p. 8.

21 Yared Tsegaye, 2018. Railway unnerves freighters, heartens importers. *Addis Fortune*, June 2.

22 Is oil money fueling war in South Sudan? *Al Jazeera*, April 6, 2019.

23 Ibid.; IMF, 2018. *Republic of South Sudan. Staff report*. Washington, DC: IMF; UN Human Rights Council, 2019. *Report of the Commission on Human Rights in South Sudan*, March 12.

24 Jeffrey Gettleman, 2009. An interview with Joseph Kabila. *The New York Times*, April 3.

25 Global Witness, 2017. *Regime Cash Machine*. London: Global Witness; Africa Progress Panel, 2013. *Equity in Extractives: Stewarding Africa's Natural Resources for All*. Geneva: Africa Progress Panel, pp. 55–63.

26 Human Rights Watch, 2015. *World Report 2015*. New York: Human Rights Watch, p. 403.

27 Zachary Donnenfeld, 2019. *Violence against Civilians is on the Rise in Africa*. Pretoria: Institute for Security Studies, October 22.

28 Robert Mattes, 2019. *Democracy in Africa*. [City unknown]: Afrobarometer.

29 Coralie Pring, and Jon Vrushi, 2019. *Global Corruption Barometer*. [City unknown]: Afrobarometer.

30 Ingrid Vik Bakken, and Siri Aas Rustad, 2018. *Conflict Trends in Africa 1946–2017*. Oslo: Prio.

31 Jason Burke Masisi, 2018. Millions flee bloodshed as Congo falls apart. *The Guardian*, April 3.

32 Congo Research Group, 2018. *Inside the ADF Rebellion*. New York: New York University, p. 5.

33 Vitus Ukoji, Abiola Ayodokun, and Victor Eze, 2019. *Eighth Report on Violence in Nigeria*. Lagos: IFRA.

34 Conversation, Niame, Niger, May 5, 2019.

35 Janani Vivekananda, Martin Wall, Florence Sylvestre, and Chitra Nagarajan, 2018. *Shoring Up Stability: Addressing Climate and Fragility Risks in the Lake Chad Region*. Paris: Report to the G7.

36 Hannah Armstrong, 2010. China mining company causes unrest in Niger. *Christian Science Monitor*, March 29.

37 Conversation, December 18, 2019.

38 OECD, Country programmable aid in constant US$.

39 Jeffrey Gettleman, 2008. An interview with Joseph Kabila. *The New York Times*, April 3.

40 Mogopodi Lkorwe, 2016. *China's Growing Presence in Africa Wins Largely Positive Popular Review*. Lusaka: Afrobarometer.

41 Top Russian legislator warns against return of neocolonialism in Africa. *Moscow Times*, July 3, 2019.

42 Léonce Ndikumana, and James K. Boyce, 2011. *Africa's Odious Debts*. London: Zed Books; Mandla Makhanaya, 2019. How neo-colonialism wreaks havoc in Africa. *Daily Maverick*, October 17.

43 Alemayehu Mariam, 2017. Chinese neocolonialism in Africa. *Pambazuka*, September 7.

44 Josephine Appiah-Nyamekye Sanny, Carolyn Logan, and E. Gyimah-Boadi, 2019. *In Search of Opportunity: Young and Educated Africans Most Likely to Consider Moving Abroad.* [City unknown]: Afrobarometer.

45 Robert Muggah, and Katherine Aguire Tobon, 2018. *Citizen Security in Latin America: Facts and Figures.* Rio de Janeiro: Instituto Igarapé.

46 Protester dies during violent clashes in Paraguay. *Financial Times*, April 1, 2017.

47 Cheng-Chwee Kuik, 2016. How do weaker states hedge? *Journal of Contemporary China*, 25(100), 500–14.

48 Lionel Barber, 2019. Vladimir Putin says liberalism has become obsolete. *Financial Times*, June 28.

49 Thomas Grove, 2012. Russia's Putin says the West is on the decline. *Reuters*, July 9.

50 Ali Watkins, 2017. Obama team was warned in 2014 about Russian interference. *Politico*, August 14; Laura Galante, and Shaun Ee, 2018. *Defining Russian Election Interference: An Analysis of Select 2014 to 2018 Cyber Enabled Incidents.* Washington, DC: The Atlantic Council.

51 Vladimir Putin, 2018. Presidential Address to the Federal Assembly. Moscow, March 1.

52 Address by President of the Russian Federation, Moscow, March 18, 2014.

53 Conversation, Saint Petersburg, December 2, 2017.

54 Speech by Recep Tayyip Erdoğan, Istanbul, March 26, 2017.

55 Three children not enough, have five: Erdoğan to Turks in EU. *Hurriyet*, March 17, 2017.

56 Mu Xuequan, 2019. Chinese president meets Saudi crown prince. *Xinhua*, February 22.

57 Private conversation, November 19, 2019.

Watershed

1 Conversation with EU official, Beijing, May 16, 2016.

2 Donald Trump, 2019. Remarks to the 74th Session of the United Nations General Assembly. New York, September 24.

3 Quoted in Saint Augustine, 2003. *Concerning the City of God Against the Pagans* (Henry Bettenson, trans.). London: Penguin: p. 44.

4 Eurostat, 2019. Travel and Tourism Database.

5 https://research.fb.com/blog/2016/11/facebook-friendships-in-europe/

6 Richard Gardner, 1962. *The United States and the United Nations*. Washington, DC: Department of State, p. 25.

7 Inis Claude, 1966. Collective legitimization as a political function of the United Nations. *International Organization*, 20(3), 376–9.

8 Pelosi Floor Speech in Support of Hong Kong Legislation, Washington, DC, October 15, 2019.

9 Russian interference highlights Britain's political failings. *The Economist*, July 25, 2020.

10 Interview with VW boss Herbert Diess, April 16, 2019. https://www.bbc.com/news/av/business-47944767

11 Remarks by HR Josep Borrell on the EU–China strategic dialogue, Brussels, June 9, 2019.

12 Conversation with senior European member state official, Brussels, January 11, 2018.

13 Hans Morgenthau, 1949. *Scientific Man vs Power Politics*. Chicago, IL: University of Chicago Press, p. v.

14 William Pitt, 1915. *The War Speeches of William Pitt the Younger* (R. Coupland, ed.). Oxford: Oxford University Press.

FURTHER READING

My hope is that this book has given readers a bird's-eye view of the last three decades that formed the West's "unipolar moment" and the growing resistance to that order. My main objective has been to offer a panorama from which the reader can opt to zoom in for more in-depth reading. With this in mind, here are some suggestions for more specific works. I have tried to structure them thematically and regionally. These are, of course, selective, personal recommendations and do not represent a complete overview of the literature available in each area.

Milestones: Big events remain markers on the timeline of history. This book started with the fall of the Berlin Wall. A moving account of this moment is Timothy Garton Ash's *Magic Lantern* (Vintage, 1999). The best account of operation Desert Storm, the first major war in the unipolar world, is Rick Atkinson's *Crusade* (Mariner, 1994). He takes the reader from the Oval Office to the desert frontlines. For the 9/11 terrorist attacks, and especially the explanations of the readiness of the terrorists to die for an extreme world view, I suggest Lawrence Wright's *Looming Tower* (Alfred Knopf, 2006). The best document about the Iraq War in 2003 is still that of the Iraq Study Group (2006). *Too big to fail*, by Andrew Ross Sorkin (Penguin, 2010), is a very complete overview of how the financial crisis from around 2008 could happen.

Global governance: Readers seeking to better comprehend global governance can consult *International Organization and Global Governance*, edited by Thomas Weiss (Routledge, 2018). It offers a comprehensive account of different organizations and challenges to global governance. Linda Fasulo's

Insider's Guide to the UN (Yale University Press, 2015) is a crisp summary of how the most important international organization works, the administrative maze, and the diplomatic elbowing. Kofi Annan's *Life in War and Peace* (Penguin, 2013) gives a first-hand testimony from the top about this organization in difficult times, its struggle to respond to humanitarian crises, and the difficulty of reforming a rusty organization. The *Stiglitz Report* (Free Press, 2010) is a sharp treatise about what goes wrong in global financial governance and how to repair organizations such as the IMF. *The WTO After Seattle* (International Economics, 2008) does a good job in elucidating the growing tensions between the main trading powers in the 1990s, while *The Great Delusion* (Yale University Press, 2018) is a blistering attack from John Mearsheimer on the very idea of peace and cooperation advanced by institutions and norms.

Environment: *How Bad Are Bananas?* (Profile, 2020) by Mike Berners-Lee is an enjoyable yet confronting work that calculates the environmental burden of matters ranging from an email to a wind turbine. It shows how big political debates have their roots in our day-to-day lives. To understand the causes and impact of climate change, there is still no more authoritative source than the *Assessment Reports* of the International Panel on Climate Change. All reports can be found on its website: www.ipcc.ch. Most interesting also is *Who Really Feeds the World?* by Vandana Shiva (North Atlantic Books, 2016), which explains how food security could be best provided by networks of small farmers and by striking a balance between nature and agriculture. *The Green Industrial Revolution*, by Woodrow Clark and Grant Cooke (Butterworth Heinemann, 2015), does the same for manufacturing and energy, although it puts much more emphasis on technology.

Poverty: In *Fault Lines*, Raghuram Rajan (Princeton University Press, 2010) states that after the financial crisis that started around 2008, the main economies still did not learn their lesson, and that in the response to the crisis, new massive economic imbalances emerged. Abhijit Banerjee and Esther Duflo advance in their *Poor Economics* (Public Affairs, 2012) the idea that poverty is primarily about impediments preventing human beings from fulfilling their potential. While this argument is in line with the previous "human development" thinking, the authors present it in a very engaging way and critically review existing anti-poverty solutions. Dambisa Moyo's *Dead Aid* (Farrar, Straus and Giroux, 2009) is another powerful criticism from Africa against the usual overlords of development cooperation. Poverty remains an important cause of migration, as Paul Collier explains in *Exodus* (Public Affairs, 2009), but migration can be bent into an economic opportunity.

Security: One can get a good general impression of the outlook of the modern battlefield and contemporary security threats in the United States from the *Quadrennial Defense Review*. This document is available online (https://dod.defense.gov/News/Special-Reports/QDR/). That nuclear weapons will not disappear and only become more lethal is explained by various experts in *Strategy in the Second Nuclear Age*, a volume edited by Toshi Yoshihara and James Holmes (Georgetown University Press, 2012). Paul Scharre explains the rise of robots and autonomous warfare in *Army of None* (W.W. Norton, 2019). P. W. Singer and Emerson Brooking's *Like War* (Houghton, 2018) offers a good discussion of how social media have become weaponized. Giles Kepel's *Terror in France* (Princeton University Press, 2017) remains the reference for understanding the spreading of radical Islamic terrorism in the Western world. *Viruses, Plagues, and History*, by Michael Oldstone (Oxford University Press, 2009), presents a good overview of the battle between humans and viruses, a battle, it appears, that can never entirely be won.

China: To understand China's historical trauma of weakness and humiliation, Stephen Platt's *Imperial Twilight* (Knopf, 2018), a book about the Opium Wars, is a good start. Zhao Zhiyang's *Prisoner of the State* (Simon and Schuster, 2010) offers a first-hand account of the debates inside the Chinese Communist Party about how to respond to the Tiananmen uprising and the future of the state. Elizabeth Economy's *The Third Revolution* (Oxford University Press, 2018) and Evan Osnos's *Age of Ambition* (Farrar, Straus and Giroux, 2014) are two fine explorations into the internal transformation of China. They could be combined with the movies of Jia Zhanke, such as *A Touch of Sin* (2013) and *Ash is Purest White* (2018). David Schambaugh's *China*

Goes Global (Oxford University Press, 2013) nicely describes China's first step as a major power with global ambitions. China's own *Defense White Papers*, released in English by the State Council Information Office (http://eng. mod.gov.cn/Database/WhitePapers), are a useful source to begin exploring China's official narrative on world politics.

Southeast Asia: Any additional reading about Southeast Asia should start with Lee Kuan Yew's *From Third World to First* (HarperCollins, 2000), which is a personal autobiography and, one could say, also an autobiography of a region in search of a balance between strong leadership and democracy, as well as between superpowers. Sebastian Strangio explains in *The Dragon's Shadow* (Yale University Press, 2020), how this search continues now that China casts a shadow over the region. ASEAN is partially advanced as a response to external influences, yet, as Marty Natalegawa explains in *Does ASEAN Matter?* (ISEAS, 2018) the tension between state sovereignty and integration is hard to handle for this rather loose grouping of states. Interesting specific country studies are Thant Myint-U's *Hidden History of Burma* (W.W. Norton, 2019), Jamie Davidson's *Indonesia: Twenty Years of Democracy* (Cambridge University Press, 2018), and Andrew MacGregor Marshal's *Kingdom in Crisis: Thailand's Struggle for Democracy in the Twenty-First Century* (Zed Books, 2015).

South Asia: Yasmin Khan's *Great Partition* (Yale University Press, 2017) is a great starting point. James Crabtree's *The Billionaire Raj* (Tim Duggan, 2018) and Katherine Boo's *Behind the Beautiful Forevers* (Granta, 2012) can help you discover the internal transformation of India, perhaps combined with a documentary from BBC Radio on the rising tide of Hindu terrorism, *India's Silent Terror* (https://www.bbc.co.uk/programmes/p04kj4fg). Anatol Lieven's *Hard Country* (Hachette, 2012) does the same for Pakistan. Robert Kaplan does a great job in his *Monsoon* (Random House, 2010) to explain the geopolitical outlook of the region.

Russia: Both *Mr. Putin* by Fiona Hill and Clifford Gaddy (Brookings Institution Press, 2015) and *New Tsar* by Steven Myers (Vintage, 2015) describe in detail how the time of troubles in the 1990s paved the way for Vladimir Putin. It is difficult to choose between them. Masha Gessen's *The Future Is History* separates Russia's recent history into four stages – unraveling, resurrection, protest, and the authoritarian crackdown – and does so empathetically by following the life of four Russians (Penguin, 2019). Vladimir Putin's speech in Munich in 2007 certainly was a milestone and deserves to be read or watched in its entirety. PBS Frontline masterfully reconstructs the growing tensions with the United States in a two-part documentary, *Putin's Revenge* (2017). As a peek into Russian society, its corruption, and violence, Andrey Zvyagintsev's *Leviathan* (a movie from 2014) can be recommended.

The Middle East: To better understand the Middle East, Albert Hourani's *History of the Arab Peoples*, James Barr's *Line in the Sand* (W.W. Norton, 2012) and Naguib Mahfouz's *The Journey of Ibn Fattouma* (Anchor, 2016) are a must. I would add to these general works like Tamim Ansary's *Destiny Disrupted* (Public Affairs, 2009), which is a lively enquiry into how the Muslim world and the West grew apart. These general introductions can be followed by country studies, such as *History of Modern Iran* by Ervand Abrahamian (Cambridge University Press, 2008), *The Rise to Power of Mohammed bin Salman* by Ben Hubbard (Tim Duggan, 2020) and *The New Sultan* by Soner Cagaptay (I.B. Tauris, 2017). PBS has some solid documentaries online about the region: *Once Upon a Time in Iraq* (2020), *Targeting Yemen* (2019), and *Bitter Enemies: Iran and Saudi Arabia* (2019).

Africa: Robert Kaplan's essay, *Coming Anarchy* (*The Atlantic*, 1994), later turned into a book, was one of the first powerful works warning that the ending of the Cold War would give way to strife propelled by poverty, extremism, and crime. Howard French's *Continent of the Taking* (Vintage, 2005) and David Van Reybrouck's *Congo* (HarperCollins, 2015) are two more important accounts of how the colonial legacy, corruption, and marginalization in the global markets prevented the continent from turning its demographic dividend and resilience into prosperity. Philip Gourevitch's *We Wish to Inform You That Tomorrow We Will Be Killed with Our Families* (Farrar, Straus and Giroux, 1999) is the most gripping account of the Rwandan genocide, while Stig Jarle Hansen's *Horn, Sahel, and Rift* (Hurst, 2019) does a good job in systematically explaining the causes of strife in the

Sahel region. Reading Nelson Mandela's *Long Walk to Freedom* (Back Bay, 1995) is the best way to understand how only a few of the hopes of a strong continent have materialized.

Latin America: A good introduction to Latin American politics is offered by Michael Reid in *Forgotten Continent* (Yale University Press, 2017). He describes accessibly the aftermath of the Cold War and how the region failed to profit from its commodity boom. Eduardo Galeano's *Open Veins of Latin America* (Monthly Review Press, 1997) takes that point to an extreme and highlights the external exploitation, and so does the wildly energetic *Brazillionaires* by Alex Cuadros (Spiegel & Grau, 2016), although the latter places its focus on the elite. The fate of the indigenous communities in Latin America and the tension with modernity are given their due attention in F. Bruce Lamb's *Wizard of the Upper Amazon* (North Atlantic Books, 1993).

The EU: In probing European politics, no one can sidestep Tony Judt's *Postwar* (Penguin, 2010), which is the most complete history of European politics and society. It tells the story of a project that was "the insecure child of anxiety" and has remained fragile since. Ideally, it is combined with Geert Mak's travelogue *In Europe* (Vintage, 2008). The more recent tremors that shook Europe are described well in Jean Pisani-Ferry's *The Euro Crisis and Its Aftermath* (Oxford University Press, 2014). His book is a dispassionate reconstruction of the crisis and its – temporary – ending. Patrick Kingsley's *The New Odyssey* (Guardian Faber, 2017) offers the best review of the migration crisis, trailing fortune seekers, and recounts the complex interactions with European societies. Peter van Kemseke's *Europe Reinvented* offers a concise assessment of the tension between national selfishness and cooperation during the corona crisis (Boeklyn, 2020). *Bursting the Brussels Bubble* offers a very useful glimpse of the functioning of the European bureaucracy (AlterEU, 2010).

The United States: In *Strangers in Their Own Land*, Arlie Russell Hochschild reveals how innate, deep expectations account for the anger and the sense of powerlessness among rightist Americans about their changing society (The New Press, 2016). George Packer's *Unwinding* does the same, but broadens the canvas to the elite (Farrar, Straus and Giroux, 2014). An unmatched look into the White House under Trump is offered by Michael Wolff in *Fire and Fury* (Macmillan, 2018). *Excellent Sheep* by William Deresiewicz (Free Press, 2015) and *Billion Dollar Whale* by Bradley Hope and Tom Wright (Hachette, 2018) are must-reads for those trying to understand how the American elite got disconnected from its society.

American foreign policy: One can start by reading two works that explain the shift from isolationism to engagement. In *American Diplomacy* (University of Chicago Press, 1979), George Kennan stresses the importance of the preservation of the Eurasian balance of power, and, in the slightly more controversial *Tragedy of American Diplomacy* (W.W. Norton, 2009), William Appleman Williams highlights the economic motivations behind American foreign policy. More recent books that brilliantly discuss the causes and consequences of interventionist hubris are Steven Walt's *The Hell of Good Intentions* (Farrar, Straus and Giroux, 2018) and Andrew J. Bacevich's *The Limits of Power* (Holt, 2009). Both authors call for a return to realism. Readers can find a good inside view of foreign policy decision making in *Holding the Line* (Sentinel, 2019), a crisp treatise on Trumpian foreign policy written by Guy Snodgrass, and *The World as It Is* (Bodley Head, 2018), in which Ben Rhodes recounts Barack Obama's struggle to balance immense expectations and America's shrinking power.

INDEX